Every Factory a Fortress

EVERY FACTORY A FORTRESS

THE FRENCH LABOR MOVEMENT
IN THE AGE OF FORD AND HITLER

Michael Torigian

OHIO UNIVERSITY PRESS *Athens*

Ohio University Press, Athens, Ohio 45701

© 1999 by Michael Torigian
Printed in the United States of America
All rights reserved

Ohio University Press books are printed on acid-free paper ∞ ™

03 02 01 00 99   5 4 3 2 1

Parts of chapters two, three, and four originally appeared in somewhat
different form in *The Journal of Contemporary History 32* (October 1997).

Library of Congress Cataloging-in-Publication Data

Torigian, Michael.
    Every factory a fortress: the French labor movement in the age of
 Ford and Hitler / Michael Torigian.
       p. cm.
    Includes bibliographical references and index.
    ISBN 0-8214-1275-2 (cloth: alk. paper)
       1. Trade-unions—Metal-workers—France—Paris—History—20th
 century. 2. Strikes and lockouts—Metal-workers—France—Paris—
 History—20th century. 3. Labor movement—France—Paris—
 History—20th century. 4. Trade-unions and communism—France—
 Paris—History—20th century. 5. Industrial mobilization—France—
 Paris—History—20th century. 6. Industrial productivity—France—
 Paris—History—20th century.   I. Title. II. Title: French labor
 movement in the age of Ford and Hitler.
 HD6688.M5T67 1999
 331.88'171'094436—DC21   98-45899
                                                                   CIP

1001811329

To my mother,
Joan O'Meara

Contents

Preface ix

Abbreviations xiii

1 Mass Production and the Industrial Working Class 1

2 The Labor Movement in the Paris Metal Industry 27

3 The Crisis 47

4 Jacobins in Blue Denim 65

5 The Occupation of the Factories 93

6 The People's Front in the Shops 121

7 Between the Hammer and the Anvil 150

8 The Battle for the War Factories 174

Excursus 191

Notes 195

Bibliography 239

Index 257

Preface

The labor movement that unionized France's mass-production industries had a long genealogy in the history of the West. It appeared with the first great wave of industrialization, whose course it altered, and lingers still as an institutional agent of some import. Its historical prominence has not, however, spared it controversy, evident in the very terms that designate it. The *mouvement ouvrier,* for example, is commonly associated with the trade unions and the *Arbeiter- bewegunung* with socialist politics, while the "labour movement" is typically seen as an institutional blend of unionism and socialism. Different political systems and different national contexts have spawned equally diverse ways of defining it.[1] Given these sundry connotations and the controversies surrounding them, any history of the labor movement ought to begin with a definition.

Mine starts with Alain Touraine's actionalist sociology, which defines the labor movement as a form of occupational solidarity that develops in opposition to the heteronomous social relations inherent in industrial production. In Touraine's view, workers challenging these relations develop a group identity (class consciousness) and an alternative vision of industrial management. Yet unlike Marxists, who believe worker struggles "contradict" the existence of industrial capitalism, Touraine sees them as "conflicts" endemic to a factory's social system, part of the process by which contending social groups articulate and advance their divergent interests. In a related vein, he differs with liberals who depict the labor movement in purely market or institutional terms. The struggle for a fairer distribution of wealth and a mitigation of managerial prerogative, he insists, causes labor to function not simply as a value-enhancing commodity, but also as a movement affecting the management of industry and the organization of society.[2]

In rooting the labor movement in the social problems of production, Touraine assumes that the trade union, reflecting the interests of workers in their shops and work sites, constitutes labor's most representative organization. Unions, though, have long been steeped in political activities remote to the social field of the factory and have had many links to the various "parties of labor." Marxists even contend that these political associations represent the highest historical manifestation of the labor movement, while liberals consider them a necessary part of labor's institutionalization. Touraine, by contrast, argues that the labor movement is inherently non-political, serving as a vehicle neither for a party nor an ideology. Socialism and unionism may therefore have developed in parallel and occasionally shared similar fates, but neither, he claims, was ever synonymous with the other. The social role of the worker and the political role of the citizen—however closely associated—were girded along different axes and addressed dissimilar issues. This did not, of course, make the worker more important than the citizen or the social realm superior to the political, but it did highlight their dissimilarities.

These dissimilarities have had a profound influence on the history of European unionism. The most powerful labor movements, such as the German and the English, were grounded in the trades, exercised considerable authority within the manufacturing process, their chief field of activity, and participated in Social Democratic or Labour politics only to promote those interests eluding their efforts in the factories. On the other hand, in countries like tsarist Russia, where authoritarian social relations and repressive laws prevented workers from challenging management on the shop floor or forming their own autonomous organizations, they had to rely on radical political actors to advance their interests, even though these actors subordinated their social aspirations to state-related projects and utopian schemes. As an actionalist rule of thumb, the history of unionism suggests that labor's politicization reflects its weakness in the factory more than its strength in society.

In France, where the state has traditionally dominated society and unions have been weak and fragmented, this rule of thumb has had particular applicability. Politics, in fact, has so influenced French workers that they have often been more inclined to defend a revolutionary barricade than attend an occasional union meeting. In the apocalyptic atmosphere of the 1930s, when the rise of fascism cast a threatening shadow over republican institutions, this inclination was particularly acute. As a consequence, auto, aircraft, and engineering workers involved in unionizing the mass-production industries in this politically charged decade were conditioned at nearly every step by forces only tangentially related to the factory. Associated with anti-fascism and the Communist party, these forces sometimes aided the labor movement and spurred it to conquer new worlds. But over time, as political imperatives eclipsed socioeconomic concerns, they tended to divert the unions from the labor process, leading them into battles that eventually divided and defeated them.

This book is about the single most important chapter in the history of the French labor movement—the chapter devoted to the unionization of mass-production workers in the Paris metal industry. Based largely on evidence found in the left and labor press of the period, it relates a story that is intended neither as an institutional history of industrial unionism nor a social history of mass-production workers, but rather as a study of how workers in the most advanced sector of their nation's economy were able to coalesce into a social movement and alter the contours of French industry. In telling this story, I attribute no primacy to the social and assume only that unions veering too far from their corporate axis and deferring to political projects remote to the problems of production are bound to lose their way, cutting themselves off from those industrial concerns that define and motivate them. Communist and anti-fascist politics might therefore have dominated the labor history of inter-war France, but, as I hope to show, they did so to the detriment of labor's social project.

Abbreviations

CFTC	Confédération Française des Travailleurs Chrétiens
CGPF	Confédération Générale du Patronat Française
CGT	Confédération Générale du Travail
CGTU	Confédération Générale du Travail Unitaire
CI	Communist International (Comintern)
OM	Ouvrier manoeuvrer (laborer)
OP	Ouvrier professionnel (skilled worker)
OS	Ouvrier spécialisé (semi-skilled worker)
PCF	Parti Communiste Français
PSF	Parti Social Français
RILU	Red International of Labor Unions
SFIO	Section Française de l'Internationale Ouvrière (Socialist party)
UIMM	Union des Industries Métallurgiques et Minière

Every Factory a Fortress

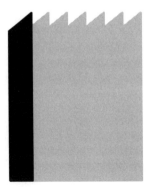

Mass Production and the Industrial Working Class

FRANCE'S MODERN LABOR MOVEMENT WAS BORN IN THE spring of 1936, when a wave of factory occupations swept across the Paris metal industry. These stay-in strikes that shook the foundations of French society and culminated in a union-centered system of industrial relations were provoked by the World Depression and the People's Front. But their origins can be traced back to the Great War and the 1920s, when the introduction of American mass-production technologies led to the creation of a new class of producers. All the various expressions of the labor movement would be affected by these changes, for unlike the craftsmen of the prewar era, mass-production workers were less concerned with the corporate world of the trades and the traditions of French syndicalism than with the Communist party and its ideological conception of their interests.

The Transformation of Metal Fabrication

The First World War revolutionized French industry. To produce the vast stockpiles of shells, artillery pieces, and planes to fight this "war of munitions," traditional craft manufacture had to give way to highly mechanized forms of production. Paris metal producers, whose earlier experiments in auto, aircraft, and electrical construction had familiarized them with many of the new technologies, were best situated to carry out this modernizing process. Under the leadership of Louis Renault, the rising star of French auto makers, these industrialists would create the largest, most advanced center of European metal fabrication.[1]

The modernization of the Paris metal industry, the core of France's armament sector, influenced virtually every facet of French production, but its initial effect was felt mainly on the workforce. Within two weeks of the war's outbreak, two-thirds of all metal workers had been called to the colors and half of all metal plants closed because of manpower shortages. This reduced the region's available workers to a mere 61,000. Once it became apparent, though, that the war would continue beyond Christmas and that industry would be vital to its success, a concerted effort was made to recruit a larger workforce. Begun in early 1915, this effort would eventually raise the number of metal workers to more than a quarter of a million,[2] a majority of whom would be concentrated in newly constructed mass-production plants.[3] Although the myriad of small shops dominating prewar manufacture did not entirely vanish in this expansion, their significance was massively diminished. The Renault auto works, whose workforce grew from 4,400 in 1914 to 22,500 in 1919, represented the most spectacular example of this expansion; it was followed by Citroen, which went from 3,500 to 12,000 workers, and by Delaunay-Belleville in Saint-Denis, expanding from 1,000 to 11,000 workers.[4] More typical of the wartime growth, however, were metal plants whose workforce rose from several hundred workers to a thousand or two.

Because the mobilization absorbed most available manpower, it was no easy task finding workers to fill the new armament plants. The army did what it could by releasing thousands of conscripted craftsmen to serve as "militarized workers" (*affectés spéciaux*), but the war's incessant demands required more hands than the army was willing or able to provide. Metal producers were consequently forced to tap previously untried labor markets, made up largely of French women and youth, as well as foreign and colonial workers. These unskilled workers posed, however, many new problems, for only by introducing methods, machines, and managerial principles to supplant traditional artisanal techniques was it possible to employ them. As a result, the poorly mechanized, decentralized factory of the prewar era, with its handiwork procedures, was compelled to give way to a different model of production.

Mechanization was key to this process. After 1915, unprecedented numbers of machine tools, whose costs had been underwritten by the state, were imported from the United States.[5] Accompanying these electrically motored machines were jigs for machining or drilling objects of awkward shape, and gauges for interchangeable parts. Tools for cutting, cupping, and stamping metal were likewise introduced and applied with greater efficiency. As automatic lathes, new milling machines, drill and punch presses spread, augmenting the supply of precision parts, the need for fitters, turners, and adjusters declined. In addition to raising output, stabilizing product quality, and reducing the need for skilled labor, increased mechanization facilitated the reorganization of manufacture. Production circuits, from smelting to mechanical assembly, were consequently extended, expediting the sequential flow of parts from one shop to the next; new forms of conveyance, although not quite the continuous mechanical conveyor of Henry Ford, were experimented with and installed; traveling cranes, hoisting devices, and electric carts for lifting and carrying heavy objects (to lighten the labor of women and adolescent workers) multiplied; work stations were specialized and arranged in logical sequences to reduce the transit time of pieces from station to station, as they progressed along the path to final assembly. Simultaneously, certain Taylorist forms of "scientific management," designed to divide tasks into operations appropriate to unskilled workers, were adopted and many customary work rules suspended. Finally, outside the plants, at a level affecting the general economy, a subcontracting system was imposed, converting some firms into producers of a standardized model (of a plane or howitzer, for example) and the firm's prewar competitors into suppliers of parts and accessories.[6] This, in turn, prompted the proliferation of interchangeable parts, as well as greater specialization, a more sophisticated division of labor among producers, and an unparalleled degree of industrial integration.

Aided by state planning, mass-production techniques succeeded in raising metal productivity by over 100 percent during the course of the war.[7] In the process, an unskilled workforce of women, adolescent boys, and foreigners was transformed into an army of machine tenders, capable of producing prodigious quantities of metal goods which craftsmen, working on universal or general-purpose machine tools, had previously manufactured in far smaller quantities.[8] France's wartime production of 90,000 airplane engines, compared to the 40,000 produced in the larger German industry, was one testament to France's successful industrial mobilization.[9] Another was the fact that when the American Expeditionary Force arrived in 1917, most of its munitions, airplanes, artillery, machine guns, and tanks were supplied by Paris producers. In nearly every category, French armament production exceeded that of her allies. According to William McNeill, it was not Britain or America, but France that constituted "the arsenal of democracy in World War I."[10] Such a role, to be sure, would have been impossible without the modernization of the Paris metal industry.

Following the Armistice of November 1918, metal producers faced another formidable challenge, that of converting "swords into plowshares." Those plants benefiting from the war's technological innovations tended to experience the least difficulty shifting to peacetime production. Within a year of the war's end, the electrical-equipment and mechanical-engineering sectors, as they busily filled the backlog of civilian orders for agricultural machinery, domestic appliances, machine tools, sewing machines, typewriters, cutlery, tinware, and other metal products, took the lead in reconverting. Some auto producers (such as Delaunay-Belleville and Mors) would falter in the transition to peacetime production, but those reconverting swiftly enough were able to capitalize on the heightened demand for motor transport popularized by the war. Only the aircraft sector of the metal industry, deprived of state orders and without alternative markets, shrank as a consequence of reconversion.[11] As early as 1920, the metal industry was employing 119 percent of its prewar workforce and 97 percent of its prewar plants had resumed peacetime production.[12]

The exceptional activity of the postwar domestic economy, spurred by the reconstruction of the battle-torn north, provided the major impetus to reconversion. As the state poured billions of *francs* into rebuilding the 9,000 factories, 6,000 bridges, and 1,500 miles of rail lines destroyed in the war, Paris producers were motivated to consolidate their wartime innovations and stake out a place for themselves in the peacetime market. One observer characterized the state's reconstruction effort as a "gigantic public-works program of which the war industries were the principal beneficiaries."[13] But while the postwar spending spree provided new markets for former war industries and facilitated a relatively painless transition to peacetime production, it took a high toll on the general economy, causing the state to augment money supplies to meet rising expenditures and setting off, in turn, a galloping inflation. By 1924, inflation had the entire economy in its grip. Only by implementing a series of drastic monetary measures, which devalued the currency and made French products a bargain in international markets, was Premier Raymond Poincaré able to return the country to financial stability.

The undervalued *franc* and the new exchange rates that came with the Poincaré devaluation created a formidable trading opportunity for French producers. To take advantage of it, they resumed their wartime experiments with assembly-line production, scientific management, and standardization.[14] As they did, much of the Paris metal industry came under the sway of a "rationalization movement," aimed at promoting greater production and productivity through better-tooled plants, the latest scientific and technical innovations, a reorganized workforce, the integration of productive processes in allied industries, and a work culture pillared on speed and efficiency.[15] Modeled on the

American auto industry, the rationalization movement prompted producers to send their engineers to inspect U.S. plants, purchase the latest American machine tools, import the latest production technologies, and increase plant investment. As a result of this movement, production routinization and product standardization introduced during the war, along with continuous-flow technologies, spread throughout the industry, significantly augmenting output. By 1927, the export of metal goods had more than doubled its prewar high, making French producers, for the first time, strong international competitors of engineering products.[16] By decade's end, auto production (concentrated in the Paris Region) stood a phenomenal 600 percent above its 1913 level, followed by similar, though less spectacular growth in other branches of the metal industry.[17] At this point, Paris metal workers made up 29 percent of the region's active population and the largest single corporate segment of France's postwar workforce.[18] Only with the arrival of the World Depression in 1931 did this surge of activity come to a halt, but not before establishing the Paris metal industry as the dominant sector in the nation's economy.

The Concept of the Metal Industry

As an economic category, the "metal industry" is a distinctly continental term, without an exact British or American equivalent. In French usage, the term embraces all factories and shops which produce, transform, or fabricate with metals. In Britain, it would apply to metallurgical and mechanical-engineering industries; in the U.S., to auto, aviation, electrical-appliance, machine-tool, and steel-making sectors. Like many French industrial terms (such as *papier, cuirs et peaux, alimentation, verriers*), the metal industry is defined by its raw materials, the category of input, and not the specific products made from metals. As such, it involves a number of distinct industrial activities that might not otherwise be considered part of a single industry. On one occasion, the Union des Industries Métallurgiques et Minières (UIMM), the principal association of metal manufacturers, described the industry as comprising the following branches:

1. Iron and steel making (*sidérurgie*)
2. Shipbuilding
3. Re-forging, or the secondary casting of metals (*fonderie de 2e fusion*)
4. Mechanical engineering
5. Electrical appliance
6. Autos, airplanes, cycles, and accessories
7. Miscellaneous metal fabrication (*fabrication métallique divers*).[19]

During the interwar period, these seven branches were sometimes arranged differently and rarely defined according to an agreed set of criteria, but the above designations suggest something of the range and character of the industry. The office of government statistics and the Labor Ministry applied equally imprecise standards in their various statistical compilations, sometimes accepting the employers' delineation of specific branches and trade groups, sometimes altering them to suit their own categories for measurement and classification. The very nature of the metal industry, however, lent itself to imprecision. Auto and airplane engines, for example, were made from cast parts taken from a blast furnace and rolled, a process distinct to steel making (or metallurgy), as well as from parts cut, planed, drilled, and stamped, activities associated with mechanical engineering. To compound matters, metal producers, concerned with maximizing market options, tended to participate in several industrial branches. As a consequence, most metal-fabricating activities were viewed according to the general concept, which grouped all enterprises smelting or fabricating with metal into a single industrial category.

Because the general concept took precedence over the specific terms defining the industry's different branches, social and economic organizations representing distinct trade groups played a subsidiary role in representing them. Industrialists (even if they belonged to specialized trade groups, like those representing auto makers or electrical-appliance manufacturers) tended to identify with the general concept and make the UIMM, representing the industry as a whole, their principal corporate representative.[20] This tendency was also replicated in the labor movement, which ignored the specific corporate expressions of the different trades and focused on industrial organization. Linguistically, the primacy of the general concept was evident in the term *métallurgiste* (and its popular derivation, *métallo*), used to denote all metal workers, whether they worked in steel plants or auto factories, were highly skilled tool-and-die makers, semi-skilled machine tenders, or unskilled laborers. There were, of course, terms to designate different trades (like fitters, boilermakers, molders, polishers, tinsmiths, turners, etc.), but it was the general term, *métallo*, that reflected the social reality of postwar industry, entered into common parlance, and eventually assumed organizational form.[21]

Paris possessed the largest segment of France's metal industry, embracing five of the seven branches listed above. (Steel making was concentrated in the east and shipbuilding in several Atlantic ports). Of the five Paris branches, auto—"the most representative sector of modern industry all over the globe"— was pivotal. In the 1920s it employed over a quarter of the region's 450,000 metal workers, making it the primary component of France's industrial economy. But mechanical engineering and, to a lesser degree, aviation (both of which were linked to car production) were closely associated with auto's hegemony; in fact, a great many producers combined two or three of these activities under a single roof.[22] As a result, the labor movement that unionized the metal industry in the 1930s would be made up largely of auto, aircraft, and engineering workers. But because there were no rigid lines dividing these various branches, events or forces emanating from one tended to be felt throughout the industry.

Constituting the nation's principal mass-production sector and the seedbed of its future labor movement, the Paris metal industry was responsible for many of the most important developments affecting interwar France. These developments were preeminently economic, but their effects could be felt throughout French society. The sheer magnitude of the industry, evident in the following figures for the year 1931, indicates one of the reasons why this was the case:

Paris (The City)
185,449 metal workers (156,979 male, 28,470 female)
186 plants of 100–500 workers
26 plants of 500+ workers

The Near Suburbs of Paris (The Department of the Seine)
213,480 metal workers (176,263 male, 37,217 female)
232 plants of 100–500 workers
56 plants of 500+ workers

The Far Suburbs of Paris (The Department of the Seine-et-Oise)
48,370 metal workers (42,009 male, 6,361 female)
59 plants of 100–500 workers
11 plants of 500+ workers

Total
447,299 metal workers (375,251 male, 72,048 female)
477 plants of 100–500 workers
93 plants of 500+ workers[23]

These imposing quantitative dimensions were further magnified by the industry's concentration; unlike prewar manufacture, spread over thousands and thousands of small shops, interwar developments concentrated two-thirds of all workers into just 2 percent of metal plants.[24] More consequently, it was in these medium (100–500 workers) and large-scale (500+) plants dominating the heights of the French economy that the most consequential technological and organizational innovations were carried out.

The Fordist-Taylorist Mode of Production

In one sense, the entire history of industrialization is a process of rationalization, based on the progressive division of labor described by Adam Smith. Nevertheless, the rationalization movement of the 1920s, taking up where the wartime innovations left off, did more than advance the fragmentation and mechanization of work tasks. Based on principles formulated by Frederick W. Taylor and Henry Ford, rationalization introduced an altogether different system of production.[25] According to Taylor's theory of scientific management, the main obstacle to higher productivity was the inefficiency of worker control and the craftsman's resistance to economic "rationality." Taylor's managerial innovations sought to circumvent these obstacles by making the craftman's knowledge accessible to the engineer, thereby eliminating his monopoly of technique and lessening the need for skilled labor. Based on an academic understanding of craft technique, the Taylorist engineer was able to divide work tasks into a number of routinized, purely executionary operations that could be performed by semi-skilled workers on specialized machines. The worker's every gesture was then analyzed and broken down into a number of highly subdivided activities—a process known as "phasing." Once this was accomplished, the engineer was able to dictate the "one right way" in which a task was to be done and according to what schedule and remuneration. Deskilling and managerial control were thus central to Taylorization.[26] Ford's strategy, by contrast, was to mass produce a standardized product with interchangeable parts. To accomplish this he introduced extensive mechanization of parceled tasks, situating them in an unbroken circuit of assembly. Coordinated with a continuously moving conveyor belt, Fordist mechanization, in its rational arrangement of space and time, brought about a qualitative increase in the order, speed, and flow of production. Greater quantities could thereby be manufactured at drastically lower costs and with less craft control of production.[27] Ford repeatedly denied that his system owed anything to Taylor—and to the degree that Taylor emphasized the managerial and Ford the mechanical, this was true—but the great auto maker nonetheless depended on Taylor's innovations to adapt labor to intensified mechanization, as well as to augment supervisory authority and enhance the rational organization of the factory.[28]

Looked at together, the innovations of Ford and Taylor had a revolutionary effect on industry, creating a system of manufacture in which the worker was reduced to the purely physical aspect of labor and where all aspects of production—men, machines, and management—were subordinated to a centrally controlled technical system responsible for organizing and coordinating the various fragmented operations linked to the main production circuit. The engineer's technical expropriation of the worker's skill (Taylor) and the worker's integration into a single mechanized production circuit (Ford), together forming the basis of the so-called rationalization movement of the 1920s, constituted what the French would later call the "Fordist-Taylorist mode of production."[29] The process through which the Paris metal industry shifted to this mode occurred in three distinct steps. First, the war years, 1914–18, saw the introduction of American production techniques, the augmentation of mechanization, the concentration and standardization of production, and the creation of an economy of scale. Second, the period of reconstruction, 1921–24, witnessed the consolidation of the wartime developments and their adaptation to peacetime markets. Third, the rationalization movement of 1926–31 generalized Taylor's managerial reforms and Ford's mass-production strategy. By the time the World Depression reached France in 1931, virtually every large-scale and most medium-size metal plants in the Paris Region had become part of the Fordist-Taylorist mode of production.[30]

Governed by a technical system subordinating all facets of production to a single overarching logic, the new productionist mode affected workers in ways entirely foreign to traditional craft systems. Work in the technical system would henceforth be defined by the social organization of the plant and the centralized directives of the methods office (or planning department) and no longer by the product fabricated, the machine used, or the professional qualities of the worker. Antonio Gramsci, one of the first to perceive the nature of this system, characterized its workers as parts of a "human complex"—whose meaning lay in the system's aggravate logic and not the sum of its various component parts.[31] The traditional links between man, his tools, and his work were, in other words, irreparably severed in this new system.

The social consequences of the Fordist-Taylorist mode contrasted sharply with the older artisanal system of production. Prior to the war, workshops in the Paris metal industry had been relatively autonomous.[32] Although orders and production schedules originated with employers and plant directors, skilled workers had considerable leeway in filling them as they saw fit. The foreman, based on his empirical understanding of technique, usually initiated the production process by assigning specific tasks to the shop's workers, who then made the necessary technical decisions for carrying them out, hired and fired their own helpers, and set their own work rhythm. Craft and shop custom played a key role in this system, dictating work rates and shaping worker behavior. Supervision, as a result, tended to be light and discipline enforced by piece rates.[33] This left the individual worker with a high degree of independence and initiative. The shop's general operation, though, revolved around the foreman, who was skilled at the tasks he assigned, knew which men were most appropriate to what jobs, and was not above getting his hands dirty to show a new man how to set up a particular machine or perform a particular assignment. Given his centrality to production, the foreman tended to enjoy the respect of his workers and rarely evoked deep animosities. Each shop was thus internally regulated and relatively independent of others. *Patronal* authority, by contrast, was responsible for establishing the enterprise's general policy, but rarely intervened in the actual manufacturing process.

With the postwar transition to the Fordist-Taylorist mode, all this changed. Henceforth, the different phases of production were subject to a single logic— the technical system—which alone controlled and coordinated the various facets of production. Individual work tasks, as well as general operating schedules, fell, as a result, under the exclusive auspices of managers and engineers in the plant's methods office. Based on a "scientific" study of work activities, the methods office was charged with setting up tasks and schedules, providing incentives for increased productivity, synchronizing the different phases of manufacture, and standardizing procedures. It also specified what machines were to be used, pre-ordered raw materials, instructed supervisors and foremen on the specifications of the assigned work, and fixed remuneration rates. Pieces produced in different shops according to the dictates of the methods office were then fed into a tightly integrated circuit that conveyed them to final assembly, after which they were inspected and prepared for delivery. Because the technical system required the harmonious coordination of numerous shops and assembly processes, it subjected all manufacturing activities to its discipline. A worker failing to perform his task within the time allowed and according to the system's overriding logic was considered a threat to the entire production process. Moreover, the imperative to coordinate time, tasks, and flow meant that supervisory control became absolutely critical to the labor process. Postwar foremen were consequently selected less for their technical competence than their ability to command—for their principal function in the technical system was to transmit orders from above. Likewise, workers were no longer seen as members of a self-regulating team, but rather as individual machine tenders, dependent on orders and schedules issued by the methods office. Foremen thus ceased to identify themselves as team organizers and instead became commanders of a given set of machines, whose operating guidelines were established outside the workshop. Not surprisingly, grievances against foremen escalated throughout the 1920s, as workers came to view them as disciplinarians whose principal role was no longer to be the shop's most astute worker but rather the long arm of management.[34]

The Fordist-Taylorist mode transformed not only the character of production, but the character of the producing class as well.[35] Since the early nineteenth century, Parisian workers had fallen into one of two broad categories: craft worker (*ouvrier professionnel* or OP) and laborer (*ouvrier manoeuvrer* or OM). By definition, a craft worker acquired his skill through a long apprenticeship which familiarized him with some mathematics and mechanical drawing, taught him how to operate a variety of machine tools, allowed him to perform fitting and assembly operations at his bench, and made him reflective about the operations of his trade. After training in a shop or municipal trade school, he usually received a certificate documenting his particular expertise and then, as a journeyman, performed tasks based on his technical knowledge—tasks that required a conscious understanding of the trade and could not be reduced to the execution of simple repetitive movements.[36] In the artisanal system, the craft worker usually began with a blueprint or a design of his own, made all the necessary parts, filed and fitted them together into a finished product, and did all this without interference from boss or foreman. The laborer (OM), by contrast, was an unskilled and hence untrained worker who performed auxiliary tasks (cleaning, supplying materials, conveyance) that freed craftsmen from menial operations, thereby facilitating the flow of materials and products, or else did heavy work in the foundries where engine blocks and other metal components were cast. Although historians sometimes date the deskilling of the Parisian working class around the mid-nineteenth century, when piece rates were introduced, skilled metal workers continued to dominate Parisian labor markets until the second decade of the twentieth century.

While prewar labor was characterized by the prominence of the OP/OM relationship, the postwar era saw the rise of an entirely new type of worker: the semi-skilled machine tender (the *ouvrier spécialisé* or OS). Mechanical conveyance and assembly-line production automatically diminished the need for laborers (OM), just as the introduction of specialized or single-purpose machine tools manned by semi-skilled operatives engaged in highly routinized tasks reduced the demand for skilled labor. This shifted the entire division of labor from a qualitative to a quantitative mode. Craft workers (OP) were consequently eliminated from many assembly shops and machine-work operations (or, like the "machine-builders" of the prewar era, turned into machine-tending OS). Skilled workers were not eliminated in the change-over to the new production mode, but their significance within the labor process sharply declined. Those refusing to suffer this affront to their autonomy could, of course, retreat to small shops subcontracted to the giant producers, where serial production remained uneconomical and where skills were needed for a variety of polyvalent tasks, but if they remained in large-scale plants, they were usually assigned to do quality work on lathes, millers, and borers, assist the OS in selecting, modifying, and adjusting machines, or run the tool room and the maintenance department of the plant, both of which were vital to production, but no longer part of the actual manufacturing process. Moreover, because Fordist-Taylorist engineers never succeeded in routinizing all tasks, skilled workers remained a necessary component of the new factory system.

But they were no longer needed to organize work teams, train apprentices, or constitute the indispensable component of manufacture, as they had before the war, when industry operated according to the artisanal mode. Not coincidentally, these workers whose skills were threatened by the new forms of production would make up the core of the small union movement of the 1920s and the nucleus around which the movement of the 1930s developed.

On the eve of the World Depression, half of all metal workers were categorized as "skilled" (although the term "skilled" at this stage, when apprenticeship had been abridged and skills more narrowly defined, possessed a less rigorous meaning). The other half were designated as non-skilled (30 percent OS, 20 percent OM).[37] The relation of skilled to non-skilled, however, varied according to sector and was in the process of evolving. In aviation, where production remained largely artisanal, the relation was two to one; the OP also outnumbered the OS in the small workshops of the mechanical-engineering sector. By contrast, in armament and electrical-appliance factories, where production revolved around the assembly of elementary parts, the OS greatly outnumber the OP. In auto, situated between these two extremes, the relation of OS to OP was close to fifty-fifty but tending toward the diminution of the OP. Touraine estimates that in 1925, several years after the Renault auto works adopted a Fordist structure, the OP made up 46 percent of its workforce and that by 1939, had dropped to 32 percent; at Peugot and Citroen, where rationalization went further, skilled workers represented no more than a quarter of the workforce.[38]

The semi-skilled mass-production worker (OS) created by the technical system was not, it needs stressing, simply a demoted OP, but a new kind of worker altogether—one who owed his existence to the spread of automatic and specialized machine tools, assembly-line operations, and the technical organization of production. As the distinctive worker of the Fordist-Taylorist factory system, the OS was employed to the degree that industry became mechanized and labor parceled. Concentrated in the assembly, machining, and mass-production departments of the new factories, he usually performed a series of elementary and repetitive gestures that were purely executionary and required no professional knowledge or creativity, only an adaptation to the rhythms of the machine or the line.[39] Because his job could be learned in a few hours or a few days and required little training or initiative, he was preeminently replaceable—indiscriminately hired in times of high demand, dismissed in periods of slack, discarded when age prevented him from keeping up with the demands of mechanization or the flow of production. Paid according to piece rates, the OS's working life was governed by the clock, which forced him to produce so many pieces, in so many seconds without reflection or respite.[40] He was consequently not allowed to stop, smoke a cigarette, or chat with his fellow workers, for if he failed to keep up with the rhythm of the machine or the minutely calibrated pace of the assembly line, he was likely to be discharged.[41] The new science of management, in fact, required that every facet of his activity be planned and controlled. He was thus always at the beck and call of the foreman. "Never do anything, even in the slightest, that constitutes an initiative," Simone Weil recalled from her experience in the Paris metal industry. "Every gesture has to represent the execution of an order." These orders, moreover, were given in a curt tone, because authority demanded it and because the OS "didn't count."[42]

The OS's lack of personal freedom was further compounded by the organizational labyrinth of large-scale production. Situated in gigantic plants, he was isolated at his post, surrounded by machines, and engaged in a highly fragmented process that was nonetheless part of a centralized totality involving masses of workers. This restricted his freedom of movement, limiting him to a simple routine performed at high speed, usually in conjunction with a machine or a conveyor belt; the noise and strain of the line further restricted the possibilities for social intercourse. His personality and intelligence were thus constantly subject to mechanical forces, just as his pride and self-respect were bombarded by the system's harsh and seemingly arbitrary dictates.[43] Moreover, the OS rarely felt a commitment to his work or found an expression of his personality in the products he created; so deprived, his personality tended to lack depth or cultivation. In this respect, he perfectly embodied the Marxist "proletarian."[44] But perhaps the most intolerable aspect of the new factory system was its anti-social character. The nature of the new labor process cut the OS off from his fellow workers, emptying the factory of sociability. Personal recollections from this period almost always stressed the sad, lonely character of the factory experience.[45] "There is no place," one worker wrote, "that is so foreign as this factory where I spend eight hours every day."[46] Finally, because he was relegated to a minutely subdivided task that was monotonous, isolating, and repetitive and because the quantitative logic of the division of labor robbed work of all personality, the OS became virtually interchangeable with every other OS. Such a system, as John Ruskin might have observed, divided labor not merely into a series of mindless operations, it divided the laborer himself, reducing him to a fragment devoid of dignity or any transfiguring element.

Unlike the OP, who experienced the Fordist-Taylorist system as a threat to his skills, the OS was mainly afflicted by the inhuman rhythms of the technical system, the insecurity of employment, the meaninglessness of work, and the degradation of his spirit.[47] Only his marginal place in French society and his lack of alternatives kept him at a job that most Frenchmen felt beneath their dignity. His consciousness, as a consequence, tended to reflect a certain type of proletarian misery, not the OP's concern for occupational autonomy or professional respect. But while the Fordist-Taylorist mode of production confined him to a low rung in the factory hierarchy and instilled in him a sense of passivity and powerlessness, it nonetheless created a work environment in which the barriers between different categories of workers were gradually broken down. The rise of the OS, in fact, helped narrow the gap separating the skilled "aristocrats" and the non-skilled. Wage differentials, moreover, began to decline after the war, as OS piece rates became increasingly comparable to skilled wages. More importantly, OS and OP each opposed the system—for different reasons to be sure—and each shared an interest in mitigating its negative effects. In time, the OS's discontent would join that of the OP and create a new alignment in the labor movement.[48] In the first postwar decade, however, skilled and non-skilled *métallos* working in the same firm were likely to belong to different worlds and have different, if not incompatible relations to the labor movement.

The Illiberal *Patronat*

The difficulties facing workers in the Fordist-Taylorist factory system were compounded by the illiberal attitudes of the French *patronat*. Louis Bergeron argues that the "France of the *chateaux*" was never really "conquered" by bourgeois France.[49] Unlike English entrepreneurs, descended from the ranks of commoners and influenced by the gnostic project of low-church Protestants, the French bourgeoisie was a relatively "closed" class, marked more by the aristocratic ethos of the Old Regime than the democratizing forces of market society.[50] This heritage did not prevent it from embracing liberal republican politics (inherent in the very nature of capitalism), but it did cause it to anchor its value system in family and tradition and to view production as a proprietary inheritance rather than a social responsibility. The fact that the Renault and Citroen works and many of the largest and most modern metal plants were closely associated with their founders and incorporated only late in the interwar period added further weight to the notion of inheritance.[51] Within this traditionalist view of the enterprise, there was little room for democratic relations or contractual norms. According to one metal worker, "the manager is like the king of France"—and the king was not expected to bargain or negotiate, only reign.[52] Yet however much the French bourgeoisie emulated the magisterial disposition of the aristocracy, it nonetheless prided itself on its own distinct character, defined in terms of industrial leadership and codified in strict hierarchies of control.[53] Even more than its preoccupation with profit and financial gain, this sense of command guided *patronal* behavior and imbued it with an autocratic sense of jurisdiction. Not surprisingly, workers in this scheme, like tenants on the manor, had neither the right nor the supposed capacity to interfere with the management of the enterprise.

The personal, familial, and authoritarian disposition of the *patronat* was likewise reflected in the management of the technical system. Because managers in this system were recruited from elite professional schools rather than from the ranks of skilled workers, class barriers that might have been mitigated through internal recruitment were replicated in the managerial hierarchy.[54] Moreover, these school-trained engineers and supervisors generally lacked familiarity with the practical aspects of production, which made it difficult for them to communicate with those responsible for production on the shop floor, understand their specific needs, or develop those personal bonds crucial to worker morale. Their exercise of authority assumed, as a result, a distant, unilateral character, offensive to the worker's democratic sensibilities. This haughty style was further buttressed by the legacy of nineteenth-century economic liberalism, which viewed workers as mere labor-providing commodities, whose rights or claims had been purchased with their weekly wages.[55]

Neither the war nor the new forms of production did much to mitigate this archaic managerial structure. Military supervision between 1914 and 1918 and the technical system introduced in the 1920s did much, in fact, to reinforce the traditionalist conception of the enterprise and magnify managerial authority. After the war, *patrons* continued to view themselves as masters to whom workers owed complete and unquestioned obedience.[56] In the face of worker grievances, which were bound to be numerous, metal employers were prone to respond with moralistic appeals to harmony and joint interests.[57] If conflicts arose in the shops, they looked to foremen, recruited from worker ranks, to mediate them. In cases where isolated trade unionists sought contractual relations, they were treated as an anathema, sacked and blacklisted when possible.[58] Collective bargaining and worker representation consequently played little role in French industry. It was also an article of faith among employers that most workers were hostile to adversarial forms of organization. Whenever disputes broke out, they attributed them to union militants and "outside agitators," never to their own policies.[59] This simplistic view of the enterprise and its workers, to be sure, ignored the social complexities of the modern factory, but it logically followed from the employer's sense that he was the *patron* of the industrial order and thus the one, like the aristocrat in his chateau, who was alone responsible for the enterprise.[60]

The war did have one significant effect on employer behavior: it revived a lapsed sense of paternalism. The verso of authoritarianism, paternalism aimed at mitigating the harsher aspects of factory life and demonstrating the master's concern for his workers. Between 1914 and 1918 and again in the course of the early 1920s, canteens, child care, housing services, infirmaries, and certain welfare schemes were introduced by the larger industrialists, while others sponsored sporting teams, recreational facilities, and cooperatives. Progressive employers, like Citroen, even experimented with American sociological methods designed to instill self-discipline and "rational" forms of behavior in their workers. In general, though, these measures had but a superficial effect on the factory's social system and rarely survived the decline of labor strife in the mid and late 1920s. Yet even these isolated displays of paternalism, constituting the more positive aspect of the employer's self-conception, were premised on the belief that workers were creatures in need of direction, dependent on the benevolence and guidance of their *patrons*.[61]

The Labor Market

Following an earlier tradition, the trade-union press characterized the new factories as penal colonies *(bagnes)* and barracks *(casernes)*, where the convict or the conscript was subjected to a supervisory system based on fear and coercion. According to one woman machine tender: "The employer imposes his will and we submit. All day long we are made to work like the damned. In every sense of the word, it's forced labor."[62] In a similar vein, a skilled metal smith described his employer's view of workers as "machines designed solely for his benefit. Too bad for those who don't produce enough. It's the door for them."[63] But perhaps the most insufferable aspect of employer dominance was its psychological effect. Whenever a manager exercised his authority in the new factory system, the worker could not help but feel humiliated, for everything seemed designed to offend his dignity. If he strayed from his workstation or wandered into another workshop without permission, if he caused a minor defect in production, made an impertinent remark, or was a few minutes late, he was likely to be treated as a lawbreaker.

Harsh, humiliating social relations, though, were not the sole affliction besetting these workers. The technical calculus of the Fordist-Taylorist system never factored in their health or humanity. The result was a repugnant, often dangerous work environment. The worker press of the period abounds in stories of workers sacrificing fingers, hands, arms, hair, even their lives to the technological innovations carried out in the new large-scale metal plants.[64] In addition to machines that mutilated and frequently operated at unsafe speeds, working conditions were blighted by noxious fumes and clouds of metal dust, poor ventilation, extreme temperatures, and cramped, ill-lit, and insalubrious shops. Rare was the enterprise whose workers did not complain of deplorable conditions. Not coincidentally, tuberculosis, respiratory disease, toxic poisoning, and injury accidents were higher in metal than in any other sector of the French economy, including coal mining.[65] These hazardous work conditions, along with the technical system's authoritarian style of control and its unvaried grind, created a social situation that seemed to cry out for redress. Yet except for sporadic outbursts of instinctive protest, metal workers were quiescent throughout most of the 1920s. Besides the normal fear of reprisal, this quiescence was a product of two related factors: the social character of the workforce and the turbulent nature of the job market.

With 20 percent of the active male population dead or permanently disabled by the war, the postwar expansion was predicated on new labor sources. Between 1921 and 1931, 1.3 million migrants from Bretagne and Normandie, Anjou and Maine, the Loire Valley and other rural provinces left the French countryside to fill urban labor markets. In the same period, 2 million immigrant workers, largely from Poland and Italy, but also from Spain, Belgium, Greece, Russia, Armenia, North Africa, and Southeast Asia entered the country.[66] Paris and her suburbs were the principal recipient of these workers. By 1926, there were 20,000 foreigners in the metal industry of Paris, 30,000 in that of her suburbs. Five years later, 10.5 percent of all French metal workers were foreign (compared to 4 percent prior to the war).[67] In addition to foreigners, women entered postwar industry in unprecedented numbers, making up 15 percent of the total metal workforce (compared to 6.7 percent before 1914 and 30 percent during the war). These women workers often did the most dangerous and difficult work, at wage rates up to 40 percent less than their male counterparts.[68] The feminization of metal work was directly linked to rationalization and mechanization, which diminished the need for skilled male workers and degraded the character of labor.[69] And wherever there were large numbers of women, there were inevitably large numbers of youth. Taken into industry as apprentices at the age of thirteen and fourteen, these adolescents were employed as laborers (OM), frequently receiving none of the training that justified their employment and earning wages a mere fraction of what women earned.[70] Together, women, youth, foreigners, and rural migrants constituted nearly half the postwar *métallos*—and a clear majority of the unskilled and semi-skilled categories.[71] Without professional training, job security, and corporate traditions, these highly proletarianized workers tended to switch back and forth between widely varied forms of employment. Because they were always moving about, gravitating to plants in whatever industry whose wages and conditions seemed attractive, they commonly failed to develop an affiliation with a particular trade or economic sector: this nomadism, with its attendant insecurities and lack of social place, was in fact their most defining characteristic.[72] And because they were restricted to the most wretched categories of labor, had harried, empty working lives, with few social attachments and low levels of "job consciousness," they lacked the human and economic resources to challenge the "rationalized" work procedures of the new factory system. As a consequence, outbursts of rage and discontent seldom disrupted their subservience in the plants, just as strikes, workstoppages, and trade unions played little role in their working lives.

The quiescence of these workers was also structurally related to the character of the job market. Industrial workers had traditionally been an unstable lot, hired and fired without much formality. This was no less the case in the postwar metal industry. A *métallo* in search of employment would usually wait outside a factory gate to see if an employer had need of someone with his skills or experience. After showing his work certificate and taking a brief medical exam by a company doctor, he might be hired—provided there was no evidence he was a trade unionist, a Communist, or a drunk. The contract he then signed was largely a formality, for it lacked collective significance and afforded few individual legal rights. It also left wage rates undefined or else based them on piecework and bonus systems, which were frequent sources of dispute.[73] In addition, the contract provided no form of redress. The sole means by which workers were able to present grievances, demand higher wages, or press for minor changes in conditions was through striking. In the absence of viable unions, metal strikes in the 1920s were usually spontaneous, without leadership or preparation; as a result, they typically broke out only in cases where accumulated tensions and frustrations bypassed the threshold of restraint. These strikes almost always focused on wage demands, even if other grievances provoked them, and rarely challenged the conditions of employment. Moreover, in large factories, strikes began and were generally limited to a single or a few related workshops, where the demands of a particular trade or work site lacked relevance to workers in other parts of the plant. Skilled workers normally had some bargaining leverage in these strikes, OS and OM only in periods when the employer could not afford to interrupt production; rarely did their struggles merge.[74]

The tight labor market, created by the industrial expansion of the 1920s and the shortage of available labor, also encouraged high rates of turnover. As long as the economy was expanding and hiring practices remained casual, workers had little difficulty jumping from plant to plant. The auto industry, with its seasonal fluctuations, annual model changes, and periodic layoffs, was especially prone to turnover. At Citroen, for instance, it exceeded 100 percent annually. High turnover, moreover, made strikes almost superfluous; it was often easier to find a new job, with a slightly better wage or a more tolerable foreman, than "to negotiate by strike." Spontaneous strikes, as a result, tended to blend into the normal turnover process, as workers found individualist solutions to their various employment problems.[75] The most qualified *métallos*, whose scarce skills were in high demand, and the least skilled, who did the hardest, most brutalizing work, were generally the ones engaging in turnover.[76] Those, therefore, who were able to organize and lead and those whose grievances were the fuel of revolt, both had outlets in this period to satisfy their respective needs.[77] In such a labor market, beset with high turnover and constant expansion, the heterogeneous components of the mass-production sector were without those individual qualities that might have enabled them to resist the technical system of production, as well as the structural cohesion to solidify into a self-conscious social entity capable of asserting their collective interests.

Deracination and Deculturation

As craftsmen were technologically demoted in the Fordist-Taylorist mode of production, traditional forms of residence and culture underwent a similar demotion. In the decade prior to the war, but especially during it, the Paris metal industry began relocating to the suburbs (*la banlieue*). In the process immigrants, peasant migrants, women, and craftsmen seeking work in the new factories were compelled to resettle in hastily developed towns north and west of Paris where they were subject to various forms of deracination and deculturation.

The life they encountered in these suburban towns was unlike anything faced by prewar workers.[78] Up until the twentieth century, when every quarter or *faubourg* of Paris had been a sort of village, skilled workers had been rooted in communities animated by their own values and traditions. The impersonal forces of liberalism and capitalism, with their utilitarian and contractual relations, had yet taken these communities fully in their grip. In his study of nineteenth-century Belleville, the most renowned of Paris's worker communities, Gérard Jacquemet found that the social and corporate identity of its workers was nearly inseparable from their communal identity. Most Belleville craftsmen, for instance, were born in Paris; the small trickle of rural and foreign workers who settled there easily assimilated into the dominant artisan milieu.[79] Through identification with their craft and the organic communities formed around it, these skilled workers aquired a body of moral resources—a sense of honor, mastery, responsibility—that freed them from many aspects of wage labor. For example, if a foreman or employer displeased such a worker, he would think little of packing up his tools and looking elsewhere for work. This autonomy made him a fierce individualist, but one whose individualism was anchored in and sustained by stable, well-defined communities whose marital, social, family, and communal life was closely associated with that of the trade. The links between the workshop, the street, and the stoop were thus closely knit. This is not to say that capitalism had not already begun to commodify and depersonalize labor prior to the war, but only that the *faubourgs'* craftsmen retained enough traditional and communal supports to minimize the weight of market relations. Moreover, the pride these workers took in their skills and in the traditions of the trade helped reinforce their sense of community, buffering them from the atomizing forces of liberal capitalism.[80] Labor conflict in the *faubourgs*, as a result, frequently took on the character of a "local struggle"—

mobilizing not merely the community of the trade, but the community *qua* community, as social, economic, familial, and communitarian identities converged along a single axis, assuming the quality of a "total conflict."[81]

In the years leading up to the Great War, the Second Industrial Revolution began wearing away the outer layers of this artisanal world; the war and the boom years of the 1920s destroyed its core.[82] Propelled away from the city center by rising rents and scarce housing and forced to relocate to its periphery and then to hastily constructed communities in surrounding suburbs, postwar workers progressively lost their identity with a particular locality. In the process, they were thrown back on their own individual devices. This would sever the ties between work and residence and undermine the older forms of sociability and community, transforming the suburban population into an amorphous mass in which each isolated atom lived only for himself. Workmates consequently ceased being neighbors and labor consciousness lost its key component. Suburban workers, as a result, would have difficulty sustaining the values and solidarities that had given craft workers in the *faubourgs* their socially durable moorings.[83] The breakdown of community and its destructive effects on labor consciousness were further exacerbated by the ceaseless incursions of rural migrants and foreigners into the new communities, for these newcomers added many heterogeneous and alienating elements to a situation in which face-to-face relations, ascribed social status, and communally rooted identities were being replaced by impersonal, mobile, and purely functional affiliations.

The inhospitable nature of the suburbs constituted another source of deracination. The hurly-burly growth of large-scale factories during the 1920s and the massive influx of workers to staff them caused suburban towns to mushroom at an astonishing rate, many of them doubling in population in the course of a five- or ten-year period. In the decade between 1911 and 1921, the Paris suburbs grew by 239,300 inhabitants; between 1921 and 1931, they swelled by over a million.[84] These figures are especially impressive if one considers that interwar France experienced virtually no population growth at all. Although Paris continued to house a significant worker population (a third of Parisian *métallos* continued to live there), the city had already embarked on a process of gentrification that would diminish the size and significance of its worker inhabitants.[85] Henceforth, the Paris working class would be associated mainly with the new suburbs. Saint-Denis, north of the city, and Boulogne-Billancourt to the west, both of which had begun to develop prior to the war, were the largest and most important of these suburban communities, but numerous adjacent towns, whose empty fields and truck gardens were suddenly inundated by factories, railroads, and improvised housing, grew throughout the 1920s, transforming the northwest sector of the Paris Region into one of the densest industrial concentrations in postwar Europe.[86]

As these suburban towns expanded and industrialized, their infrastructures strained to assimilate the influx of new workers. A pervasive housing shortage represented the most serious consequence of this growth. During the war, there had been little constructions anywhere in France and in the following decade French building efforts were concentrated mainly in the war-devastated north; moreover, it was not until the late 1920s that the government realized housing was a social problem that had to be tackled on a national scale. As postwar workers were left with little option but to crowd into existing suburban facilities, all the problems of uncontrolled urbanization proliferated in the new communities. One prominent historian of the period claims the Paris working class was the worst housed in all Europe.[87] In addition to a shortage of adequate housing, transportation, electrification, water, sanitation, and schooling were also appallingly inadequate. As population growth outpaced available services, parts of the Paris suburbs were transformed into shanty towns, full of the privations and miseries that we today associate with the squatter settlements surrounding the burgeoning cities of the Third World. One depressing testament to the wretchedness of these suburban towns, where "neither air, space, cleanliness nor beauty" had a place, was the fact that in the mid-1930s, 600,000 people in the Paris Region were infected with tuberculosis, a disease associated with unhealthy living conditions, and nearly 200,000 lived in tenements condemned by public health officials.[88] Child mortality rates, diphtheria, and other health problems were also unusually high. Given the housing shortage, most single workers had little choice but to live in dreary, ill-kept residence hotels, which housed up to a third of the population in some towns, while family men either built poorly constructed houses that lacked running water and indoor toilets or else squeezed their families into a rented room or two. Both types of housing were overcrowded and hive-like, offered little in the way of amenities, and gave the suburbs a drab, dingy appearance.[89] Not surprisingly, the inhabitants of these tenements, shacks, and residence hotels, haphazardly thrown together, felt little sense of solidarity or community. The arrival of 500,000 immigrants to fill the breaches in the postwar labor market affixed strains of another sort.[90]

Between the two world wars, various efforts were made to remedy the problems of rapid, unplanned suburban development and recapture something of the sociabilities, traditions, and identities that had been lost with the break up of the *faubourgs*. Suburban workers, however, had been torn from their former existence and deprived of the roots and branches that might have enabled them to rebuild their world. They suffered, moreover, from the psychic effects of deracination, isolation, and the absence of stable social networks, all of which made them vulnerable to what was probably the most deculturating and deracinating of the postwar forces, the "culture industry."[91]

As consumption in the 1920s succumbed to the same market forces responsible for routinizing work in the new factories and as "culture" became a commodity to be peddled like other commodities, customary values and modes of behavior began to give way in the surburbs to mass-produced standards that altered the character of popular life and homogenized its externals. The standardization of manufactured products, in a word, entailed the standardization of those who produced them—for the mass production of identical objects was intended for the use of men who were supposed to be no less alike. This was conspicuous in numerous facets of postwar existence, but particularly so in the new forms of dress, made possible by the advent of cheap, ready-made, but fashionable clothes. Except for the persistence of the peaked cap, few articles remained to denote the worker's social position. Female fashions were especially devoid of class insignia. Off the job, women factory workers were inclined to "turn coat," becoming almost indistinguishable from their middle-class counterparts. Silk stockings, elevated hem lines, bobbed hair, the latest styles—all within reach of modest pocketbooks—would henceforth ensconce working women in a fashionable world removed from the styles and mores of their communities.[92] Given the tremendous social significance of clothes, the new female fashions, with their suppression of local color and their uniformity, did much to "emancipate" working women from the cultural confines of their class.

Men were no less affected by the new forms of consumption. This was particularly the case with sports. In the 1920s, spectacles of professional cyclists, race-car drivers, and footballers, organized by market forces and accompanied by fabricated fanfares, gave rise to sporting cults that no religion or tradition could rival. The most avidly consumed papers in this period—and it was only in the 1920s that the mass-circulation press took off in France—were devoted to athletic events and all the great heroes of the age were athletes. Sports in fact came to dominate popular discourse, providing one of the most important reference points for social life. Just as working-class women assimilated the commercialized standards of the postwar world through fashionable affordable clothes, their male counterparts were lured into the commercialized realm of sporting spectacles, where activity was willed for its own sake, performance was judged according to purely quantitative criteria, and individual achievement took priority.[93] Unlike the athleticism fascinating fascists in the 1930s, the French sports craze of the 1920s was foreign to any belief in honor or self-discipline, any love of combat or courage, based as it was on the spectacular obsessions of those seeking escape in entertainments that were inherently passive and affirmative, promoting adjustment, rather than transcendence.

Sports and fashions were by no means the sole postwar forces reshaping the worker's cultural universe. The cinema, the phonograph, the mass-circulation newspaper, the glossy magazine, and soon the radio were equally significant.[94] The motion picture, for example, exerted an unprecedented effect on popular tastes and values.[95] Its powerful imaginary world, with its emphasis on "sex appeal" and its exaltation of pleasure-seeking, probably did more than any other factor to reorder the mind and senses of those enmeshed in the new forms of production and culture. As George Orwell notes, "movies and the mass production of cheap smart clothes" thoroughly refurbished the mental world of the popular classes. "You may have three halfpence in your pocket and not a prospect in the world and only the corner of a leaky bedroom to go home to; but in your new clothes you can stand on the street corner, indulging in a private day dream of yourself as Clark Gable or Greta Garbo. . . . Whole sections of the working class who have been plundered of all they really need are being compensated, in part, by cheap luxuries which mitigate the surface of life."[96]

As film fantasies, electronic music, mass-produced opinions, standardized clothes, advertised tastes, and radio programs began reshaping popular sensibilities, workers became increasingly subject to outside influences and values. Unlike former periods, when the real world was a man's village or neighborhood and his mental connections were governed by a locally generated consensus governed by tradition and common purpose, the postwar culture industry created a situation in which a few hubs of information, taste, and entertainment, controlled by the money powers, were able to mold the opinions and mores of millions. Torn from their former communities, overwhelmed by the new forms of production, and concerned with buying a movie ticket, workers now had their heads turned by hucksters and influence peddlers marketing tardy goods, vulgar life styles, and manufactured illusions.[97] In undermining the old traditions of popular culture, the vulgarity and mass-mindedness fostered by these developments did little to raise cultural standards or deepen the quality of life. Moreover, whenever workers in this period sought to satisfy their needs through the new forms of cultural consumption, they were inevitably led back to the artificial and atomized relations they had sought to escape, for the packaged products of the postwar culture industry inevitably replicated the forms and principles underlying the new economic system. In characterizing these trends, one trade unionist disparagingly concluded that: "Today, life in and outside the factories is similar to life in America [and] has no other aim than the pursuit of crass material satisfaction. . . . To achieve this satisfaction, people seem willing to accept any kind of servitude."[98]

Because the culture industry colonized everyday life in ways comparable to labor's demotion in the new factory system, social role and cultural identity began to diverge in the 1920s.[99] While workers on their way home from the tedious grind of the factory continued to escape in bistros and retained much of the rough, informal manners distinct to their class, their view of and their relation to the real world was progressively taken over by the culture industry. As worker life succumbed to these forces, hostility to the impersonal, class-privileged tendencies of liberal society tended to give way to submissiveness and passivity, or else took the form of cynicism and individualism. One especially well-positioned observer noted that the Parisian worker who talked of nothing but socialist and anti-clerical politics before the war now seemed concerned only with sports, film, and women.[100] This, of course, did not herald the extinction of cultural diversity or the erosion of all communal forms, but it did affect those forms of struggle and resistance which traditional culture and interdependent social relations free of market-defined socialization had once made possible.

The Red Belt

The passivity and powerlessness fostered by mass production and the culture industry were not at all comparable to the sensibilities of the trade-union militant who lived for the pride taken in his craft and the communal virtues it fostered. Yet without the trades to provide an alternative model of how the world ought to be organized and without the solidarities provided by stable, identity-defining communities, the standardized individuals of the Fordist-Taylorist system, severed and thus excluded from organic forms of meaning and value, were easily influenced by the life-molding forces exerted by mass culture and mass production. The "little platoons," which Edmund Burke considered the "first principle of public affection," would consequently give way in this period to anonymous collective forces that defined freedom in purely materialistic terms, opposed all that tradition and community had formerly revered, and turned society into an atomized collection of individuals.[101] Accompanying this process of cultural expropriation and communal breakdown was the rise of mass politics. As José Ortega y Gasset trenchantly observes, the socially alienated "mass man," uprooted from the securities and customs of the past and cast adrift in a world where quantitative principles ruled, was prone to "redemptive politics," whose myths and mystiques helped compensate for the alienating conditions of impersonal market relations.[102]

It seemed, moreover, to make little difference if these myths and mystiques—the false promises of mass society—were peddled by democratic opportunists or by idealists associated with an Asiatic dictatorship.[103] Shortly after its formation in 1920, the Parti Communiste Français (PCF) sought to make the Paris suburbs and their great factories the principal focus of its activities.[104] One of the party's first and most important achievements was its depiction of the suburbs as *une terre ouvrière,* home to the revolutionary proletariat that one day was expected to encircle and supplant the capital of the French bourgeoisie. In portraying the suburbs as special enclaves representing the society of the future, communists endeavored to convert a sense of deprivation into a source of pride and hope, arraying the workers' tribal "us" against the evil "them." To whatever degree the disparate inhabitants of the suburbs would come to imagine themselves as a community, it would largely be in these ideological terms—that reduced the problems of proletarianization and rapid social change to problems of economics and "class struggle."[105] The communist myth of a proletarian counter-society was, though, less an alternative to liberal society than a mass or democraticized version of it, derived as it was from Marx's neo-Hegelian appropriation of liberal, materialist tenets.[106] But even in this derivative vision of mass society, the myth of a *terre ouvrière* offered workers a symbolic recourse to the existing order, evoking an age when the good life was defined not in terms of a fair wage or the primacy of economic satisfactions, but according to those non-quantitative fundaments underlying organic communities, such as work, mutual aid, and communal solidarity.

The party's appeal, however, went beyond the ideological. In the absence of local elites and with state neglect of suburban growth, the PCF was nearly alone among French parties in addressing the various social pathologies associated with postwar suburban developments. During the 1920s, Communist electoral politics was able to achieve a certain success as a form of "sewer socialism." In many suburban municipalities, it was the PCF that was responsible for installing water mains and drainage systems, introducing electricity, building schools, extending bus lines and tramways, paving streets, developing public housing, and providing a variety of welfare services. The party also took the lead in forming clubs, sporting associations, youth groups, and vacation colonies that provided the suburbs with their first organized forms of sociability. In thus looking out for the "little guy," furnishing those social supports that family, work, and community once supplied, the party was able to capture the electoral allegiance of an ever-growing number of suburban workers. As early as 1924, it held nine town halls in the Paris Region, was politically influential in a dozen others, and had become closely identified with the political and social life of the suburbs.[107] One historian claims that "in some Paris suburbs, to grow up Communist [was] as natural as to grow up French."[108] This did not mean that the rootless, deculturated suburban masses, whose sensibilities and social models had been taken over by mass production and industrial culture, suddenly turned to political activism to escape the meaningless routines of their working lives. Most, in fact, remained passive, marginal figures who

The Labor Movement
in the Paris Metal Industry

FRENCH UNIONS WERE ONLY REMOTELY COMPARABLE TO their counterparts in other industrial countries. The absence of a general political consensus, the persistence of an artisanal system of factory production, and the illiberal character of the employer class tended to favor unions whose economic axes were weak and political orientations strong. French unions consequentially oriented to agitation and mobilization more than to organization and contractual agreement. These extra-institutional orientations were further exacerbated by the ideology of revolutionary syndicalism, which reflected the libertarian aspirations of skilled workers in small factories and shops. Unsurprisingly, little in this union tradition spoke to the concerns of mass-production workers in the postwar factory system.

The Heritage of Revolutionary Syndicalism

Trade unionism appeared relatively late in France. *Compagnonnages*, mutualities, and *sociétés de résistance*—forms of worker organization bearing the imprint of pre-industrial society—persisted long into the nineteenth century. Only in 1862, after encountering British unionists at the Universal Exposition

27

in London, did French workers take up modern forms of trade unionism, and only in 1884 did their unions achieve legal recognition. Yet long after their introduction and legalization, unions failed to attract more than a handful of followers. This was largely due to the character of French industry, which was dominated by small and medium-size enterprises situated in labor markets with inelastic wage rates, limited employment options, artisanal forms of production, and employers resistant to negotiations. In such a market, unions could offer workers neither material advantage nor shop floor leverage.

When national unions, like those affiliated with the Confédération Générale du Travail (CGT), began to emerge at the turn of the century, it was more for political than economic reasons. France's long history of popular insurrection and violent constitutional revision had fostered a situation in which the existing order could never be taken for granted. In the words of one historian, "A revolution seemed almost a normal way to affect political and social change."[1] Because barricades and toppled governments became the "normal way" of achieving reform, much of nineteenth-century political life succumbed to a cycle of reaction and revolution—in which a defensive right, hostile to republicanism and liberalism, vied with an insurgent, but anti-social left. The result was a fragmented political system, dominated by unresponsive institutions that required major social upheavals to redress grievances and bring about reform. Toward the end of the century, this tradition of political strife was grafted onto the social and class conflicts provoked by the Second Industrial Revolution.[2] In the process, working-class identity was fused with republicanism and the radical traditions of democracy, while the labor question was posed in terms of the revolutionary heritage.

Besides politicizing social antagonisms, the revolutionary heritage complicated the organizational tasks of unionism. In the 1880s and 1890s, a host of rival socialist sects identified with this heritage vied with one another in an effort to mobilize workers behind their particular political projects. In competing for popular allegiances, Guesdists, Allemanists, Possibilists, and Blanquists ended up cultivating deep political cleavages within the worker elite, severely compounding the problems of unionization.[3] To overcome these sectarian rifts and enhance worker unity, unionists eventually took up the anarchist slogan of "no politics in the unions."[4] Parties, they concluded, "artificially" divided workers along ideological lines, while economic interests united them on common ground. As Emile Pouget put it, "the union's purpose is to make war on the bosses, not engage in politics."[5]

Yet however much unionists resisted party interference in their affairs, they remained committed to goals that were as political as those of the anarchists who cried "no politics." Like their libertarian mentors, the first generation of CGT unionists believed direct action at the point of production, not parliamentary electioneering, was key to overcoming bourgeois dominance and eliminating commodity production based on wage labor. *Votards* pinning their hopes on ballots rather than barricades, even if their votes went to socialists, were a frequent object of scorn. In union eyes, liberal-democractc institutions were inherently plutocratic, weighed against the interests and aspirations of the popular classes. If workers were ever to free themselves from "wage slavery" and achieve power and social mastery, they had to rely on themselves, not middle-class politicians affiliated with the bourgeois state. Unlike the working class as a whole, which tended to support liberal republicans and moderate socialists, the CGT's artisan elite, the sole proponent of the class's will to power, viewed the established parties as agents of an opposed class and "Lib-Lab" alliances as a betrayal of class loyalties. True to the revolutionary and anarchist influences shaping their world view, these CGT'ers considered class war the only viable way of overthrowing the established order. Then, in 1906, at the CGT Congress of Amiens, the anti-parliamentary politics of these revolutionary unionists was codified in a charter that defined the CGT as an ersatz "class-party"—abstentious toward bourgeois institutions, yet bent on their radical transformation.[6] This would give the CGT a distinct political coloration, even if it formally reputed electoral activity.

Those identifying with the 1906 charter adhered to a form of unionism known as *syndicalisme révolutionnaire,* which ideologically reflected the world view of highly skilled workers in small shops in the building and metal trades who were hostile to the dominant forms of state and society. Proud of their technical knowledge, these craftsmen were convinced that they, better than the "parasitic" *patronat,* could manage production in a rational and socially progressive manner and that their values and institutions represented a higher form of organization than those of the money powers. Revolutionary syndicalism was not, however, merely an expression of craft egoism; it also reflected the realities of an economy dependent on skilled labor, for this was an age in which "the mechanic was still the master, not the servant of the machine."[7] Thus confident of their ability to run industry, they looked to the unions to overthrow the money-driven institutions of bourgeois society and reorganize them on the basis of mutuality and self-management.[8]

Because they believed "the emancipation of the working class was the task of the workers themselves," revolutionary syndicalists refused to delegate their interests to individuals or institutions foreign to their class. In distrusting intermediaries of all kinds, they opposed procedural methods of negotiation, favoring instead boycotts, sabotage, wildcat strikes, and other forms of direct action that rooted popular struggles in worker ranks. Inherent in this disposition was a disinterest in organizational issues and a disdain for the various encumbrances of an institutionalized labor movement. Union dues were consequently nominal and recruitment erratic. This, to be sure, kept membership low in relation to the workforce, but numbers, they felt, were of little matter—they valued the militant, the heroic individual devoted to the cause, not the sheep who followed where led. Union membership was thus tantamount to a revolutionary commitment, limited to a select minority who would prepare the day when the awakened masses would follow them in overthrowing the state, expropriating the economy, and establishing a free association of producers. In orienting to decentralized unions run by small bands of inspired militants who lived for the *Grand Soir* and the distant goals of the labor movement, revolutionary syndicalists focused most of their energies on the corporate community, where it was possible to mobilize workers around agitational issues.[9] Whenever strikes broke out, they were usually the ones to lead them. But given their disdain for organization, they rarely possessed the funds to sustain these conflicts and strikers usually had to fall back on the solidarity of the trade or the community.[10] Strikes were consequently short, sporadic, yet frequent. But whether successful or not, strikes were valued as a means of nurturing worker consciousness, preparing the way for the general strike that one day would topple the bourgeois order and establish a socialist commonwealth. As Victor Griffuelhes put it, the strike "is worth more than the contents of whole libraries; it educates, it hardens, it trains and it creates."[11] Although it is difficult to judge the degree to which these syndicalists, with their libertarian contempt for reformist modes of actions and their heroic conception of militancy, influenced the working class as a whole, their impact on the union movement was immense.[12]

Yet despite its formative influence, the heyday of revolutionary syndicalism was shortlived. In the years leading up to the First World War, numerous debilitating strains began disturbing its ranks. As the CGT proved less and less able to satisfy the evolving needs of the labor movement, especially as they were shaped by the modernization of industrial technique and the decline of small artisanal shops, these strains tended to assume divisive ideological forms, eventually culminating in a *crise du syndicalisme*. In the Paris metal unions, this crisis took the form of a growing polarization between the corporate and political axes of the unions: *métallos*, in small shops, closer to the older forms of the trade and concerned with corporate issues, gradually came to be identified with the "right wing" of the *syndicats*, while skilled workers in the new large-scale factories, like auto, concerned with mobilizing workers around radical agitation, constituted the "left."[13] Both wings remained attached to the syndicalist goal of a union-managed economy, but the "right" tended to emphasize the counter-hegemonic task of education and professional enhancement, while the "left" advocated revolutionary mobilization.

This *crise du syndicalisme* was especially prominent at the organizational level. In the half-dozen years leading up to 1914, as syndicalist ideology underwent a severe self-examination, union membership, already low, further declined, strikes became less successful, and union factionalism more contentious. On the eve of the Great War, only a tiny splinter of metal workers had any organizational attachment to the CGT. In the new large-scale industries anticipating postwar developments, such as the nascent automobile factories, a mere splintering of a splinter. At the Renault auto works in 1914, there were, for example, only fifty unionists out of 4,400 workers; of the nearly 10,000 Paris auto workers in the same period, only 300, almost all of whom were highly skilled and unrepresentative of the mass-production workers who would constitute the growth sector of postwar industry.[14] Moreover, the new large-scale firms contained not merely a smaller number of militants, their workforces were qualitatively less militant. In their study of French strikes, Shorter and Tilly found that between 1910 and 1914, large-scale plants with an average of 1,200 workers had 75 percent fewer conflicts than small factories with an average of 130 workers.[15] The types of solidarities and emotional ties favoring collective action in small shops simply did not exist in the massive, anonymous workforces of the new factories. In response to these trends, metal unionists attempted to develop organizational forms appropriate to the new mode of production. In the years leading up to the war, several of the more important craft unions fused into a single industrial federation which sought to unite skilled and unskilled workers in large-scale metal plants. But because this federation remained tied to the artisanal milieu, the principles of industrial unionism failed to resolve the larger problems facing métallos in the advanced sectors.[16] The crise du syndicalisme thus deepened, spreading in time from the metal unions to the CGT national office, where sharp and acrimonious polemics pitted a growing majority of unionists favoring a prudent reevaluation of labor's relationship to French society against a strident minority loyal to the revolutionary tradition. By 1914, the CGT was in the throes of a paralyzing internal struggle, as craft and industrial, reformist and revolutionary unionists vied for control of the labor movement. The war's massive restructuring of industry and the formation of a new class of mass-production workers would help transform these struggles into two opposed conceptions of unionism.

The Union Sacrée

Instead of calling a general strike to resist the "capitalist war" which socialists and syndicalists had anticipated, the CGT in August 1914 succumbed to the irrefutable patriotism of the French working class, joined the union sacrée, and ignored its previous jabber about workers having no country. In doing so, unionists were obliged to acknowledge the workers' primordial identification

with the *patrie*.[17] This patriotic turn immediately upset the balance of power between revolutionaries and reformists in the unions. As moderates championing the national cause gained control of the confederation, they proceeded
to elaborate a new ideology and a new practice to accord with national defense.
Under the direction of its general secretary, Léon Jouhaux, the CGT refrained
from joining the "bourgeois government" of René Vivani, as did several prominent socialists, but it unreservedly supported the government's war effort by
recruiting labor to staff the new armament factories, advising the state on
planning and production problems, sanctioning the introduction of new technologies, and attempting to minimize labor strife. At the same time, union officials agreed to participate in various public agencies responsible for war production and Jouhaux accepted a position as a government commissioner,
entrusted with representing labor at the highest levels of the state. The
wartime government, especially the Armaments Ministry of Albert Thomas,
granted the CGT a voice in ministerial deliberations and entrusted labor with
many new responsibilities. Although these measures did not translate into direct influence over the economy as they did in England and Germany, they did
bring the unions into a closer working relationship with the state and helped
mitigate their former pariah status. Moreover, in turning from confrontation to
cooperation, the CGT developed a qualitatively more cooperative relationship
with French society. But its participation in the war effort did not, as some have
argued, cause unionists to abandon their vision of a labor-centered economy.
The war and the *union sacrée* did little to lessen class antagonisms, change their
negative view of the *patronat*, or cause them to accept the principles of the capitalist market economy.[18] What changed after 1914 was the CGT's rejection of
direct action for institutional modes of mediation and negotiation. As André
Marchal describes it, CGT leaders hoped their collaboration with the wartime
government would "eliminate the *patronat*, conquer the state, reorganize industry according to its own designs, [and] make the state an economic rather
than a political institution—in a word, destroy capitalism by installing a syndicalist regime."[19]

   If the CGT leadership remained committed to the historic goals of the labor
movement, it nonetheless had difficulty convincing its membership in the war
plants. In fact, the more it participated in the common effort and implicitly put
industrial mobilization ahead of rank-and-file welfare, the more it alienated
workers champing at the bit of wartime conditions. Because these workers
began flocking to the unions after 1917, they had a critical effect on unionism.[20]
Since the CGT lacked the personnel and the organizational structures to assimilate them and had little power to prevent the downward pressure on wages and
conditions, it also had difficulty controlling and influencing them. To compli-

cate matters, most wartime recruits were unskilled machine tenders, new to trade unionism as well as to factory work. Lacking ties to the prewar traditions, they instinctually sought "mass unions" to champion wage demands, redefine job classifications, and mitigate the onerous conditions of armament production—just as they showed little interest in issues of workers' control, craft autonomy, or the maintenance of skill categories, which had occupied prewar artisans. Hoping to secure immediate reforms through collective action, these unskilled war workers forced the old craft leaders into many areas where they were reluctant to tread.[21]

This became strikingly evident in the spring of 1917, when the regimented cogs of the armament sector staged the first concerted rebellion against the war effort.[22] In a period when the army was wracked by mutinies and anti-war sentiment had taken more vocal and visible forms, spontaneous workstoppages erupted in 171 Paris metal plants. As 60,000 *métallos*, mainly women, joined noisy demonstrators from textile, chemical, and food industries in the streets to protest declining wages, brutal work rules, exhausting twelve-hour days, and the high cost of living, a large part of the armament industry came to a halt. Union leaders intent on sublimating the strikes to the common effort were immediately challenged by the strikers, who rejected their willingness to compromise and their right to represent them. Friction between the ranks and the leadership was especially heated when the latter tried to protect skill categories from those seeking advancement through an elimination of craft rights. Although skilled male workers under military requisition had a somewhat different agenda and could not strike, they too sympathized with the strikers because they resented the life-and-death power that management had acquired over them and because they opposed the deskilling inherent in the war effort.[23]

As the carnage at the front continued, the differences dividing the recent recruits from the reformist leadership took increasingly divisive form. In March 1918, the Paris metal industry was rocked by another round of spontaneous strikes, this time involving more than 100,000 workers. Led by dissident shop stewards and rank-and-file militants loyal to the revolutionary spirit of the Chartre d'Amiens, these strikes openly questioned the legitimacy of the war effort, rejected the established CGT leadership, which opposed the workstoppage, and at points assumed a character reminiscent of the St. Petersburg metal strikes of the previous year. The mystique of the Russian Revolution had in fact begun to affect Paris metal workers at this point, for they could not help but view the Bolshevik experiment as a possible alternative to the hardships and miseries of their own war-torn world.[24] As these strikers gravitated toward radical political goals and mass industrial unionism in the closing months of the war, their leaders rededicated themselves to reformist politics and craft principles. Such antinomies would have a profound effect on labor's subsequent development.[25]

The Two Red Years

The war, which Lenin called "the mighty accelerator of events," transformed nearly every facet of French life.[26] Between 1914 and 1918, as millions perished and empires fell, the order sustaining the libertarian aspirations of skilled workers gave way to an entirely different system of social organization—based on a highly centralized state, a mass-production economy, and a sensibility alien to the civilities and customs of the earlier age. In the face of these changes, syndicalist visions of the withering away of the state and its replacement by the workshop seemed increasingly unrealistic. Moreover, the rising generation of workers, having come of age while their fathers were at the front and their mothers at work, now faced a future full of uncharted and uncertain possibilities.[27] In the Paris working class, these developments gave rise to the feeling that one world was on the wane and another struggling to be born.[28]

In view of its transitional character, unionists differed in their orientation to the postwar world. Those in control of the CGT national office, after having collaborated with the wartime state, believed it was no longer necessary to assault capitalism frontally in order to create a union-centered regime. By allocating labor, subsidizing certain forms of production, requisitioning raw materials, introducing financial and social regulations restricting capital's dominance, and mobilizing millions of people for the common national effort, the state displayed what seemed like a limitless potential for large-scale economic reform. The confederation's reformist leadership was thus inclined to believe that the socialist economic forms implicit in the war effort might be fully realized if it maintained its close association with the political system.[29] In the final months of the war, it codified these beliefs in a "Minimum Program" proposing the nationalization of key industries, collective economic management, and the implementation of contracts and labor laws to regulate industrial relations—all of which seemed possible on the eve of the Armistice. Although this program would orient the reformist wing of the labor movement throughout the interwar period, it was almost immediately thwarted. In early 1919, the state abruptly retreated from the economy, dismantled its wartime regulatory system, restored the "free market," and returned unilateral control of the factories to their owners. Without state intervention and government-mandated tripartism, the unions were divested of whatever influence they had gained during the war. At the same time, CGT leaders were challenged by revolutionary syndicalists and proponents of the new Soviet model of labor organization, both of whom would outshout and outmaneuver the quieter forces of reform.[30]

The revolutionary wing of the labor movement had grown stronger and more influential in each year of the Great War. The strikes of 1917 and 1918 had given it a mass audience, the Bolshevik Revolution an ideal. After the Armistice and the spread of revolution in Central Europe, anti-reformist union-ists endeavored to push the labor movement leftward, challenging the confed-eration's accommodation to the state, and advocating an overthrow of the ex-isting order. The difficult transition to peacetime production and the influx of returning veterans further augmented their ranks and created many potential flashpoints in the plants. Then, in the spring of 1919, while the victors were sowing the seeds of another world war at the Versailles Peace Conference, the relationship between the CGT's two wings took a turn for the worse. As war factories facing reconversion laid off large numbers of workers and the gov-ernment refused to make a meaningful accommodation to postwar labor, dis-gruntled *métallos* began venting their frustrations in the streets. May Day 1919 was the occasion for bloody clashes with the police. A month later, as tensions continued to mount, the metal industry erupted in a wave of spontaneous workstoppages protesting the "sabotage" of a recently passed, but highly flawed eight-hour bill. Led by anarchist shop stewards, these strikes lasted over a month and involved nearly 180,000 metal workers. They also challenged the "bourgeois government." In Saint-Denis, the epicenter of the conflict, the strike committee proclaimed itself a "soviet"; similar revolutionary aspirations were expressed in other suburban towns.[31] Although the authorities never lost con-trol of the situation, the turbulent workstoppages immediately exacerbated so-cial tensions and evoked fears of a Bolshevik conspiracy. Even after the union leadership refused to endorse the strikes and the government sent troops into the factory districts to arrest their rank-and-file leaders, strikers kept up their demands, hopeful their struggle would culminate in the sort of upheaval then shaking Central Europe. While the strikers failed to overthrow the established order, they nonetheless managed to usher in an era of acute labor-capital hos-tility, ending any possibility of developing a more cooperative factory regime.[32]

Following the unsuccessful strikes, relations between reformist and revolu-tionary unionists approached the breaking point. In May 1920, strikes similar to the 1919 metal conflict broke out among railroad workers and spread to the rest of the organized labor movement. At this point, as industrial strife assumed an even more threatening amplitude, the government and employers closed ranks in a massive counter-offensive that nearly crushed the CGT. This caused unionists disillusioned by the CGT's failure to influence national polices to seek out alternative means of advancing labor's revolutionary agenda. This alternative was found sooner than anyone expected. Partly as a result of the failed strikes of 1919 and 1920 and the political conflicts issuing from them, and partly from the heritage of the war and the Russian Revolution, the Socialist party (SFIO) split in late 1920, giving birth to the PCF.[33] The formation of this new "workers' party" instantly altered the factional alignment inside the unions. As revolutionaries strengthened their forces and threatened to capture the CGT national office, reformists proceeded to purge them from the confederation.[34] This schism would have an immediate and devastating impact on the unions, splitting them into two bitterly opposed and disabled blocs.[35]

The CGTU

Following *la grande scission,* in a period of defeat and retreat, the expelled revolutionaries founded the Confédération Générale du Travail Unitaire (CGTU). The CGTU was no sooner formed then it, too, became the site of bitter factional strife. Communists, anarchists, and revolutionary syndicalists, previously united in opposition to the reformist CGT leadership, now divided over the new confederation's programmatic and organizational orientation. Anarchists in control of the CGTU's first executive body attempted to give it a federalist, anti-political structure faithful to the spirit of the 1906 Chartre d'Amiens. Within a year, however, they were outflanked by the better-organized communists, who had a different notion of unionism. Unlike anarchists or revolutionary syndicalists, whose revolutionism stemmed from the artisanal traditions of the French past, communists represented a new type of militant. Forged in the war and the two red years that followed it, communists retained aspects of the French revolutionary tradition, but unlike other tendencies in the labor movement, defined themselves exclusively in terms of Russian Marxism (alien to the doctrinal heterogeneity of French socialism), Leninist organizational norms, and an unbending (some would say, slavish) loyalty to the new Soviet state. More critically, they identified with the interests and aspirations of mass-production workers in the new Fordist-Taylorist factory system. After consolidating their hold over the CGTU executive in late 1923, communists proceeded to affiliate the new confederation to the Moscow-based Red International of Labor Unions and remodel it according to Bolshevik principles. But their efforts to communize the CGT were doggedly resisted by their anarchist and syndicalist rivals.

The heated factional struggles that henceforth divided the CGTU, as communists and their opponents struggled to define the character of labor's revolutionary wing, revolved around numerous organizational and programmatic differences, but ultimately boiled down to a question of party/union relations—a question which pitted the Russian conception of unionism against that of the French syndicalist tradition. Since the 1890s, French unionists had rejected all forms of party interference. Believing that politicians, even socialists, were an alien class force threatening labor's autonomy, syndicalists had kept union affairs strictly in their own hands. Politics, they deemed, was the province of the bourgeoisie, unionism that of the working class. But with the postwar formation of the PCF and the CGTU, this pattern of party/union relations underwent a fundamental alteration. After 1921, the economic field (i.e. the unions) was no longer solely occupied by worker revolutionaries nor the political field (the parties) by middle-class reformists. This led communists, inspired by an argument developed in Lenin's *What Is To Be Done?*, to claim that politics and unionism were not autonomous spheres distinct to different forms of class action.[36] Implicit in this argument was the contention that unions ought to serve as "transmission belts" to convey the worker masses into the PCF. This political conception of unionism, however, rubbed against the grain of the French labor tradition, for most syndicalists continued to believe that a party, even an ostensibly revolutionary party like the PCF, had no business interfering in the shop or the strike. Only unionists, they believed, had the right to lead labor struggles; otherwise, they predicted, workers would end up exchanging one set of masters for another.[37] In this spirit, syndicalists and anarchists fought off communist efforts to subordinate the new confederation to the Bolshevik political project.[38]

It is worth noting that these conflicting models of unionism were not confined to different economic and political approaches to class struggle, but went deeper, expressing competing visions of state and society—and ultimately contrasting notions of freedom. Factional strife, as a result, would remain an endemic feature of CGTU organizational life, finding its way into internal bulletins, newspaper polemics, union meetings, and consuming energies that could have been spent organizing the factories. Yet as contentious and divisive as these factional struggles were, they were nonetheless held in check by the fact that each CGTU tendency saw "class war" and direct action as the sole means of advancing working-class interests.[39] In adhering to these common principles, rival factions succeeded not only in maintaining the new labor confederation, but in perpetuating three of the most distinct prewar traditions: refusing institutionalization within the capitalist system, extolling labor's marginalization on the fringes of French society, and fracturing the labor movement along ideological lines.

Unitaire Unionism in the Fordist-Taylorist Factory System

After the defeats of 1919 and 1920 and the schism of 1921, those who had inundated the union ranks during the war and the two red years massively abandoned them. Throughout the 1920s, memory of these divisive struggles, enhanced by CGT–CGTU rivalries and CGTU factionalism, did much to tarnish labor's image, causing workers to look on the rival confederations with indifference or skepticism. Henceforth, the diminished ranks of both the reformist and revolutionary wings of the union movement would be filled almost exclusively by a core of sectarian activists drawn from the skilled trades.[40] In the metal industry, these activists tended to share numerous common traits, differing mainly in age, experience, and temperament. Broadly speaking, CGTU *métallos*—or "*unitaires*" as they were known—were somewhat younger and more ideological than their CGT counterparts. Their education in the war, their lack of prior union experience, their greater vulnerability to turnover and unemployment, and their youthful idealism gave them a greater disposition to revolutionary politics and direct action. As a consequence, they showed little interest in the old craft traditions of syndicalism (although most were craftsmen), championed the "proletarian masses" created by the Fordist-Taylorist mode of production, and took their inspiration from the new forms of charismatic leadership emanating from the former land of the tsars.[41]

Although the CGT Metal Federation retained two-thirds of the union offices after the schism, a majority of its ranks voted with their feet. In 1922, an estimated 50,000 to 60,000 metal workers cast their lot with the *unitaires*, while the parent organization retained less than 20,000.[42] *Unitaires* were particularly strong in Paris, where 5,000 to 8,000 *métallos* joined the local CGTU Metal Union, against a mere 500 for the CGT. Neither union tendency, however, was able to retain the big battalions. Up until the mid 1930s, the combined membership of both the CGT and CGTU Metal Federations would never amount to more than 5 percent of the total French metal workforce.[43] These figures contrast sharply with the 200,000 *métallos* who filled the Paris metal unions in 1919 and 1920 and suggests the degree to which the post-schism labor movement reverted back to the small "spark plug unions" of the prewar era.[44]

The CGTU Metal Federation was formally constituted in April 1922 at the Congress of St. Etienne, but it was not until late 1923 that internal factional struggle subsided to the point where it was possible to orient outward. The Unitaire Metal Union of Paris, the largest and most important of the federation's municipal unions, was likewise stymied by factionalism.[45] Anarchists initially dominated the union (as they had the CGTU and federal offices), but they were a minority able to lead only by playing on communist-syndicalist rivalries. Once communists succeeded in wresting control from them, they sought to refashion the union according to the Soviet organizational model. But until 1931, when the last major oppositional tendency split from the CGTU, the Paris metal union was wracked by factional battles that prevented communists from carrying out many of their intended policies.

Given these persisting disputes, *unitaire* metal unionism was fraught with numerous problems throughout the 1920s. These problems, however, were not entirely the result of factionalism. A great many followed from the PCF's effort to communize the union. In his unpublished memoirs, Albert Vassard, one of the communist architects of French metal unionism, describes the metal union of the 1920s as "a sort of . . . union guinea pig [*syndicat-cobaye*] and union sieve [*syndicat-passoire*], regularly used for all kinds of [political] experiments."[46] The highly politicized and unstable character of the Paris metal union would distinguish it not only from the CGT, but from other CGTU unions. For unlike their metal counterparts, *unitaires* in tertiary, railway, and mining unions were primarily concerned with enforcing the various public statutes governing these sectors. Thus, despite their radical rhetoric, a great many of the new CGTU unions practiced a brand of unionism not unlike that of the CGT. Because these unions constituted the PCF's largest trade-union constituency and demanded a specific kind of leadership, they were generally spared the kind of party interference that affected the metal union. As a result, whenever communist leaders in Paris or Moscow thought of "mobilizing the masses" or applying a new line, they inevitably looked to the Paris *métallos*, whose small, highly political union, soon reputed to be the most communist of all French unions, had little to lose from political experimentation.[47] Party interference was not, however, merely a matter of expediency. For communists, metal workers, especially those in the mass-production sector, represented the archetypal "proletarians" and thus the ones most likely to respond to the party's revolutionary appeal. From its inception, then, the metal union was singled out by party leaders as a political guinea pig. Every change of line, every new directive, every political imperative cooked up by the French and international communist movement would thus find its way into the union's daily operations. But because this guinea pig was frequently prey to political experimentation and party interference, it tended to burn up its membership—making it a regular sieve in terms of the numbers who flowed in and out of it. Vassard estimates that in the years between 1922 and 1927, 35,000 *métallos* passed through the union and that of its 3,000 members in the late 1920s, only half were stable.[48] This meant that a sizable number of workers joined the union, played an active role for a while, and then left, perhaps disillusioned with its failure to bring about the *Grand Soir* or become a force in industry.[49]

If party interference was responsible for turning the metal union into a guinea pig and a sieve, communists nonetheless played a significant role in equipping it with the organizational forms appropriate to mass-production unionism. This was especially the case with the Communist International (Comintern) and the Red International of Labor Unions (RILU), both of which were instrumental in helping *unitaire métallos* make the transition from minority to mass and from craft to industrial unionism. Of the innovations most pertinent to this transition, the most important came in June 1924, when the Comintern's Fifth World Congress ordered the reorganization of its various national sections. This reorganization was mainly intended to "bolshevize" (i.e. Russianize) Western Communist parties and make them more pliant to Moscow directives, but it also had far-reaching implication for the PCF's relation to the working class.[50]

Organizationally, bolshevization shifted the party's membership base from the section, defined by political geography and concerned with electoral activity, to the factory cell, rooted in the workplace and oriented to the economy.[51] Prior to bolshevization, party influence in the workplace had been exerted mainly through the activity of individual communists.[52] In implanting the party in the factory, bolshevization aimed to sever the PCF from its "social democratic" roots, make it into an organization of factory workers, and ensconce communists in industrial affairs.[53] Key to this process was the formation of factory cells, which were to be established wherever three party members were employed in the same enterprise. Cell members were then expected to carry out agitation in the plants, distribute propaganda, publish a journal, and intervene in various day-to-day struggles. In the process, cell members were to build a following among their fellow workers and transform local conflicts into struggles promoting the communist revolutionary project.

The shift to the factory was not, however, entirely successful. Rather than abandon their political section and take up revolutionary activities in the workplace, foreign to the socialist tradition, many communists quit the party. Only 30 percent of the party's sections converted to cells—and of these, many had but a phantom existence or else continued to function in the old way.[54] Vassard reports that his cell, attached to a small polishing plant in Paris's tenth *arrondissement*, had not a single member employed in the plant it was suppose to represent and only the most superficial connection to its workforce. Cell formation was also hampered by the political battles that still raged between communists and their factional opponents inside the union, by the influence of the socialist and syndicalist traditions, both of which preferred agitation in the community to organization in the factory, and, not least, by the novelty of assimilating an economic model of party organization.[55]

Even after their introduction and formation, factory cells continued to be plagued with problems. Because a cell's success depended largely on its secretary's organizing skills, those lacking militants capable of filling this office rarely acquired the organizational aplomb to function efficiently.[56] At the same time, logistical problems created problems of another kind. For example, finding an appropriate time and place to meet for members who worked different shifts and commuted from different parts of the suburbs was an on-going problem. There were also numerous complaints about cell meetings being irregularly held, "too long, badly prepared, and without interest." Another problem was victimization; for fear of losing their job, cell members had to keep a low profile, which made it difficult to carry out party work or integrate the cell into the life of the enterprise. Because police and employer repression drove most cells underground, their existence was often unknown to the workers they hoped to influence.[57] Equally deleterious, the party tended to impose general orders that ignored specific factory conditions and caused many cells to develop an artificial, if not a dysfunctional relation to their workplace. Vassard estimates that by the late 1920s, the party possessed less than 210 cells in the Paris metal industry, many without a real functional life.[58] Broadly speaking, the factory cells created in the wake of the Comintern's order were badly organized, lacked the cadre and the autonomy to function properly, and neglected specific workshop concerns.[59] Yet despite these admittedly grievous shortcomings, bolshevization was anything but a failure, for in establishing the cell and rooting the party, however partially, in the plants, the PCF gained an unprecedented access to industry and a potential although yet unrealized means of recruiting the new mass-production workers.[60]

Following the party's bolshevization, which created the cell and rooted the PCF in the industrial sector of the economy, the Unitaire Metal Federation underwent a similar reorganization, shifting its basic unit of organization from the *section locale,* which grouped workers by neighborhood, to the *section syndicale,* designed to represent the union in the factory.[61] Like bolshevization, the *unitaire* reorganization was designed to exchange a residential for a purely economic mode of organization. When revolutionary syndicalists complained that the reorganization represented a compromising departure from the French union tradition, communists defended it as an indispensable response to the rise of large-scale production and the changes wrought by suburban developments.[62] In principle, a *section syndicale* was to be formed wherever ten (later three) unionists worked in a factory. Led by an elected secretary and linked to a *union locale* that situated it geographically, the *section* was intended to represent workers in their daily struggles, organize solidarity, propaganda, and factory-level actions, and carry out general CGTU policy.[63] Practically, however, the *sections* suffered the same kinds of problems plaguing the party's cells: persecution, lack of cadre, logistical failures, and a reluctance to agitate in the economic arena.[64] And because *section* and cell activities inevitably overlapped and duplicated one another, *section* and cell members, often the same people, were uncertain where party work ended and union work began. There was thus a good deal of confusion between political and union priorities and, in such cases, union issues usually took a back seat to those of the cell. Moreover, *section* activities tended to reflect party concerns more than those of the workers it sought to represent.[65] In fact, beginning with bolshevization, the metal union became increasingly subordinate to the party—evident not merely in the priority given to political issues, but also in the increased politicization of worker grievances.

The main problem besetting the *section syndicale*, however, was adapting and assimilating a form of union activity previously unknown to the French union experience. Like the first generation of French communists, *unitaires* recruited from the ranks of revolutionary syndicalism preferred communal and corporate agitation to "education" in the shops. They thus had difficulty distinguishing between ideological and economic issues. This created a major obstacle to union growth, for metal workers, like workers everywhere, viewed the union mainly as a means of defending and improving their conditions of employment, not as a vehicle for overturning the established order. Again, like their syndicalist predecessors, *unitaires* tended to emphasize politics (that is, anti-parliamentary or revolutionary politics) to the detriment of economics, neglecting in effect the most basic motivation for unionism.[66] In this vein, they devoted more energy to exposing the injustices of French society and the shenanigans of the bourgeois state than in struggling against wage cuts and speed-ups. The "industrial" orientation imposed by Moscow might therefore have given unitaires the means of implanting themselves in the metal industry, breaking with the revolutionary syndicalist model of unionism, and focusing on workshop issues, but it would take years before they succeeded in assimilating its tenets and longer still to make it pay dividends. Even at the end of the 1920s, the metal union and its *sections* had barely a toehold in any of the major metal plants

Since the *section syndicale*, like the cell, demanded relatively high levels of commitment, few *métallos* showed an interest in joining them. To develop a rank-and-file following in the plants, *unitaires* were compelled to experiment with less demanding forms of organization. The factory or shop committee was probably the most significant of these. First in 1923 and then more seriously after the onset of bolshevization, implanted *unitaires* appealed to metal workers to elect committees.[67] These committees (which would never number more than two to three hundred in the Paris metal industry) then formulated demands for improved wages, hours, and conditions, around which they tried to rally the rest of the workforce. The committees' agitation (carried out more often in cloakrooms, lavatories, and bicycle sheds than on the shop floor) aimed to rouse workers and develop a union following. In this, they were not entirely unsuccessful, for in the mid-1920s they managed to set off several strike waves that forced employers to raise wages. For a moment, it even looked as if the committees might become a force in the industry. But, over the long haul, they had only an ephemeral success. Workers reluctant to join a union were no less reluctant to join a factory committee. Initial interest was thus generally followed by indifference and apathy. Then, after it became apparent that factory or shop committees had failed to galvanize the *métallos*, the union began experimenting with other kinds of front groups—"action committees," "combat committees," "committees for proletarian unity," etc.—in another futile bid to accomplish what the union itself had failed to achieve. At the same time, *unitaires* resorted to leafleting and soapbox speeches at factory gates, which not infrequently roused a commotion in the plants and drew attention to union issues, but police harassment and arrests made this sort of intervention costly.[68] Moreover, a quick leafleting or a five-minute speech at the start or change of a shift might alert workers to the union's latest slogans or aggravate tensions in the shops, but it was rarely enough to win the hearts and minds of those the union hoped to recruit. *Unitaires* were thus left with the strike as the sole means of enhancing their standing in worker ranks.

But even here they faced daunting obstacles. Because spontaneous workstoppages in the metal industry did not lend themselves to organization, it was difficult for the union to gain their leadership. Throughout the 1920s, *unitaires* participated in most strikes only after they broke out, which meant they did more following than leading. Often they did not even participate as followers. The wave of metal strikes arising in response to the 1926 devaluation of the *franc*, the largest strike action of the decade, almost completely escaped them.[69] To foster struggles that lent themselves to union recuperation, unitaires tried to prepare and foment strikes. Implanted militants (with the aid of the factory committee, the cell, or the *section*) were thus instructed to sound out workers, draw up lists of demands, and agitate in their favor; wherever they evoked a responsive cord in the shops (and often in situations where they were ignored), they would call a strike.[70] But because their *sections* were weak and their members feared reprisals, it was frequently necessary to smuggle "commandos" into the shops to instigate these strikes, even if this evoked the charge of "outside agitators." In plants with accumulated grievances and in periods of unrest, such methods occasionally set workers in motion. Significantly, though, the most successful communist-led strikes in this period were not the result of union action in the workplace, but rather the outcome of municipal or political agitation. This, for example, was the case during the general strike of 12 October 1925, called to protest the Rif War. In Saint-Denis, a PCF stronghold, 50 to 75 percent of the workforce participated in the communist protest. But it was the party organization, entrenched in the local town hall, not the cell or *section*, that was responsible for bringing the workers out; in those parts of the suburbs where the PCF lacked municipal influence, there was little movement in the factories.[71]

Even in cases where *unitaires* focused on legitimate labor concerns or responded to genuine workshop grievances, workers rarely responded to their appeals. Sometimes, after a particularly emotional strike, the union might reap a harvest of new recruits. But those flocking to the union in the hour of combat were likely to slip away once the struggle subsided. Only the militant, inspired by political or corporate ideals, was likely to risk his job for the illusive goals of the labor movement in the 1920s. There was simply no incentive to be a unionist and much potential disadvantage: the union lacked bargaining power with the employers, had no authority on the shop floor, and could offer its membership little except possible persecution or blacklisting.

Yet despite these failings and the fact that political, rather than corporate concerns dominated their activities, *unitaire* organizing efforts were not totally without effect in this period. If communists failed to mobilize the big battalions, they at least pioneered methods and organizational forms (such as the *section syndicale*, the cell, and the factory committee) that helped root them in the factories and clear the way for more meaningful forms of industrial implantation. In the process, they accumulated a repertoire of agitational experiences, developed a small but committed cadre of organizers, and got to know something about the economic and social geography of the industry. The Paris metal union might thus have had little to show for its various efforts during the first decade of its existence, but it had nonetheless prepared the ground and nurtured the seed, whose later ripening would be bountiful.

Confederal Unionism

The Unitaire Metal Union of Paris was the single most significant force attempting to organize the mass-production sector, but it was not without rivals. After the schism which led to the founding of the CGTU, *métallos* rejecting *l'esprit politicien* reaffirmed their allegiance to the amputated CGT. These unionists—known as "confederals"—tended to be older than their CGTU counterparts, less political, if not apolitical, and concerned mainly with corporate issues. Although not necessarily imbued with revolutionary-syndicalist ideology, they remained attached to prewar forms of craft unionism, expressed as much in their loyalty to the Old House as in their unwillingness to adapt to the new economic realities. The Confederal Metal Unions of Paris were thus basically middle-age organizations, inclined to caution and compromise, and with few roots in the growth sectors of the industry. More seriously, because the CGT as a whole had lost most of its industrial membership in the schism, particularly in metal, its most important unions and federations after 1921 were made up of workers in sheltered or regulated trades, such as teachers, postal workers, civil servants, miners, and railroad workers, all of whom had a vision of unionism different from those in private industry.[72]

Nowhere were the implications of these different visions more evident than in the CGT's attitude to economic conflict. While the post-schism confederation continued to pay lip service to the strike as the specific instrument of worker action, its national office studiously avoided workstoppages, preferring legal or institutional activity to economic confrontation.[73] Even when strikes spontaneously broke out, the CGT rarely intervened, preferring to pressure public authorities into finding a political remedy. This reluctance to strike was, of course, conditioned by the CGT's reformist orientation and the dominance of its tertiary membership, which had procedural alternatives to striking, but it also arose from fear that direct action might veer out of control and create an opportunity for their *unitaire* rivals. Given this attitude, local unions in the post-schism CGT were required to get authorization from their federations before striking. Not surprisingly, most strikes after 1921 occurred without CGT initiative or leadership.

Given their decimation during the schism, the first task facing confederals in the Paris metal industry was to rebuild their shattered organization. This, however, was a path strewn with obstacles. The bitterness of the schism and the fierce polemics that followed made public meetings and organizing campaigns the object of numerous disruptive *unitaire* interventions. Confederals were also handicapped by a lack of cadre and auxiliary organizations. To overcome these obstacles and create a niche for themselves in the postwar metal industry, they decided to revive certain forms of craft unionism privileging corporate issues neglected by the *unitaires*.[74] In 1922, confederal *métallos* organized two craft unions in Paris (*Tourneurs en optique* and *Instruments de précision*) and one general industrial union *(Mécaniciens)*.[75] During the 1920s, each of the craft unions grew to 600 or 700 members, while the industrial union, whose ranks were also entirely skilled, acquired 1,000 to 2,000 members, climbing to 3,000 by the mid-1930s.[76] In addition to retreating from the principles of industrial unionism, confederal *métallos* refused to adapt to the altered realities of the Fordist-Taylorist factory system. After the schism, membership and union activity continued to be determined by residence and inspired by craft concerns. If residential forms of union organization *(unions locales)* grouping workers where they lived and not where they worked had been feasible in the prewar *faubourgs*, they lacked all relevance to the industrial geography of the new industrial suburbs, where the links between work and residence had been severed and where the factory replaced the neighborhood as "the epicenter of the labor movement."[77] Needless to add, this confederal brand of unionism had little pertinence to the new mass-production workers.

Official CGT policy constituted another detriment to confederal organization in the Paris metal industry. With a membership vastly reduced by the schism and without a well-organized base in private industry, the CGT national office came to rely on a *politique de présence* to compensate for its lack of authority on the shop floor.[78] Through participation in various consultative bodies or through lobbying in governmental ministries and local *prefects,* the postwar CGT hoped to make itself "present" in all situations where labor interests were at stake. This institutional orientation did not, however, sit well with metal unionists attached to syndicalist notions of self-reliance and worker control.[79] Moreover, in contrast to public-sector workers, *métallos,* like other workers in the private sector, knew the state mainly through its strike-breaking police and its failure to enforce social legislation in the factories. Unsympathetic to lobbying activities in ministerial corridors, confederal *métallos* preferred the prewar model of unionism which privileged the "moral community of the trades."[80] In addition to their discomfort with the *politique de présence,* the craft-conscious leaders of the Confederal Metal Unions were suspicious of, if not opposed to rationalization and industrial modernization, which the top confederal leadership touted as the best means of elevating living standards and improving working conditions. Therefore, while the CGT's national office converted lock, stock, and barrel to the new Yankee religion of efficiency in the 1920s, believing that enhanced production would do away with traditional conflicts born of scarcity, the craftsmen in charge of the Confederal Metal Unions disapproved of the new technologies, which threatened their skills and undermined the cultural-intellectual character of their working lives.[81]

Despite these reservations—to rationalization, the *politique de présence,* and the CGT's general orientation—confederal metal leaders remained too disoriented by the war and schism to challenge their national leadership or put forward an alternative strategy for organizing the Paris metal industry. Drastic changes in the character of metal unionism, as well as the metal industry, had first to occur before they—or their *unitaire* rivals—would have any chance of playing a more meaningful role in the Fordist-Taylorist factory system.[82]

The Crisis

NOT UNTIL THE WORLD DEPRESSION REACHED FRANCE IN 1931, taking its toll on wages, conditions, and employment opportunities, did mass-production workers begin to unionize. Besides providing an incentive to organize, the economic crisis facilitated the possibility of organization. The slowdown in migration, immigration, and turnover following in the depression's wake helped homogenize their ranks and diminish the centrifugal pressures that had previously hampered their cohesion. As they became more cohesive and amenable to organization, *unitaire* unionism underwent a change of comparable significance, adopting an orientation that demoted its ideological conception of unionism and enhanced its sensitivity to workshop issues. With workers spontaneously resisting deteriorating conditions and unionism becoming more pertinent to the world of work, the unorganized and those hoping to organize them gradually started finding their way to one another.

Advent of the Depression

France was the last major country touched by the World Depression. Although American and German production indexes began dropping as early as June 1929, French indexes did not reach their postwar high until nearly a year later.[1] This led many Frenchmen to believe that their country was a "happy island" in a swelling sea of crisis. Even after 1931, when this illusion gave way to grimmer realities, the French would be spared many of the depression's more devastating effects. It was, for example, qualitatively less earthshaking than the social cataclysms set off in Germany and the U.S. Stagnation and creeping paralysis, not massive unemployment and economic breakdown, were its worse manifestations. The initial drop in production was a "manageable" 10 percent, compared to nearly 25 percent in Germany and the U.S.[2] Unemployment and social dislocation were likewise less severe. At its nadir in 1935, French unemployment touched only 12.5 percent of the active population, less than half the German or American rate.[3]

The depression, however, had a particularly devastating effect on the mass-production sector. In the metal industry, the hardest hit branches were auto and mechanical engineering, both dependent on foreign markets. With the exception of aviation and armaments, which continued to grow, especially after Hitler's accession to power in 1933, metal employment fell well below the national average.[4] Between 1931 and 1936, a third of all *métallos* were permanently eliminated from the active workforce.[5]

Metal Employment[6]

1930	100%
1931	89.6%
1932	74.1%
1933	72.0%
1934	70.5%
1935	68.8%

This contraction of the labor market, in an industry that had experienced full employment for more than a decade, had a jolting effect on workers, making them justifiably insecure about their jobs. Unemployment, moreover, was compounded by underemployment. Of those managing to hold on to their jobs after 1931, nearly half experienced a sharp cut in hours—for most employers preferred to reduce hours and spread work rather than lay off entire sections of their workforce.[7] With underemployment came lower piece rates and diminished incomes. Wages, which had gradually but progressively risen in the course of the 1920s, now stagnated, undermining living standards and exacerbating the problems of shorttime.[8] The CGT Metal Federation estimated that by 1936, real wages had shrunk to more than 30 percent of their pre-depression level.[9]

Although not as catastrophic as elsewhere, the French depression was nonetheless severe enough to strain numerous facets of national life. These strains were especially acute inside the factory system. While a third of metal workers lost their jobs and another third experienced a significant reduction in hours and wages, they all confronted a more grueling labor process, for employers had no choice but to stave off insolvency through higher productivity and lower labor costs, attained not through technological innovation, which required scarce investment capital, but through speed-ups and sweating. This was especially the case in auto, where the production index dropped from 627 in 1929 to 400 in early 1935.[10] As car makers and other metal producers began imposing prodigious new quotas on lines operating at unprecedented speeds, nervous anxiety and exhaustion, recorded in no statistical table but graphically detailed in the labor press, soared to record-breaking levels.[11] Some workers were wont to characterize the depressed factory regime as "a reign of terror," where employers were able to make impossible demands without the slightest regard for the limits of human endurance.[12] In such an environment, *métallos* cowed by the prospect of unemployment were expected to submit "like slaves."[13] Each new attempt to reduce production costs by raising productivity levels consequently subjected them to progressively more stringent production norms, based on a rigid quantification of labor capacity, the multiplication of time and motion studies, and the enhanced role of the methods office. The stop-watch and the use of various piece-rate systems—particularly the exhausting Bedaux system—now came to dominate the metal industry as never before. In fact, it was only in this period that workers truly became "analyzable objects," whose every movement was "broken down and then counted, according to the universal unit—time."[14] As piece rates and production norms rose to unattainable levels, as conveyors manned by fewer workers reached unprecedented speeds, as work rules became more flexible and foremen more capricious, workers were forced to labor longer and harder for lower wages. This created a work environment full of grievance and discontent—and sometimes perplexity. At the Lioré-Olivier aviation plant in Argenteuil, for example, a worker achieving the established quota was so dismayed that he could only attribute it to a horrendous mistake on the part of the *chrono* (the stop-watch engineer).[15]

Along with speed-up, employers sought to augment their repressive powers and impose more strenuous forms of discipline. Giant auto works, like Renault and Citroen, which had their own private police forces, tightened controls after 1931 and rewrote work rules; others introduced paid informants to act as the eyes and ears of management on the shop floor and weed out potential dissenters, heightening the atmosphere of suspicion and mistrust in the shops.[16] It soon became so that one could not tell if one's neighbor was a friend or a company agent. To compound matters, employers introduced new rules against talking, smoking, or going to the toilet without permission.[17] Then, in

February 1932, the French Parliament legalized the use of workshop fines for disciplinary offenses.[18] The cumulative effect of these measures was not only to threaten the worker's well being, but his dignity, his sense of security, and his attitude to work.

Yet despite its deleterious impact on the labor process and the terms of employment, the depression had a not altogether unfavorable effect on the labor movement. Besides giving workers an incentive to organize, the depression made them more amenable to organization. Throughout the war and the 1920s, in fact since the turn of the century, the industrial population of the Paris Region had grown without respite. The depression brought the first major stabilization in three decades. With layoffs and plant closures, immigrant workers were reduced in number and prevented from entering the country.[19] Rural migrants, no longer finding the cities potential sources of employment, remained in the countryside. Family men, rather than youth and single women, were given a priority in employment. Skilled workers, always in demand, were retained in preference to others, thereby securing the most conscious elements of the workforce within the production system.[20] Moreover, as surplus choked the depressed labor market, the incessant turnover central to the boom economy of the 1920s came, if not to a halt, to a drastic slowdown, causing metal workers to take a greater interest in retaining their jobs. That residency was required for municipal doles also contributed to stabilizing the workforce, making workers think twice before picking up roots and relocating. And because family and kinship ties, along with some forms of neighborhood, had had a chance to develop during the previous decade, workers faced the economic crisis with a greater sense of communal identity. Finally, the crisis was a great leveler, diminishing the significance of ascriptive differences by universalizing the threat of unemployment and the need for unity. As these various forces weighed on the depressed job market, Paris *métallos* became qualitatively "more French, more skilled, more mature, more urban, more stable"—and consequently more likely to see themselves as a collectivity in need of organization.[21]

Confederal Responses

Unlike many liberal economists and industrialists, who viewed the depression in terms of overproduction and waited for the inevitable upturn,[22] the national CGT office claimed it was consumption's decline in relation to the enormous productivity gains made since 1914 that was at the root of the economic disorder.[23] If overproduction and underconsumption were responsible for the market's collapse, then it was absolutely imperative to introduce structural reforms to reduce hours and augment mass purchasing power. Capital, in other words, had to share its productivity gains with labor. "Egoistic" efforts by employers to "protect their privileges and profits" by lowering wages and laying off workers could only exacerbate the economic downturn: mass production dictated mass-consumption and without it the system would remain permanently "out of sync." In this spirit, they called for a forty-hour week, annual paid vacations, earlier retirement, and a lengthening of the years of obligatory schooling.[24] More consequently, they proposed the nationalization of key industries and financial institutions and the formation of a managed economy at both the national and international levels.[25] Not surprisingly, these proposals rejected the liberal market and reflected the demands inscribed in the Minimum Program of 1918.

Following the depression's onset, CGT leaders sought to popularize their view of the crisis. In public meetings and through their press, they propagated the message that the depression represented a "crisis of regime," that the old liberal solutions were no longer viable, that employers were pursuing short-sighted policies, and that the depressed labor market had to be structurally reformed. The confederation's emphasis on structural reforms, however, put rank-and-file activists in a bit of a bind. As the depression started exacting its toll on employment, wages, and conditions, and as factory workers instinctively resisted attacks on their standards, shop floor issues took on a sudden urgency. Yet by focusing on structural reforms and engaging in lobbying and education to promote them, the national CGT office tended to neglect the unrest stirring in the plants, isolating confederals at the very moment workers were beginning to seek out leaders for their struggles.

This abstentionism provoked some CGT'ers to wonder if their leadership had not lost its working-class soul by lingering overly long in ministerial antechambers. Motivated by the rising agitation on the shop floor, rank-and-file confederals began calling for a more activist approach to the depressed economy.[26] At both the 1931 and 1933 congresses of the Confederal Metal Federation, the CGT's institutional orientation, particularly its *politique de présence*, came under attack, as militants demanded a more aggressive policy oriented to the shops. The 1933 Congress even produced a resolution rejecting the substance of the CGT's institutional orientation, proposing in its stead a strategy for factory recruitment.

To implement the 1933 resolution, confederals tried to establish a more conspicuous presence in the communist-dominated suburbs.[27] This represented a major departure for them. Throughout the 1920s, confederals had avoided the red heartland for fear of divisive *unitaire* interventions. But the organizing opportunities created by the depression spurred their ambitions. Communists, however, had not been the sole nor even the principal obstacle to confederal implantation. More fundamentally, the CGT Metal Unions lacked the organizational equivalent of the *section syndicale* and possessed only the residence-based *union locale* to carry out its organizing activities. This made it extremely difficult for confederals to contact suburban *métallos* or connect with them in the plants. As one activist put it: "Once the worker leaves the factory, it's nearly impossible to reach him."[28] To compensate for their lack of workplace organization and facilitate their implantation, confederals decided to set up Centres Syndicaux de Propagande. These centers were designed to offer certain social services (such as job placements), engage in elementary forms of solidarity, and hold evening meetings to promote the union cause. By the spring of 1934, confederals had organized seventeen of these centers in the suburbs and ten in Paris, but it was soon evident that the centers were no substitute for shop floor organization.[29] Without the equivalent of the *section syndicale*, it was nearly impossible to reach, let alone organize workers in the plants or convince them they had something to gain by joining the union. To make matters worse, confederals had but three fulltime officers for the entire Paris Region and a membership unaccustomed to economic intervention. They thus failed to capitalize on the favorable organizing opportunities opened by the depression, thereby leaving the task of unionizing the depressed factory system almost entirely to the *unitaires*.

The Third Period

If confederal organizing efforts had been hampered by the CGT's institutional orientation, *unitaires* were disadvantaged by the PCF's sectarian policies. In the CGTU's early history, as communists wrestled with anarchists for control of the confederation's leadership, the PCF kept a respectful distance from union affairs, exerting its influence mainly through the individual activities of its militants. Then, beginning in the mid-1920s, as the party shifted to the factory cell and the CGTU to the *section syndicale*, the PCF began systematically subordinating corporate and union concerns to its political project. This process would reach its zenith in 1928, when *unitaire* politicization took its most decisive turn.

At its Sixth World Congress in July, three years before the World Depression reached France, the Comintern propounded an interpretation of the international situation that radically reoriented the PCF and its union supporters. According to the new line propounded by the Congress, the period of revolutionary upheavals following the World War (1917–23) and the "Second Period" of stabilization (1923–27) that succeeded it were about to give way to a "Third Period" marked by "the growth of the general crisis of capitalism and the accelerated accentuation of its fundamental . . . contradictions."[30] As capitalism became dysfunctional in this Third Period, economic crisis was expected to usher in an era of imperialist war and renewed capitalist attacks on the Soviet Union. At the same time, Social Democrats, no longer acting as "the right wing of the labor movement, but the left wing of the bourgeoisie," would behave as "social fascists." And workers suffering the brunt of capitalism's decline would gravitate toward increasingly radical politics. This interpretation of the international situation, it is significant to note, had virtually no foundation in contemporary events, but originated solely from Stalin's need to create a revolutionary smoke-screen for the murderous terror accompanying the Five-Year Plan of 1928. The new line, accordingly, made nonsense out of the situation it was designed to explain.

To marshal the PCF behind the Comintern policy, the Soviets installed two young *métallos*, Henri Barbé and Pierre Célor, co-opted from the Jeunesses communistes, to lead the party. The "Barbé-Célor group," guided by the ultra-left implications of the Third Period line, promptly reoriented the PCF from a siege to storm tactic. In doing so, it ordered programs that were impossible to implement, organized anti-government actions that brought down police repression on the party, called strikes on the slightest pretext, and attacked fellow communists who wavered in their enthusiasm.[31] It was not long before André Tardieu's right-wing government, whose battle cry was *Le communisme, voilà l'ennemi!*, countered with a full-scale repression. By the spring of 1929, the entire Political Bureau was in prison, underground, or in exile, and nearly half the PCF ranks illegal or clandestine.[32] Not surprisingly, party membership took a precipitous fall, reducing the PCF to a virtual *secte de masse*.[33]

As for the worker radicalization that was to follow the advent of the Third Period, it existed only in the minds of those inclined to interpret the slightest agitation as the onset of capitalism's collapse.[34] Although opposed by realities that refused to bend to their ideological expectations, militants now attempted to link strikes and other labor struggles to the "general class tasks of the proletariat." Every party and union action was thus treated as a possible opportunity for igniting a social conflagration that would lead to the revolutionary seizure of power.[35] Then, in September 1929, at the height of French prosperity, the annual CGTU Congress claimed that labor conflicts were about to "turn into political struggles." *Unitaires* were consequently advised to lead the working class with an eye to preparing the final battle for class power. "It is absolutely necessary," the CGTU Congress resolved, "to condemn the erroneous conception which limits worker actions to the economic plane, to purely corporate questions. . . . [E]very struggle engaged by the proletariat for the improvement of its conditions of existence [must] transform itself into a battle against bourgeois power."[36] In assuming that strikes would inevitably pass from the defensive to the offensive, communists now prepared for an insurrectional assault against the state.[37] As they did, they expected "every workshop, every factory . . . [to] become our fortress."[38]

At this point, the politicization of *unitaire* unionism came full circle: under the aegis of the Third Period line, the CGTU Metal Union discarded all pretense of being an economic organization and abandoned itself to the expected revolutionary apocalypse. It thus began calling strikes for a "class offensive against capitalism," even if such strikes resulted in futile struggles that dissipated its ranks.[39] It politicized the smallest workshop issues and framed them as part of the impending economic catastrophe.[40] It brushed aside the daily concerns of the shops, arguing "the fight [had] passed beyond the stage of struggle for better conditions."[41] It dismissed the contract (or collective agreement) as "a reformist deviation" and opposed all efforts to maintain "industrial peace."[42] It raised economic issues only when they were codified in party offices (rather than gleaned from the workshops) and treated all strikes as if they were "a step on the road leading to proletarian insurrection."[43] Moreover, it was not content with sabotaging its own work, for it tried to wreak havoc with the rest of the left by abandoning united-front activities with non-communists (stigmatized as "social fascists") and splitting, destroying, and undermining any group that resisted its leadership.[44] At the same time, the non-communist left was characterized as "an integral part of the capitalist system" and the term "reformist" made synonymous with "fascist."[45] Public encounters between communists and socialists, *unitaires* and confederals, became, as a result, increasingly factious. The Third Period's theory of "social fascism" led, in fact, to a kind of civil war within the ranks of labor and the left, for only by uncompromisingly decimating socialist and confederal organizations were communists, it was argued, going to prevent a fascist onslaught.[46] In such a situation, as socialists became agents of capitalist reaction and insignificant shop conflicts the harbinger of world revolution, "lies, slanders, insults, duplicity, hypocrisy, perfidy reigned, [just as] "honesty, loyalty, truth, justice [were] cynically or obliquely dismissed as bourgeois virtues," irrelevant to the impending struggle.[47] Finally, *unitaire* opposition to "militarism" and "imperialism," central to the tactical orientation of the new line, found little resonance in an industry constituting the backbone of French armament production. Typical of the growing misalignment between the party's strategic orientation and its link with factory realities was the PCF's much-touted National Day of Struggle Against the Threat of Capitalist War on the USSR, held on 1 August 1929, which brought out on strike a few thousand CGTU'ers prepared for the "final struggle," while the majority of *métallos* reacted with indifference, if not dismay.[48]

The disastrous implications of the new Comintern policy were not long in coming. Instead of turning the mass-production plants of the Paris Region into revolutionary fortresses, as the Third Period line envisaged, *unitaires* ended up estranging themselves from the very workers they hoped to lead.[49] Accordingly, 1929 and 1930 were black years for the CGTU and its Paris metal union. By compelling militants to violate the most elementary tenets of trade unionism and behave in ways that undermined their credibility in the ranks, the adventurous line wreaked havoc with the union's implantation. Some of the younger, tougher metal workers, it is true, enthusiastically propounded it, but they did so at the cost of marginalizing themselves in the plants or setting themselves up for victimization. Militants anxious to maintain their standing on the shop floor, as well as hold onto their jobs, were obliged to add nuance to the new line or tone down its excesses.

From Sectarianism to Economism

By the summer of 1930, French communist leaders and their mentors in Moscow were no longer able to ignore the dwindling membership rolls, demoralized ranks, ineffective interventions, and general organizational malaise produced by the new line.[50] Soviet leaders were thus prompted to make an immediate, though indirect, reevaluation of their policies in the West. The first hint of this occurred in June 1930, at the Sixteenth Russian Party Congress, when Stalin's mouthpiece, V. M. Molotov, cautioned against making war "on the whole body of social-democratic workers" and came close to characterizing Third Period sectarianism as "adventurous."[51] Shortly after Molotov's pronouncement, PCF leaders were summoned to Moscow, where they were ordered to apply the social-fascist epithet with greater subtlety and to distinguish between sincere but misguided rank-and-file reformists and their supposedly treasonous leaders. They were also chastised for their "defective implementation" of Comintern directives, as if the application, not the content, of these directives had been at the root of their recent failures.[52] Then, at the Fifth Congress of the Red International of Labor Unions in August 1930, the national sections of the trade-union international (of which the CGTU was the largest and most important) were instructed to implant themselves in the factories and concentrate on economic struggles. Unlike previous orders of a similar tenor, RILU leaders now stressed that successful implantation depended on daily work in the shops and attention to worker demands raised in the production process, not militant verbiage and frantic posturing.[53] Several months later, RILU chief Alexander Losovsky, who two years earlier had called for revolutionary strikes, rebuked *unitaires* for focusing on *la haute politique* and neglecting the small, everyday concerns of the workshop. "Many comrades," Losovsky added, "think the struggle for immediate demands is reformist and that they, the great revolutionaries, are only responsible for the major political issues [*haute politique*]."[54] After admonishing them for ignoring the "profound differences" separating party work from union work, Losovsky ordered *unitaires* to expand their factory-level operations and do so by focusing on the daily concerns of the shops.[55] Although these various measures helped mitigate the more extreme aspects of the Third Period line and demote the political dimension of their workshop activities, *unitaires* by no means disavowed revolutionary strikes. They did, however, start treating "economist" struggles as the *sine qua non* of, no longer a detraction from, radical class struggle.[56] In fact, given the depression's destabilizing effect, it gradually dawned on them that economic strife had an inherent political significance.

As the PCF reigned in its sectarianism, its labor policy underwent a corresponding modification. The key change came at the Comintern's Eleventh Plenary Session in March 1931, when the PCF was criticized for being overly identified with the CGTU and for neglecting the practical aspects of trade-union work.[57] Implicit in this criticism was the understanding that *unitaires* in the shops should have more freedom in responding to specific economic issues. Then, in July 1931, as part of Moscow's reevaluation of the French and international situation, the ultra-left Barbé-Célor group was blamed for the party's decline and Maurice Thorez, with a "mandate" to create a more "democratic" party regime, installed as the new PCF chief.[58] Thorez's ascension to power was accompanied by the installation of a team of Comintern agents who assumed control of the party's daily operations and did so in ways that made them more realistic.[59] By 1932, de facto Soviet policy, although still confused and muddled, was increasingly oriented toward rebuilding communist bridges to the "masses" (which Third Period sectarianism had destroyed)—and doing so by focusing on the practical tasks of unionism. This economist reorientation was further buttressed by a Comintern directive issued in July 1932 which called on communists to win the working class by engaging in "well-organized, systematic, day-to-day work" based on "methods of persuasion and not mindless sloganeering."[60]

Although the Third Period line remained formal party policy until June 1934, its gradual mitigation between 1930 and 1932 helped French communists curb their sectarianism and take a more pragmatic approach to the workplace.[61] As they did, party organs learned to differentiate between the separate spheres of party and union work and to emphasize the distinct economic tasks of unionism.[62] The economist implications of these changes were then formalized at the March 1932 PCF Congress, where the party resolved to focus more resolutely on the factories, take up daily struggles in the shops, and make factory interventions the concern of the entire apparatus.[63] As a means of implementing this resolution, the PCF ordered its factory cells to assist the CGTU in constituting new *sections* and making industrial implantation their foremost priority. According to the party's chief theoretical organ, "Factory work is decisive, without it there cannot exist a real Communist party, capable of organizing the great class battles of the proletariat. It is in the plants that the party can and must establish its links with the masses and do so by fighting for the daily demands of workers in the shops."[64] Finally, in October 1932, Benoît Frachon, a former metal worker favoring the economist turn, was made general secretary of the CGTU, replacing Gaston Monmousseau, a staunch proponent of the Third Period line. Frachon was particularly concerned with the situation in the Paris metal industry and his appointment would inaugurate a new era in *unitaire* unionism.[65] Generally speaking, these changes helped reorient communists toward labor's corporate agenda and enhance their ability to intervene in the depressed economy. Although it is true that some militants continued to agitate in a noisy, sectarian manner, acting as if workshop actions were part of the more general struggle to overthrow capitalism, the PCF in this period gradually stopped viewing labor conflict as the prelude to insurrection and sought to lead workers by championing their daily needs.[66] In the factitious language of the new party chief, "nothing which affected the workers could be treated as a matter of indifference to us."[67] And this was exactly the image the party now hoped to convey in the plants.

The party's overheated sectarianism had done its greatest damage in the CGTU; its revision there would be especially consequential. In September 1931, the Sixth CGTU Congress, in response to the altered signals coming from Moscow, resolved to dedicate itself to the "energetic struggle against negligence in preparing the economic struggles of the proletariat." It then condemned sectarian policies that privileged political over economic issues.[68] In a related vein, the Tenth Congress of the Paris metal union, meeting in October 1932, resolved to provide workers "the means to conduct their movements to victory"—by advancing a business-like approach to economic issues. In this spirit, *sections syndicales* were ordered to discard strident language and extremist tactics, orient to the corporate peculiarities of their plants, and connect with workers spontaneously resisting the deterioration of their conditions.[69] By late 1932, the *Unitaire* Metal Union had almost entirely discarded its previous political demands and made the forty-hour week, the guaranteed hourly wage, health and safety delegates, paid vacations, and the collective contract the centerpieces of its agitation. Instead of imposing revolutionary political objectives on worker conflicts, as it had at the height of the Third Period, the union now viewed economic conflict as a circuitous but necessary means of furthering communist objectives in the workplace.

As this economist orientation took hold in 1931 and 1932, a new type of labor policy, focused on corporate issues that only indirectly advanced the party's political project, emerged to guide *unitaire* efforts in the mass-production sector.[70] This policy would be buttressed by two concomitant developments. The first of these involved the exit of the non-communist opposition. Since its formation in 1922, the CGTU (and especially the metal union) had been torn by sharp and acrimonious factionalism. Largely identified with revolutionary syndicalism, the opposition had been organized under several different banners. In the late 1920s, it was concentrated in the Comité pour l'Independence du Syndicalisme and propagated its views in the weekly *Le Cri du Peuple.* In November 1930, the Comité pour l'Independence du Syndicalisme merged with the Comité des 22, an ad hoc group advocating the reunification of the labor movement on the basis of "political independence."[71] These oppositionists, however, were so smothered by the Third Period line that in September 1931 they felt compelled to quit the *Unitaire* Metal Union and join the CGT.[72] Their exodus eliminated the last significant factional obstacle to the communist leadership and marked the final step in the CGTU's communization. Once free of their critics, *unitaire* metal leaders were—paradoxically—free to take up limited economic demands and distance themselves from the party's political objectives, which had been at the heart of the opposition's program.

The second development consolidating the CGTU's economist turn was less concrete, but no less consequential. It involved the emergence in the early 1930s of a new generation of militants. Forged in the crucible of bolshevization and the Third Period, these young, sometimes unscrupulous militants constituted a tried and disciplined cadre, full of crusading ardor, and conditioned to accept the most extreme demands of Stalinist organization. Because they had "organically" emerged from the worker milieu and assimilated communist principles in ways the first generation, schooled in the critical anarchist spirit of revolutionary syndicalism, had never quite managed, they would be particularly effective proponents of the *unitaire* cause. They would consequently provide the union with a nucleus of activists whose significance would be out of all proportion to their small number. Ambroise Croizat, general secretary of the Metal Federation, Robert Doury, later general secretary of the Paris metal union, Alfred Coste, later union president, Jean-Pierre Timbaud, union secretary and the most powerful of its agitators, and a handful of others with energetic and inspiring personalities, began in this period to assume important leadership roles.[73] As they did, they prepared to make the union a force in the Fordist-Taylorist factory system.

Progress

The "decisive turns" aimed at rooting the PCF and CGTU in the factories were not entirely successful.[74] Top PCF officials, like the new party chief Maurice Thorez, continued to appraise aspects of the political scene in terms of the Third Period line, which had been modified but not discarded. At lower levels, in the union and the party, there remained militants who persisted in propounding the political strike, ignoring mundane workshop issues, and denouncing reformists as "social fascists." More seriously, *unitaire métallos* were slow in vitalizing their *sections* or implanting themselves more widely in industry. In mid-1932, there were only twenty functioning *sections* in medium and large-scale factories, most of which suffered from ineffective organization, unstable membership, inadequate cadre, meager recruitment, and a lingering prejudice against economic interventions.[75]

Not withstanding these on-going problems, the CGTU Metal Union of Paris became noticeably more effective after 1931.[76] The appeal for insurrectional strikes, for instance, gave way to more realistic demands and militants found they automatically increased their audience in worker ranks if they focused on corporate issues. The union also began experimenting with new organizational forms, such as the *section industrielle*, which was set up for specific sectors (such as auto, aviation, electrical appliance, etc.) in order to collect information pertinent to that sector, ascertain its specific demands and grievances, and designate actions to deal with its peculiarities—acknowledging in effect that corporate issues were central to union activities, not simply the general class tasks dictated by previous communist labor policy.[77] Perhaps the best example of the *unitaires'* economist reorientation was their use of labor tribunals *(Prud'hommes)* to contest employer violations of individual work contracts. Throughout the first decade of the CGTU's existence, *unitaires* had consistently disdained the use of judicial action in the name of revolutionary principle. Beginning in 1932, however, they actively took up this "reformist" mode of action, making a great ado about it inside the CGTU and in their press.[78] These various efforts to intersect the workers' corporate world soon led to results, as *unitaires* halted the drain of their membership and their *sections* started to grow in number and influence.[79] Although still weak in large-scale plants, those factory *sections* concerned with limited economic actions, not pie-in-the-sky rhetoric, began now to grow in size and significance, becoming tribunes for *métallos* prepared to resist the depression's onerous impact on wages and conditions.

Unitaire Strikes

When the first jolts of the World Depression hit the Paris metal industry in 1931, not a few workers shrugged off the apathy of the 1920s and began defending their standards. Their readiness to act collectively was much facilitated by the growing homogenization of the labor market and the fact that the Paris suburbs now offered communal and political resources that had not existed in the years following the Great War. More importantly, workers were encouraged by the CGTU's economist turn: for once the *unitaires* subordinated their sectarian notion of unionism to the imperatives of economic defense (which the depression elevated to a new status), *métallos* were inclined to follow their lead. In this situation, previous efforts at industrial implantation began to pay dividends.

Events moved rapidly once the larger structural and organizational changes were in place. This was evident as early as March 1931, when the union intervened at the Chenard-et-Walker auto works in Gennevilliers. Shortly after management announced a wage cut, CGTU agitators appeared at the factory gates—none of the Chenard workers were unionized—and urged workers to resist the cuts by staging a sitdown strike. The sitdown had long been a feature of the RILU program, but *unitaires* had never previously applied it. Two months earlier, however, 400 bodyshop workers at the Talbot auto works in Suresnes had engaged in a spontaneous sitdown; it was not entirely successful, but *unitaires* hailed it as a model for future labor action.[80] When they arrived at Chenard, they tentatively proposed the novel strike tactic. The Chenard workers immediately sensed its appropriateness. As the production index was in the process of falling from 136 to 96 that year, unemployment dominated their concerns; fear of lock-out and a labor market clogged with surplus made the sitdown seem like an ideal way to prevent scab-herding and pressure management.[81] On 6 March 1931, 800 bodyshop workers downed their tools and refused to leave their shop; at the same time, 200 workers from other shops walked out. While two-thirds of the Chenard workers ignored the strike call, the sitdown by the highly skilled bodyshop workers, use to good wages and decent conditions, created a rare organizing opportunity for the *unitaires.*

After management called the police, the sitdown strikers were forcibly evicted from the plant and threatened with dismissal if they did not immediately present themselves for rehire. The metal union then attempted to continue the struggle from outside the plant, but the odds were stacked against it; not only had most of the workforce ignored the strike call, a massive police presence quickly rendered union picket lines ineffective. Because the struggle failed to develop, strikers were forced back on the employer's terms. But not all was lost, for the strike represented the first significant application of the union's new economist orientation and brought *unitaires* in contact with newly-roused workers. Following the conflict, a party cell was formed at Chenard, and the cell, in turn, helped establish a *section syndicale,* which eventually recruited a hundred members. Over the next year, the *section* would go on to gain a certain authority at Chenard, leading fourteen union actions over the next year, most limited to a workshop or two, but all focused on corporate demands, which were in the process of becoming uppermost among *unitaire* organizing concerns.[82]

Although the Chenard-et-Walker strike of March 1931 owed more to the combativeness of the bodyshop workers than to improvements in *unitaire* techniques, it nonetheless convinced communists that economist demands were a powerful mobilizing force and the sitdown a viable method of struggle.[83] Armed with this conviction, they prepared to intersect future struggles. In August, they staged another sitdown strike, this time at the Babcok-et-Wilcox plant in La Courneuve, where they succeeded in forcing management to retract a recently introduced Bedaux piece-rate system.[84] During the next six months, they went on to organize more than thirty such sitdowns, mostly in small shops and factories. While not all these strikes were successful, they nonetheless created many new organizing opportunities for the *unitaires*.[85]

In late 1931, the union took another leap forward, this time at the heart of the Paris metal industry. For a decade, it had sought to implant itself in the giant Renault auto works in Boulogne-Billancourt, but could count barely sixty *unitaires* among its 30,000 workers. The union's prospects, however, were about to change. In response to the economic crisis, which had an especially severe impact on auto makers, Louis Renault had speeded up production, diminished piece-rates, and increased time-and-motion studies. Then, in November 1931, he decided to impose a hefty wage cut. This decision was made with perfect business acumen, but it failed to account for the shift in union tactics or the evolution in worker spirits. When the wage cut was initially imposed in the chassis-assembly shop, a spontaneous workstoppage by the shop's highly skilled workers forced its retraction. Undaunted, Renault tried in other shops. At this point, the *unitaires* intervened. Rather than call a general strike of the entire factory, with its 300 workshops, as they had tried and failed to do in the past, they decided to resist the cuts shop by shop, as they were announced. In this way, the union sought to root the struggle in worker ranks and concentrate its forces at the strategic points. Whenever a shop in the giant auto works was notified that the old rates were to be lowered, *unitaires* urged workers to elect a strike committee and stage a sitdown. The union lacked the cadre to intervene in all shops, but by thinly spreading its forces and using sympathetic, usually skilled workers contacted at factory gates or in nearby canteens, it managed to organize strikes or support spontaneous workstoppages in nearly half the shops with scheduled cuts, successfully mitigating many of them.

The two-month-long series of cat-and-mouse skirmishes which *unitaires* carried out at Renault constituted a limited but unprecedented riposte to France's most powerful industrialist. Although their actions were limited to skilled workers and management soon purged many of the strike leaders, *unitaires* nonetheless demonstrated their ability to lead. Contrary to the pessimism of the CGT national office, which thought it impossible to wage economic struggles in the crisis-ridden economy, they proved that such struggles were not only feasible but could be extended to the factory interior. Their application of the sitdown tactic, moreover, turned many of the strikes into prolonged union meetings, considerably inflating worker spirits. Finally, the Renault struggle imbued the *unitaires* with a sudden credibility in worker ranks.[86] By avoiding political issues and concentrating on the wage cut, they were able to shed their sectarian image and enhance their appeal to the unorganized. Over the course of the next year, with its reputation much revamped, the *Unitaire* Metal Union went on to apply its Renault strategy in other sectors of the industry. If its actions only partially stymied employer attempts to manage the economic crisis according to business interests, they at least provided *métallos* a means of defending their conditions and doing so under increasingly competent *unitaire* leadership.

It was not until the Citroen auto strike in the spring of 1933 that the metal union took another leap forward. Shortly after André Citroen, *le Napoleon de l'automobile*, announced a massive wage cut, 300 craftsmen in the tool shop of his Javel plant spontaneously stopped work, elected a delegation, and asked management to rescind the cuts. Before the conflict was resolved—and it was likely these highly skilled auto workers would receive some sort of satisfaction—the *unitaires* intervened. Agitators were dispatched to the factory gates, where they harangued workers going to lunch or changing shifts. At the same time, leaflets were distributed and organizers smuggled inside the giant plant. That afternoon several workshops responded to the agitation and soon 4,000 auto workers were in the factory courtyard demanding that the rest of the workforce join them. Next day, as the protest grew, Citroen was compelled to lock out 18,000 workers at his seven Paris plants. For the first time in its history, the *Unitaire* Metal Union found itself at the head of a mass strike.

For the next thirty-five days, communists mobilized all their resources to bear on the momentous Citroen conflict. L. Monjauvais, a PCF parliamentary deputy, used his political connections to set up meetings between the Citroen strikers and the labor minister; he also got the chamber, with its Radical-Socialist majority, to pass a bill permitting strikers to collect unemployment benefits. In various metal-working towns of the suburbs, the party mustered its membership to collect 200,000 *francs* in strike support, one of the largest fund raisers up to this period, and its press network helped rally the suburban population behind the strikers. At the same time, CGTU militants in other factories, particularly Renault, tried to spread the strike and put additional pressure on Citroen.

The most important facet of the union's strike activity came with its organization of a strike committee, made up of elected delegates from the various Citroen shops. From the start, the committee took charge of the movement, giving it a democratic veneer and providing a crucial link between the union leadership and the strikers. A key task of the committee was to deploy mass pickets at the factory gates to discourage scabbing and maintain striker élan. Mounted police repeatedly dispersed these pickets and on several occasions the strike turned bloody. The much-discussed and highly visible strike did not, however, end in a union victory. On 24 April, after police regained control of the streets, Citroen reopened his works. Although 80 percent of the strikers voted to continue the struggle, the tide turned against them once the unskilled workers broke ranks and accepted Citroen's offer to return without reprisal and with a mitigation of the proposed wage cut. In another break from precedent, the union ordered the remaining strikers to return *en bloc*. As production resumed, a sizable number of workers followed the union's lead in engaging in slowdowns, temporary workstoppages, and various disruptive measures designed to pressure management into rehiring victimized strikers and fulfilling the promised mitigation of the wage cuts. Only at the end of May, after the successful reintegration of the victimized strikers, did the seven Citroen plants return to normal.[87]

The metal union lost the Citroen strike, but few considered it an outright defeat. The strike's level of violence, its impressive organization and duration, and the numerous political and social forces involved made it the most significant industrial action since the revolutionary metal strikes of 1919 and 1920. During its course, one of the most powerful French industrialists had been challenged and put on notice that his anti-labor policies would henceforth be resisted. If Citroen emerged victorious, most workers attributed it to the police powers of the state, not the inadequacies of the union. *Métallo* solidarity forged during the strike now dramatically ended a dozen years of worker passivity, signaling what would be a resurgence of worker initiative and union growth.

The *unitaires*, it is important to note, did not suddenly overcome all their previous shortcomings during the Citroen strike. Their five implanted *sections* had failed to coordinate their activities, most organization and propaganda was carried out by the union's Paris office, which was not always up to the task, and there was a general lack of coordination between local and municipal levels of the union leadership.[88] Yet by focusing on the corporate dimension of the conflict, soft-pedaling its politics, and catering to the strikers' organizational needs, the union succeeded in winning the leadership of those willing to fight in defense of their conditions.

In the Balance

Unitaire strike activity in the period 1931–33, especially its leadership of the Citroen strike, considerably broaden the union's influence, validating its economist "turn." Although its *sections* remained relatively few in number, its factory journals overly political, and the majority of *métallos* still indifferent to union organization, the CGTU Metal Union had nonetheless begun in this period to emerge from its isolation and make an impression on the industry.[89] More significantly, larger forces were moving in its favor. By late 1933, the depression had created an ever-expanding audience for union agitation, even though the union was still poorly rooted in the plants. If the situation had evolved "naturally," the union would likely have gone on to organize a significant minority of metal workers, particularly among skilled workers able to defend their standards. The situation, however, did not evolve naturally. As was so often the case in French social history, a crisis in the political system suddenly overshadowed whatever issues the union was beginning to address in the factory, shifting its concerns to the state.

Jacobins in Blue Denim

IN FEBRUARY 1934, THE STREETS OF PARIS BECAME A STAGING
ground for a series of violent right-wing assaults on the state. As the republic
teetered, a massive CGT mobilization succeeded in warding off further attacks.
This immediately changed labor's standing in French national life, transforming the unions into bulwarks of republicanism and unionists into latter-day
Jacobins. Workers, as a consequence, acquired the sudden confidence to challenge management, the "progressive" parties rallied to their corporate demands, and the rival confederations found the common ground on which
to reconcile. Republican defense thus automatically imbued labor with a new
calling and a new authority. But it did so at the cost of subordinating the
unions to a political logic foreign to their traditional project.

6 February 1934

The 1932 legislative elections gave the Radical and Socialist parties a majority in the Chamber of Deputies, but neither party was able to agree on how
to tackle the various disorders precipitated by the depression. Radicals representing the liberal petty bourgeoisie favored a deflationary policy aimed at

cutting state expenditures and reducing budgetary deficits, while socialists advocated a strategy of greater popular purchasing power—and higher deficits—
to stimulate markets. In the face of these incompatible policy orientations, six
different cabinets rose and fell in the first year and a half of the new chamber.

While failing to resolve problems related to taxes, deficits, and economic
stagnation, Radicals and socialists nonetheless agreed on the need to dismantle the political legacy of André Tardieu. As premier several times between 1928
and 1932, Tardieu had curtailed parliamentary prerogatives, enhanced the executive powers of his office, and introduced reforms appropriate to the new
managerial forms of capitalism, all of which threatened Radicals opposed to
state intervention and socialists resentful of his social program. In reversing
Tardieu's innovations and reviving the "stalemated" political forms of the
Third Republic, the Radical-Socialist coalition inadvertently created the impression that the government was more concerned with defending ministerial
privileges than aiding peasants whose crops could not be sold, functionaries
facing state-mandated pay cuts, and workers without prospect of employment.[1] As this impression gained ground, public opinion took a decidedly anti-
government turn, intersecting the growing disillusionment that had followed
in the depression's wake. The victory of 1918, the unprecedented postwar
growth, and French hegemony in European affairs had fostered the illusion
that France was master of her destinies. When this illusion came crashing
down after 1931, the public could not help but feel "betrayed." These feelings
were further exacerbated by Hitler's accession to power in 1933, for it revived
the fear of German militarism and cast suspicions on the heavy sacrifices of the
First World War, which brought the French victory but little apparent gain. By
the early 1930s, talk of "the decline of Western civilization" and the general
crisis of the moral order achieved a certain currency, just as hatred for lawyers,
parliamentary deputies, and cabinet ministers became a fashionable part of
public discourse. Some newspapers and periodicals (and not merely those of
the far right) even began reevaluating the state forms advocated by Hitler and
Mussolini, finding praise for their energetic response to the depression.[2] With
this decline of public confidence, sections of the populace started to look beyond parliament for an alternative solution to the crisis. Protofascist organizations, as a result, began to grow and anti-republicanism, largely dormant since
the war, gained a second breath. Then, at the end of 1933, after the press un-
covered criminal financial links between several high-ranking cabinet ministers and Serge Stavisky, a swindler of Ukrainian-Jewish origin, the political
crisis turned explosive.

For many, the Stavisky affair, the latest in a series of governmental scan-
dals, was the last straw. Feeling that drastic measures were needed to prevent

the parliamentary regime from leading the country to ruin, they now flocked to various leagues and veteran groups opposed to the republic. In January 1934, the Action Française, the Croix de Feu, the Solidarité Française, the Jeunesses Patriotes, and other far-right groups organized a series of demonstrations demanding the resignation of the "Judeo-liberal government." Although not "fascist" in the German sense, these anti-republicans, following in the bonapartist tradition of French politics, operated outside the parliamentary framework as paramilitary pressure groups hostile to the nineteenth-century heritage of liberal democracy, parliamentary government, and Jewish emancipation.[3] Made up of monarchists, admirers of Mussolini, and intervening gradations between these extremes, the leagues and veteran organizations were united only in their anti-communism, anti-Semitism, and ardent nationalism, but this was enough to make them a formidable source of disorder.[4] Emboldened by the recent collapse of the Weimar Republic and the declining fortunes of the Third Republic, these far rightists viewed the Stavisky scandal not only as another sign of liberal decadence, but as an opportunity to bring down the government. Their violent street protests now infused Paris streets and squares with an atmosphere of impending civil war.[5]

On 3 February, Edouard Daladier, the recently appointed premier, inadvertently ignited the first volley in this civil war by dismissing Jean Chiappe, the Paris *prefect* of police. The far right, with whom the *prefect* sympathized, took Chiappe's dismissal as a direct affront. "To drive the republican thieves" from the chamber, the leagues and veteran groups called the population of Paris to a day-long series of demonstrations scheduled for 6 February. As tens of thousands responded to their appeal, Paris was besieged by a wave of violent street skirmishes. For a moment, as buses burned in the streets and pitched battles broke out with the police, it seemed as if the demonstrators might topple the regime. Subsequent studies have shown that, despite its hatred for the republic and the money powers that controlled it, the far right was not intent on insurrection. Its actions, however, had the appearance of one.[6] This especially seemed the case on the evening of the 6th, when 100,000 rightists massed in the Place de la Concorde, across the river from the Palais Bourbon, seat of the Chamber of Deputies. Armed with pieces of cast iron and paving stones, and in some cases with knives and hand guns, the demonstrators tried to gain the Left Bank of the Seine and literally sweep the "republican bandits" from their parliamentary benches. Only the clubs and rifles of the police prevented them from doing so. When the din and dust cleared that evening, eighteen lay dead, 1,600 wounded, and untold others injured and in need of medical assistance.[7] Not since the Commune of 1871 had so much blood flowed in the streets of Paris.

Although the rioters failed to overthrow the republic, they succeeded in forcing the Radicals from power. Lacking the full support of his party and fearing a renewal of disorder, Daladier felt obliged to resign.[8] This sent an immediate shockwave across France. For the first time in the republic's history, the streets had brought down a government. As the ramparts of constitutional legality teetered, it seemed as if the "Republican synthesis" of the 1870s might wholly unravel.[9] In this tense situation, the conservative Gaston Doumergue, a former president, was called on to form an all-party or National Union government, made up of Radical and right-wing deputies—a government which some characterized as bonapartist.[10] This created further cause for alarm. If the demonstrators had not overthrown the *république des scandales*, they had at least destroyed parliamentary morale and brought the right to power, in effect annulling the center-left victory of the 1932 election.[11] One liberal Catholic captured the prevailing mood in the capital when he described the anti-republican demonstrations as proving "that a civil war was not impossible. In the shadow of this horrifying obsession, people became panic-stricken, hatreds grew more and more bitter, the gullibility of the public took on fantastic proportions, and the number of those whose fear, anger, [and] credulity made them ready for anything increased unceasingly."[12] What this "anything" might entail was particularly unsettling to the left. With Adolf Hitler's recent triumph in everybody's mind, the violent rightist demonstrations appeared to herald an impending clash between republicanism and reaction.[13] Leftists now anxiously wondered if they could rally their scattered forces to defend the threatened republic.

The Moment of Decision

Throughout January, the CGT national office had monitored the rightist demonstrations. Of the progressive forces in France, it was the most acutely conscious that European democracies were succumbing to the disorders and miseries of the world economic crisis and that unions were likely to be the first to suffer from democracy's demise. Shortly after Hitler liquidated the Marxist trade unions, the CGT vowed to defend republican liberties by "any means necessary."[14] A year later, when the far right began disturbing the public spaces of Paris, the CGT reiterated its pledge.[15] Then, on 6 February, as the leagues squared off with the police outside the chamber, the CGT alerted its Paris membership for possible emergency action. The decisive confederal action came, however, only after Daladier's resignation on the 7th, when the confederation announced a twenty-four-hour general strike to rally labor and the nation in defense of the threatened republic.[16] Although this announcement followed from the CGT's earlier position, it constituted a remarkable act of bravado. For a dozen years, the confederation had stood on the periphery of French national life; now, at the moment when democratic liberties were imperiled, it—and it alone—stepped out of the shadows to take up the mantle of republican defense.

Unlike the CGT, the PCF and CGTU reacted to the anti-republican tumult with considerable ambiguity and indecision. Throughout the Stavisky scandal and the events leading up to 6 February, communists had been guided by the Third Period line.[17] Although the line's more extreme aspects, particularly in respect to the unions, had been modified, the party still refused to distinguish between the forces of the democratic left and those of the anti-republican right, both of which were characterized as facets of the capitalist order and thus manifestations of fascism. At the height of the crisis, L'Humanité had even called for demonstrations against the government, the socialists, and the "fascists" (i.e., the anti-republican leagues), suggesting that no significant difference lay between them.[18] In a speech he was unable to deliver to the Chamber of Deputies, Maurice Thorez had been prepared to tell his fellow deputies that "there is no difference between bourgeois democracy and fascism. They are two forms of capitalism. . . . Between cholera and the plague, one does not choose."[19] Then, on 7 February, as the fateful impact of the rightist attacks became apparent, the PCF's Political Bureau repulsed a socialist proposal to form a united front in defense of the republic.[20] At this point, it looked as if French communism would follow its German counterpart in acquiescing to the destruction of republican institutions.

The PCF would be spared this fate, but little credit was owed to the top party leadership. Throughout the events leading up to the anti-republican riots, rank-and-file communists had resisted the leadership's opposition to the "bourgeois Republic" and its simplistic equation of republicanism and fascism.[21] Years of bolshevization had evidently failed to destroy their ingrained sympathy for the traditional republican patriotism of the French left and its time-honored slogan: Pas d'ennemis à gauche. The ranks, as a consequence, were not unreceptive to SFIO and CGT appeals for "unity of action"—appeals which the party leadership dismissed as feeble efforts to prop up "the tottering capitalist regime." More seriously, the charismatic communist major of Saint-Denis, Jacques Doriot, a former metal worker, dramatically broke party discipline after the 6th and advocated a PCF–SFIO united front to repel the anti-republican menace.[22] As the party's greatest worker-revolutionary, Doriot's indiscipline directly challenged the PCF leadership (and soon led to his expulsion).[23] To counter him and the republican current in communist ranks, Thorez announced a mass demonstration for 9 February to demand the arrests of the "fascists," as well as Daladier's "murderous cabinet." Such a demonstration was bound to result in an adventurous confrontation with the authorities and aggravate the dangers facing the republic. But, unbeknown to the top party leadership, it would also prove to be the Third Period's swan song.[24]

The General Strike

The communist demonstration of 9 February was banned by the government and 20,000 police and troops were mobilized against it. As communists went ahead with the prohibited demonstration, it rapidly degenerated into a bloody street battle which left six dead and thousands injured. Despite their "admirable courage," communist demonstrators were as decisively crushed as the anti-republicans had been on the 6th.[25] This, however, did not detract party myth-makers from portraying the demonstration as a great and heroic resistance to the "fascization" of France. What they could not dismiss, however, was the fact that the PCF had failed to shape events according to its extremist agenda. As sectarian illusions momentarily lifted after the 9th, the CGTU leadership displayed a sudden receptivity to the general strike planned for 12 February.

The actual details accounting for this change of heart have left few traces in the historical record, but Russian concerns were undoubtedly paramount. By early 1934, Hitler had taken Germany out of the League of Nations, abrogated certain disarmament conventions, and signed what the Soviets considered a worrisome non-aggression pact with Poland. These early stirrings of German nationalism, combined with Japanese aggression in Manchuria, had forced Stalin to contemplate a rapprochement with the Western democracies, especially France.[26] Although Hitler was in no position as yet to threaten the Soviet regime, Stalin had ample reason to fear, for the famine and economic dislocations provoked by the first Five-Year Plan had made the USSR weaker than at any time since the Civil War. He thus sought some sort of counterweight to a resurgent Germany. This was evident as early as December 1933, when the Central Committee of the Russian Communist party endorsed a resolution favoring collective security and admission to the League of Nations. Stalin, however, realized that a rapprochement with the Western powers, aimed at enmeshing Germany in a web of multilateral restraints, was possible only if these powers maintained political systems hostile to fascism. Although PCF leaders were oblivious to the soul-searching then taking place in the Kremlin and showed not the slightest interest in defending the republic, their obtuseness would have little ultimate effect, for the party's fate lay, as always, in the hands of Moscow, not Paris.[27]

Albert Vassard claims a telegram from the Comintern led to the PCF's decision to support the CGT general strike. Orthodox party accounts maintain that the CGTU decided to participate in the strike as early as 7 February, when it was announced.[28] Whatever the exact source of the decision, the PCF had been shaken by the fiasco of its 9 February demonstration and concerned about its restive membership. If the SFIO had called a "united front from below," communist ranks, as a number of party stalwarts warned, would likely have succumbed to it.[29] In Saint-Denis, "capital of the Red Belt," Doriot's united front with the SFIO and the CGT had already won the enthusiastic support of local communists, as did united fronts formed by several PCF cells in the northern suburbs and in a dozen provincial cities.[30] With or without party approval, the CGT general strike was bound to attract communist ranks and could not but worry party leaders. The irrepressible pressure for "anti-fascist unity," combined with the failure of their demonstration and perhaps orders from Moscow, now pushed the PCF leadership toward the CGT and the non-communist left. On 11 February, in what Henry Ehrmann called a "revolutionary somersault," *L'Humanité* announced that the PCF and CGTU would support the CGT action.[31]

The general strike of 12 February turned out to be one of the *grands journées* of the French labor movement—"a mass movement without precedent," according to communist historians.[32] Four million workers across France observed the strike, many of them participating in the 350 provincial demonstrations that accompanied it. But it was the strike in the Paris Region that was decisive and here the republican mobilization assumed its greatest success. From 50 percent to 75 percent of the region's workforce struck, registering a powerful vote of confidence in the republic. This impressive turnout caused one socialist to note that "in the face of the fascist menace, the Parisian working class was able to rediscover all its élan, all its combativity."[33] What was not noted, however, was that workers, despite their general economic discontent, responded mainly as defenders of their republican identities rather than as class-conscious opponents of a potentially anti-labor regime. The republic— with its popular association with the figure of Marianne, the Sacred Value, the Social Republic[34]—constituted the most potent symbol of their cultural identity as Frenchmen and thus of their affiliation to the national community. This was especially the case with suburban workers who had lost a sense of historical continuity and were uncertain of their place in the larger social world. Republicanism would now serve as a tonic to the "identity crisis" provoked by the deep-going economic transformations of the past two decades and a means of socially grounding workers in a world where everything—work, neighborhood, norms—had shifted under their feet.[35] As a consequence, the general strike to defend the republic, in affirming their republican identity and their place in the national community, had a powerful effect on their sensibilities.

Press accounts indicate that in many of the small metal shops of the eleventh, nineteenth, and twentieth *arrondissements*, the strike turnout was nearly total. Aircraft plants with their large skilled workforce also had a better-than-average turnout. But in the larger suburban towns, it was the political configuration, not the character of the workforce, that seemed to matter most. Saint-Denis, Doriot's stronghold and the site of an effective united front of left and labor organizations, had nearly a 100 percent observance, even in the large-scale plants. Elsewhere, it was the presence of *sections syndicales* or organized leftists that made the difference.[36] But everywhere, concern for the declining fortunes of the republic appeared decisive.

Like its provincial counterparts, the general strike in Paris was accompanied by numerous street demonstrations. In the suburbs, where feelings were especially tense, several of these demonstrations led to bloody clashes with the police.[37] In the capital, though, the street mobilization was a disciplined, peaceful event of unprecedented scope. As 150,000 demonstrators in two merging contingents, one led by the SFIO, the other by the PCF, manifested a common concern for the republic, years of divisive strife came to a momentary halt—for the first time since the schisms that had split the labor and socialist movements. This sudden, if temporary alliance of rival left and labor organizations, it was commonly agreed, made the 12th a day of unparalleled significance, giving many the feeling that they had achieved a great victory and that this victory would be a prelude to others.[38]

The Turn

The general strike, in turning labor into a mainstay of democratic liberties, immediately revived the flagging fortunes of the French left and helped bridge some of the numerous cleavages running through it. Yet however many rifts were suddenly overcome on 12 February, the principal ones remained. Central to any meaningful reconciliation of the progressive forces was the suspension of the Third Period line, which characterized "reformists" as "social fascists" and prevented communists from joining them in common fronts against the right. At this crucial juncture, the Russian leadership intervened to facilitate just such a reconciliation. As noted above, Russian fears of a resurgent Germany had already caused Stalin to inch toward a change of course and was probably responsible for the PCF's participation in the general strike. In contemplating a collective-security alliance with the Western democracies, the Soviets were obliged to reevaluate their theory of "social fascism." In the week following the general strike, a bloody rightist coup in Vienna that culminated in the crushing of the Austrian labor movement helped convince them that fascists—that is, those advocating the policies of Hitler and Mussolini—represented something quite different from the "social fascists" of the social-democratic left. By the spring of 1934, after the publication of the new German military budget indicated the Reich was rearming and after the French government responded positively to a Soviet proposal for collective security, the theory of "social fascism" began to give way in Moscow to demands for an anti-fascist front of the "progressive forces."[39] This shift was almost immediately felt in the international communist movement. Halfway through the PCF's National Party Conference of June 1934, a Comintern telegram ordered a change of course. With little explanation and no recantation, the PCF leadership jettisoned the Third Period line and executed a 180-degree turn.[40]

On the basis of the Moscow directive, Maurice Thorez (who was proving to be an astute adapter to the twists and turns of Soviet policy) informed the Party Conference that fascists on the right, not the "social fascists" on the non-communist left, were the greatest danger facing the working class. He then redefined fascism as the "terroristic dictatorship" of the most retrograde and militaristic elements of finance capitalism—implying that all forms of bourgeois rule no longer fell into this politically incorrect category, that significant differences existed between liberal democrats and fascists.[41] To build the anti-fascist movement dictated by the new line, the working class, he argued, would need to ally with social democrats, reformist unionists, and the liberal middle class, just as the PCF would have to give up its quest for Soviet power and its opposition to republican institutions. Although not all the implications of the new line were immediately apparent, the alliances and policy changes dictated by it would have a momentous impact on the party, transforming not only its relation to the left, but the very nature of French communism: for if fascism was the greatest danger, then the main task in the coming period was no longer the revolutionary class struggle, but the defense of republican liberties and the creation of the broadest possible anti-fascist front.[42]

The first step in the party's transformation—and the first consequence of the new line—involved a reconciliation with the Socialist party. On 27 July 1934, after a brief series of negotiations, the PCF was able to work out a "united action pact" with the SFIO. In accepting this pact, each party agreed to stop attacking the other, participate in joint actions against the anti-republican right, defend democratic liberties, and oppose the unpopular deflationary policies of Doumergue's National Union government; they also agreed to form an alliance in the up-coming cantonal elections. From the start, the PCF–SFIO pact opened many new organizing opportunities for the left. The PCF, however, had even more ambitious plans for the anti-fascist movement.[43] In late October 1934, shortly after the Soviet Union joined the League of Nations, Thorez appealed to the Radical party, the principal French bearer of the liberal-democratic tradition, to join communists and socialists in a *Front populaire*—a People's Front[44]—dedicated to defending the republican order from fascist and reactionary attacks.[45] This was a radical departure from all previous communist policy, for never before had the PCF advocated a multi-class alliance. The top Radical leadership quickly dismissed Thorez's appeal, but the Young Turks on the Radicals' left wing, at a loss as to how to emerge from the political quagmire in which their scandal-ridden party was stuck and anxious to revive their flagging parliamentary prospects, were not unsympathetic to the idea of an alliance that would reaffirm their association with the republican cause.[46] The PCF had only to demonstrate its respect for the institutional parameters of "bourgeois France" before they too would march in the ranks of the anti-fascist front.

The Question of Trade-Union Unity

In the popular mind, the general strike of 12 February meant more than republican defense. The successful mobilization of the left and labor organizations seemed to suggest that the labor movement might achieve great things if only it were united. Following the strike, the sentiment for unity spontaneously spread through the organized and unorganized ranks of the working class, becoming something of a mystique.[47] This mystique was considerably magnified by the PCF's new labor policy, which called for the reunification of the two labor confederations. At the National Party Conference in June, when the change of line was introduced, Thorez had argued that CGT–CGTU reunifi cation needed to be achieved "at any price," for a viable anti-fascist movement was allegedly possible only on the basis of an united working class.[48] This argument now set the tone for the PCF's new labor policy. Following the National Party Conference, Benoît Frachon, the CGTU chief, asked the CGT to put aside its differences with the *unitaires* and join the CGTU in a single unified confederation.[49]

Confederal leaders, however, had no intention of allowing the temporary alliance of 12 February to evolve into something more consequential, for they believed it was neither possible nor desirable to reconcile with those whose highest loyalty was to an Asiatic dictatorship. If communists wanted to unify the labor movement, confederals suggested they dissolve the CGTU and apply for CGT membership.[50] This, of course, was not the sort of unity that communists had in mind. To circumvent CGT resistance, they promptly devised a series of alternative measures, the most effective of which was the *syndicat unique.* Without quitting their own confederation, confederal and *unitaire* unionists were urged to join a single union permitting dual affiliation and constituting the first step toward trade-union unification. CGT leaders summarily dismissed the *syndicat unique,* but their ranks, many of whom would flock to the "dual unions," were not only less critical, but had already begun to contemplate a labor movement infused with the spirit of 12 February.[51] Two hundred twenty-two of these *syndicats uniques* were formed by early October and twice that many two months later. Significantly, these dual unions were concentrated in the public sector or in trades regulated by public statute; of the 222 organized in October, 160 were among railroad workers and 49 among postal workers, teachers, and lower civil servants; there were none in the metal or textile trades, and only three in construction.[52] Tertiary workers drawn to the *syndicats uniques* had not only been hit hardest by the austerity program of the new National Union government, but their unions were not unlike *unitaire* ones, which made reconciliation there considerably easier than in private industry.

Because these tertiary workers constituted two-thirds of the CGT membership, the proliferation of the dual unions brought new pressure to bear on the confederal leadership. *Unitaire* proposals rejected out of hand in July, when they were initially proposed, were, by the fall of 1934, as the *syndicats uniques* gained ground, treated with considerably more circumspection.[53] Fearing an estrangement of their membership if they continued to resist the *unitaire* overtures, CGT leaders finally agreed to sit down with CGTU representatives and consider their propositions. At the same time, the Confederal Metal Federation was ordered to follow the confederation's lead and set up talks with its *unitaire* counterpart. But like the CGT national officers, confederal *métallos* entered these negotiations with a good deal of cynicism, hoping, in effect, to sabotage them—even if they now duplicitously joined the chorus bemoaning the lack of unity. Indeed, talks had no sooner gotten under way than confederal leaders stipulated that they would consider unification only on terms corresponding to their conception of unionism. Because these terms were so unfavorable to the *unitaires*, they thought an agreement impossible, the prospect of which displeased them not in the least.[54]

Mobilization in the Streets

As a movement born in the strikes and demonstrations of 12 February, the republican union linking labor and the left took its first hesitant steps in the streets and in the streets it grew to stature. Emblematic of the public sphere and the state, the streets were hotly contested after February. Whoever mastered the streets, it was commonly held, would master the nation's fate. As the right rallied around the leagues and the "popular forces" gathered under the broad banner of what would shortly become the People's Front, the streets were transformed into a symbolic battlefield where each side struggled for the higher ground.[55] Between February 1934 and May 1936, more than a thousand demonstrations would prolong the debate begun on the 6th.[56]

These demonstrations had a particularly galvanizing effect on the working class. As workers assembled in the "red towns" of the suburbs and the popular *arrondissements* of Paris to demonstrate their support for the republic or prevent rightists from holding meetings, there gradually emerged a new community based on labor's alliance with the "republican union." In this community, heralding the emergence of Popular France, the worker was given the opportunity to become a man again, "not just a cog in a machine, and not just a 'hand' to be discarded and abandoned."[57] Not uncommonly, a "star," a celebrity, or a local notable would make an appearance at these mobilizations, lending it his authority and instilling in demonstrators a sense of their importance. At the same time, newspapers were hawked, leaflets distributed, revolutionary and patriotic songs sung, slogans chanted, red flags and tricolors waved; gradually, a repertoire of popular rituals arose to celebrate the republican ideal and reaffirm the worker's identification with the nation and its populist republican traditions. Not coincidentally, *Vive la France!* and *Vive la République!* began to crowd out the older communist slogan of *Les Soviets partout!* In the process, workers rediscovered not only French nationalism, but infused French nationality with the concerns and longings of their class. No less important, these animate mobilizations helped invigorate their spirits. In the words of one confederal, they "led us to expect better days . . . by generating energy, confidence, hope."[58] In marching to the local war memorial or gathering in their town squares to hear speeches and participate in colorful pageants organized by the SFIO, the PCF, and then the People's Front, the human flotsam of the Fordist-Taylorist factory system experienced not merely a festive outing, but also, for the first time, the breath and depth of its collective weight. This offered it a sense of identity and purpose absent in virtually every other avenue of national life, returning the worker, in effect, to a "society" where he was offered fellowship and a meaningful place. These "festivals of fraternity," in a word, helped revive the worker's kinship with the national community, foster a more elevated sense of his role in that community, and, in some individual cases, allow him to discover sources of personal renewal and dignity. Although these republican mobilizations rooted labor issues in a terrain foreign to the factory, they nonetheless imparted a significance to them that was not to be found in the production process.

Labor after 12 February

Between the general strike and the advent of the unity discussions, the CGT national office formulated a plan to remedy the political and economic ills of the depression. Like groups in virtually every nation touched by the economic crisis, whether they stood on the right or the left, represented social organizations or corporate interests, confederals looked for salvation in government intervention, for the depression had discredited liberal principles and popularized the idea of centralized economic management. Influenced by the works of Henrick de Man and the recent *Plan du Travail* adopted by the Belgian Labor party, confederal leaders now called for interventionist measures to attack the underlying causes of the economic crisis. In this connection, they advocated a series of structural reforms to supplant the market economy. Then, in March, the CGT "brain trust" codified these proposed reforms in a plan that called for the nationalization of credit institutions and key industries, the enhancement of the state's economic powers, the augmentation of popular consumption, and the curtailing of "oligarchic privileges."[59]

As unity negotiations got under way in late 1934, confederal leaders began canvassing suburban metal-working towns with meetings to publicize the CGT Plan. A consistent theme at these meetings was the argument that the moment was revolutionary in scope, that great measures were needed to prevent a fascist takeover, that meaningful reforms were only possible on the basis of major structural alterations in the economy. As a corollary to this argument, they claimed *unitaire* economism, in focusing on bread-and-butter issues, represented an opportunistic rehabilitation of reformism and a dangerous flirtation with demagoguery, totally inappropriate to the crisis facing the nation and the labor movement.[60] Their argument, however, had little apparent effect on workers then being swept up in the rising tide of republicanism.[61] For despite its claim of being the one means of treating the social and economic roots of fascism, the CGT Plan failed to account for the surging movement in the streets, which offered workers sources of meaning and commitment not to be found in the plan's dry economic tenets. This boded ill for the CGT. After the general strike, the apathetic ranks of industry had suddenly come to life. Convinced that they alone had "barred the route of fascism" and saved the republic, workers now eagerly readied themselves for subsequent mobilizations—but showed not the slightest emotional concern for the plan's structural reforms. Confederals, as a result, would reap few benefits from the movement inspired by their general strike.

Unitaires, by contrast, excelled in exploiting the growing republican agitation. Following the general strike, their *sections* began to grow in number and authority[62] and they found themselves at the head of anti-fascist committees that had spontaneously sprung up in the plants.[63] More importantly, they were increasingly called on to lead strikes and workshop actions. In late February, they led 800 aircraft workers at Lioré-Olivier in a three-week strike over a wage dispute that ended in defeat, but nonetheless dramatically ended the long dormancy that had reigned in the aviation sector of the metal industry. Several weeks later, at the Rosengart auto works in Neuilly, 500 workers, almost all of whom had observed the general strike, staged a sitdown against a proposed wage cut and then, after being locked out, waged a militant twelve-day struggle under *unitaire* direction until police violence crushed their picket lines and forced them back on employer terms. In the same period, a series of workstoppages at several Citroen plants resisted proposed wage cuts (at Grenelle) and the installation of new machines threatening the elimination of several work teams (Saint-Ouen).[64] While these actions attracted little public attention, they nonetheless reflected a changing mood in the factories. As several contemporary observers noted, the revival of the republican ideal in the general strike seemed to have bolstered the *métallos'* courage and given them the confidence to contest the conditions of their employment.[65]

By the summer of 1934, *unitaire sections* had grown from 109 to 143 and the union was able to put out a new monthly paper, *Le Métallo*.[66] Their most important breakthrough in this period, though, would come at the Bloch aviation plant in Courbevoie. Shortly after the general strike, *unitaires* succeeded in establishing a *section* there. Then, after a good deal of preparatory work, promotion of the corporate interests of the aircraft workers, and a major dose of patriotic republican rhetoric, they managed to recruit a large part of the workforce and force management to recognize their delegates. This was followed by another bout of organization and a brief sitdown strike, which gained them an "English week," a guaranteed hourly wage, and an improvement in piece rates.[67] These successes, which turned Bloch into a model of *unitaire* organization, were greatly facilitated by the change in worker spirits. But they also reflected the boom in armament production that had followed in the wake of the Nazi triumph: the aircraft sector, benefiting from new state orders, would grow 20 percent in 1934 and another 50 percent in 1935. As plants began augmenting their workforces, Bloch and other aviation plants became especially viable arenas for *unitaire* recruitment.[68]

The Chenard-et-Walker Strike

The anti-fascist front, the campaign for trade-union reunification, and the republican conquest of the streets had an extremely curative effect on *unitaire* unionism, encouraging it to tap into the deep currents of worker republicanism and presenting it with many new opportunities for intervention. Under the aegis of the People's Front line announced by Thorez in late 1934, *unitaires* continued to emphasize economic issues—the eight-hour day, wage hikes, paid vacations, resistance to layoffs—and do so without bending these issues to specific communist goals. Yet in promoting economist demands, they associated them with republicanism and the anti-fascist movement, instilling in *métallos* the sense that their corporate struggles were part of the larger effort to defend the nation's democratic patrimony. Although their focus remained on economics, the lessons were preeminently political, as worker solidarity in the plants was touted as the verso of republican defense in the streets.

The *unitaires'* new labor policy, which would orient them throughout the remaining years of the 1930s, achieved its first effective realization at the Chenard-et-Walker auto works in Gennevilliers. Since the advent of the depression, the Chenard management had sped up production and repeatedly lowered wages, provoking a good deal of discontent in the workforce and setting off a series of erratic ripostes. The failed strike of 1931 represented the first of these.[69] Then, in the spring of 1935, the hundred members of the Chenard *section*, buoyed up by recent union successes at Bloch and elsewhere, decided to counter the managerial offensive. After a general meeting of the workforce, *section* leaders asked management to grant a guaranteed hourly wage, improve health conditions, and establish a shop-steward system. Following the rejection of their demands, the entire Chenard workforce staged a sitdown.

As production came to a halt on 12 March, management wasted no time reasserting its authority. Police were called and the strikers forcibly expelled from the plant. They then formed a contingent and marched along the main street of Gennevilliers, to the public square, where they voted to continue the strike. During the next twelve days, the union rallied the strikers in daily marches and demonstrations and organized a strike committee that saw to the practical details of the strike.[70] Associating the conflict with republican defense, Gennevilliers's communist mayor provided various supportive services, such as communal kitchens and meeting facilities. Not to be left out, the local PCF branch launched a propaganda campaign that depicted the strike as a community project designed to curtail the employer's "parasitic appetites." In parliament, communist deputies accompanied worker delegations to the labor minister, set up negotiations, and tried to involve the state in mediating the strike.

Although these measures brought an unprecedented legitimacy to the strike and magnified its social impact, they failed to defeat the employer. With a massive police presence at the factory gates and frequent, sometimes bloody clashes between the two warring sides, the Chenard strikers were unable to maintain their picket lines. Then, as management began recruiting another workforce, the strikers were forced to retreat. In returning to work, however, they felt anything but defeated. For twelve days they had carried out a disciplined action that succeeded in every way but one: neither the *unitaires* nor the communist municipality nor the striking pickets were able to counter the police and prevent scabs from crossing their lines.[71] Only the neutralization of the state (which alone had full control over local police powers) offered the possibility of evening the balances in such struggles. Neutralization, though, was achievable only at the national level—where events now seemed to favor it.

May 1935

May 1935 was a crucial month in the fortunes of French unionism—due, characteristically, to developments in the political system, not industry. On the 2nd, following a rapprochement that had gotten under way with the rise of Hitler, Pierre Laval, foreign minister to the second National Union government, flew to Moscow to sign a Franco-Soviet Pact of Mutual Assistance, in which both powers promised to engage in mutual consultation if threatened by enemy attack. The pact implicitly linked the two countries in a common alliance against Germany, even though it lacked a military clause.[72] Moreover, by reconciling the "workers' state" with what was previously considered the most errant of the imperialist powers, the pact had direct implication for the PCF and its labor policy. If France were to serve as a useful Soviet ally in the struggle to preserve the Versailles order and contain a resurgent Germany, it had to be well armed. Stalin, "the genius of toiling humanity," thus ordered the PCF to help maintain France's "armed forces at a level consistent with its security requirements." This, however, entailed a major about-face. After fifteen years of attacking militarism and the international system created at the 1919 peace settlement, French communists were now expected to take up imperialism's mantle and demand bigger armament budgets, instant war against "aggressor nations," and a defense of the international system which they had formerly characterized as a product of predatory oligarchic interests.[73] While others might have balked at this sudden role reversal and the inference that principle had been sacrificed on the altar of *Realpolitik*, the disciplined proponents of French Stalinism dutifully accepted it in the name of the international working class—identified, as always, with the imperatives of Soviet foreign policy.

The signing of the Franco-Soviet Pact gave new significance to the People's Front line. As Soviet international interests suddenly coincided with those of imperial France and the PCF rallied in support of French militarism, communists were obliged to embrace the cause of "bourgeois democracy" and all the various nationalist ideals and symbols they had formerly attacked.[74] The party, as a consequence, not only began to privilege the priorities of the state to the detriment of labor, but to shift the class struggle to the international level—by transforming France into the brave opponent of the "plutocratic fascist powers." While rightists interpreted this as another sign of the PCF's subservience to Moscow, it greatly facilitated the party's reconciliation with the Radicals, the supposedly "progressive" wing of the bourgeoisie, thereby preparing the way for the formal organization of the People's Front. The Franco-Soviet Pact also affected the way the PCF defined (or redefined) itself in the public arena. Before long, it was presenting itself as a *parti de la nation* and the most ardent proponent of French national interest. Just as U.S. communists were about to proclaim communism "twentieth-century Americanism," their French counterparts now identified workers, formerly without a fatherland, as France's true-born sons and daughters.[75] This would lead them to accept the workers' membership in the historic community of the nation, and, in the process, wrap themselves "so tightly in the French flag that the hammer and sickle would barely be visible."

Although the Franco-Soviet Pact and the People's Front line helped transform the PCF into a quasi-reformist party of national cohesion, able and anxious to transcend class affiliations in the name of collective security and anti-fascism, it did not make the PCF like other democratic parties operating in the parliamentary arena.[76] It remained a "party of the new type," committed to Leninist organizational norms and Soviet foreign-policy interests, even if communists now heralded the virtues of French democracy and portrayed themselves as ardent patriots. What changed after May 1935 was the party's willingness to work within the established institutional framework and express its interest in the republican idiom. This, to be sure, constituted a major change in the party's form and affected the nature of its daily operations, but it did nothing, as later events demonstrated, to alter its loyalties or long-term objectives. Yet for contemporaries, especially liberals and other *bien-pensants* mistaking the fuzzy sentiments of anti-fascism and republicanism for an analytical validation of liberal democracy, this was less clear. Many of these types would abandon their anti-communism, henceforth incompatible with anti-fascism, and come out in support of PCF demands for national unity and collective security—as if the PCF had never been anything other than a patriotic supporter of the French political community.

May 1935 was also significant in that it was the month of the municipal elections. In the first significant electoral application of the People's Front line, Radicals, socialists, and communists agreed to observe "republican discipline" and desist to the highest leftist vote-getter on the second ballot. As a direct consequence of this discipline, communists were able to make spectacular gains in the elections, virtually doubling the number of city and town halls under their command (from 150 to 297). These gains were especially prominent in the Paris Region. In the Department of the Seine (Paris's "near suburb"), PCF–controlled town governments rose from 9 to 27, embracing 719,000 inhabitants; in the Department of Seine-et-Oise (the "far suburb"), the party went from 6 to 29 municipalities, with a population of 300,000.[77] Besides enhancing the party's political weight, the newly captured municipalities laid an entirely new foundation for union work. From their bully pulpits, communist mayors would now be able to spread the union gospel and give it greater legitimacy. The Hôtel de Ville would also provide facilities for organizational activities and a network of personal contacts and clients. But most importantly, municipal patronage

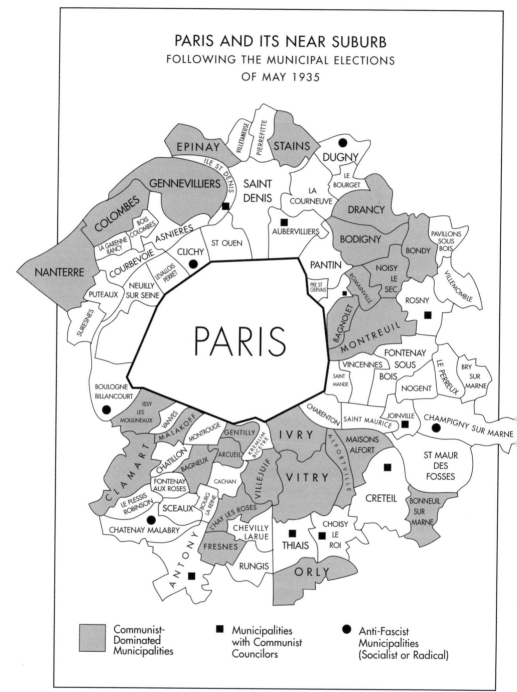

PARIS AND ITS NEAR SUBURB
FOLLOWING THE MUNICIPAL ELECTIONS
OF MAY 1935

VILLETANEUSE
PIERREFITTE
EPINAY
STAINS
DUGNY
ILE ST DENIS
LE BOURGET
GENNEVILLIERS
SAINT DENIS
COLOMBES
LA COURNEUVE
DRANCY
BOIS COLOMBES
ASNIERES
ST OUEN
AUBERVILLIERS
BODIGNY
PAVILLONS SOUS BOIS
LA GARENNE RANCY
COURBEVOIE
CLICHY
BONDY
NANTERRE
LEVALLOIS PERRET
PANTIN
NOISY LE SEC
VILLEMOMBLE
NEUILLY SUR SEINE
PRE ST GERVAIS
ROMAINVILLE
PUTEAUX
ROSNY
SURESNES
BAGNOLET
MONTREUIL

PARIS

FONTENAY SOUS BOIS
VINCENNES
BOULOGNE BILLANCOURT
SAINT MANDE
LE PERREUX
BRY SUR MARNE
ISSY LES MOULINEAUX
NOGENT
VANVES
CHARENTON
SAINT MAURICE
JOINVILLE
CHAMPIGNY SUR MARNE
MALAKOFF
MONTROUGE
GENTILLY
IVRY
CLAMART
CHATILLON
ARCUEIL
KREMLIN BICETRE
MAISONS ALFORT
ST MAUR DES FOSSES
BAGNEUX
VITRY
FONTENAY AUX ROSES
CACHAN
VILLEJUIF
ALFORTVILLE
LE PLESSIS ROBINSON
BOURG LA REINE
SCEAUX
CRETEIL
BONNEUIL SUR MARNE
CHATENAY MALABRY
L'HAY LES ROSES
CHOISY LE ROI
ANTONY
CHEVILLY LARUE
FRESNES
THIAIS
RUNGIS
ORLY

Communist-Dominated Municipalities

■ Municipalities with Communist Councilors

● Anti-Fascist Municipalities (Socialist or Radical)

Source: La Voix de l'Est, 18 May 1935.

would enable the union to recruit and maintain a cadre to carry out the agitation and activity that the clandestine members of the cells and the *sections* could not. Because these municipally employed organizers, usually blacklisted militants assigned to pork-barrel jobs, had little to fear from employer repression, they would equip the *unitaires* with a powerful new means of reaching the *métallos*.[78]

The *Métallo* Offensive

Between the general strike of February 1934 and the municipal elections of May 1935, the republican mobilization in the streets continued to make itself felt in the factories. Shop actions, not coincidentally, escalated in this period, achieving a new boldness and a new effectiveness. The first half of 1935, for example, had a strike rate higher than the entire year of 1934, while the number of solidarity strikes and strikes of a purely offensive nature more than doubled.[79] At the same time, *unitaire* membership grew two-fold and many new *sections* were organized.[80] PCF support of national defense also enhanced the union's audience in the booming armament sector of the industry.[81]

The first major *unitaire* triumph of 1935 accordingly came at the Gnome-et-Rhône works in Paris, France's largest aircraft manufacturer. After the May municipal elections, the thirty-seven members of the Gnome-et-Rhône *section* began organizing workshop meetings, circulating petitions for union demands, and electing shop delegates. It then threatened to strike if management did not grant a guaranteed hourly wage, respect the forty-eight-hour week, and permit workers the right to refuse overtime. With mounting orders to fill, management prudently bowed to these demands.[82] The Gnome-et-Rhône victory was then followed by an action at the Panhard-Levassor auto plant, also in Paris, this time for a 10 percent pay hike; after an eight-day struggle, in which Panhard workers engaged in a series of partial walkouts and "quickie" sitdowns, management again conceded their demands.[83] *Unitaires* next extended their campaign to the Chausson auto works and to Hispano-Suiza, where they won another wage increase. In late June, struggles among aviation workers at Bloch, CAMS, and Lioré-Olivier led to similar gains.[84]

Union struggles in the first half of 1935 focused largely on economic demands. Then, in July and August, a second wave of *unitaire* strikes convulsed the industry, this time in solidarity with victimized militants, fired in a concerted employer effort to halt the union offensive. As these strikes shifted from struggles over wages and conditions to questions of solidarity, they revealed an increasingly combative spirit in worker ranks. Emboldened by the rising power of the left in its struggle against "fascism" and their identification with republican defense *métallos* at this point started addressing long-suppressed griev-

ances. At Gnome-et-Rhône, for example, the entire night crew walked out of
the plant after a worker was dismissed for smoking on the job and refused to
return until the fired worker was reinstated. The following day, the *section
syndicale* organized a "smoke-in" in defiance of the company's anti-smoking
rule. As workers willfully lit up, the union threatened to halt all production if
anyone else was fired, in effect forcing management to abandon its anti-smoking policy.[85] This did not suddenly render management powerless, but its authority was beginning to slip, and the union was becoming, if not a power in
the industry, at least a factor to be reckoned with. The formal organization of
the People's Front would further tip the balance in the *métallos'* favor.

The Republican Union

After a series of aggressive right-wing demonstrations in June 1935, which
republicans characterized as a "rehearsal for insurrection," a group of ten left
and labor organizations—including the PCF, the SFIO, the Radicals, the CGT,
and the CGTU—came together to form the Comité de Rassemblement
Populaire. This committee was delegated to organize a massive demonstration
for 14 July, Bastille Day, to counter the rightist mobilizations. In the spirit of 12
February, the *comité* promoted its scheduled demonstration in classic Jacobin
style, calling on the "people" to defend the republic against the Bastille—the
Bastille that once protected the "parasites" of the old regime, the Bastille that
now supposedly protected contemporary economic privileges.[86] This sort of appeal, with its populist conception of the nation, struck a responsive cord in the
Paris working class, bringing out more than a half million participants.
Because the Bastille Day demonstration constituted a forceful riposte to the on-
going rightist agitation and thereby strengthened the republican union, the
Comité de Rassemblement Populaire decided to maintain itself as a center of
republican activity. Before long, it was serving as the organizational headquarters of the People's Front which Thorez had proposed in October 1934, rallying
the left parties to the anti-fascist cause and marshaling them in an electoral
coalition for the up-coming legislative elections.

The People's Front alliance emerging from the Comité de Rassemblement
Populaire would represent the single most significant political movement of the
interwar period and exert a powerful influence over the subsequent development of the labor movement. From the beginning, however, this coalition combined a number of ambivalent, if not contradictory orientations. As mentioned
above, it began rather inauspiciously as an ad hoc organization to organize the
Bastille Day demonstration, but it rapidly evolved into a formidable electoral alliance; it was constituted as an instrument of the three major left parties and
their politicians, all of whom had quite different notions of the alliance's pur-

pose, but it quickly galvanized the popular classes and assumed the trappings of a mass movement; it pursued negative aims of a purely defensive nature, yet introduced an entirely new spirit into French political life. Finally, it posed as the defender of peace and brotherhood, but did much to popularize the Soviets' anti-German policy of collective security, thereby preparing the way for the Second World War.[87] These antinomies, which would later foil and fracture the People's Front, were initially a problem, however, only when Radicals, socialists, and communists attempted to translate their newfound affiliations into a program of concrete demands.

True to their liberal principles, Radicals wanted the People's Front to avoid social or economic issues and focus on republican defense, while socialists and confederals viewed the left coalition as an opportunity to promote "structural" reforms that would address the various social pathologies fostered by the depression. Because communists valued the People's Front as a means of promoting Soviet foreign policy and achieving broad national support, they were inclined to accommodate the alliance's lowest common denominator, which meant siding with the Radicals on most policy disputes. The People's Front Program, to which all the parties eventually subscribed, would consequently remain abstentious on the key issues facing the country.[88]

Following five months of often contentious deliberations, the coalition partners finally published their program on 11 January 1936. While codifying the coalition's anti-fascism, the People's Front Program offered few specifics for resolving the larger problems facing the country; in the words of one Trotskyist, it was full of "utopian illusions" and contained "nothing that would serve the interests of the proletariat."[89] Two of the program's three sections pertained to questions of domestic freedom and foreign affairs, calling for the suppression of the leagues and the creation of collective-security system against international fascism. The third section, labeled "Economic Demands," promised to restore the "purchasing power destroyed or reduced by the crisis" by establishing a national unemployment fund, reducing the work week, reversing previous governmental deflationary policies, and introducing collective-bargaining rights, old age pensions, and public works.[90] *Le pain, la paix, et la liberté,* summing up the economic, international, and domestic sections of the People's Front Program, would henceforth serve as the coalition's main organizing slogan. As principles, bread, peace, and liberty were suggestive enough to placate socialists and labor leaders and vague enough not to offend Radicals, but they lacked substance and would offer future People's Front governments few practical guidelines. The program also promised more than it could deliver. By committing the left to collective security, the pacifist majorities in the SFIO and the Radical party inadvertently endorsed the PCF's aggressive anti-German policy—although this had not been their intent. More seriously, the People's Front Program, in affirming the prevailing liberalism, neglected the structural origins of the crisis, which were at the root of the republic's disorder. In time, these programmatic failings would play havoc with the left coalition, but at the moment of its formation, in a period of strife and uncertainty, its shortcomings seemed less significant than the emotional energy it generated in rallying the French left to an old-style "republican union."

The New Jacobins

In championing the left alliance, the PCF displayed a remarkable ability in adapting to French national institutions. Key to this adaptation was its identification with the "revolutionary traditions of democracy" and the Jacobin legacy of 1793.[91] With its repertoire of republican symbols, its opposition to "reactionaries," and its forceful defense of the underprivileged, Jacobinism furnished the party a banner that was easily flung to the breezes of popular favor. Throughout the nineteenth century, Jacobinism had been associated with the legacy of the Great Revolution, to which every republican considered himself an heir. When communists nailed their colors to its mast in 1935, it was already part of the mainstream conception of the nation: republican, secular, and populist. As Maurice Thorez put it, the Jacobin heritage implied "the values of the nation"—values that fraternally united all Frenchmen, regardless of class or social status. In embracing this heritage, with its validation of liberal democracy and its appeal to national, not class identities, the PCF acquired an idiom that was second nature to most Frenchmen—unlike the language of Asiatic Marxism, whose categories and principles were almost completely jettison in this period.[92]

Jacobinism also implied the revolutionary traditions of 1793, with its aggressive assault on established hierarchical principles. This would allow the party to promote its egalitarian politics in terms agreeable to liberal opinion. In a manner not dissimilar to the revolutionaries of the National Assembly, the "new Jacobins" would make a cult out of the "people," the "little ones" (les petits), without power or ambition, who stood at the mercy of the "great" (les gros), the monied aristocracies with all the power. In this language, they would succeed in conveying messages that never would have gotten a hearing if expressed in the class-specific vocabulary of Marxism.[93] The Jacobin idiom, to be sure, came with certain limitations that diluted the PCF's social agenda and forced it to abide by the parameters of existing liberal institutions, but it did little to divert it from its long-term objectives. More importantly, it created a vast audience for the party—not only in the working class, but in all the popular classes.[94] Only those oligarchic industrialists and bankers, the "200 families," who selfishly defended their privileges at the nation's expense, willfully making and breaking governments to serve their particular interests, were demonized as "enemies of the people."[95] The struggle against the 200 families—*la lutte des petits contre les gros*—was, in fact, presented as if it alone would restore the nation's vitality and bring the various crises afflicting the republic to an end. Yet in marshaling the "people" against the financial aristocracy, communists conveniently neglected the central contradiction of bourgeois society, that between labor and capital—for the defense of liberal democracy, synonymous with capitalism, was now treated as the best defense against "fascism."

While the communist flame burned brightly in the Jacobin ambiance of the left alliance, with the PCF becoming *le parti républicain le plus dynamique et le plus conséquent*, confederals experienced a dimming of their influence. Despite their commitment to republicanism and their postwar orientation to the state, they continued to distinguish between their trade-union responsibilities and their obligations to democracy.[96] Mixing politics—even pro-labor politics—and syndicalism instinctively disturbed and, over the long run, debilitated them. At the 1935 congresses of both the Confederal Metal Federation and the CGT, their fears of political entanglements assumed programmatic form, as large majorities passed anxious resolutions stipulating that union involvement in the left coalition did not constitute an abandonment of labor's traditional political independence or a neglect of its social project.[97] These resolutions failed, however, to still their doubts. Between the formation of the Comité de Rassemblement Populaire in June 1935 and the parliamentary elections of May 1936, confederals would repeatedly return to argue the pros and cons of labor's participation in the left alliance.[98] In debates carried out in the pages of *Le Peuple* and *L'Union des Métaux* and in various deliberative bodies, CGT'ers both favoring and opposing the People's Front jointly acknowledged that the parties and the unions possessed distinct domains of activity, that it was crucial for labor not to lose its "personality," that the first concern of the unions had to be the reform of social relations in the factory, not the defense of republican institutions.[99] Each side in these debates differed only in its ordering of union priorities. For those rooted in the revolutionary-syndicalist tradition, the People's Front represented the second coming of the *union sacrée*, the alliance that bound labor to the war aims of the French bourgeoisie in 1914; the class-collaborationist character of the People's Front, along with its implicit militarism and pro-Soviet sympathies, gave these syndicalists much to worry about.[100] Other confederals feared the coalition's unwillingness to adopt the CGT Plan or commit itself to structural reforms implied an opportunist evasion of the country's most pressing needs; these confederals were inclined to view the People's Front as just another electoral fraud. Both sorts of critics, however, represented a minority. Most confederals believed a rightist triumph at the polls would spell the end to any kind of unionism and had little hesitation supporting labor's participation in the left alliance; for these unionists, there was simply no alternative. Because each side in this debate constituted a well-established strand in the French labor tradition, reconciliation between them was nearly impossible. And without reconciliation, confederal commitment to the People's Front would remain tempered with doubt and division.

Paris *métallos*, however, had no such qualms. They enthusiastically supported the coalition's defense of the republican political community.[101] As Frenchmen, republicanism was virtually synonymous with their sense of nationality. As citizens, republicanism enfranchised them. As workers, republicanism promised them, if not a reputable place in French society, at least a potential voice in its polity. Republicanism, in fact, was all they had. Unlike virtually every other social stratum, workers entitled to vote had no other attachment to French social life—not to its higher values, thought, art, or leisure—only its political process. This one tie to the national community consequently had a significance for them that was greater than it was for those whose social integration was greater. An alliance to defend the republic could not but appeal to them, especially those in the Paris Region, who in every generation since the popular mobilizations of 1789 had been called on to reaffirm—often with their lives—their dedication to republican principles.

Like Jacobinism, however, republicanism was full of varied connotations. In the popular mind, republicanism was synonymous with political liberty and equality, which had been won with the overthrow of the Old Regime. Workers, however, did not quite understand that republicanism had other implications, not all of which favored them. The Old Regime, for all its numerous failings, had actually opposed the reign of money and many of the things they now associated with the "200 families." Because demands for "freedom and equality" were originally liberal bourgeois slogans aimed at eliminating the old non-economic hierarchies obstructing the full play of the market's monetary calculus, their realization had the effect of "emancipating" the money powers, leading to the creation of a social structure based entirely on economic domination. Republicanism thus not only made the money powers supreme, it duped the popular masses into serving an oligarchy that was arguably more egoistic than any of the Old Regime.[102] Working people rallying to the republican union did not, however, see this; for them, republicanism—freedom and equality—represented a categorical liberation for *all* men, not the basis for a specific form of class rule.

While the republican union failed to distinguish between these different conceptions of republicanism and thus put workers on a collision course with the politicians of the People's Front, it nonetheless infused workers with a sense of meaning and purpose denied by the postwar economic order, affiliating them with a national project that promised to reestablish their place in the national community. Almost as a matter of course, they believed a change in government, especially one devoted to the demotic republican order, would improve their standing in French society and, perhaps, serve as a panacea for the ills afflicting them in the factory.[103] In this spirit, they were inclined to believe that the left alliance spoke to the problems of caste and class in the factory system, for if fascism was incompatible with the republican order and had to be resisted, it seemed to follow that the authoritarian order in the factories, which *unitaires* frequently characterized as fascist, was likewise unacceptable.[104] It was not unreasonable then for workers to think that the People's Front made anti-*patronal* resistance, like anti-fascism, synonymous with republicanism.

The left alliance, however, had not the slightest intention of altering the underlying character of liberal capitalist society. The PCF, to be sure, hoped to advance its own fortunes on the basis of the mass movement mobilized by the People's Front, but it remained committed to defending republican France—and republican France, product of the Bourgeois Revolution of 1789, was preeminently a parliamentary regime undergirded by capitalist social relations. The workers' support of the People's Front was therefore based on an illusion, for the social aspirations they projected onto the left alliance contradicted the very things the republican union was committed to defending. This, however, only became apparent later. Until then, the People's Front received their unqualified support.

Agitation in the Factories

Throughout 1935 *unitaire* organizing efforts focused on the aviation sector of the Paris metal industry. Victories at Bloch, Gnome-et-Rhône, Farman, Lioré-Olivier, Caudron, Hispano-Suiza, Salmson, Lorraine-Dietrich, and Amiot, all aircraft producers experiencing rapid growth, eventually encouraged union actions in other sectors, particularly in auto and mechanical engineering, where increased defense expenditures were stimulating employment as well as organizing opportunities. In these economically healthy plants, the implanted *section*—aided by the PCF's municipal, parliamentary, and press apparatus—began connecting with *métallos* energized by the republican mobilizations. The result was a powerful resurgence of union activity.

When the production index dropped slightly in late 1935, the union turned to defending fired militants, resisting layoffs, and protecting wage standards. In this period the key struggle occurred at the Fiat auto works in Nanterre. Provoked by a cut in piece rates, the Fiat workers staged a sitdown, followed by a lock-out and a twenty-five-day strike. Like the Chenard-et-Walker strike of

March 1935, large contingents of police enabled management, identified with Italian fascism, to break union picket lines, introduce scab labor, and beat back the strikers.[105]

Notwithstanding this setback, *unitaire* activities attained unprecedented levels in the months leading up to the legislative elections of April–May 1936.[106] As its *sections* addressed increasingly larger audiences in the workplace, the *Unitaire* Metal Union highlighted its demands for a collective contract, a forty-hour week, a minimum wage, suspension of overtime, the right to unionize, and paid vacations. It also enlisted the support of various politicians from the People's Front (largely but not exclusively from the PCF) to promote and popularize these demands. According to one syndicalist, this had the effect of turning the left alliance, the metal union, and the labor movement into a sort of "Russian salad"—in which corporate demands mixed with and were subordinated to electoral issues.[107] Not coincidentally, the far left began reporting cases of *unitaires* refusing to give "a class struggle" character to certain conflicts (at Bloch), refraining from combating employers who speeded up armament production (Gnome-et-Rhône), and avoiding actions against employers affiliated with the Radical party (Peugeot).[108] But however opportunistic, *unitaire* activities continued to escalate with the approach of the legislative elections. In early 1936, the number of strikes doubled from that of the same period in 1935, with 81 percent ending in complete or partial victories.[109] *Unitaires* also stepped up their activities in the suburbs, bombarding the metal plants with tracts, agitation, and *section* meetings aimed at rallying the *métallos* to the People's Front. These "revivalist" actions would do much to galvanize unorganized workers, generating a feeling of fraternity and a vision of new things to come.

Reunification

The "unity of the working class in the struggle against fascism" roused not only the previously quiescent ranks of industry, it also helped reconcile the rival confederations. Although CGT–CGTU talks had broken down between February and June 1935 over the question of "political independence," trade-union unity remained foremost among worker concerns. In this spirit, *unitaires* conceded virtually every confederal proposition. They balked, however, at giving up their fractions; without fractions, they felt they would be unable to influence the ranks in a unified organization—which was why confederals wanted them dismantled.[110] On this issue, trade-union unity faltered. To surmount this last obstacle to unity, CGTU chief Benoît Frachon decided to seek out the Comintern's advice. In Moscow, he learned that *unitaires* had an overly formal notion of fractional activity; factory cells, he was told, could assume fractional duties if need be—and the CGT could not ask the PCF the abolish its basic unit of organization.[111] When Frachon returned to Paris in early June, the CGTU publicly disavowed its fractions, agreeing in effect to every CGT condition for unity.[112]

Although still distrustful of *unitaire* intentions, confederals were once more forced back to the negotiating tables. Again, outside pressures made themselves felt. International events—the newly signed Franco-Soviet Pact, the pro-Nazi plebiscite in the French-occupied Saar, and Italian plans to invade Abyssinia—along with domestic developments—the continuing provocations of the right-wing leagues and the formation of the Rassemblement Populaire—imparted new urgency to the question of unity, making resistance correspondingly unpopular. Then, on 24 July 1935, ten days after the massive Bastille demonstration united the left in a grandiose celebration of republicanism, CGT leaders at last gave in to the various pressures arrayed against them and accepted the principle of trade-union unification. Political imperatives at this point prevailed over incompatible principles. While it would take another seven months of negotiations to iron out the remaining differences between the two confederations, the accord signed on 24 July cleared the biggest hurdle to unity.

Fourteen years of division in the labor movement were not, however, easily surmounted, particularly in the metal unions, where fusion entailed not merely the acceptance of the unification principle, but numerous organizational, strategic, and programmatic differences that were not at issue in the public-sector unions.[113] On 29 July 1935, the two metal federations signed an accord similar to the one adopted by the confederations, yet confederal *métallos* refused to resign themselves to unity and, in fact, did everything possible to sabotage its implementation.[114] In the second half of 1935, while ostensibly preparing the final terms of an agreement, they practiced a variety of stalling tactics, avoided joint actions, disagreed over the character and purpose of the unity congress, and, in time, raised intractable questions about financial arrangements, political involvement, and craft unionism.[115] While the CGT national office had left them with little choice but to fuse, they could not bring themselves to finalize the merger. Only in late October, a month after the two confederations and most of their respective federations had scheduled fusion congresses, did confederal metal leaders, again under pressure from the CGT national office, consent to fuse. But all sorts of problems, quite real in themselves, yet ultimately reflective of confederal resistance, continued to delay the unification.[116]

Because it appeared these problems would not be solved before the CGT–CGTU unity congress, the Comité National Inter-fédéral des Métaux decided to arrange a fusion by fiat. The two Paris unions were then ordered to merge by June 1936, the national federations by October.[117] One measure of the confederals' ongoing resistance was their demand for fifty-fifty representation at every level of the provisionally-unified organization: outnumbering confederals better than three to one, *unitaires*, for the sake of unity, were again forced to make another major concession simply to get the confederals to join them. (The CGT, whose membership outnumbered the CGTU seven to two, did not have the same problem, for here fusion was mainly on confederal terms).[118] Christian and anarchist unionists observing the negotiations from afar both noted that fusion came about mainly because of political imperatives, which glossed over rather than resolved the numerous differences dividing *unitaires* and confederals.[119]

The Consolidation of the Labor Movement

The CGT–CGTU Unity Congress met in Toulouse between 2 and 5 March 1936. However much the two wings of the labor movement remained latently at odds with one another, their formal merger on the eve of the parliamentary elections did much to consolidate and rearm the unions. This fusion, it bears repeating, was mainly the product of political pressures. The anti-fascist mobilizations in defense of the republic had revived worker confidence, overcome bitter divisions on the left, diminished union rivalries, and created a favorable climate for unification. It had also made the daily problems of the shop floor— the bread-and-butter issues of industry—matters of general political concern. Despite the long-term problems inherent in labor's politicization, its initial effect was to invigorate union ranks and expand their opportunities. *Unitaires*, with their factory-based organizations and recently acquired sensitivity to worker demands, and confederals, with their artisanal traditions and labor-centered vision of industry, together now acquired the means to function within the limits of the existing regime—as well as the potential to reshape its fundamental contours. In this spirit, Léon Jouhaux described the Unity Congress as the dawn of "our emancipation."[120]

The Occupation of the Factories

GIVEN THE SEVERITY OF THE ECONOMIC CRISIS AND THE various forces mobilized in reaction to it, a change in government could not but entail a change in social relations. This especially seemed the case in the Paris metal industry, where republican politics had served as a surrogate for unaddressed social issues in the factory. While it was thus commonly assumed that a victory for the People's Front would have a major impact on labor, no one quite imagined just how immense that impact would be.

"Things Have to Change"

The parliamentary elections of April and May 1936 took place under a specter of civil war. During the campaigning, the right-wing parties, aligned in a National Front, predicted that a left victory would bring chaos and revolution.[1] The left warned of fascism. As the election approached, tensions and expectations assumed a feverish pitch. The first ballot of 26 April saw the left tally up a slight majority. Then, on the second round of 3 May, as the parties of the People's Front observed "republican discipline," the left turned its slight numerical lead into a massive 378 majority—against 214 for the right.

Communists came away from the elections with the most spectacular gains, leaping from 10 to 72 seats (with 15.3 percent of the total votes).[2] This automatically turned the PCF into a powerful parliamentary force and a factor with which all future governments would have to contend. Less spectacular but no less consequential was the electoral shift from the Radicals to the socialists. The SFIO, with 147 new deputies (and 19.3 percent of the vote), became the largest party in the new chamber, while the Radical party suffered a mutilating reduction, falling from 158 to 116 seats. The triumph of the People's Front was thus largely a victory of the two "worker parties," which suggests something of the degree to which the elections had polarized the country; (among the parties of the National Front, those of the extreme right made analogous gains). The socialist Léon Blum, as leader of the largest party, was then called on to form a government based on the new parliamentary majority. Instead of doing so immediately, as his left wing urged, Blum opted to respect constitutional procedure and wait till early June, when the new chamber was scheduled to convene.

In the anxious month between the elections and the convening of the new chamber, the social confrontation, which had simmered below the surface of the electoral campaign, dramatically shifted to the factories. This shift began before the final votes were even counted. May Day, falling between the two rounds of balloting, was observed by 120,000 Paris metal workers, making it the largest strike since 1920.[3] It was also carried out with an audacity and élan rarely before seen, presaging a greater upheaval.

When it came, this upheaval began not in Paris, where it seemed most likely, but in the provinces. When management at the Bréguet aviation works in Le Havre fired two militants for their role in the May Day strike, a union meeting of the workforce resolved to fight the victimizations. On 11 May, the plant's 600 production workers laid down their tools and refused to leave their shops. When the *gardes mobiles* arrived to evict them, the strikers barricaded themselves in the shop housing the plant's prototype. Fearing a clash that might jeopardize the firm's future, the plant's director prudently called off the police. This did not, however, end his troubles. The union next announced that the strikers would spend the night inside the struck plant to avoid being locked out the following morning. At this point, the director decided to go to the bargaining tables. The Radical mayor of Le Havre then intervened to set up talks and serve as chief negotiator, while Louis Eudier, the communist secretary of the Le Havre metal union, and Ambroise Croizat, general secretary of the Metal Federation, were called on to represent the strikers.[4] Other, less visible forces also made themselves felt. The caretaker government in Paris, fearful the strike might turn violent, urged local officials to arrange a quick settlement, which, of course, put management at a distinct disadvantage.[5] Within two days, the strikers walked away from the bargaining table with all their demands satisfied:

the fired militants were reinstated, a particularly disliked supervisor was dismissed, and, almost without precedent, they were paid for the days of the strike.[6]

As the Bréguet strike was being settled on 13 May, an identical conflict broke out in a second provincial city, in Toulouse at the Latécoère aviation plant. Although there is no extant evidence to prove that the Metal Federation, headquartered in Paris, instigated the Latécoère strike, it seems unlikely that its timing and character were purely coincidental, especially considering that the PCF's Toulouse branch had recently called for a renewal of social struggle.[7] Like the Bréquet conflict, the Latécoère occupation was provoked by the firing of militants and decided at a union meeting of the workforce. The organization and leadership of the Latécoère strike also followed a similar pattern: production was halted, fire guards were posted, and an elected strike committee took charge of the occupation. The local PCF then opened a soup kitchen for the strikers and local politicians affiliated with the People's Front intervened to set up negotiations. More importantly, the interim government in Paris refused to use its police powers, which made the strikers nearly unconquerable. After a single night barricaded in their plant, Latécoère workers emerged with terms comparable to the Bréguet settlement.[8]

The next day, the 14th, the occupations invaded the capital, as the Bloch aircraft works was struck. The strike was ostensibly provoked by management's refusal to receive a shop delegation demanding a wage increase, but given the nature of the two provincial strikes, the Paris metal union undoubtedly sensed a turning of the tide and decided to take the initiative. The occupation of Bloch thus marked the advent of the purely offensive use of the sitdown tactic. If not for the paucity of historical studies, it should also have dispelled the ensuing myth that the budding strike movement originated as a spontaneous outburst of the most oppressed, unorganized sectors of the working class.[9] *Unitaires* had long been a force at Bloch, having established a *section syndicale* in early 1934 and organized 500 of the plant's 700 workers by early 1935.[10] As the most unionized plant in the Paris metal industry, the highly skilled Bloch workers enjoyed wage rates and contractual rights that were among the best in the industry. It is difficult to imagine that these workers, the vanguard of the Paris *métallos*, launched what was to become the most consequential strike movement in French history purely by coincidence.[11] When police arrived to evacuate the occupied plant on the 14th, Bloch workers, like their counterparts in Toulouse and Le Havre, barricaded themselves in the shop housing the prototype, again forcing management to call off the eviction. Several hours later, local PCF deputies arrived to set up negotiations. They were accompanied by the communist mayor of Courbevoie, who offered to feed the strikers and provide logistical supports. The Labor and Air Ministries also volunteered to arbitrate the conflict, but the uncharacteristically confident strikers preferred to argue their own case, which they would do with considerable success, emerging after two nights with a new contract and a significant pay raise.[12]

In the week following the Bloch strike, there were occupations at a small aircraft works in Villacoublay and in several trades outside the Paris Region, but none of these strikes seems to have been instigated by the Paris metal union. This has often been taken as proof of the spontaneity thesis. These minor strikes, though, represented a mere lull in the gathering storm. The massive wave of occupations that was about to sweep across the metal industry, as will be shown, would be the handiwork of unionists bent on taking advantage of the propitious political situation. But it should also be noted that the situation was primed for a labor upsurge. The events leading up to the elections—the conquest of the streets, labor's identification with the Jacobin conception of the nation, the reconciliation of the rival confederations—had prepared workers for a new, more assertive role in French life. Then, during the election campaign, various union issues had been addressed and the left politicians promised a "new deal" in the plants. Workers were thus led to believe that a left victory would constitute a mandate for labor reform.[13]

As a "breath of hope and confidence" swept through the factory districts in early May, workers nonetheless feared that the People's Front might follow the path of previous left-of-center governments, such as those elected in 1924 and 1932, which had similarly roused popular expectations only to disappoint them.[14] Numerous signs gave credence to these fears. Following the elections, the premier-designate, in an effort to calm jittery financial markets, called on the people to have patience, to "master themselves," and put their faith in republican law.[15] In one well-publicized statement, Blum made a point of emphasizing that "we do not aim to transform the social system."[16] This kind of talk had prepared working people for disappointments in the past; perhaps they were being prepared again. Communists also sought to dampen popular expectations. As Blum was busily reassuring the business community, the PCF's parliamentary faction issued a statement affirming its commitment to private property and its Political Bureau proposed certain conservative monetary measures to protect the *franc*.[17] Then, in *L'Humanité*, Marcel Cachin called on workers to be calm and refrain from "wild revolutionary gestures." Finally, on 14 May, the PCF announced its decision to decline a post in Blum's cabinet (supposedly because it could better serve the People's Front, to which it pledged its whole-hearted support, but actually because it feared alarming the center-right parties, whose support for an anti-German front it hoped to win).[18] Given these pronouncements, the soon-to-be-installed government seemed bent on caution and moderation, comparable to former coalitions whose campaign promises were forgotten once the ballots had been counted. Workers, however, in a period of desperation and rising expectations, had voted for change—immediate and consequential change. The longer the left politicians refrained from enacting the promised reforms, the greater their anticipation.[19]

If Blum and his forthcoming government held out an uncertain future, the elections had at least neutralized many of the old fears. Besides giving workers the sense that the tide of history had turned in their favor, the left victory created a situation in which the boss now stood alone in his factory, unlikely to be aided by police or public official.[20] "L'Etat, c'est nous maintenent"—and this seemed to make all the difference, for the old politicians had been chucked out and the in-coming government at least claimed to stand on their side. This could only enhance the possibilities of worker action.[21] In the words of the "proletarian writer" Tristan Rémy, the working class suddenly felt "ready for any resistance, any responsibility, any adventure."[22] Uncertain of what to expect from the newly elected government, but increasingly confident of their own abilities, workers now unconsciously readied themselves for a new role in French national life.[23] Although few realized it, the factory occupations in Le Havre, Toulouse, and Courbevoie had served as a dress rehearsal for this new role.

Avenging the Commune

Sunday, 24 May, marked the annual commemoration of the Paris Commune. Instead of the usual demonstration of 10,000 or so celebrants, a vast crowd of 600,000 turned out to march up the windy cobblestone path to the Mur des Fédérés, where in 1871 the last of the Communards had taken their final stand. Unlike previous demonstrations organized by the People's Front—perhaps because the Radicals refrained from participating—this one had a distinctly plebeian character, complete with red flags, revolutionary songs, and banners reading "Soviets Everywhere" and "We Will Avenge the Commune Dead."[24] Not the "people" nor the "citizen," but the worker and his numerous links to France's revolutionary past were celebrated in this tribute to the Commune.[25] In fact, the assumption that the working class was the "people" and that the people were ready to take their rightful place in the national community was now made explicit.[26]

This unprecedented display of labor solidarity did not pass without consequence. The conservative Le Figaro, after observing the size and spirit of the Mur des Fédérés demonstration, was quick to note that a "new factor"—the working class—had entered French public life.[27] As to be expected, it was the Communist party—which had suddenly become a mass party with six times more deputies, a membership nearing a third of a million, and a press and support network larger than any other French organization—that was the first to draw out the implications of this "new factor." Speaking to the PCF Central Committee on Monday, 25 May, Maurice Thorez announced that the "masses" would henceforth play a leading role in Blum's government: "We well know that our struggles, our mass actions allowed the [people's] front to succeed. It will be the same for the government's program."[28] If, in other words, their actions had stopped the rightists in the streets and made possible the electoral victory, they would continue to play a similar role in supporting the new government and insuring the implementation of its program. Implicit in Thorez's announcement was the notion that through its leadership of popular mobilizations and its forceful concentration of working-class power, the PCF would serve as the tribune of the entire populace, becoming in effect the "minister of the masses" within the new governing coalition. Eugène Hénaff, chief of the Paris Trade Assembly (Union Departementale), then specified that: "Union action to develop the struggle for labor demands has to be . . . the most important task for party members—if parliamentary illusions are to be dispelled and communist influence enhanced."[29] Results in the factories would thus be key to maintaining and extending the party's tribunary role.

While Thorez and other party leaders were mapping out their plans for the days to come, metal workers prepared to make their entrance on the historical stage. The imposing demonstration at the Mur des Fédérés had set the scene. As the old syndicalist Pierre Monatte observed, "When you feel strong in the streets, you can no longer feel like a slave in the factory."[30] The occupations at Le Havre, Toulouse, and Courbevoie now suggested what it might mean to feel strong in the factory. On the Monday following the Mur des Fédérés demonstration, the workshops and courtyards of the Paris metal industry bustled with activity and agitation. Then, on Tuesday, the industry witnessed an unprecedented assault on employer prerogatives, as six metal plants, touching 4,000 workers, were seized and occupied.

The *métallo* offensive began at the Nieuport aviation works in Issy-les-Moulineaux. On the morning of 26 May, a worker delegation headed by the local communist mayor (Cresson) and the union's general secretary (Doury) presented the Nieuport management with demands for a wage increase, the abolition of overtime, a forty-hour week, and the recognition of union delegates. The union had previously posed similar demands, all of which management had rejected. This time, however, it was not to be put off. When management again rebuffed its demands, a courtyard meeting elected a strike committee and the plant was occupied. A strike committee then took charge of the occupation. Sentries were posted at the factory gates, workshops were prepared for possible assault, and fire guards assigned to supervise the safety of the works. Taken aback by the character of the strike, management promptly called the interior minister, but he declined to send the police. At this point, the plant director decided to negotiate—provided the strikers evacuated the factory. The Nieuport workers, though, refused to budge. For the next five days, until 30 May, they remained encamped in their shops, until management bowed to their demands and signed an accord that granted a eight-hour day, an annual two-week paid vacation, shop stewards, and three-days strike pay. With considerable justice, the union would hail the accord as a *belle victoire.*[31]

The Nieuport occupation was accompanied by other strikes, the most important of which was in Levallois-Perret, where 2,000 *métallos* occupied the Hotchkiss armament works after management fired sixteen union militants. The unprecedented occupation immediately forced management to reconsider its action. The fired militants were then reinstated, the union recognized, and some economic concessions made. That night the Hotchkiss *métallos* evacuated their plant singing the "Internationale."[32] In nearby Saint-Ouen, 500 metal workers in the Levallete plant, which produced sparkplugs, also struck. Resisting an announced wage cut, these workers confronted a determined management and would have to spend two weeks in their occupied plant before receiving satisfaction.[33] Other occupations on the 26th were more easily resolved. At Sautter-Harlé, at a branch plant of the Amiot aviation works, and in a shop at Renault, short three-hour sitdowns beat back threatened wage cuts or firings.[34] All these strikes, it is worth noting, occurred in healthy metal plants connected with national defense, where the union had previously implanted itself. Equally significant, they were all instigated by *unitaires*, conformed to the order announced by Thorez on the 25th, and supported by union officials from the Paris union office and politicians from local communist-controlled municipalities.[35] This is not to suggest that communists foresaw the massive strike movement their actions were about to provoke, but there can be little doubt that they were responsible for setting it in motion.

On Wednesday, 27 May, the occupations maintained the previous day's momentum. Strikers who had gone out on the 26th were reported in high spirits, despite having spent an uncomfortable night on makeshift beds. Moreover, new strikers joined the movement. Hotchkiss workers in Clichy and in Gennevilliers, after learning of the effortless victory won by their counterparts in Levallois-Perret, seized their plants and within hours gained similar concessions. The budding strike movement also touched the Farman aviation works in Boulogne, occupied after management refused to receive a worker delegation headed by Alfred Costes, the union president. Farman was one of the most important aircraft plants in the Paris Region, but its proximity to the giant Renault auto works made its occupation especially significant. As the most conspicuous metal plant in the industry, Renault was important both in itself and as a key psychological factor determining the possible fate of the gathering movement. When the Farman strike committee posted Renault's walls with an appeal for solidarity, the sitdown strike arrived at the gates of the largest auto maker outside North America.[36]

Still, the second day of the strike movement had more the potential than the reality of a mass movement, although it was already bolder and more audacious than anything previously seen in the metal industry—or in any other French industry—and had already made an impression on the political system. At this point, Jacques Duclos, *numero deux* in the PCF hierarchy, felt obliged to visit the acting premier, Albert Sarrault, and request that he do nothing to "aggravate" the situation. A delegation from the metal union made a similar request to the labor minister.[37] Sarrault's interim government agreed that an exercise of police powers might provoke unforeseen consequences and promised not to evoke them.[38] Duclos then issued a statement declaring the PCF's sympathy with the strikers and its willingness to offer them whatever assistance they might need.[39]

While the government and the PCF tried to maintain calm, others began to take alarm. The Paris dailies, for one, denounced the revolutionary character of the occupations and alerted the public to the "looming specter" of proletarian expropriation, which, of course, had a disturbing effect on conservative opinion.[40] The *unitaire* and confederal command structures of the two metal unions, while still in the process of merging, were quick to refute the alarmist press accounts. Representatives from both tendencies claimed the *patrons*, who had consistently refused to discuss worker grievance, were alone responsible for the strikes.[41] These unionists stressed the spontaneity of the strike movement and underplayed their own involvement. In *Le Populaire*, the former secretary of the Confederal Metal Federation, Marcel Roy, described the "tempest unleashed in the enterprises [as] the result of all the suffering accumulated during these last years." The left electoral victory, he explained, had made possible the venting of this suffering. In contrast to the hue and cry raised in the dailies, Roy emphasized the corporate character of the workers' demands and castigated employers for having left workers with no other option but to strike.[42] The former *unitaires* also emphasized the spontaneous character of the strikes and the *patrons'* reponsibility for them. Yet what Roy and other ex-confederals failed to realize was that communists in the *sections* and the cells had taken advantage of the propitious political situation to instigate the movement and spur it forward. With few, if any connections to the occupied plants, these reformists saw only the strikers' legitimate grievances, not the hand of their former rival.

On Thursday, 28 May, 33,000 Renault auto workers joined the strike movement, giving it a qualitatively more imposing amplitude. Renault went out in two phases. At 10 A.M., the workshop producing artillery pieces—the most unionized shop in the giant factory and the workplace of Marcel Vigny, Renault's highest-ranking communist—stopped production. When the morning shift began on the 28th, militants circulated among the shop's highly skilled workers, informing them that a sitdown was about to occur and urging them to "join forces to get the forty-hour week and a paid fortnight's vacation." The bolder workers promptly responded to the strike call, the more hesitant once the electricity was cut off.[43] At this point, Costes, Timbaud, Frachon, and Doury—the elite of the former *Unitaire* Metal Union—entered the auto plant to bring out the other workshops. Within two hours, all production had come to a halt.[44]

An ad hoc strike committee then took charge of the occupation. Dominated by communists, the committee immediately replaced Renault's executive office as the factory's nerve center. As it did, red flags with hammers and sickles were hoisted over the factory gates.[45] The committee's first task was to draw up a list of demands for a contract, a guaranteed minimum wage, suppression of overtime, and a promise not to speed-up production. It then addressed the various practical problems of the occupation—safety, food, entertainment, defense, etc. Surrounding municipalities under communist and socialist direction were also called on to help feed the strikers, although some would be fed by the local labor population or by families who brought food parcels, while others were left to fend for themselves in local bakeries, groceries, and tobacco shops.[46] The strike committee, to be sure, only gradually mastered the logistics of the occupation, but in the face of numerous inconveniences and some frustrations, the strikers' mood remained buoyant. Symptomatic of the festive spirit taking hold of the strike movement, amateur musicians arrived to entertain the strikers and many factory courtyards were transformed into improvised dance arenas. Finally, at 5 P.M. the committee ordered women and adolescent workers to leave the factory so that the men could prepare the overnight occupation.

The Renault occupation instantly doubled the size—and significance—of the strike movement. Besides Nieuport, Farman, and Lavellete, which remained occupied, the occupations on the 28th touched auto plants at Rosegart, Chausson, Talbot, Citroen's Grenelle plant, and Fiat, aviation plants at Gnome-et-Rhône, Salmson, Harriot, and Caudron, and the armament manufacturers Brandt and Gevelot. The strike movement also started to affect other trades and reach beyond the Paris Region, to Toulouse and elsewhere. The movement, however, was still essentially a metal strike, centered in the auto and aviation plants of the capital. And although launched by communists, all the strikes were carried out with "order and discipline," supported by the popular classes, and animated by a festive atmosphere more akin to a holiday than a mass upheaval. Yet however calm and well-disciplined, the strikes were cause for alarm—to the industrialists who had suddenly lost control of their enterprises, to the general business community which feared a possible breakdown of order, to the Paris dailies which saw the red hand of Moscow behind the movement, and, not least, to Léon Blum, whose future government was presented with an unprecedented social challenge before it had even taken power.

Although some strikers could be heard uttering the word "revolution," most seemed concerned only with utilizing the propitious political situation to rectify long-standing grievances. This was evident in the nature of their demands, which varied from factory to factory, but rarely transcended corporate issues. In some plants, strikers focused on purely local matters (wages, overtime, work rules), while others, especially those led by unionists, took up wider demands of a social but not a political character (the forty-hour week, collective bargaining, paid vacations). In no plant were explicitly political demands posed. Hysterical outcries from the *patrons* and the conservative dailies about the strikers' revolutionary designs were all far off the mark (just as earlier left-wing assertions that 6 February had been a fascist conspiracy to overthrow the republic). By tapping worker enthusiasm for the People's Front and exploiting grievances that had accumulated in five years of depression, *unitaires* had succeeded in provoking the metal strikes, but they were hardly plotting revolution. Their sole ambition, as one communist paper put it, was "to be wherever workers had need of their assistance"—which is to say they wanted to become the chief representative of the working class, not the leader of an insurrection.[47] A revolutionary mobilization was, in truth, the least of the PCF's concerns, for an attempted seizure of power would almost certainly have led to civil war or a German invasion—which was not at all what France's Soviet ally wanted.[48] Instead of overturning the existing order, communists—or at least their leaders—saw the novel occupations mainly as a means of augmenting their trade-union following and extending their social influence. Nearly every public statement issued by the reunified metal union would emphasize that the strikers' demands were "purely economic" and that their movement persisted solely because of employer intransigence. At the same time, union leaders made a concerted effort to maintain "calm, discipline and order" in the occupied plants, avoid provocative actions, and isolate far leftists trying to enflame the movement.[49] For the PCF, a powerful union movement held out the best prospect for achieving the mass influence that Thorez had called for on 25 May. Social clout, not the imperatives of revolution, seems to have been the party's guiding concern during the strikes—indeed, no other policy would have been reconcilable with the Soviet need to consolidate its diplomatic alliance with France.[50] As Marcel Gitton, in the name of the party secretariat, declared: "We regard as unacceptable a policy, which, in the face of the Hitlerite menace, would put French security at risk."[51] The revolutionary potential of the factory seizures might therefore have tormented conservatives and excited isolated leftists, but it had no place in the party's strategic orientation.

The strikes were nonetheless anxiously monitored by the government. Shortly after the movement gained momentum, the acting premier, Albert Sarraut, and his labor minister, Ludovic-Oscar Frossard, scrambled to set up negotiations and divert the movement into institutionally amenable channels. Negotiations, however, were a bitter pill for the employers. Just before the advent of the strikes, Pierre Richemond, head of the metal employers' association (UIMM), declared that it was impossible to bargain with the union because "labor leaders base their actions on class hatred."[52] Yet once Renault succumbed to the gathering storm, the *patrons* were quick to reverse themselves and accept the principle of government-sponsored talks—class hatred or not. Yet before they would sit down at the negotiating tables, they insisted on the evacuation of the factories and the resumption of production.

Although the metal union hoped to establish itself as the strikers' bargaining agent and wanted to accept the employers' terms, only a meeting of factory delegates had the authority to terminate the strike movement. When this meeting convened on the morning of 29 May, 130 delegates representing 50,000 strikers considered the union's request for an evacuation. Few of the delegates, however, fully understood the significance of a collective contract and were obviously uncomfortable with the prospect of presenting their fellow strikers with a decision to end the novel occupations. A small handful of non-communist delegates (and most of the delegates were reputedly either PCF members or sympathizers) even argued that it was foolish to terminate the struggle for the mere promise to negotiate. But against the delegates' hesitation, union leaders pressed for an acceptance of the employers' terms, claiming that without a contract recognizing their right to act as the workers' collective bargaining agent, the union would never become a power in the industry and the strikers would fail to consolidate their gains. The resolution concluding the meeting handed union leaders what they wanted, but delegate concerns, which had been ardently expressed and defended, were also respected: evacuations were to take place only after local agreements specified the exact terms for the resumption of production and after individual employers agreed to consider the specific demands of their own workforce.[53]

Following the delegate meeting, the metal union got to work facilitating the various individual agreements that would empty the factories. Late on the afternoon of the 29th, local agreements were reached at Gnome-et-Rhône, Nieuport, Citroen-Javel, Brandt, and several smaller plants. Some of these agreements actually satisfied the strikers' initial demands; most merely postponed matters to future talks in the interest of speeding the evacuations. At

Renault, the union mounted a special effort. While management made few concessions, union leaders characterized its offer in terms vague enough to suggest otherwise.[54] Some Renault strikers were not taken in by this and accused the union of selling them out. In the more militant workshops, the union had to resort to its most persuasive speakers to get the strikers to desist.[55] One Trotskyist report claimed that Alfred Costes, the union president, was literally chased from several workshops when he tried to impose the back-to-work order.[56] Another report, however, indicated that strikers were anxious to reach an agreement in order to take advantage of the upcoming three-day Pentecost weekend.[57] Contrary as they seem, both reports have the ring of truth and probably reflect the diverse sentiments motivating the strikers.

Once the evacuations commenced on Friday night, Richemond of the UIMM agreed to sit down with the metal union. Because of the upcoming Pentecost holiday, work at Renault and elsewhere was not scheduled to resume until Tuesday, 2 June—long enough, employers figured, for the strike fever to subside. That Sunday, negotiations got under way at the Labor Ministry. Employer representatives from the UIMM and strike representatives from the Metal Federation, the Paris metal union, and the Paris Trade Assembly (Union des Syndicats Ouvriers de la Région Parisienne), joined by the labor minister, quickly agreed to two common principles: recognition of trade-union rights and the establishment of a shop-steward system. They then decided to continue negotiating until a final agreement could be worked out. Frossard, the labor minister, hoped an accord would be signed by 4 June, before the formal installation of Blum's government.

Then, on Monday, 1 June, employers brought a number of material concessions to the bargaining tables, but balked at signing a contract, foremost of the union demands. They also complained that several factories had yet to be evacuated. *Le Peuple*, the CGT daily, estimated that only nine small plants remained on strike, although the business journal *Usine* claimed sixteen with a total of 8,000 workers. These differences, quite minor in themselves, reflected the employers' reservations in establishing contractual relations with the union. From their side, unionists viewed the complaints as a veiled threat to break off talks now that the strikes had receded.[58] Both sides were thus unable to finalize an agreement. This would prove a disastrous misjudgment on the employers' part, for the strike wave was far from spent.

"Everyone Is Doing It"

On Tuesday, 2 June, following the three-day holiday, workers returned to their plants. Rather than tempering their spirits, as employers had hoped, the long Pentecost weekend seems to have encouraged them to resume the novel strike movement. Battle positions were almost immediately retaken. By noon, sixty metal factories were occupied; by nightfall, a substantial part of the entire Paris metal industry had come to a standstill. At the same time, the strikes began to spread to other trades and regions.

The unexpected extensions on the 2nd, which gave the strikes a mass character, caught the metal union completely off-guard. Publicly, union leaders attributed them to the employers' refusal to grant "decent wages, human work conditions, and the right to unionize."[59] Privately, they wondered if the strike movement had not begun to take on a life of its own. The strikes' extension, moreover, seemed to have little to do with specific grievances. In plants with relatively decent wages and conditions, workers enthusiastically occupied their plants.[60] Many of the strikes had in fact begun without any direct provocation or any stipulated demands. The mere appearance of a left politician or union activist at the plant gate was often enough to provoke a stoppage. Some workers were indeed so anxious to enter the fray that they visited the local union office or, in communist municipalities, the town hall in order to find out how to occupy their plant.[61] In a display of what was probably the prevailing sentiment behind the strikes' extension, one *métallo* explained that he was striking because "everyone is doing it."[62] The will for change, it seemed, was in the air. Moreover, given the *patrons'* vulnerability and their sudden readiness to bargain, workers could not resist the opportunity to take them down a notch and assert their own claims. But more than the forces of imitation and contagion, workers sensed the propitiousness of the moment.[63] Employers who had ruled like feudal lords and denied the most minor reforms were suddenly making concessions at the mere threat of a strike. As workers succumbed to these various forces, the metal union struggled to regain the leadership of a movement that was beginning to veer beyond its control. And struggle it was. On the evening of the 2nd, 500 delegates from the occupied plants brushed aside a union recommendation to terminate the strike, insisting on staying out until all their demands were met.[64]

The Strike Committee

Once occupied, a factory had to be organized. Organization was usually delegated to an elected strike committee. Where there were well-established *sections syndicales* or party cells, their members tended to form the core of the strike committee. In plants without a *section* or a cell, isolated union militants or left-wing activists, mainly communists, came forward to assume command of the movement. Elsewhere, union officials and local red notables were called on to aid the strike committee. But whether composed of cell members or isolated militants, the strike committees were dominated by skilled workers,

whose habits of self-assertion, self-reliance, planning, and technical competence imbued them with the individual authority and the knowledge to organize their fellow workers.[65] The mass of unskilled and semi-skilled workers who
gave the strikes their magnitude simply lacked the personal credentials to assume these positions of responsibility. Their passive place in the industrial order
would thus go largely unchanged by the occupations.[66] Although some may
have resented the way they were now required to observe the OP's leadership,
they generally lent the committees their unqualified support. In contrast to
their work experiences in the early 1920s, the OS and OM had absorbed the values of urban industrial society, set down roots, and realized they occupied a
menial place in the dominant social hierarchy. The strikes held out to them the
prospect of an elevated status in the factory and perhaps a more dignified idea
of themselves in the larger society.[67] If they delegated authority to others and
occasionally chaffed under the OP's lead, they nevertheless fully identified with
the common struggle. Moreover, they had little cause to think about larger issues, for the strike committees would keep them occupied with dances, concerts, sporting events, and other group activities—all designed, of course, to
help the shepherds herd their flocks.[68]

Once organized, the strike committee was on permanent duty. Usually it
possessed a double structure: vertically, it assembled delegates from the plant's
workshops, acting as the representative body of the factory workforce; hori-
zontally, it divided up into subcommittees to resolve the logistical problems inherent in the occupations.[69] In this latter capacity, it resembled the command
structure of an army, responsible for appointing fireguards, supervising the entrances, feeding the ranks, providing entertainment, maintaining order and
calm, and insuring that the occupation not degenerate into chaos. Virtually
every contemporary observer would remark on the high degree of organization achieved at this level. Finally, the committee was entrusted with the task of
formulating strike demands, dealing with management, and maintaining relations with the Paris union office. Union influence over the strike committee,
however, was tenuous at best, mainly exerted through delegate meetings, the
union locale, or indirectly through PCF and CGT members. In fact, most red municipalities tended to exert a greater influence over the strikers than did the
Paris union office. But even in cases where red notables assisted or advised
them, the committees remained jealous of their powers, tolerant of no rivals,
and careful not to excite actions that might undermine their own authority.

"The Cry of Joy"

While the factory occupations shook the nation's social foundations, they
were carried out in a holiday spirit—*une véritable kermesse populaire.*[70] For

many, the workstoppage constituted their first break since the age of thirteen or fourteen, when they had left school—unless they had experienced unemployment, which is never a holiday. With time on their hands, the strikers had the opportunity to get acquainted with one another and develop a group consciousness that had never been part of their job experience. They were also able to attend sporting events, accordion concerts, courtyard dances, and other improvised activities organized by the strike committees. These activities not only allowed them to escape the humdrum of their regular working lives, but to participate in what was already recognized as an extraordinary, if not glorious moment in modern social history. The implanted intellectual Simone Weil, in the first and most celebrated account of the occupations, has left us a particularly vivid picture of this aspect of the strike movement.[71] In her reckoning, the occupations represented a festive respite from the soulless drudgery of the modern industrial inferno. Once they upset this authoritarian regime and the daily grind came to a momentary halt, all the workers' longings and pent-up desires burst forth, expressed in what she called a "cry of joy."[72]

This joy, however, was not, as Weil suggests, merely relief from the drudgery and humiliation of industrial life. Just as the mobilizations of the People's Front had served to integrate the mass-production workers into the republican political community, the occupations now redefined their role in the modern factory, transforming the existing system of industrial relations into one that better accorded with the ideals of the labor movement. While the strike committee took charge of the occupation and accordion sounds replaced the roar of engines, workers found time to socialize, learn the names and opinions of those they had worked beside for months or years, engage in various recreations, and absorb the fact that their collective social weight constituted a powerful counter-authority to the employer's "divine right." In the process, there emerged a surrogate community that brought mass-production workers together in entirely novel ways, cultivating affective ties, which the technical system of the Fordist-Taylorist factory, with its deleterious effects on group morale and its atomizing processes, had previously impaired. By living together in their fortified factories, new forms of solidarity and cooperation had a chance to emerge and these, in turn, altered their relations to one another and to the employer. Moreover, once the killing weight of apathy and despair momentarily lifted and workers experienced the sociability and fellowship of the "sitdown community," they instinctively demanded to be treated as free men and allotted a more dignified place in the industrial hierarchy. These demands, to be sure, did not constitute a revolutionary assault on the prevailing order, but they did challenge the traditional social structure in the plants and the contractual, egoistic, and impersonal relations governing liberal society. The joy accompanying the occupations thus derived as much from the ways in which workers redefined their role in the factory's social system as it did from the momentary respite from industrial routine described by Simone Weil.[73] For this reason, one historian rather convincingly depicts the labor revolt of June 1936 as "the delayed political repercussions of the new organization of work" introduced during the war and the 1920s.[74]

The French Revolution

On Wednesday, 3 June, the strike wave again lurched forward. Three hundred metal plants in the Paris Region, employing 150,000 *métallos*, were now occupied. An equal number of workers in other trades—particularly in the chemical, building, textile, and transport industries—were also out.[75] These strikes, as they shut down middle and small-size firms untouched by the first wave, further complicated the contract negotiations. Metal employers, upset with the progressive breakdown of order, threatened at this point to terminate the talks if the occupations continued to spread. Caught between their desire to secure a contract and to retain the leadership of the burgeoning strike movement, union leaders felt themselves pulled in contrary directions.

On Thursday, 4 June, the strike wave advanced another step. At this point, the Renault workers rejoined the movement. Like other plants where hasty agreements terminated the strike prior to Pentecost, the Renault accord of 29 May had resolved nothing. When work resumed on 2 June, the factory simmered with turmoil. Disputes flared up over minor issues; worker delegations refused to tolerate employer temporizing; and numerous shops spontaneously stopped production. Alfred Costes was finally compelled to call the workers back out on strike. That evening, red flags reappeared over the gates of the massive auto works.

Nearly a half million workers in all trades were on strike on the 4th. For the first time, the general population began to feel the strikes' effect. As truck drivers joined the movement, food distribution was disrupted, causing hoarding and depleting food stocks. Gas works closed and cast parts of the suburbs into darkness. Gasoline deliveries were interrupted. All newspapers, except those of the left and labor movements, ceased publication. Although not yet paralyzing, the economic situation was becoming a matter of general concern, especially to those who thought the occupations bore an alarming resemblance to the general strike of syndicalist myth.

The strikes' spontaneous extension also troubled the union leadership. Costes, for example, had not wanted to bring Renault out a second time: it jeopardized the contract negotiations and compounded the tasks facing the soon-to-be-installed People's Front government. Yet if union authority in the giant auto plant was to be maintained and a more chaotic and perhaps violent out-break prevented, Costes had no alternative but to sanction the occupation.[76] He and other union leaders were also aware that the strike wave was succumbing to forces over which they had little control. The entire metal industry, in fact, was beginning to yield to its contagion. Non-striking workers were reportedly in a state of nervous agitation, wondering if and when they too would go out. When communists, like Costes, intervened to promote the strikes, they now did so to preserve their authority in the movement, no longer to control it.

On the evening of the 4th, the union convened another meeting of factory delegates, attended by 800 representatives from the occupied metal plants. Most of these delegates were young, under thirty, and without former trade-union experience. Their radicalism, of relatively recent creation, threatened to overwhelm the union leadership. Some delegates had even begun to urge the union to announce a general strike in order to turn the movement into a con-certed assault on employer privileges and prerogatives.[77] Others proposed a re-sumption of production under worker control, as had been done in the revolutionary Italian occupations of 1920.[78] Union leaders gingerly side-stepped these demands, claiming the strike movement "was developing by it-self" and needed no assistance. It was becoming increasingly evident, however, that the cautious leadership and the impatient delegates were beginning to move in contrary directions. In an effort to channel their militancy into insti-tutionally amenable forms, union leaders asked that delegates avoid "provoca-tive" actions, establish closer communication links with union headquarters, and accept union guidelines for resolving individual conflicts. But these mea-sures thrown in the path of the strikers' headlong gallop would be of little avail, for the delegates at this juncture had begun to head toward goals quite differ-ent from the ones pursued by their leaders.[79]

The movement's extension on the 4th brought the contract negotiations to a halt. In abandoning the bargaining tables, industrialists appealed to the gov-ernment "to fulfill its duties."[80] The interim government of Sarraut, however, had thoroughly depleted its authority. Albert Lebrun, the republic's president, at last decided it was time for Blum to assume power and assert his leadership over the troubled situation. As Blum bowed to the exceptionalism of the mo-ment and accepted the president's request, many, including Blum himself, wondered if the former Proustian aesthete possessed the strength of character commensurate to the tasks at hand.[81]

On 5 June, in his first act as chief of the People's Front government, Blum took to the airwaves to address the nation. The new premier called on striking workers to be patient, respect the law, and give his administration a chance to attend to their demands. Disorder and paralysis of public functions, he cautioned, would only hamper his ability to act. He did not, however, ask strikers to evacuate their factories, only to be calm and cooperative. He then promised working-class France a forty-hour week, an annual paid vacation, a pay raise, and a system of collective bargaining, if he were only allowed to legislate such reforms. At the same time, Blum criticized employer intransigence and appealed to the *patronat* to examine worker demands with a "spirit of equity."[82] His broadcast, carefully monitored in boardrooms and occupied factories, reportedly incensed employers, who resented the insinuation that they were somehow at fault, and, more surprising, had little apparent effect on strikers, who were unconvinced that "true strength lay in patience" or that this was the moment to halt their movement. On 5 June there was even another extension of the strikes.

The premier's failure to tame the movement could not but alarm employers, many of whom were beginning to fear that the situation was becoming revolutionary.[83] On the 5th, Alfred Lambert-Ribot, a member of the influential Comité des Forges, decided that drastic measures were needed. In contacting Blum (a fellow Mason), he managed to arrange a conference between him and the heads of the principal employer associations.[84] With red flags fluttering over their factories, employers like Lambert-Ribot had given up the idea of "outright resistance" and begun contemplating a compromise, even if major concessions had to be made. In the conference he arranged, the new premier and the *patronal* representatives decided that a tripartite meeting between the Confédération Générale du Production Française (CGPF), the CGT, and the government ought to work out a strike settlement.[85]

Before the scheduled 7 June meeting could get under way, Blum first had to present his government to the new chamber. In his address to the assembled deputies on the 6th, he proposed legislation to establish the forty-hour week, a system of collective contracts, union rights, public works, and annual paid vacations. To those on the right aisle of the chamber who might have contemplated a repeat of the June Days of 1848, he ruled out forceful action and committed himself to a peaceful resolution of the conflict. He did not, however, totally ignore rightist concerns. With hair-splitting subtlety, he tried to cajole the conservative deputies into viewing the occupations as "installations"—as if this semantic distinction mattered.[86] Then, before adjoining, the chamber's new majority passed a vote of confidence in Blum's government, hopeful the premier's proposed legislation would soon calm the situation. Blum, though, realized that the new laws would take days, if not weeks to enact and that the best chance for resolving the conflict lay with the tripartite meeting scheduled for the next day.

On Sunday, 7 June, in the first meeting of its kind, union and employer representatives met at the Hotel Matignon, the premier's residence, to discuss a settlement that would bring the strike movement to a peaceful conclusion. In the small hours of the 7th, after a good deal of debate and deliberation, an agreement known as the Matignon Accords was reached.[87] Constituting the first step toward a collective contract, the accords granted union recognition, a system of shop stewards, and a 7 percent to 15 percent wage hike. Demands for annual paid vacations and a forty-hour week were left to the chamber to work out. The government, the unions, and the employers now hoped the psychological impact of this unprecedented agreement, promising a complete reformation of labor-management relations, would bring the occupations to a halt.[88]

The following day, the papers of the left hailed the Matignon Accords in huge banner headlines. *L'Humanité* proclaimed: "Victory Is Won." The CGT's *Le Peuple* announced: "Victory Over Misery—Eight Million Workers Get Satisfaction." The socialist daily *Le Populaire* declared: "Victory to the Working Class." With the exception of anarchists and Trotskyists, the left and labor movements were unanimous in praising the settlement. They also expected it to bring the strikes to an end. That evening, in a radio broadcast, Léon Jouhaux heralded the accords as "the beginning of a new era." "For the first time," the CGT chief told his auditors, "an entire class has obtained an improvement in its conditions of existence." Jouhaux then asked workers to honor the terms of the agreement and terminate the strikes.[89] The next morning, Benoît Frachon, speaking for the former *unitaires* in the reunified CGT national office, made a similar appeal on the front page of *L'Humanité*.[90]

Employers, by contrast, were already having second thoughts about the accords. In the business press they complained that the agreement placed intolerable burdens on French industry, for the wage hike, along with the shorter work week and the annual paid vacation, automatically increased labor cost by 35 percent, while union recognition and shop stewards threatened the traditional exercise of *patronal* authority. In a representative expression of employer discontent, the leading business journal discussed the accords in an article titled "La Route du Fascisme."[91] Owners of small and medium-size firms, unaffiliated to the CGPF and unable to afford the additional social charges mandated by the accords, were particularly unhappy and openly disavowed it.[92] Even the employer representatives who signed the accords complained that they had had little choice but to accept them, given Blum's refusal to use force against the strikers. In no uncertain terms, they characterized the accords not as a possible foundation for a new labor-management consensus, but only a tactical concession to stave off revolution.[93] One conservative deputy captured the prevailing discontent in calling the accords a *Diktat*, the term the defeated

Germans had applied to the punitive peace settlement of 1919.[94] The agreement hailed by labor and the left was thus thoroughly repudiated in *patronal* ranks.

For different reasons, striking workers displayed a similar lack of enthusiasm. On 8 June, after reopening talks between the metal union and the UIMM, the labor minister announced that only fifteen middle-size metal factories had been evacuated. This was a mere fraction of the total and was dramatically offset by 150,000 coal miners who joined the strike movement at this stage, along with clerks in banks, insurance agencies, and department stores. In the occupied plants, the consensus seemed to be that the Matignon Accords were a moral victory, but hardly cause to abandon the struggle. Some far-left workers even labeled the accords a betrayal—*Matignon, maquinon*—because they lacked legal status and had settled for too little.[95] Although it was not apparent at the time, communist labor leaders were also divided. In a 1976 interview, Robert Doury, the union's general secretary, indicated that he and several others in the top leadership shared rank-and-file reservations about the accords and thought they should go for the "maximum." Frachon, the highest ranking communist in the CGT hierarchy, took, however, the opposite stance and insisted on immediate compliance to avoid endangering the People's Front and alienating the Radicals.[96] Similar differences divided the PCF ranks, where "some excellent revolutionary workers" (i.e., loyal party members) considered the accords a sham and refused to accept them as a basis for a settlement.[97] One well-connected observer claimed that not a few communists were prepared to continue the strikes until "the armed insurrection."[98] Given these reactions, it is not surprising that the Matignon Accords failed to do what Blum, Jouhaux, and the CGPF leadership hoped they would: assuage the strikers and empty the occupied factories.

On Tuesday, 9 June, the CGT made another futile effort to gain control of the strike movement.[99] Over two million French workers, a quarter of the French working class, were on strike, most in occupied plants. As these strikes spread to trades and regions with little or no trade-union traditions, they became increasingly difficult for the CGT to influence. They were also all spurred on by the Paris metal workers, who remained the storm center of the movement and showed little sign of abating.[100] On the night of the 9th, at a meeting of 587 metal delegates from 243 occupied plants, union leaders again called for a return to work on the basis of the accords. Skeptical of the settlement and insistent on their own specific demands, especially the elimination of low wage rates, the delegates again rebuffed their leaders.[101] Following the meeting, communist unionists privately complained of the delegates' lack of cooperation, even though most of them were reputedly affiliated with the party.[102] That same evening, independent of the union, Hotchkiss workers in Saint-Denis, encouraged by a Trotskyist in their ranks, convened a meeting of delegates from

thirty-three of the largest Paris metal plants. These delegates, whose convoca-
tion demonstrated a certain mistrust of the CGT, vowed to continue the strike
until they had won a contract and a guaranteed wage. They also resolved to set
up a "central committee of delegates" to give direction to the occupations, implicitly challenging the established union leadership.[103]

The next day, 10 June, after issuing an anxious communiqué deploring the
strikers' refusal to accept the Matignon Accords, the metal *patronat*, for the
third time, broke off negotiations, refusing to surrender more than what the
CGPF had conceded in the Matignon Accords. This presented union leaders
with another dilemma. At a delegate meeting that evening, they attempted to
take some of the wind out of the strikers' sails by proposing a resolution threatening the employers with nationalization of armament production and a government-mandated contract in the non-military sector, if a significant wage
increase were not granted within forty-eight hours.[104] This threat, combined
with the employers' refusal to negotiate, dangerously raised the stakes.

As the warring sides failed to reach a compromise and the economy approached paralysis, Leon Trotsky, who was following the strike movement by
radio in faraway Norway, published an article titled "The French Revolution
Has Begun." In this piece written 9 June and appearing in Paris on the 11th, he
argued that the strike movement was beginning to transcend purely corporate
issues. "These are not craft strikes that have taken place," he wrote. "These are
not just strikes. This is A STRIKE. This is the open rallying of the oppressed
against the oppressor. This is the classic beginning of the revolution."[105] The
only thing lacking, he claimed, was a revolutionary party to lead the insurgent
masses to power. Blum's government lost no time confiscating *La Lutte Ouvrière*,
the paper in which Trotsky's article appeared, for his remarks, however hyper-
bolic, expressed what many communists, socialists, and CGT'ers feared to
admit in public: the situation was becoming revolutionary. This fear, however,
had already taken hold of the conservative *Le Temps*, which had no qualms in
characterizing the strikes as "the practice maneuvers of the revolution." Yet in
surveying them today, one is struck by the absence of radical political demands
and the relative immunity of the existing institutional structures. Trotsky's
Bolshevik expectations, the fears of union and party leaders, as well as those of
the employers and the dailies, all seem off the mark—for the strikers showed
not the least intention of toppling a government they considered "theirs."
These fears, however, were not completely unfounded. The strikes might not
have challenged the institutional parameters of the state, but they unques-
tionably threatened the nation's social structural underpinnings—insofar as
they assaulted the "*patronal* dictatorship" in the plants—and this could not but
alarm all who had a stake in preserving the existing order, including the PCF
leadership.

The specter of revolution loomed up again on the afternoon of the 11th, when strike delegates were convened to consider the employers' latest contract offer. The previous evening, bowing to the union's forty-eight-hour deadline, the metal *patronat* made several concessions that union leaders urged the delegates to accept. The delegates, however, "vehemently" rejected the employers' offer, dismissing it as "insufficient." They then specified four conditions that had to be met before they would consider a cessation of their movement: a "serious" wage adjustment, an explicit contract clause on paid vacation (on which the chamber was scheduled to vote), payment for the days of the strike, and satisfaction of the demands raised by striking technicians.[106] In posing these "non-negotiable" demands, delegates again rebuffed the union's effort to terminate the strikes, once more raising the ante.

Against this background of failed negotiations and escalating tensions, the social crisis deepened. The increasingly desperate government strained to satisfy striker demands and empty the factories. Between 10 and 12 June, the chamber hurriedly passed laws establishing the forty-hour week, a system of collective bargaining, and annual paid vacations. "We are facing circumstances," Blum declared, "in which every hour counts."[107] Even rightist deputies, eager to stem the strike wave, rallied to these bills, in effect supporting the most progressive social legislation in the Western world. Yet despite these measures, the situation continued to grow steadily more precarious. On the 10th, the government requested that the People's Front Committee of Paris cancel a 14 June demonstration planned to celebrate the election victory; a massive street procession, it feared, might turn explosive. Roger Salengro, the socialist interior minister, had already used the police to break up a demonstration of cafe, restaurant, and hotel workers, in an effort to maintain order. The government did not know quite what to expect and feared the worst. On the 11th, rumor had it that the *métallos* were preparing to evacuate their occupied plants and march on the city. Another rumor held that Renault strikers were planning to use the tanks produced in their plant.[108] These stories were entirely fictitious, but they testify to the nervous state of mind gaining ground in the capital.[109] Also on the 11th, in a sign of the mounting tension, a Paris employer shot and killed one of his striking employees. The government meanwhile was besieged with messages from veterans, small businessmen, financiers, and the Chamber of Commerce, imploring that it do something, anything, to stave off the threat of revolution. Edouard Daladier, the new defense minister, epitomizing the concerns of middle-class France, demanded at this point that Blum prepare the government for a possible use of force. On the evening of the 11th, in response to Daladier's demand, Blum brought several legions of *gardes mobiles* into the Paris Region, stationing them throughout the suburbs, along the principal thoroughfares leading into Paris, and in front of government ministries. Powerless to halt the strikes, Blum and his fellow politicians were becoming increasingly desperate—acting, in the words of one deputy, like "a ship without a rudder."[110] For fear of risking a potentially violent confrontation, the government refrained from using force; yet without forceful action, it remained a prisoner of the strike movement.

As the government floundered and the crisis reached critical levels, the PCF decided to intervene. The party at this point had come to an important juncture: it could either champion the increasingly militant demands emanating from the occupied plants and adopt a strategy of revolutionary assault, or it could reaffirm its parliamentary ties with the People's Front and attempt to resolve the social conflict in terms of the Matignon Accords.[111] Given its fidelity to the anti-fascist alliance and its fear that the occupations were alienating the Radicals and their middle-class constituency, communists unsurprisingly opted for the People's Front.[112] We know nothing of what was transpiring in the minds of the top PCF leadership at this moment, but on the 9th, as the strikes reached their crescendo, some sort of decision was apparently made to intervene against them. That day, the party assembled the secretaries of its factory cells and rallied them in support of Blum's government; on the front page of *L'Humanité*, Frachon appealed for a return to work. On the 10th, the party called for vigilance and resistance to "provocative actions," instructing communists to maintain calm in the movement. Then, on the night of 11 June, in a mass meeting of the party's Paris membership, Maurice Thorez rendered homage to the strikers; but against those who thought the hour of revolution had struck, he stressed that "everything is not possible." At the present time, he argued, there could be no question of expropriating industry and seizing state power. The highest priority remained the anti-fascist front, which had to be preserved and defended against all who sought to destroy or bypass it. Then, in the most important part of his speech, Thorez said communists "had to know how to end a strike." "If all the essential demands of the metal comrades are satisfied, if the lowest wages have been sufficiently raised, if the better paid workers have received acceptable increases, if the paid vacation is specified in the contract, we can, we must, sign the agreement that will bring the present movement to an end."[113] Thorez thereby threw the weight of the Communist party against the extreme wing of the strike movement.[114]

As long as the PCF had supported and encouraged the strikes, communists in the cells and strike committees had considerable leeway to urge their fellow workers in whatever direction they wanted—provided they eschewed explicit political action.[115] Thorez's speech on the 11th, which ordered party members to become proponents of compromise and bring the strikes to a peaceful conclusion, imposed a completely different orientation.[116]

Their influence—and communists alone seemed to have any authority over the strikers—made itself felt the very next day, at a meeting of metal delegates. For the first time since the beginning of the strikes, the delegates retreated from their intransigent position and bowed to the demands of the union leadership. Even though the employers had still not conceded their four "nonnegotiable" demands, 500 delegates (minus seventeen dissenters) voted to accept a compromise agreement.[117] Thorez's *mot d'ordre* had obviously been heeded, for nothing else accounts for the delegates' sudden about-face. As the delegates relented, the way immediately opened for a termination of the strike movement. On the evening of 12 June, the metal union signed a collective contract with the UIMM. Raises, paid vacations, and shop stewards were written into the contract and the union was recognized as the *métallos'* sole collective bargaining agent. The new contract, covering workers in the Departments of the Seine and the Seine-et-Oise (i.e., the greater Paris Region), was to last a year, with production scheduled to resume on Monday, 15 June.

On the basis of the departmental contract, individual factory contracts were worked out on the weekend of 13 and 14 June. Once these local agreements were finalized, strikers evacuated their plants—usually in procession. The most impressive of these took place at Renault. On Saturday evening, 13 June, 20,000 auto workers marched out of their factory, and down the principal street of Boulogne-Billancourt, to the town's central square, accompanied by floats decorated with red CGT flags, the hammer and sickle, and busts of Thorez and Blum. As the triumphant auto workers spilled into the streets of the industrial suburbs, bands played the "Internationale" and the "Marseillaise," the worker anthem and the national anthem, just as the red flag and the tricolor, the clenched fist and the Phrygian bonnet, mingled in an indiscriminate mix of communist and French motifs. For two and a half hours, the Renault workers paraded through their town in what can only be described as a jubilee of communal redemption. In other suburban metal-working towns that weekend, the streets were filled with similar corteges, flowing out of the occupied factories and onto the byways of the nation, whose social and institutional course had now been fundamentally altered.[118]

The following Monday, the Paris metal industry resumed production. Some metal plants and some trades had yet to resolve their disputes, but with most Paris *métallos* returning to work, the remaining strikes were soon drawn into the ebbing tow of the great tide.

The Inundated CGT

Throughout the June movement, confederal leaders occupied a sideline position. When the first strikes erupted after the Mur des Fédérés demonstration, they reacted with surprise and some confusion. In their view, the strikes were simply a spontaneous revolt against the intolerable conditions of the modern factory system.[119] They knew nothing of the communist role in launching the strikes nor did they have much understanding of what was happening in the occupied plants, even though they projected a public image of confidence and control.[120] Among railway, postal, and public-service workers, to whom the old CGT leaders had long organizational ties, there were, significantly, no strikes at all.[121]

On 16 June, after the subsiding of the movement in the Paris metal industry, the Comité Nationale, the CGT's highest deliberate body, convened. Since its last deliberation, the CGT membership had climbed from one to over two and a half million. By year's end, the membership would reach five million. This unprecedented expansion, which overnight turned the CGT into the authentic representative of the French working class, disturbed the old confederal leaders, who were organizationally and psychologically unprepared for it. Yet it was not simply the sudden, unanticipated inundation that troubled them, although it certainly disturbed their sleepy routines, but rather the implications of the expansion—for most of the new recruits were mass-production workers, whose influx automatically shifted the confederation's axis from the public to the private sector.

Of even greater concern were the political consequences of the expansion. The three largest industrial federations (metal, construction, and textile)—making up nearly half the post-June membership—were now dominated by communists. Through the factory cell and the *section syndicale*, through their previous efforts to implant themselves in the shops, and with their centralized organizational structure, the ex-*unitaires* had been best situated to capture the allegiance of the new recruits. They were also favored by their association with the PCF. In the Red Belt, which had fallen to the communists in the municipal elections of May 1935, the party possessed not only a well-oiled municipal, mayoral, and parliamentary machine, but also an apparatus capable of distributing leaflets, transmitting orders, gathering information, mobilizing sympathizers, and organizing demonstrations. Once the June inundation made the old union structures obsolete, this apparatus was in position to fill the organizational vacuum. In this and in other ways, the former confederals were simply no match for the communists, whose augmented influence would have great consequence for the labor movement. The reunification at Toulouse in March 1936 had given the confederals, with their large tertiary unions, a secure majority of the CGT membership, but after the June occupations, as the industrial federations mushroomed, the balance swung decisively toward the ex-*unitaires*, who would henceforth dominate the reunified confederation.[122]

Nowhere was this more the case than in the metal union. Transported by the enthusiasm born in the strike movement, the union grew by leaps and bounds in June, becoming the single largest French union. The most impressive growth came at Renault, where union membership went from several hundred in May to nearly 25,000 by the end of 1936.[123] Because so many *métallos* at Renault and elsewhere sympathized with the PCF and were influenced by its cells, *sections*, and strike committees, communists easily won their allegiance. In the words of André Marty, the *métallos* had become "the spirit and force of the Parisian proletariat and of our party."[124] In fact, many metal workers now looked on CGT membership as a first step toward PCF membership, which was hardly surprisingly considering the way communists had linked the labor movement to their conception of the People's Front and given it a political coloration.[125] Significantly, though, the new unionists seemed less interested in communist ideology per se, of which they could have little understanding, than in broader agitational issues related to anti-fascism, economic reform, and Jacobin populism.[126]

The problematic implications of the June inundation were further compounded by the reunification process. In late May 1936, before the strikes swelled up into a vast wave, numerous *unions locales* of the CGT and CGTU Metal Unions had begun to fuse. On the weekend of 13–14 June, as the occupied plants were being evacuated, the two unions formally merged their leadership apparatus. Two weeks later, on 27–28 June, a Fusion Congress of the membership was held.[127] Because the June occupations fundamentally altered the relation between the two wings of the labor movement, massively augmenting the forces sympathetic to communism, the ex-confederals were largely marginalized in the newly unified organization. Before the strikes, metal *unitaires* had outnumbered confederals three to one; afterwards, the proportion was closer to twenty to one. This lopsided relation became strikingly evident at the Fusion Congress, where the overwhelming majority of the 243 delegates (representing an estimated membership of 183,000 *métallos*) identified with the ex-*unitaires* and their conception of unionism. In the election of the executive officers, communists or ex-*unitaires* captured every position.[128] The few ex-confederals elected to the union's bureau achieved their posts only with communist compliance—for the party sought to maintain an image of unity and diversity. Likewise, in the vote on the new statutes, the ex-*unitaires* had everything their way, which allowed them to reconstitute the union on the basis of their highly centralized, politicized model of organization.[129] Given this realignment of forces, the reunified metal union, like other industrial unions, would henceforth be guided almost exclusively by communist labor policy.[130]

Colonization

During the June occupations, the strikers had been a captive audience for union organizers. At Renault—and in most large factories—two tables were set up in the plant's main courtyard. One sold CGT membership cards, the other PCF ones.[131] Because of conformism or contagion, but hardly out of attachment to the syndicalist tradition, an overwhelming majority of Paris *métallos* flocked to the metal union. It would take several months to tabulate the exact results of the June recruitment, but when the tabulations were finally released they confirmed what was already evident, that union membership had dramatically escalated during the strikes. Prior to June, only a small percentage of the industry's workforce had been unionized; after the strikes, the number soared to nearly 90 percent. The most reliable sources offer the following figures:

Paris Metal Union Membership[132]

1935	7,000
May 1936	14,000
June 1936	180,000
Dec. 1936	250,000

This expanded membership—as it embraced both skilled and unskilled workers, large-scale factories and small shops—would have an enormous impact on the subsequent character of metal unionism. Above all, it terminated the era of minority unionism and opened the way to mass unionism, centered on the organization of the Fordist-Taylorist factory system. This implied a qualitative as well as a quantitative change. Hereafter, the kinds of organizational ties linking union leaders with the ranks would no longer be based on the militant's devotion to the labor movement but rather on the sort of relations that had arisen between the strikers and the strike committees—even if the new unionists were inclined to view the union as a counter-society to the one they rejected in the market, looking to it for more meaningful forms of fellowship. The June recruits would thus assume a largely passive, non-participatory role in the union, animated more by the ideological community forged by the People's Front and the occupations than by the direct-action traditions of prewar syndicalism.[133] Lacking a *conscience syndicale*—being "unionized and not unionists"—these recruits would need a leadership which only a bureaucratic apparatus could provide.[134] Bureaucratic unionism, though, would do little to instill union principles in them, elevate their consciousness, teach them the responsibilities of active membership, or generate more genuine forms of community. And because the June recruits identified less with the union than with populist republican politics, they would be easily lured by political mystiques that obscured the social foundations of the labor movement and confused union imperatives with those of the state and the PCF.[135] One ex-confederal later described the essence of this sort of unionism as involving nothing other than singing the "Internationale," paying one's monthly dues, and attending an occasional union meeting—all of which, of course, simply reinforced the membership's passivity and its confusion of syndical and political goals.[136] Given the recruits' political malleability and their ignorance of the union tradition, the ex-confederals took a rather dim view of their human qualities. Even communists, who rose to prominence on the basis of the June recruitment, acknowledged that their propensity for spontaneous actions and political mobilizations, combined with their lack of trade-union discipline, added many unpredictable and unreliable elements to metal unionism.

Because the new recruits—*la promotion Blum*—were "slaves of political ritual," conditioned to salute with the raised fist and disposed to local communist notables rather than experienced union leaders, they naturally gravitated to the *unitaire* style of leadership. This further disturbed the former confederals, who resisted but did not fully understand these developments. In their view, communists achieved their influence through a process of "colonization," which enabled them to infiltrate into positions of power and authority.[137] What the ex-confederals refused or failed to grasp, however, was that communist "colonization" was not the product of underhanded scheming (which, of course, was not foreign to party practices), but rather followed from the recruits' mass-mindedness and their affinity with an ideological conception of unionism.[138] The term "colonization," with its sinister connotations of communist machinations, reveals more about the confederals' organizational shortcomings and their prewar mindset than it does about the changes affecting the labor movement before, during, and after the June strikes.[139] More seriously, it would anticipate the sort of internal disputes that later divided and polarized the union along ideological lines.

The People's Front in the Shops

BY OVERTHROWING THE PATRONAT'S "DIVINE RIGHT" AND turning the CGT into the workers' collective bargaining agent, the Matignon Accords revolutionized the French system of industrial relations. But because this system rested on the new political alignment, it would be imperiled whenever union interests clashed with state exigencies. Given the character of the People's Front and the problems besetting it, these clashes were bound to be frequent and far-reaching.

Regrouping the *Patronat*

Once the storm had passed, the *patrons* surveyed the damage. In their eyes, the sitdown strikes, and the social laws that followed, made France more like the "collectivist dictatorships" of Soviet Russia and Nazi Germany, for the new system of industrial relations impaired their authority on the shop floor, invalidated the individualistic premises of the liberal economy, and endorsed certain anti-capitalist propositions that had long challenged their right to manage.[1] Henceforth, wages, work conditions, health and safety requirements, and a host of things that had formerly been the sole prerogative of management, became subject to contractual arrangement.

But more than upsetting the traditional hierarchy of authority, the Matignon Accords bore the stigma of capitulation and defeat. This made it nearly impossible for the *patronat* to accept them as a tenable foundation for industrial peace, for few employers would forget the indignity of having been sequestered in their offices during the occupations or the lack of deference that came with the new contractual system. Finally, most employers, given their nineteenth-century mindset, refused to accept an adversarial relationship with the unions. In their view, labor-management conflict was neither inevitable nor unavoidable, but an aberration that ought not to be a normal part of industrial relations. A system premised on the free play of such conflict seemed totally unnatural to them. One exasperated employer in the electrical-appliance sector gave vent to the prevailing sentiment when he announced that: "We have to decide whether an employer is master in his own house in France—whether there still are employers left. . . . I prefer death to surrender."[2] Like many industrialists, this *patron* could not imagine a system of industrial relations in which he alone was not the boss and where conflict was accepted as part of the normal institutional process. Only a counterattack to humble the unions and restore the old prerogatives seemed an appropriate response to the post-June regime. Prerequisite to any counterattack, however, was a regrouping and rearming of *patronal* ranks.

Prior to 1936, French employer associations included only the largest, most powerful industrialists, and served largely as clearing houses for cartel arrangements. The slightness of their organization, compounded by the loose federation of regional and trade groups, was in fact sign of *patronal* hegemony. It was only after the Matignon Accords "enfranchised" the unions that the need for more comprehensive and effective association became apparent.[3] Accordingly, in the fall of 1936, several new employer organizations were founded and the CGPF, the largest and most important association, underwent a radical transformation. This transformation began with a rechristening; in changing its name from the Confédération Générale du Production Française to the Confédération Generale du Patronat Français, the CGPF announced a shift from a purely economic to a social and political conception of its role, redefining itself as a class organization able to counter the politically enhanced capacities of the labor movement.[4]

There next occurred a "palace revolution" in the CGPF leadership. C. J. Gignoux, replacing René Ducheim as president, was given a mandate to reform the organization and wage a concerted struggle against the unions. As an anti-labor publicist and a former politician without ties to any single faction of industry, Gignoux possessed the ideal credentials to lead the reconstituted CGPF. With the assistance of a group of young, assertive businessmen ready to face down the People's Front, Gignoux would mobilize the *patronat* in a solid front against the unions and the state. His project sought to bring small and middle-size employers into the CGPF fold, develop a social policy to counter that of the government, sabotage the new contractual regime in the plants, resist demands for additional concessions, and rally the middle class against the left coalition.[5] Gignoux would ultimately fail to realize all these objectives, but his aggressive leadership set the standard for other employer associations, particularly the UIMM, which represented the metal industry inside the CGPF. In the fall of 1936, the UIMM embarked on a similar revamping, replacing its president with a militant anti-union employer, extending and tightening the links between Paris and the provinces and those between small and large-scale producers, creating new offices to handle collective contracts, arbitration, propaganda, and public relations, and, indicative of the conflicts that lay ahead, preparing its members for an anti-union offensive.[6]

Under the reformed leadership of the CGPF and the UIMM, metal employers avoided a frontal assault on the new contractual regime. Instead their line of march began with a series of flanking maneuvers, *une guérilla sociale*, designed to stymie its function in the plants.[7] In the fall and winter of 1936, employers began firing stewards, retributively laying off workers, reclassifying skill categories, refusing to pay certain wage rates, forming company unions, and delaying the application of the contract.[8] They also made literal or tendentious interpretations of the new social laws, sabotaged their implementation, and temporarily closed plants. In the face of these attacks, five thousand worker complaints were lodged in the first four months of the Matignon system.[9]

The New Order in the Factories

For different reasons, workers took issue with the new Matignon system of industrial relations. Having shattered the employers' "divine right" and brought a "new deal" into the shops, they suddenly considered themselves equal to their masters and insisted on being treated as such.[10] Because the occupations had overcome their isolation in the production process and forged a new community—identified with the various projects of the Communist party, the CGT, and the People's Front—they now thought that solidarity and direct action held the key to a host of complex and intractable social problems. What need was there then for compromise or institutional forms of conflict-resolution when their collective struggles would suffice? Worker impatience with the new system of industrial relations was not, however, simply an expression of unrealistic expectations; something else had changed during the occupations which made it impossible for them to accept the old routines or adjudicate their claims through the procedural mechanisms of the Matignon system. In addition to securing a rationalized wage structure, workshop representation, and the legal codification of union rights, the June strikes prefigured an alternative system of social relations—in which labor interests dominated, labor leaders called the shots, and labor needs dictated the rhythms of production.[11] After such an experience, with its implication of a wider emancipation, workers felt restrained even by institutional arrangements favoring their interests.[12] Like employers, they found it impossible to compromise and accept a system in which each side "agreed to disagree."

And here the contradictions of the republican union became insupportable. The general strike, the street mobilizations, and the appeals of populist republicanism had given the anomic masses of the Fordist-Taylorist factory system a powerful identity and a sense of place denied by the economic innovations of the earlier period. Buoyed up on their successful political campaign, they were at last able to assert themselves within the factory's social system and alter it in ways that undermined its liberal foundations. The result was the June strikes, the new social laws, and mass unionism, all of which empowered them in the plants and challenged the individualistic premises of the existing order. This empowerment, however, threatened not only the managerial policies of the *patronat* and the "totalitarian" logic of the technical system, it also beckoned the syndicalization of industrial relations, reviving earlier ideas of worker-control and self-management and implicitly refuting the liberal-democratic principles that the left coalition was committed to defending. As a result of these rising expectations, the period of the People's Front would see not only a gradual estrangement between the working class and the government, but a growing confusion between its political and social aspirations.

More immediately, the workers' defiant state of mind, combined with the employers' resistance to the new contractual regime, spawned many new conflicts after June. Soon conflicts fed on conflicts. Because these clashes in the factory had an adverse effect on the political situation, communist union leaders feared they would undermine the People's Front, as well as the Matignon system. They were, however, uncertain how to cope with them. Part of their uncertainty stemmed from the fact that the metal union was not in complete control of its ranks. Having overnight expanded from a few thousand to a quarter million members, the union lacked the seasoned cadre to discipline the new membership and police the contract. Much of the union's factory-level leadership had in fact fallen into the hands of recruits without previous trade-union experience and with ideological convictions of an extremely agitational character. Accordingly, the union would encounter its most acute problems on the shop floor, where newly elected shop stewards and *section* secretaries, attuned to the heady atmosphere of the occupied factories, sought to bypass the union's Paris office and pursue politically inexpedient social goals.

Considering themselves representatives of a dual power, not obedient cogs in the lowest rung of an institutional system, these stewards and secretaries presented a formidable counter-authority to the *patrons* and created numerous disciplinary problems for the union. Rarely would these lower-level unionists hesitate to threaten a slowdown or production delay if disliked piece rates were imposed, if labor-saving machines were installed, if the tempo of production increased, and especially if anything was done to threaten the new union-centered order in the plants, including the refusal of fellow workers to purchase their monthly union stamp. Stewards and secretaries also felt entitled to en-croach on employer hiring-and-firing practices, for which they had no author-ity. Except in the recently nationalized aviation sector, the contract restricted the secretary's power to union representation and the steward's to the settle-ment of individual worker grievances, the supervision of contract provisions, and health and safety issues. But because workers saw them and they saw themselves as agents of a new order, they instinctually sought broad supervi-sory powers within the production process, which inevitably led to confronta-tions with management—and sometimes with their own union leadership. Thus, in addition to rectifying the workers' traditional lack of industrial repre-sentation, these new shop representatives would serve as further sources of discord.[13]

Given the altered power relations in the plants, the slightest issue—speed-up, firings, safety violations, misinterpretation of the contract, piece-rates dis-putes—was likely to provoke a conflict. When conflicts turned into strikes, workers frequently had trouble formulating their demands, which suggests that these conflicts were more the expression of a newfound power than an at-tempt to remedy a particular grievance. In a related vein, brawls between unionists and foremen were on the increase, just as punctuality and discipline, associated with the old regime, were on the decline.[14] Because these conflicts often culminated in occupations, social tensions inevitably escalated, as *métal-los* barricaded in their plants felt duty-bound to make a higher level of com-mitment.[15]

In the months following the June strikes, the Paris metal industry seethed with dispute. At the Hotchkiss armament plant in Clichy, workers struck after an announced layoff and stayed on strike until it was rescinded. At Franco-Belge, another munitions manufacturer, workers protested the introduction of several advanced German rollers threatening certain job categories. At SECM in Colombes, aviation workers resisted management's effort to reclassify skill categories. At Nieuport, aviation workers struck until stopwatch engineers were removed from the shops and management promised not to alter piece rates. At Chenard, Babcok-et-Walcox, CAMS, and Lavellet, strikes broke out over contractual issues and in defense of fired stewards. The most consequential conflict in this period (and I have mentioned only the more representative ones) occurred at SACEM in Argentreuil, a mechanical-engineering firm contracted to the armament industry, where six hundred workers occupied their plant after management "arbitrarily" dismissed six workers, reclassified certain skill categories, and refused to observe the terms of the contract. This strike would last fifty-four days and require the intervention of several cabinet ministers before a compromise could be worked out.[16]

Because such actions—at SACEM and elsewhere—troubled the economy, disrupted the contractual system, and complicated the tasks of the People's Front, the metal union discouraged them and tried to get workers to redress their grievances through procedural means.[17] This, however, put union leaders in a bit of a quandary. On the one hand, they wanted to avoid conflicts that might undermine the Matignon system or compromise the left government, which entailed a policy of conciliation, social peace, and labor discipline. On the other hand, they needed to remain sensitive to the ranks or risk alienating them, which meant supporting direct actions aimed at defending the new order in the shops. In this contradictory role—as responsible member of the left alliance and as leader of a newly empowered working class—communist labor bosses usually disappointed both their constituencies. By providing leadership to spontaneous strikes and occupations (if only to head them off or keep them moderate), they tended to antagonize the *patronat* and trouble the politicians, but by playing the moderate and restraining worker actions, they failed to consolidate their authority over the impatient ranks or secure labor gains on the shop floor.

Caught on the horns of this dilemma, the metal union resorted to a dual strategy. First, it sought out the assistance of the Labor Ministry and the Blum government, with the aim of introducing greater state supervision of the workplace and bringing political pressure to bear on the *patronat*. At a second level, it made a concerted effort to publicize worker grievances and document contractual violations in the hope public opinion would compel *patronal* compliance.[18] In adopting these measures, the union leadership strained to preserve the peace and normalize production, for without normalized production, economic recovery would be out of the question—and without recovery the People's Front was certain to flounder.[19] The leadership, as a result, ended up devoting more attention to matters of political expediency than to corporate defense.

Because the Matignon system, as well as the left alliance, hinged on subordinating direct action to the contract's procedural forms, the leadership was frequently compelled to bring out the bit and the bridle.[20] Shortly after the June occupations, Benoît Frachon publicly admonished *métallos* for failing to reconize that "the strike was not the sole means of obtaining satisfaction."

Workers, he insisted, should use the provisions of the contract to enforce observance of the new regime rather than let employers "maneuver" them into actions that discredited the labor movement and embarrassed the government.[21] Frachon's admonitions, like others articulated in the months ahead, represented an attempt to divert the newly awakened labor movement into institutionally amenable channels. These admonitions, it is worth noting, specifically targeted the cells and *sections*, which were prone to transforming orders issued by the summit into actions that agitated the base.[22]

Like their communist counterparts, Jouhaux and the former confederal leadership exhorted workers to ignore "employer provocations" and put their faith in procedural methods. In July, after the socialist interior minister promised conservative critics that Blum's government would no longer tolerate factory occupations, Jouhaux used the occasion to offer CGT assistance in "neutralizing" (evacuating) occupied plants on condition that the government step in and arbitrate the disputes.[23] The CGT chief hoped neutralization would get the state involved in monitoring industrial relations and bring new pressure to bear on the *patronat*. In mid August, in a first attempt to implement his proposal, the metal union convinced striking workers at the Dehouse metal works to evacuate their plant and let government arbitrators resolve the conflict. Dehouse was no sooner evacuated, however, than neutralization backfired. For three weeks the employer refused to negotiate and the government wavered in its promise to intervene.[24] As unrest at Dehouse and elsewhere persisted, the union floundered and industrial peace became increasingly tenuous.

Rifts in the Left Alliance

If the failure to harmonize the new system of industrial relations troubled the People's Front and complicated the union's relationship with the ranks, international events introduced an entirely different order of difficulty. On 18 July 1936, General Francisco Franco and a sizable part of the Spanish Army, supported by the fascist powers, rebelled against the People's Front government of Spain. The Spanish working class responded with armed resistance. The ensuing civil war, which drenched the Iberian peninsula in blood, threatened the peace of Europe, and captured the world's attention, had an immediate and divisive impact on French domestic politics. Following the rebellion, the Spanish Republic appealed to France for arms. Azaña, the premier, believed fifty planes would suffice in crushing the franquist uprising.[25] Sympathetic to the Spanish People's Front, ideological kin to his own government, Blum was inclined to grant Azaña's request, but opposition from Radicals in his cabinet and right-wing deputies in the chamber, both of whom feared intervention would touch off a larger European war, forced Blum to reject the request. In its stead Blum

devised a policy of non-intervention, designed to prevent the internationaliza-
tion of the Spanish conflict. All the major powers then formally agreed to observe his non-intervention policy, even as they prepared to ignore its
provisions.[26] This would have the effect of allowing aid to reach the rebels and
placing obstacles in the way of suppressing them. Its domestic consequences
were no less dismal. Although non-intervention appeased critics on the right,
it profoundly shocked anti-fascists in the left alliance and in the unions, who
expected Blum, as a matter of course, to support the Spanish Republic in every
way short of war. The struggle against fascism, they insisted, could not be com-
partmentalized: "the border between Paris and Madrid is only apparent."[27]
Their insistence became especially strident after Italy and Germany began
sending arms and troops to aid the Nationalist rebels. For these anti-fascists,
Blum's policy was tantamount to a betrayal of the People's Front.

The ensuing controversy over the Spanish Civil War would create deep and
acrimonious divisions within both the left coalition and the CGT. For Jouhaux,
non-intervention was objectively pro-fascist. Like many unionists, he viewed
the Spanish conflict through a manichean lens, seeing it as a battle between
light and darkness.[28] No one who took anti-fascism seriously, he believed, could
abstain from aiding the Spanish Republicans. Their cause "was the cause of
workers of all countries." If the arms embargo were not immediately lifted, he
prophesied a terrible tragedy for France.[29] Jouhaux's view was shared by many
in the CGT ranks, who in each of the four months following the war's outbreak
donated a million *francs* to the beleaguered Spanish Republic—the greatest single fund-raising campaign yet waged by French labor. Paris metal workers,
whose union mounted a similar campaign, displayed an even greater sympathy
for the Spanish cause. They contributed a part of their weekly earnings to the
republicans and not a few of them joined the 9,000 of their countrymen who
would make up the French section of the soon-to-be-formed International
Brigade. More importantly, it was in the workshops of the Paris metal industry
that "Blum's treason" was frontally challenged.

From the start, the PCF characterized non-intervention as a capitulation
to the most retrograde elements in the French political system and a failure to
pursue those forms of collective security needed to contain fascist aggression.
Yet for nearly a month and a half the party's criticism was offered in a spirit of
"national unity." This restraint was largely due to the new *Front Français* to
which the PCF was rather unsuccessfully luring Catholics, right-wing republicans, and virtually anyone, however reactionary, who was willing to support
an anti-German foreign policy.[30] In the spirit of the *Front Français*, communists
directed *métallo* opposition to non-intervention into safe and legal channels.
This moderation was maintained even in the face of bitter worker demands for
action. In August, for example, Renault workers tried to purchase a Renault

tank for the Spanish Republic; at Gnome-et- Rhône and at Hispano-Suiza, air-craft workers sought to buy a warplane; at Hotchkiss and at Brandt, armament workers proposed machine guns and shells. Communists prudently steered these proposals for military assistance into less inflammatory measures, such as food and medical aid, but did so to the disappointment of their supporters in the plants.[31] Later, on 13 August, a meeting of a thousand Paris metal dele-gates, called on the government to lift its arms embargo. A similar meeting a week later issued another such call, which Doury, the union's general secre-tary, delivered to Blum. All these actions, reflective of the PCF's "loyal opposi-tion," were designed to persuade rather than pressure the government into changing its Spanish policy.

Persuasion, however, soon gave way to pressure. In early September, just before the Soviets decided to ship arms to Spain, the PCF adopted a noticeably more confrontational stance.[32] At a hastily assembled meeting of several thou-sand communist auto workers, Maurice Thorez saluted recent union resolu-tions at Bloch and Hotchkiss condemning non-intervention and calling for "mass actions" in support of the Spanish People's Front. Then, on 5 September, a delegation from the metal union formally requested that Blum lift the arms embargo. To show that this was more than a symbolic gesture, 2,000 arma-ment workers at the Hotchkiss plant in Levallois staged a thirty-minute strike "in solidarity with the Spanish people," threatening more consequential ac-tions if Blum did not immediately lift the embargo.[33] Finally, that evening, after the news reached Paris that the Nationalists had overrun Irún, a meeting of metal delegates voted a union-sponsored resolution to hold a one-hour "gen-eral strike" to protest French neutrality vis-a-vis Spain, as well as focus public attention on the ongoing contract violations.[34] For the first time since the in-stallation of Blum's government, communists lined up in opposition to the so-cialist premier.

According to L'Humanité, the one-hour general strike of 7 September was "practically total." The government estimated an 80 to 85 percent rate of ob-servance.[35] Either assessment suggests a successful strike. Reports from the metal factories, however, give a slightly different picture. Because the strike had been called for political as well as corporate demands, workers were not alto-gether certain why they were striking. The public assumed it was to protest Blum's Spanish policy, but inside the metal factories things were less clear. Métallos sympathetic to socialists and Radicals did not want to support an im-plicitly anti-government strike, even if they opposed non-intervention. For example, three-quarters of the workforce at the Rameau metal works in Courbevoie stopped production for the first five minutes of the strike and then resumed work once a socialist in their ranks convinced them of the strike's anti-government implications. In plants where socialists outnumbered communists, union delegates were careful to emphasize the strike's corporate demands (defense of the contract) and downplayed the political (Spain).[36] In most cases, though, workers struck simply because the union had called them out, irrespective of their attitude to Blum's Spanish policy.

Not surprisingly, the general strike provoked numerous rumblings in union ranks. In a sharply worded criticism, revolutionary syndicalists associated with *La Révolution Prolétarienne* characterized the one-hour protest as "a masterpiece of disorganization" that threatened the stability of the People's Front coalition, jeopardized the terms of the union contract, and subordinated the union to communist political objectives. This, they claimed, could only confuse the *métallos* and undermine labor unity. As evidence, they pointed to factories (Latil, Solex, Seignol, Hispano-Suiza, Livry) where political differences between striking and non-striking workers had erupted into counterprotests and fisticuffs. A few more experiences like this, they warned, and the metal union could say good-bye to its quarter-million members.[37]

Although the strike failed to deter Blum in his Spanish policy, it had a major impact on Radicals and socialists in the People's Front and non-communists in the CGT leadership. The Radicals were largely responsible for the non-intervention policy and the communist-inspired strike cast immediate suspicion on their coalition partner, strengthening the party's conservative wing, which was still reeling from the June occupations. The strike also alarmed the large pacifist wing of the Radical party, unsympathetic to the belligerent sentiments of the anti-fascists. At this point, the Radicals' fear of war, allied with their aversion to social disorder, began to crystallize into an anti-communist tendency—which would grow steadily more pronounced as issues of social reform and foreign policy became increasingly contentious. The former confederals in the CGT national office were no less disturbed by the strike, not because they supported non-intervention (although the pacifists among them thought it was not such an unreasonable policy), but because the PCF, in violation of syndical policy, had used the metal union to promote its political agenda. On 9 September, two days after the strike, the CGT's Commission Administrative informed its affiliated federations that it alone had the authority to decide "a general action of the labor movement." All future actions, the Commission Administrative ordered, had to abide by CGT statute. Communists were thus put on notice that the national CGT leadership would oppose any subsequent union mobilizations on behalf of their political objectives.[38]

The most consequential reaction to the general strike, as might be expected, came from socialists, although a significant number of them, especially in the Paris Region, opposed non-intervention. For the national SFIO leadership, the strike constituted not merely a challenge to Blum's Spanish policy, but an affront to the party. After the 7th, socialists from the region's metal plants began sending *Le Populaire* (the SFIO daily) various resolutions informing the public of their opposition to the strike, even if many of them had honored it out of trade-union discipline.[39] A week later, the SFIO organized a series of meetings to urge its members to form Amicales Socialistes d'Entreprise. This proposal to create factory-level organizations constituted a major watershed in socialist history.[40] Never previously had they attempted to implant themselves in industry, but after the 7 September strike, they felt it imperative to counter communist influence in the shops.[41] Once launched the Amicales quickly spread. By February 1937, 110 Amicales had reportedly organized 30,000 socialist metal workers in the Paris Region.[42] Amicales leaders soon claimed their organization touched the entire metal industry. This may, indeed, have been the case, but the socialist organization nowhere reached the depth of the PCF implantation. At Renault, for example, the Amicales succeeded in organizing less than 2,000 of the auto workers and only a few hundred at several large plants for which we have figures (Hotchkiss and Hispano-Suiza).[43] These figures represented only a third of what communists had in these plants; Amicales membership, moreover, lacked the Leninist discipline and conviction that made the cells such a force. Nonetheless, by implanting themselves in the factories, socialists became a potential, though unequal, rival to the communists.[44]

The organization of the Amicales further politicized the labor movement. This could not but upset the former confederals, however much they might have welcomed a counterweight to communist influence. Politics of any variety, they believed, diverted workers from their corporate struggles. If differences over foreign and domestic policies should henceforth become matters of general union concern, they feared worker unity would fracture along ideological lines. The more energetic and resourceful ex-confederals now decided it was time to form an organization of their own in order to re-center the labor movement on social issues. Following the general strike, ex-confederals began coalescing around René Belin, a former postal worker who was the number-two man in the CGT hierarchy. In mid-October, Belin launched a weekly titled *Syndicats* to which he rallied his followers. His "*Syndicats* group" would henceforth define itself in terms of anti-communism, union independence, pacifism, and a willingness "to defend the working class irrespective of [political] considerations." Similar to the way in which the Amicales contested communist influence in the shops, the *Syndicats* group now took the anti-communist struggle to the CGT national office, where it sought to defend traditional union principles compromised by the reunification and June expansion.[45]

With the formation of the *Syndicats* group in the fall of 1936, the CGT divided into three rival factions. The largest of these, made up of communists, was centered around Frachon in the CGT national office and supported by nearly half the CGT ranks, mainly in private industry and rail. The Paris office of the metal union, along with the majority of its ranks, aligned themselves with Frachon. Opposed to his faction was the *Syndicats* group, made up of a third of the CGT membership. Its constituency was recruited mainly from among CGT'ers sympathetic to socialism, revolutionary syndicalism, or pacifism. In the metal union, the *Syndicats* faction had only a splinter of rank-and-file support, but attracted an extremely articulate following from the ex-confederal leadership. Marcel Roy and Léon Chevalme, two of the six federal secretaries, adhered to the *Syndicats* line, as did Jean Dupaquier, Albert Lemire, Maurice Cuissot, and several dozen former leaders from the pre-unified metal union.[46] The third and smallest CGT faction, which had little support in private industry, was led by Jouhaux and derived most of its rank-and-file following from the public-sector unions; Jouhaux's faction shared the *Syndicats'* concern for union independence, but supported communists on issues related to foreign policy and the People's Front. Henceforth, as the *Syndicats* group contested communist hegemony in the reunified CGT, the conciliatory efforts of Jouhaux's centrist tendency played a crucial part in holding the labor movement together.

Skirmishes on the Shop Floor

The escalation of union factionalism took place against a backdrop of protracted labor strife. As early as September 1936, after returning from their first two-week paid vacation, *métallos* encountered a series of challenges that set off another round of strikes.[47] The calculated intransigence of employers (discussed above) provided one source of these conflicts, the general economic situation another. Between June and November 1936, wholesale prices rose 22 percent, wiping out much of the wage increase won during the factory occupations. This inflationary surge was partly due to increased labor costs resulting from the June accords and partly to the insecurity of capital, which was exported or hoarded in an effort to escape the volatile political situation. Then, at summer's end, after Blum devalued the *franc*, inflationary pressures rose again. As incomes succumbed to the mounting cost of living and workers discovered their pockets were lighter, they pressed for new wage rates.

By the fall of 1936, France had slipped into a widening spiral of uncertainty —as a result of the government's failure to resolve its various social, financial, and international problems. Created out of fear of fascism, the People's Front, as one historian describes it, had "no blueprint to revive a sagging economy and no formula for dealing with the sudden intrusion of foreign affairs as an ideological issue in [domestic] politics."[48] Although non-intervention temporarily defused the Spanish crisis, the government still lacked a viable economic strategy. In August, a price-control bill failed to remedy the inflationary situation. The Senate then refused to pass a cost-of-living bill. When wage disputes erupted in the fall, the government proposed a "second Matignon Accord," but government, business, and labor representatives meeting in mid-September failed to reach an agreement.[49]

The deteriorating economy, combined with dissension over the Spanish Civil War and employer attacks on the Matignon system, cast a pall over worker spirits. Yet throughout the fall of 1936, *métallos* continued to defend the terrain conquered in June, refusing to heed party and union appeals for restraint. Fearing the destabilizing effects of this unrest, the CGT and PCF did their utmost to calm the factories, but once strikes were launched, they were normally obliged to support them. Union and party leaders, however, adopted a reactive role in a situation demanding resolute leadership. This boded ill for the labor movement, for it blunted union influence in the political system and left workers undefended in the plants. The negative impact of this hesitant leadership was nowhere more evident than in the occupation of the Sautter-Harlé armament plant. Initiated by the *section syndicale* on 14 September, the Sautter-Herlé strike was launched in solidarity with twenty laid-off draftsmen—who were, not coincidentally, among the plant's most active unionists. Prior to the strike, the metal union had proposed an overall reduction of hours to spread the available work, but management preferred its own arrangement—which, in light of previous actions, suggested it was looking for a way to attack the union. As the union temporized over the dispute, afraid to provoke an action that might embarrass the government, a courtyard meeting of the plant's 1,200 *métallos* voted to strike. The subsequent occupation, in which embittered workers anxiously armed themselves against possible police attack, stood in stark contrast to the festive June strikes. Moreover, there was cause for concern even within their own ranks. Communists in the *section*, who had tried to head off the conflict, refused to provide adequate strike support once it began and acted as a brake on its development. According to one revolutionary-syndicalist observer, communists displayed a greater "patriotic" concern for the government's welfare than did socialists and were qualitatively less supportive than conservative Catholic unionists.

The strikers nonetheless persisted in their struggle. For thirty-five days, they occupied their factory. The shutdown of a key armament plant eventually forced the government to intervene. Yet it took over thirty worker delegations to the Ministries of Labor and War before the dispute could be resolved. According to the government's arbitrated settlement, the laid-off draftsmen were to be employed in another state arsenal and a tripartite committee set up to mediate future disputes. The government then requisitioned the plant and re-opened it under military supervision. While employers at Sautter-Harlé and in the CGPF fumed at this abridgment of their property rights, strikers viewed the settlement as a distinct victory, for it satisfied their original demands and gave them new powers over hiring and firing. Yet if communists in the Paris office and the *section syndicale* had had their way, the strike would never have occurred. This contradictory state of affairs, in which the workers' corporate interests were subordinated to the union's political concerns, was proving to be a problem not only at Sautter-Harlé but throughout the industry.[50]

Antinomies of the People's Front

Blum's government initially approached the depressed economy with the conviction that if wages and popular purchasing power were augmented, then production would rise to meet increased demand.[51] This purchasing-power strategy, however, was as impractical as it was ill-defined. Besides inheriting a large deficit (which alone consumed 35 percent of the government's income) and generating new costs by restoring state pensions and salaries cut by previous National Union governments, Blum's economic program was hampered by a lack of state controls and an executive with limited powers of intervention. Blum also missed his most important cue. Unlike Franklin Roosevelt, who used the struggles of the American labor movement to undermine the entrenched economic powers and facilitate the transition to a neo-capitalist system (by abandoning market mechanisms, introducing economic regulation, and enhancing the powers of the central government), Blum's alliance with the Radicals prevented him from tampering with the liberal economy.[52] This was not a strategy for success. As early as September 1936, it was obvious that the June reforms had disrupted, not stimulated production. Inflation, production bottlenecks, declining business confidence, and a continuing deflation of the economic structure, rather than reinvigorated markets, seemed to follow as a result of the new social laws. To complicate matters, the ailing economy caused tax revenues to contract, which meant fewer funds for increased public expenditures. The troubled political situation, in turn, caused capital to flee the country and investment to fall off, setting off alarm bells in financial markets.[53] Before long, the government faced an ever-dwindling treasury. To stave off insolvency it needed to borrow, but the only way it could meet the stringent terms set by the banks was by devaluing the *franc*, cutting back on public expenditures, and reconsidering the retrenchment and deflationary policies of previous center-right governments. These measures adopted in the last quarter of 1936 would effectively terminate the purchasing-power orientation and whatever economic strategy the People's Front had for remedying the crisis.[54]

Blum's economic retreat, following the rancor over Spain, represented the government's second major rout. This time, however, the premier would have his feet held to the fire. During the June occupations, the Chamber of Deputies had passed a forty-hour law. Because the details of the law's implementation were left to future negotiations, the government hesitated to apply it once it rethought its economic policies. Union leaders, however, hoped the shorter work week would reduce unemployment and refused to sacrifice it for the sake of the state's finances. Throughout the summer of 1936, numerous resolutions from the factory *sections* of the Paris metal industry demanded the full and immediate application of the forty-hour law.[55] While workers mobilized in support of the shorter work week, the UIMM pleaded with Blum to consider the difficulties the law would have in the metal industry and the national economy. The employer association warned that, by raising production costs another 15 to 20 percent, the forty-hour week would effectively price French products out of international markets, lead to shortages of skilled labor, increase training and benefit costs, and prevent employers from responding to sudden increases in market demand. If the new law were to be applied, the UIMM asked that it be done with flexibility, allowing special dispensation for certain forms of production, overtime provisions, and a long-term calculation of the work week.[56]

Alert to these industrial imperatives and the declining viability of the purchasing-power strategy, Blum was not unsympathetic to employer concerns.[57] When he met with labor leaders in the fall to work out the law's application in the metal industry, he tried to wheedle them into mitigating and delaying its implementation. But neither the Paris metal leadership nor the CGT national officers was prepared to compromise. They remembered the eight-hour law of 1919 that had been sabotaged by qualifications, and had no intention of allowing a similar process to rob them of their shorter work week.[58] Moreover, they believed the forty-hour week was crucial to resolving the problem of unemployment.[59] In no uncertain terms, Blum was informed that this was an issue over which labor was prepared to fight. Thus, despite his reservations, he was at last forced to bow to labor's version of the forty-hour week, which was scheduled to begin in metal on 6 December, with other French industries to follow in successive months.

Labor's victory, however, was a Pyrrhic one. Instead of generating new jobs and stimulating markets, the inflexible application of the new law created bottlenecks that disrupted parts of the economy and motivated employers to maintain production levels with existing labor forces. As a consequence, unemployment rates in metal and other industries remained unaffected (and in some cases actually climbed), while the economy as a whole continued to stagnate.[60] This embittered labor leaders, but because they considered the shorter week an inviolable tenet of their creed and attributed the law's failure to employer hiring policies, they refused to consider a compromise.[61] This, in turn, provoked employers to counterattack with a public-relations campaign to discredit and anti-union actions to stymie the law's implementation. The forty-hour week, the crowning achievement of June, thus set off another round of conflicts, further weakening the economy and the new system of industrial relations.

Metal employers were not the only ones disturbed by the new social legislation. As the June reforms took their toll on the fortunes of small businessmen and traditional market mechanisms failed to halt successive labor gains, Radicals became increasingly disenchanted with the left coalition. In October 1936, on the eve of the Radical party's annual congress, rumors began to circulate that they were contemplating a withdrawal from it. Not only was the conservative wing of the Radical party alarmed by the coalition's pro-labor bent, but the party's moderate center had lost interest in republican defense once the "fascist" danger had passed. Only the Radicals' left wing, situated in that fuzzy region between socialism and liberalism, remained steadfastly loyal to the government.

Radical disaffection was a matter of the utmost concern to the PCF. Addressing the Central Committee on 17 October, Maurice Thorez called on communists to do everything possible to avoid "alienating" the middle class.[62] This could only mean one thing: redoubling PCF efforts to quiet the factories.[63] Not coincidentally, the final months of 1936 saw a gradual tapering off of strike activity and a calming of the industrial situation. This temporary peace paid immediate dividends. Although the Radicals' congress witnessed an extremely contentious struggle between the party's left and right wings and heard a good deal of anti-communist rhetoric, they nonetheless reaffirmed their ties to the left alliance.[64] These ties, however, were likely to be maintained only as long as the labor movement moderate its demands and respect Radical sensibilities.

The Federal Congress

Between 25 and 27 November 1936, the Metal Federation's biennial congress was held—the first since the unification. With 600,000 members (growing to 825,000 by early 1937), the Metal Federation now constituted the largest and most important of the CGT federations. Like the Fusion Congress of the Paris metal union in June, the federal convention was dominated by ex-*unitaires*, who outnumbered confederals better than twenty to one. To the dismay of non-communists, their former rivals approached the congress not as unionists guided by corporate concerns but as political activists bound by party discipline. Whenever ex-confederals offered criticisms of communist-sponsored resolutions or departed from policies prescribed by the former *unitaire* leadership, they found themselves faced with threatening jeers or party discipline that stifled discussion. This immediately revived the fears that had motivated their earlier resistance to *unitaire* unification overtures. Albert Lemire, a veteran syndicalist disdainful of the Russian model of labor organization, characterized the communist-controlled event as a *congrès spectaculaire* and worried that "if we don't soon resist certain *unitaire* practices, [then] union congresses will become nothing but conformist parades, complete with flags, clenched-fist salutes, and songs, but without free ideas."[65] The ex-confederals were especially alarmed by the vote on the federation's new statutes, for the federalist, antipolitical conception of unionism was replaced by the centralist, politically motivated conception that had previously guided the CGTU Metal Federation.[66] Communists, however, went out of their way to preserve the tarnished mystique of unity. In electing the federal officers, they "reserved" two of the six executive positions for the ex-confederals (Roy and Chevalme) and thirteen of the thirty-five seats on the Commission Executive.[67] These measures helped preserve the confederal presence in the union leadership, but at the cost of formalizing their minority status.

The congress also departed from previous union tradition in proposing a unionism with *les bases multiples*. Since the June inundation, the older syndical forms, geared to the trades and to interventions by "active minorities," had ceased to accord with the needs of the new mass-production recruits. Unlike prewar craftsmen, these workers looked to the union not only to defend their interests in the factory, but to integrate them into industrial society. Sensitive to these concerns, the congress authorized the Metal Federation and the Paris metal union to develop a means of addressing these needs. Following the congress, union leaders proceeded to set up sporting, musical, and theatrical clubs, establish "vacation colonies" for the children of metal workers, purchase several country *chateaux* for the membership's recreational use, found a health clinic, offer several types of insurance, create a center for job training, and open a placement center.[68] Characteristically, these programs constituting *les bases multiples*, unlike earlier social democratic efforts to emancipate the working class from bourgeois cultural forms, were less an "alternative" than a complement to the recreational and social-security provisions of mass society.[69] Many, in fact, were simply organizations taken over from the employers.[70]

Compulsory Arbitration

In late 1936, the only major conflict the union failed to defuse occurred at the Panhard auto works. In mid-October, management announced a layoff of 825 of its 2,900 workers. Unionists thought it was designed to decapitate the local leadership, but the employer cited economic exigencies, particularly delays in delivery schedules caused by strikes at suppliers. Panhard's management was undoubtedly hamstrung by the new contractual system. Yet, as was so often the case in these disputes, there was evidence that the employer's economic argument camouflaged anti-union intentions—for management had recently turned down orders which would have made the layoffs unnecessary.[71] From the extant evidence, it is impossible to determine if these orders were turned down because of anti-union motives or because they simply could not be filled. But whatever the underlying truth, this conflict highlighted the strained nature of labor-management relations and the tendency for disputes to resist procedural forms of resolution.

When management refused to rescind the layoffs, Panhard workers occupied their plant. After a week, the union managed to neutralize the factory and government experts stepped in to arbitrate. Once these experts arrived at a decision, however, the employer refused to apply it and the strike dragged on another two weeks, despite repeated interventions by the Labor Ministry. Blum himself was eventually compelled to intervene and force the employer to comply with the arbitrated settlement.[72] This finally brought the conflict to an end, but it also perpetuated the failings of the new contractual regime, for if the state had to broker every major labor-management conflict, then the Matignon system would never take root and function on its own accord. And this indeed seems to have been the case. Joel Colton estimates that half of all strikes in the months following the June occupations were mediated by government officials and that 260 of these had to be settled by cabinet ministers.[73] And because workers and employers began to rely on state efforts to settle their differences, industrial disputes became increasingly politicized—and increasingly unsolvable.

The failure of the Matignon system to maintain social peace—at Panhard and throughout industry—eventually prompted the government to seek an alternative means of conflict resolution. In November, Blum submitted a compulsory-arbitration bill to the Chamber of Deputies. In a sharp break with tradition, the CGT came out in support of this legislation. Here again was evidence of labor's desperation. Not even in the darkest days of the Great War had the CGT accepted the principle of compulsory arbitration, which was traditionally considered a compromising abridgment of union independence.[74] Union leaders, however, felt exceptional circumstances justified exceptional measures. They had little control over their ranks, management remained aggressively uncooperative, and the persisting cycle of unrest threatened the existence of the People's Front and its collective-bargaining system.[75] Business leaders, though, waged a heated campaign against the proposed legislation and only Blum's promise to prevent future occupations managed to overcome stiff opposition in the Senate.[76] On 31 December 1936, the arbitration bill, the government's last significant piece of social legislation, passed into law.

The new law's first test came in the Paris metal industry. In early December, the union presented the UIMM a request for a cost-of-living adjustment. Claiming wages had eroded 18 percent to 20 percent since June 1936, it asked for a 15 percent raise and a cost-of-living clause.[77] Because employers wanted labor to live with the inflationary consequences of the June reforms, they rejected the union demand. In early January 1937, as the courtyards of the metal industry filled with workers demanding "our 15 percent," the union submitted its wage request to state arbitrators.[78] A month later, William Oualid, a law professor sympathetic to labor, rendered an arbitration granting a 8.5 percent wage hike. Oualid acknowledged that the cost-of-living was more than the 15 percent requested by the union, but he believed an increase geared to the cost-of-living might set off an inflationary spiral detrimental to both labor and the economy.[79] Neither the union leadership nor the ranks, however, were willing to accept this line of reasoning. Protests immediately broke out in the shops, giving vent to demands for a more favorable arbitration. Union leaders then met with Blum, who agreed the union could submit another request to appease the mood in the plants.[80] Through February and into March, while arbitrators considered the second wage demand, metal workers engaged in a series of five-minute workstoppages. When some workers called for more forceful actions in support of their demands, union leaders preached calm, denounced proponents of such action as "Trotskyites and other agents of the Gestapo," and asked workers to put their faith in the arbitration process.[81] The second arbitrated decision, though, was as disappointing as the first. Rendered in mid-March, it granted a mere 4 percent raise, not the requested 10 percent. Together, the two arbitrated wage adjustments amounted to half the actual cost-of-living increase. Yet despite the rank-and-file grumbling that followed and the rising level of disappointment in the shops, the arbitration system nonetheless enabled the union, however partially, to defend wages, vent a layer of frustration, facilitate a settlement, and avoid a general action that might otherwise have disturbed the political situation.[82]

The Pause

Although compulsory arbitration resuscitated the ailing Matignon system, the government's ongoing travails continued to undermine the stability of the new factory regime. As the "Blum Experiment" began to flounder in the fall of 1936, prices rose, capital fled the country, unemployment lingered, and popular disillusionment deepened. In numerous public arenas, employers and financiers aggressively criticized the government's bungled economic policies, further discrediting the People's Front in business circles. Desperate to secure the good will of financial interests and improve the budgetary situation, Blum cut back on public works and adopted certain conservative monetary policies. These measures enabled his government to survive the fiscal crisis of late 1936. Nevertheless, the worsening economic situation was forcing socialists to reevaluate the liberal economic policies they had spent decades criticizing and retreat even further from the purchasing-power theories that had been at the heart of whatever strategy they had for treating the depression.

When state coffers scraped the bottom for a second time in late January 1937, Blum again had to choose between pleasing the banks, which alone possessed the funds to cover state deficits, and the unions, which demanded greater government intervention in the economy.[83] On 7 February 1937, he took to the airwaves to announce a "pause" which would "temporarily" hold off on further reforms for the sake of fiscal stability. Despite the premier's disclaimer, it was widely assumed that the pause represented a return to orthodox budgetary policies and a renouncement of new initiatives. In the words of the conservative *Le Temps:* "this was more than a pause, it was a conversion."[84]

Blum's left and labor allies were dismayed by his announcement. Jouhaux and his fellow centrists characterized the pause as an emergency measure and critically supported it. Privately, though, they feared it beckoned a wholesale retreat. Rank-and-file militants in the shops were much less understanding and openly denounced it.[85] The *Syndicats* group believed the government's return to liberal orthodoxy was proof that "distributional reforms [i.e., the June gains] were impossible without structural reforms," and criticized Blum for abandoning rather than strengthening economic controls.[86] For communists, already angered by Blum's Spanish policy, the pause was a "sell-out" to the "big trusts" and a "betrayal" of the People's Front; only for the sake of anti-fascist unity did they grudgingly accepted it.

While the pause helped the government shore up its shaky finances, it did little to improve the general political situation, which continued to veer from bad to worse. Alienated by the government's rightward drift, sections of the left began to distance themselves from the People's Front. At the end of February 1937, Marceau Pivert, influential leader of the SFIO's Paris Federation, resigned his government post to protest "Blum's submission to the banks." The large revolutionary minority in the SFIO which saw Pivert as its spokesman now contemplated a split. As it did, the socialist left became increasingly fractious, pushing its trade-union supporters toward radical actions. At the same time, communists intensified their invective against the premier, criticizing his concessions to the "200 families" and his failure to abide by the spirit of the People's Front.

The failings of the left alliance had an especially deleterious effect on labor unity. As noted above, the autumn of 1936 saw the formation of the Amicales Socialistes and the *Syndicats* group. After the announcement of the pause in February 1937, several hundred anarchist and Trotskyist unionists, along with some disillusioned ex-communists, such as Gustave Galopin, formed the Cercle Syndicaliste "Lutte de Classes" to resist the "collaborationist" policies of both

Jouhaux and Frachon, who, they claimed, threatened to incorporate the labor movement in the bourgeois state. Comprising some of the most experienced and respected unionists in the Paris metal industry, these revolutionary militants advocated "a class-struggle defense" of the June reforms and a break with the left alliance.[87] The formation of the Cercle Syndicaliste, along with the ongoing activities of the Amicales and the *Syndicats* group, now added another chink to the consensus that had brought rival union factions together in March 1936, heightening the prospect of fratricidal strife.

As oppositionists started making inroads in the factory, communists took measures to silence them, prevent their newspapers from being sold, and annul their resolutions—all of which were done in the name of keeping politics out of the union.[88] Despite their efforts, however, pressure for a change of line kept reemerging.[89] The inflationary erosion of wage gains (estimated at between 15 percent and 25 percent), combined with rank-and-file discontent, employer attacks, and the government's increasingly conservative policies, locked labor relations into a spiraling cycle of strife. In heading off strikes, which they characterized as employer maneuvers designed to discredit the People's Front, communists nonetheless failed to prevent lock-outs and occupations from occurring at J. J. Carnard in Boulogne, Chausson in Asnières, Fiat (SIMCA) in Nanterre, and Société d'Outillage in Val d'Or.[90] In late February 1937, additional conflicts broke out in a number of other Paris plants.[91] In all these disputes, the politically motivated union leadership refused to mobilize the *métallos* in a direct counteroffensive.

In this troubled period, the anti-republican right made another fateful appearance. Although the "fascist" leagues had been outlawed after the elections, they continued to exert a forceful influence over French political life. The Croix de Feu, the largest and most influential of the leagues, had, for example, circumvented the government's prohibition by transforming itself into a political party. With a membership of 600,000 (twice the size of the PCF), the new Parti Social Français (PSF) almost immediately became a major player in the political system, although as a parliamentary force it did not constitute the same kind of danger as the street-mobilizing leagues. Nonetheless, it continued to disturb the routines of the liberal polity. Shortly after the announcement of the pause, the PSF organized a series of meetings in the Paris Red Belt which further strained the already tense situation. On 17 February in Montreuil and on 21 February in Suresnes, violent clashes broke out between anti-fascists intent on breaking up the PSF meetings and the police, charged with maintaining order. Communists feared these clashes might embarrass the government and tried to avoid violence, but they also hoped the protests would divert the labor movement from the intractable problems besetting it in the factories.

Anti-fascism, however, had lost much of its potential for recuperation at this point and become something of a liability.[92] When the so-called *fachos* of the PSF announced a meeting to be held in the suburban town of Clichy, socialists and communists responded by organizing a mass counter-demonstration. But instead of shoring up the People's Front, this counter-demonstration would sound its death knell. On the night of 16 March, a loud, angry crowd of 10,000 anti-fascists gathered in Clichy's main square to "greet" the PSF'ers encroaching on this working-class bastion of the left. Between the "fascists" assembled in a local movie theater and the anti-fascists massed outside, a thousand police and *gardes mobiles* attempted to keep the peace. Soon rocks began to fly and barricades were raised. By evening's end, after hundreds of shots had been exchanged, six workers and two policemen lay dead and two hundred others wounded. Whether the murderous riot was ignited by an agent provocateur—the PCF pointed to a tobacco merchant associated with the PSF—or (more likely) by unruly demonstrators escaping the control of the left organizations, Paris streets were again filled with blood, this time spilt by the police of the left government.[93] Contrary to the intentions of the top PCF leadership, which had sought to channel social conflicts into innocuous anti-fascist demonstrations, "the bloody night of Clichy" immediately widened the chasm between the People's Front and its working-class constituency.[94]

As news of the Clichy killings spread through the metal-working districts on the following morning, factories were turned topsy-turvy with agitation. Wildcat strikes, occupations, confrontations with management, and fisticuffs with suspected "fascists" spontaneously broke out, disrupting the flow of production in numerous plants.[95] To the angry workers carrying out these actions, the Clichy murders seemed to parallel what they were experiencing in the factories, confirming their suspicion that the People's Front was distancing itself from the needs and interests of the labor movement.[96] Symptomatic of these growing anti-government sentiments, the Pivertist wing of the SFIO placarded Paris walls with posters accusing Blum of using the killings to implement the policies of the trusts and banks.[97] In a similar vein, Trotskyists characterized the ripostes of the 17th as "an immense protest against Blum's policy of capitulation."[98] More seriously, the Clichy killings again blurred the line between corporate and state concerns, confusing issues of industrial relations with those of the political system.

A wave of local demonstrations accompanied the spontaneous strikes and agitation on the 17th. At Boulogne-Billancourt, 40,000 attended a union meeting in the town's main square; 15,000 assembled outside Citroen in Paris, 5,000 in Gennevilliers, 6,000 in Issy-les-Moulineaux, and 3,000 in Argentreuil. Numerous smaller rallies and demonstrations, some spontaneous, most called by the CGT or the PCF, took place in nearly every metal-working town of the Paris Region.[99] At these demonstrations, a single worker voice demanded a riposte to the killings, and in some cases, the resignation of the socialist interior minister, Marx Dormoy.

Overwhelmed by these outbursts of popular rage, the union strained to prevent workers from disrupting the factories. The local demonstrations had, in fact, been called to vent this rage. Yet fearing the People's Front might fall victim to popular retribution, PCF and CGT leaders looked for more consequential outlets. In characterizing the shootings as a plot by the big trusts to discredit the government, *L'Humanité* sought to focus public attention on its campaign to purge "reactionary elements" from the police and state bureaucracy. At the same time, communist deputies in the chamber denounced the PSF and called for the arrest of its leaders. The most serious effort to defuse the situation came, though, when the CGT's Commission Administrative announced a half-day general strike to protest the killings. This proposed strike immediately alarmed the government. When Blum got word of it, he threatened to resign if it was not called off. Although union leaders were eventually able to convince him that the strike was needed to deflect the workers' rage, this did little to lessen the sting of the scheduled protest. He then petulantly ordered a crackdown on Trotskyists and anarchists accused of instigating the Clichy tragedy.[100]

The CGT's half-day general strike of 18 March was total. From seven in the morning, the great factories were still and the principal squares of the suburbs "black with demonstrators," but this hardly dissipated their rage. At noon, when the strike was scheduled to end, many refused to return to work. Outside the gates of Renault, Citroen, and elsewhere, as acrimonious debates broke out over whether the half-day strike should be respected or extended to the whole day, union delegates pleaded for discipline and angry workers insisted on more consequential actions.[101] In this situation, the union and the PCF strained to control its ranks. One old communist in the eighteenth *arrondissement* is reputed to have said: "They massacre the workers, they let revolutionary Spain perish, and it's *L'Humanité* and the party that makes us swallow it all."[102]

On the evening of 18 March, mass demonstrations were again held throughout the suburbs: 20,000 gathered in Saint-Denis, 15,000 in Clichy, 15,000 in Colombes, 12,000 in Saint-Ouen, 7,000 in Nanterre, 18,000 in Gennevilliers, 10,000 in the tenth *arrondissement*, and many smaller ones.[103] The PCF and the metal union once more used these demonstrations to vent popular rage, but at this point many workers began turning a deaf ear to communist appeals. Three days later, the five workers killed at Clichy were buried. Over a million people attended the funeral cortege, making it one of the largest demonstrations in French history. As the "people of Paris" buried their dead, the People's Front, once a symbol of hope, began to lose its luster. This disillusionment would grow even greater, as the political imperatives of the left alliance continued to clash with the social aims of the labor movement.[104]

Once the slain workers were in their graves, another wave of ripostes swept across the Paris metal industry. At Chausson, Laffy, SAGEM, Continentale des Compteurs, Bourget, Geoffroy-Delore, and elsewhere, protests turned violent.[105] Workers in these plants lashed out at those deemed responsible for the killings, beating up and purging anyone who lacked the patina of anti-fascist fidelity. The victims of these ripostes, it is significant to note, were less often "fascists" than non-conformists—Catholics, conservatives, and others unaffiliated with the CGT, the PCF, or the People's Front. The we/they mentality of the CGT ranks, exacerbated by the emotional context of the killings, precluded such distinctions—they were all denounced as enemies of the people, responsible for the erosion of union rights on the shop floor and the spilling of worker blood in the streets.[106]

The End of the Blum Experiment

Encouraged by the ineptitude of Blum's government and the self-restraint of the metal union, employers stepped up their attacks on the contractual regime. Lock-outs were the preferred method, but the firing of militants, the refusal to hire unionists, non-respect of the contract and the forty-hour week, and other means were also used to diminish union power in the plants. These assaults were accompanied by a press campaign aimed at discrediting the metal union and exploiting the growing middle-class impatience with labor unrest. Secret CGPF documents obtained by the union revealed that Gignoux was orchestrating an industry-wide offensive to undermine the metal union and defame the government.[107] In plants locked-out since Clichy (Continentale, Geoffroy-Delore, Chausson, J. J. Chanard, Société d'Outillage) and in plants locked-out subsequently (Néoton, Jouet, Bennes-Pillot, Forges de Commentry, Electro-Méchanique), managers consistently avoided a settlement in order to weary the public and wear down the ranks. Even in cases where government arbitrators rendered decisions to resolve these conflicts, employers refused to apply them. On several occasions, labor leaders threatened a general strike to force employer compliance, but their concern for the instability of Blum's government mitigated every threat.[108] The *Syndicats* group now called on labor to defend its interests irrespective of governmental imperatives.[109]

In April, labor leaders decided to break the seemingly endless cycle of strife by pushing for a national metal contract.[110] The regional contracts signed in June 1936 were due to expire in May 1937. A national contract, it was hoped, would bring the state into the factories and restrain intransigent employers. The union also thought a national contract would lead to a regulated system of hiring and firing, a sliding scale of wages, and laws to enforce arbitrated sentences. The UIMM, however, refused to consider any of these demands and contract negotiations quickly broke down. Because neither side was able to work out at a compromise, the government was compelled to intervene and prorogue the existing contract. This, however, did little to resolve the underlying differences separating labor and management.

Throughout the spring of 1937, the metal union kept up its agitation for a national contract and the *patrons* just as consistently resisted it. As contract talks again stalled, the union looked to the government to break the impasse, but its hopes of governmental intervention were wearing increasingly thin. After a year in office, Blum had overspent his moral capital, failed to engineer an economic recovery or create a climate of confidence, and done nothing to heal the wounds on the body politic. Moreover, capital remained scarce, deficits continued to mount, "the bloody night of Clichy" panicked financial markets, and Blum's standing in the business community continued to decline. At this point, the conservative wing of the Radicals prepared to bring down his government. When the premier faced another fiscal crisis in June, he turned to the Radical-dominated Senate—"the symbol of the egoistic oligarchies"—for special decree powers to stave off insolvency. When these powers were refused, he felt obliged to resign.[111] With this, the first French experiment in socialist rule, begun with such hope and optimism in the summer of 1936, came to an anticlimactic halt.[112] Although Blum's fall was widely seen as a conservative victory—part of "a planned offensive of the banks and big capital"—and although the PCF had called on him to hold his ground against the "reactionary Senate," his resignation provoked hardly a protest in the factories, sign of the disillusionment that had begun to take hold of the Paris working class.

The government's collapse did not formally terminate the left coalition. It would take nearly another year for the parties in the chamber to dissolve the existing system of alliances and form another. In the meantime, the Radicals, led by Blum's fellow Mason, Camille Chautemps, were called on to form a second People's Front government. Because Chautemps's cabinet contained many of the socialists who had served under Blum and had Blum as its vice-president, it did not look that different from the previous government. But the spirit of the People's Front, as the embodiment of popular aspirations and a new current in French politics, had clearly died with its installation. As Radicals reoccupied the heights of the French political system, it was commonly assumed that they would restore "orthodoxy" to French affairs and retreat from the positions occupied by Blum.[113]

Following the change in government, factional tensions mounted, as communist and non-communist unionists clashed in defining labor's relation to the new government. After declaring that Chautemps, a professional politician with all the vices of his ilk, did not inspire the same confidence as Blum, Jouhaux sent out a circular in July condemning the divisive intrigues fostered by these internecine struggles.[114] Then, at a meeting of the CGT Comité National in August 1937, the opposed factions openly squared off in what was taken as a potentially schismatic confrontation. The ex-confederals affiliated with Belin's *Syndicats* group aggressively criticized communists for subordinating the CGT to the People's Front and failing to safeguard the June reforms. They proposed a new course for the labor movement: "The government is powerless to defend the working class, it's [now] up to us to defend ourselves." Labor, in other words, had to separate itself from the left parties, put its own priorities foremost, and stage a resolute defense of the Matignon system, regardless of the political repercussions. They also called for an end to communist "colonization" and a revival of the CGT Plan.[115] With equal conviction, communists rebuffed the *Syndicats* supporters, asserting that Blum's failures and the on-going difficulties of the labor movement followed from an insufficient application of the People's Front Program, not a failure of the People's Front per se. If labor were to withdraw from the left alliance, they warned the right would assume power and carry out a wholesale retraction of the June reforms. Certain tactical concessions, they acknowledged, might be needed to appease the Radicals, but any retreat from the People's Front would spell almost certain disaster for the labor movement. They thus urged workers to do nothing that might weaken the present government or dissolve the left alliance. On this contentious point—whether the unions should maintain their ties with the People's Front or go their separate way—it was impossible to reach an accord. Centrists around Jouhaux now struggled to hold things together, but the specter of schism had fallen over the CGT, as ideological differences began to overshadow workshop concerns and the labor movement divided along political lines.[116]

Undercurrents of Civil War

During the fall of 1937, as the new Chautemps government considered a variety of measures to modify the social legislation of June 1936, metal *patrons* stepped up their anti-union offensive, chipping away at bigger and bigger sections of the Matignon Accords. The layoff—sometimes for genuine seasonal adjustment, sometimes because of disruptions in the economy, but most often as a means of ridding the plants of "troublemakers" and restoring discipline— was the most frequently used weapon in this offensive. The Metal Federation estimated that two-thirds of the labor conflicts in this period were due to abusive layoffs and firings.[117] Shorter hours, wage cuts, lower piece-rates, neglect of seniority, a selective interpretation of the contract, the victimization of stewards and delegates, and other methods were also employed to circumvent the June reforms or undermine union influence on the shop floor.[118] In addition, *patrons* started forming company unions or encouraging the PSF and other right-wing groups to organize in their plants. Caught between its contradictory obligations to the ranks and the ailing People's Front, the union again disappointed its membership. In the name of maintaining the social peace and preserving the left government, which it designated as labor's highest priority, the union refused to wage a concerted counterattack. In doing so, it kept hoping that state intervention would somehow come to its rescue.[119] Yet by looking to the state and discouraging direct actions, the union, as one oppositionist put it, ended up "chloroforming" workers in the shops.[120]

This abstentionism further widened the gulf between the leaders and the led. Although the PCF's vast network of factory cells and its control of the *sections syndicales* meant that communists were in little danger of losing control of the union apparatus, they were beginning to lose support in the ranks. By the summer of 1937, as they became a force for restrain and retraction rather than for struggle and reform, the far-left Cercle Syndicaliste "Lutte de Classes," left-wing socialists in the Amicales, and the anti-communist *Syndicats* group began to attract new adherents and serve as tribunes for the mounting discontent in the ranks. Right-wing unionists in the Catholic CFTC and in the PSF's Syndicats Professionnel Français, although less conspicuously, also attracted new members.

While policing the ranks and suppressing conflicts, union leaders nonetheless sought to defend wage rates whose erosion was the most pressing grievance of all. In mid-June, prior to Blum's fall, the metal union had submitted a third request for an adjustment, this time for a 10 percent raise. By August, the demand grew to 12 percent and somewhat later to 15 percent. It took three months for the union request to work its way through the arbitration process and another month before arbitrators actually considered it. By mid-October 1937, both the leadership and the ranks had lost patience with the slow pace of arbitration. Every union meeting in this period produced a resolution critical of it. Finally, on 16 October, a conference of 2,500 secretaries from the industry's *sections syndicales* voted a resolution threatening "mass action" if an arbitrated sentence was not forthcoming.[121] This brought immediate, though disappointing results. The arbitrated sentence of 23 October granted not the requested 15 percent but only a 6 percent wage raise. This set off another wave of agitation, culminating in a rank-and-file demand for a twenty-four-hour general strike. The leadership was quick to embrace the strike demand in order to vent the mounting anger, but within a week it managed to approve the arbitrated sentence, reduce the general-strike proposal to a one-hour symbolic protest, and then associate the protest with the party's campaign to lift the Spanish embargo.[122] Once again political considerations prevailed. A general strike at this juncture would almost certainly have driven a wedge between the Radicals, who were preparing their annual congress, and the CGT. If the anti-fascist alliance was to be maintained and the People's Front preserved, the metal union was obliged to backpedal on the general strike and keep the factories calm.

The one-hour workstoppage of 10 November 1937 was observed by 95 percent of the *métallos* and hailed by the union as a *belle victoire*.[123] Reports from Catholic metal workers, however, offered a less sanguine view, suggesting that workers had little interest in the symbolic protest, participating in it only after being pressured by the *sections syndicales*.[124] The strike, moreover, did nothing to change the arbitrator's mind and was followed by punitive lock-outs and the firing of an estimated 400 *métallos*.[125] To add insult to injury, the leadership refused to defend the victimized strikers. Reports difficult to verify, but suggestive, reveal that many workers had now stopped purchasing their monthly union stamp and become openly critical of the union's indecision.[126]

This was not the end of the union's problems, however. Since late 1936, employers had waged an unrelenting campaign against the People's Front's social legislation in an attempt to win public approval for its retraction. In one typical example of this campaign, the CGPF placarded Paris with a large, red-colored poster that rhetorically asked: "Who is responsible for devouring billions in taxes? Workers and their high wages! Who is responsible for our lack of airplanes and armaments? Workers and their forty hours!"[127] National and international developments now lent an ominous dimension to these attacks. The ongoing war in Spain, along with German rearmament, was turning metal production, especially in the defense-related sector of the industry, into a political concern of the highest order. In the name of national defense, criticism was increasingly directed against the negative effects of the June reforms. Every union demand raised in this period was stridently countered by government and business demands for a modification of the forty-hour week. Union leaders publicly vowed to uphold the integrity of the shorter work week.[128] But like the wage question, they walked a tightrope on this issue. They realized the ranks were committed to what was considered the crowning achievement of the June strikes and determined to safeguard it; they thus continued to pay it lip service. Because their highest priority remained the People's Front and the party's anti-fascist crusade, it was not at all clear, however, if, in the name of national unity, they would not yield one and then another of the June reforms.

The *métallos* were not the only section of the labor movement troubled by the duplicity of their leaders. In the final month of 1937, labor strife was rife in all trades. Chautemps's coolness to the CGT had invited further employer assaults, provoking, in turn, numerous counter-assaults—usually without union sanction. At the end of 1937, Paris labor relations were in a state of turmoil, riled by "agitation, rumors, and an undercurrent of civil war."[129] In Colombes, this tense situation nearly turned bloody when 30,000 metal workers (against the wishes of their union leaders) rushed to defend rubber workers occupying a Goodrich tire factory that the government had surrounded with police and threatened to evacuate.[130] A violent confrontation was only narrowly avoided. The Goodrich dispute was no sooner settled than subway, bus, and truck drivers struck, followed by water, gas, and electricity workers. In the absence of resolute leadership, formerly quiescent sections of the working class began turning to direct action.[131] These public-service strikes were quickly resolved, but they shook the government to its foundations. Chautemps, who attributed the workstoppages to the PCF, lashed out at the entire Marxist left, reshuffled his cabinet, dismissed his socialist ministers, and antagonized communist deputies, who ceased supporting his government.

This had a particularly dampening effect on the Paris metal industry. Although the contract was now six months overdue, metal producers continued to stall. Trotskyists, left socialists, anarchists, and revolutionary syndicalists again raised their voices to denounce the leadership's inertia and demand some sort of action to break the deadlock. Union leaders, however, simply redoubled their appeals to the state. Finally, after the expiration of the prorogued contract on 31 December 1937, the government intervened to set up talks at the Labor Ministry, but they broke down almost immediately. Rather than impose a definitive settlement, the government once more prorogued the existing contract.[132]

In the opening months of 1938, as the Paris metal industry headed for a major showdown, the CGT continued to look to the state for a solution to its problems, but faced with disorder in the general economy and mounting dissension in the chamber, Chautemps's government had to contend with more serious problems. Then on 10 March 1938, with the employers and the metal union still at loggerheads, the premier unexpectedly submitted his resignation. As he did, it looked as if the People's Front and all it had achieved in the field of industrial relations might also collapse.

Between the Hammer and the Anvil

CHAUTEMPS'S FALL DID NOT QUITE FINISH OFF THE LEFT coalition. Following his resignation, the republic's president called on Blum to form another People's Front government. No one expected it to survive, but it was necessary to invoke in order to dispel further socialist claims to rule. While Blum was designating his cabinet, Hitler sent his army into Austria, annexing it to the Reich. This was the first armed invasion since the end of the Great War and it immediately evoked visions of marching columns and droning airplanes. It also signaled the end of the state system created by the 1919 Versailles settlement and implicitly challenged France's European hegemony. Henceforth, the highest priority of the French state would be to rearm and reposition itself in an international order imperiling its security. Yet in shifting its attention from social reform to national defense, the state automatically threatened its fragile alliance with labor.

The War Psychosis

For two years, French political life had centered on questions of domestic reform.[1] Whatever attention foreign policy had gotten was filtered through dreamy pacifist schemes of international arbitration or, in the case of Spain, non-intervention.[2] After the Austrian *Anschluss* and Germany's restoration as the dominant power in Central Europe, France confronted an international situation that made guns, not butter, the single overriding priority.

To forge a common front against the looming German danger, Blum tried to form a government of National Union, made up of politicians from all sides of the chamber.[3] The parties of the right, however, refused to join a cabinet containing communists, whose loyalty, they claimed, was to the Soviet Union, not France.[4] Rightist deputies also thought Blum incapable of disciplining the working class and hence preparing an adequate mobilization. For want of an alternative, Blum reconstituted the Radical-Socialist cabinet that had accompanied him to power in 1936. He then turned to the international and military exigencies facing the French state. But as he did, he was almost immediately distracted by the social question, which refused to abate.

Throughout the ministerial crisis culminating in Chautemps's fall, the metal union had pressed for state intervention in the stalled contract talks. In early March, it threatened to strike if a new contract was not forthcoming.[5] Then, with Hitler's revision of the international order and the installation of Blum's second government, the union coupled its contractual demands to demands for a foreign policy of anti-fascist resistance.[6] If collective security against revisionist assaults on the international order were not implemented, it claimed the Western democracies could expect another retreat in the international arena and French labor a similar retreat on the shop floor.[7] By linking diplomatic normality to domestic reaction, the union acted as if social and international questions were inseparable. The propensity to mix the two had always been a part of Marxist ideology, but beginning in March 1938, as a resurgent Germany sent fears through Soviet officialdom, this mix became a systematic feature of communist labor policy, reducing all social questions to matters of international relations.

Immediately following the *Anschluss*, the Nationalist forces under General Franco launched an offensive on the Aragon front that marked the beginning of the end for the Spanish Republic. As the international situation took another turn for the worse, the metal union joined the PCF in a series of demonstrations aimed at mobilizing public opinion for intervention in Spain and for collective security—all the while insisting that the government broker a new contract.[8] These demonstrations also demanded a government reflecting the tripartite character of the People's Front—i.e., one that would include the PCF. When Blum proposed an all-party government of National Union in which they would have a role to play, communists had rallied to it. After the right rejected his proposal, the union organized a demonstration of 20,000 *métallos* in Billancourt-Boulogne to protest the "maneuvers" that had excluded the PCF from the new government. Then, with the installation of Blum's cabinet on 13

March, unionists lobbied the premier for communist "inclusion" and a more steadfast posture on the international front.[9]

Several days later, Blum announced a massive increase in defense spending and a new financial program to pay for it. As part of his defense effort, Blum asked the metal union for a relaxation of the forty-hour law. In exchange for a tougher foreign policy, union leaders were prepared to make a deal.[10] The March issue of the *Cahiers du Bolchevisme* had called on workers to curtail their corporate demands for the sake of higher armament production. Other PCF publications and politicians had designated increased defense preparation, and, by implication, relaxed work rules as the highest priority facing the country. Communist unionists were thus willing to grant Blum's request. But to maintain their influence in the plants, they insisted on a new contract, for without one, they feared a rank-and-file rebellion in defense of the June reforms.[11] Because Blum failed to lift the Spanish embargo, take a stronger stand against Germany, or deliver a new contract, nothing came of the proposed trade-off. Nevertheless, the fact that union leaders had been willing to sacrifice the forty-hour week revealed the double game that they were then prepared to play—a double game in which trade-union interests became exchangeable for pro-Soviet policy changes.

As the communist leadership of the Paris metal union contemplated a mitigation of the June reforms, the opposition mobilized. Led by Marcel Roy of the *Syndicats* group, the opposition warned that communists were preparing the way for a *union sacrée* between the labor movement and the imperialist bourgeoisie; this, it warned, would lead to war—and war would entail the end of all existing reform.[12] Joined by oppositionists from the Amicales and the Cercle Syndicaliste, the *Syndicats* group now openly contested the leadership's association with Soviet foreign-policy objectives, rallying their forces against what they called the "war psychosis."[13]

The Second June

While the different union factions positioned themselves vis-à-vis the international situation, a wave of strikes swept across the Paris metal industry. On 23 March 1938, five days after the installation of Blum's new government, the metal union held a conference of politicians from the People's Front to document the ways in which the employers were "sabotaging" defense production. Union leaders claimed the armament sector was in disarray, that the employers were unwilling to modernize production, and that contractual violations were having a disastrous effect on the economy. While making their case, workers in twenty large metal plants staged twenty- to ninety-minute strikes in favor of a new contract and the opening of the Spanish border.[14] The next day, as protests again rippled through the industry, they assumed more consequential form. At Citroen's Javel branch, a full-scale occupation was launched. When *section* leaders went through the giant auto factory calling out the shops, they announced that the occupation was to be part of an industry-wide general strike for a wage adjustment and a new contract.[15] They made no mention of the foreign-policy issues uppermost among their concerns, nor did they give Citroen workers a chance to vote on the strike. By day's end, 20,000 workers at Citroen's seven Paris plants were barricaded in their occupied factories, supported by several hundred strikers at the Lockheed and Ferodo aviation plants in Saint-Ouen.[16]

Publicly, Paris metal leaders acted as if the strikes were purely spontaneous, resulting from worker impatience with the stalled contract talks. The employers, the Paris dailies, and the general public, however, had not the slightest doubt that the strikes were part of a larger PCF project to force Blum's government into a confrontation with Germany and open the border with Spain, even though *section* leaders had raised no political demands or made any overt reference to the international situation.[17] However political they might have been, the motivations for the strikes were nonetheless multiple. At the time of the *Anschluss,* a crucial juncture had been reached in French industrial relations. If a new contract were not forthcoming and if the Matignon system preserved, the union's very existence would have been jeopardized. Whatever the international situation, a showdown between the employers and the metal union was overdue. This showdown just happened to coincide with the PCF's need to pressure the government into a more aggressive foreign policy. The international realignment bore out the party's worse fears and communist leaders believed France had a leading role to play in containing fascist expansion in Central Europe and Spain. In such a situation, international and syndicalist concerns became inseparably mixed. This mixture, however, was extremely combustible. Given the nature of the international situation and the instability of the People's Front, neither the party nor the union was quite certain how to proceed. The factory *sections* had already been warned to avoid incidents that might undermine the new government or cause it to tilt to the right. The carefully orchestrated occupations at Citroen and the two aircraft plants were undoubtedly carried out to determine if the contractual dispute could be used to advance the party's foreign-policy objectives.

The union, though, had failed to anticipate the perilous course on which it had embarked. The strike sent a shock wave through the political system and instantly inflamed public opinion. The shutdown of the second-largest auto maker, in a period of national emergency, seemed utterly irresponsible, if not treasonous. The evidence is sparse,[18] but union leaders apparently reconsidered their action immediately after the strikes began. Once initiated, however, the strikes were difficult to call off. And because union leaders failed to move Blum closer to the PCF's foreign policy or the employers to the negotiating tables and because it would have undermined their standing in the labor movement to have simply abandoned them, they were left with little choice but to extend and enlarge them. On 25 March, the occupations at Citroen, Lockheed, and Ferodo were spread to Nieuport, Flertex, Air Liquide, SKF (Ivry), and, most importantly, to the 6,500 aviation workers at the Paris branch of Gnome-et-Rhône.[19] Within two days, 30,000 metal workers, including those at the second largest auto maker and the largest aircraft producer, were encamped in their plants. Though still relatively modest in size, the international and domestic situation automatically imbued these strikes with national significance.

Given the political factors motivating them and the hostile public reaction that followed, the leadership declined to take responsibility for the occupations and insisted they were a spontaneous response to *patronal* intransigence. This duplicity, however, only confused the strikers and weakened their resolve. When called out by their *section* leaders on 24 and 25 March, many strikers thought they were embarking on a "second June." They raised red flags over the factory gates and organized accordion concerts in their courtyards. But it was soon evident that the strikes were not another June. Hopes of beating back the employer offensive and winning a new contract were dampened by anxiety over the domestic and international situations.[20] The right-of-center *Le Matin* reported that 4,000 of the 10,000 workers at the Javel plant walked out on 24 March rather than participate in an occupation that seemed totally political and at odds with the country's most pressing concerns.[21] Strikers were also reportedly disturbed by the way in which the occupations were organized. The *sections syndicales,* under orders from the Paris office, had instigated the strikes, but the top leadership refused to take responsibility for them, give them direction, or announce a general action that might insure their success. If this were not distressing enough, the leadership failed to provide adequate food provisions, hold meetings, elect strike committees, or pay strike support.[22] Isolated in their occupied factories, in a situation demanding resolute leadership, the *métallos* were left in effect to fend for themselves.

To complicate matters, Trotskyists hoping to stage a concerted defense of the June regime intervened and tried to generalize the workstoppage. Fearful an industry wide strike would undermine the economy and weaken Blum's government, communists strenuously resisted their agitation. PCF deputies in the chamber called for their arrest and Stalinist thugs beat them back whenever they approached the factories. Their noisy agitation, however, raised numerous disturbing questions about the leadership's sincerity.[23] Even more disquieting, right-wing and fascist unionists associated with the PSF or Jacques

Doriot's Parti Populaire Français (the one significant expression of French fascism) made an unprecedented attempt to turn the strikers against their leaders—a particularly serious threat given the confusion and discontent in the ranks.[24] Doriotists and PSF'ers set up some fifty *Comités Independants* in cafés adjacent to large plants, organized a back-to-work movement based on a petition drive and factory-gate rallies, distributed several hundred thousand anti-strike leaflets in the shops, and stationed sound trucks outside occupied factories in an effort to rally the disaffected. When local CGT leaders tried to intimidate these rightists, they let their revolvers be seen and indicated their unwillingness to desist.[25] In several cases, confrontations turned violent.[26] Although they failed to halt the strike movement, the *Comités Independants* managed to break the strike in those plants where they were able to force a secret vote, which suggests the degree to which communists were beginning to deplete their credibility in worker ranks.[27] In the face of these interventions by the far right and the far left, the strikers' initial confidence and enthusiasm started giving way to doubt and uncertainty.[28] In a related vein, the local union leadership sent many strikers home and left the occupations in the hands of party militants.

Unwilling to build a self-conscious strike movement to win a new contract and force Blum into a more aggressive international stance, metal leaders nonetheless allowed strike pressure to mount.[29] This, however, was an inherently flawed strategy. Blum floundered in the face of the occupations and employers showed not the slightest sign of bending. Within days of their origin, it began to dawn on union leaders that the strikes were alienating the Radicals, antagonizing the public, and confusing the ranks.[30] If employers had offered to negotiate or presented the union with a face-saving means of ending the conflict, the strike movement almost certainly would have been brought to a halt.[31] Yet management at Citroen and other occupied plants, conscious of the union's predicament, held fast.[32] Buttressed by the CGPF and the UIMM, employers aggressively stared down the union, refusing to negotiate as long as their factories remained occupied.[33]

As the situation deteriorated, communists resorted to increasingly desperate measures. On 27 March, in a front page article in *L'Humanité*, the PCF tried to deflect public criticism by accusing the Amicales of having instigated the strikes—in effect giving up their spontaneity thesis.[34] The Amicales (whose members included a strong contingent of Trotskyists and left socialists) were indeed a force at Citroen, where they had grown in number and influence as a result of the union's passivity. But fingering them was simply a diversionary ruse to camouflage the political origins of the strikes and shift the blame onto others. Led by socialists loyal to Blum, the Amicales had not only opposed the embarrassing strikes, they actively intervened against them.[35] Moreover, it was Citroen's *section syndicale*, firmly in communist hands, which had brought the workers out.[36] By casting suspicion on the Amicales, communist union leaders rather unscrupulously sought a scapegoat for the enraged public.[37]

Following the party's attack on the Amicales, union leaders offered to evacuate the plants if Blum would arbitrate the dispute and mandate a token wage adjustment.[38] On 1 April, Blum took up their offer. To aviation workers, he proposed a 7 percent raise in exchange for a forty-five-hour week, and to auto workers, he promised a fair consideration of their demands. Presented with a face-saving means of terminating the strikes, the metal union jumped at the premier's modest offer.[39] Employers, however, refused the bait. This put the union in another quandary, again forcing it to raise the ante. On 5 April, Chausson, Caudron, Chaise, Panhard, Rosengard, and Messier were occupied. On 6 and 7 April, eight other factories joined the movement.[40] On 8 April, the strike movement grew to forty factories and 68,000 workers. Still, the employers refused to budge and, in fact, went on the offensive, aggressively attacking the strikers in a press and radio campaign that focused public attention on the political motives of the union leadership.[41] Torn by their desire to terminate the conflict and their need to appease the restive ranks, union leaders again begged Blum to impose a settlement. The premier, however, had come to the end of his tether. Faced with a conflict in the country's vital defense sector and denied plenary powers that would have allowed him to rule by emergency decree, his government was at last forced to resign (8 April).[42]

Defeat

With Blum's fall, Edouard Daladier was called on to form a cabinet—one that was expected to get things "back to normal."[43] This change of government freed the union from the need to restrain the strikers—although it still desperately sought a resolution of the conflict and was perhaps already secretly negotiating with Daladier. On the weekend of the 10th, as Daladier put the finishing touches on his ministerial arrangements, the union ordered plant delegations to approach management in a final effort to resolve the conflict.[44] It left open what would follow if the delegations came away empty handed—as everyone expected they would. For this reason, it was commonly assumed that the union was laying the basis for a general strike. At the same time, the PCF mobilized its supporters in a street demonstration demanding the opening of the Spanish border and the reinforcement of the People's Front, again emphasizing the strikes' political character.[45] Then, on Monday, the 11th, supposedly in response to management's refusal to resolve the conflict, Renault and a dozen other plants joined the strike wave. This extended the strikes to fifty-four factories and 130,000 metal workers, vastly amplifying their magnitude. Like the earlier occupations, these too were bureaucratically ordered by local union leaders, without consultation of the ranks and with little or no preparation. Again, the movement's extension seemed designed to get the government involved in brokering a settlement, force the employers to negotiate, and nudge Daladier's new government closer to the party's foreign-policy objectives.

Daladier took office on 12 April. His cabinet, composed of Radicals, not all of whom supported the left coalition, four moderate right-wing deputies, and no socialists, was technically not a People's Front government. In fact, he had now begun to distance himself from the left coalition, although he refrained from openly breaking with the parliamentary majority. The ambivalent character of his government provided, though, a necessary illusion, for it allowed all sides of the chamber to view the new formation according to their own lights. Given the deep divisions within the political system and the nature of the international crisis, it was unlikely a government could have been formed otherwise. The People's Front had nonetheless become a thing of the past, although it would take several months for this to become clear.[46] In the meantime, Daladier announced two overriding priorities for his government: resolution of the social problem in the metal industry and intensification of defense production. To address these related issues, he demanded and received special plenary powers recently denied to Blum. He then ordered troops into the capital.

With a speed suggesting closed-door bargaining, Daladier was able to resolve part of the dispute in his first day as premier. In the arbitration known as the Jacomet Sentence, aviation workers in the nationalized sector were given a 7 percent wage hike in exchange for their acceptance of a forty-five-hour week—terms identical to the ones Blum had offered on 1 April.[47] The Jacomet Sentence did not halt the movement in the rest of the industry; 150,000 Paris *métallos* in 220 plants unconnected with nationalized aviation remained out and new factories continued to join the movement. But its days were numbered, for union leaders welcomed Daladier's intervention.

On 13 April, Daladier extended the Jacomet Sentence to aviation plants in the private sector, formally terminating the aviation dimension of the metal strike. Union leaders immediately hailed the sentence as a great victory and urged workers to accept it. Their critics, though, condemned it, for it met none of their demands, compromised the June gains, and left the remaining strikers in a weaker bargaining position. Some aircraft workers actively opposed it. At Lioré-Oliver, Bloch, Gnome-et-Rhône, Potez, and other especially militant plants, workers voted down the Jacomet Sentence and defiantly continued the strike.[48] Elsewhere, union and party officials were needed to convince and, in some cases, connive workers into accepting the arbitration.[49] If the majority of aircraft workers finally agreed to the meager arbitration, it was mainly because they had lost faith in the misled strike. On 14 April, the aviation settlement was ratified, with work scheduled to resume on the 19th.

Paul Ramadier, the Radical labor minister, then asked the metal union to accept his arbitration of the remaining strikes. Without consultation of the ranks, union leaders accepted his offer, bringing the strike wave to an anticlimactic halt.[50] Over 200 occupied metal plants were then evacuated, with no reported cases of worker resistance. On 19 April, the entire Paris metal industry resumed operation. At this point, the government presented the arbitration known as the Giraud Sentence for the non-aviation sectors. This arbitration, which lacked a wage adjustment, put all metal plants connected with national defense on a forty-five-hour week.

The government-brokered settlement pleased employers, who thought its terms, especially the extension of the work week in the defense sector, heralded a more favorable work environment. For similar reasons, it upset workers. New work rules and more stringent codes of conduct had been surreptitiously slipped into the settlement and the *patronat* was authorized to dismantle significant parts of the Matignon system. The settlement also curtailed the union's freedom to function inside the plants, prohibiting or restricting *section* meetings, the posting of union announcements, the collection of dues, the distribution of union literature—rights that the union had won in 1936. Finally, the principle of the forty-hour week, the key labor reform, was severely compromised.[51]

After discovering what their leaders had agreed to, metal workers rubbed their eyes in disbelief.[52] The strike had not only put a dent in their pocketbooks, it led to the retraction of many hard-won conquests. Moreover, despite the terms of the arbitration which expressly prohibited it, there followed numerous punitive layoffs and firings. Some aviation plants even refused to pay the meager wage increase stipulated by the settlement or else lowered piece rates in violation of it.[53] Consternation was particularly sharp where the arbitration was used to victimize militants. At Gnome-et-Rhône, Nieuport, and Caudron, abusive firings were so blatant that workers spontaneously re-occupied their works.[54] Again, for political reasons, the metal union refused to defend these militants or mount a riposte in the plants. For many, this was the last straw. Disheartened or disgusted with the inept strike leadership and the disastrous settlement that followed, many workers now stopped paying their monthly dues or tore up their union cards. Somewhere between 70,000 and 80,000 *métallos*, a third of the total union membership, are estimated to have quit as a result of the strike.[55] With this massive hemorrhaging of the ranks, communist union prestige plummeted.[56] The union leadership would have had a full-scale rebellion on its hands, provoked by its political subordination of worker interests, if the disaffected *métallos* had rallied to the union opposition instead of reverting to their previous apathy.[57]

The strikes' single success was in getting the government to reopen contract talks (which might have been part of a secret deal arranged between the union and Daladier). Following the strike settlement, talks between the union and the employers were set up by the Labor Ministry and soon resulted in a new contract (30 April). For many, however, this contract was another source of grievance, for it duplicated the terms of the old agreement, addressed none of the former's inadequacies, conceded none of the union's new demands, offered a 3 percent pay raise that was significantly below the cost-of-living increase, and restricted union activities in the plants.[58] With some conviction, union leaders argued that the new contract was not so bad—considering the war danger, employer intransigence, the change of government, and declining public sympathy—but this was little consolation to the ranks. To deflect the criticism they expected from the opposition, union leaders warned of "super-revolutionaries"—*les professionnels de la révolte*—who thought "anything possible."[59] They then tried to coax the ranks into believing that the strike settlement and the new contract represented a major victory. Yet however it was framed, the lackluster agreement constituted a major setback for the *métallos*, who were now on retreat and being pushed from defeat to defeat.

Disarray

The climate of disaffection setting in after the April strikes made the mass production sector ripe for another retraction of the Matignon system. Disaffection in fact acted like the undertow of a spent wave, sucking employers into positions that the union had formerly occupied. With government sanction, employers reasserted their authority on the shop floor, restricting the areas of consultation and regulation, and, on occasion, ignoring significant provisions of the new contract. While union leaders kept a low profile, licking their wounds from the mishandled strikes, workers encountered conspicuous changes in their conditions. In the spring and summer of 1938, many plants reimposed the systems of surveillance that had existed prior to June 1936. Work rules were redefined, discipline tightened, and supervisors resumed many of their previous prerogatives.[60] More seriously, a great many stewards and *section* secretaries were fired or transferred in an effort to erode union power in the shops.[61] The metal union estimated that abusive employer dismissals were responsible for the loss of 40,000 man hours in the first two months following the April strikes.[62] Buttressed by the public's growing hostility to reform, employers also launched an aggressive campaign to recruit "fascist" and right-wing workers to fill company unions.[63] Shop-steward elections in June and July 1938 saw, as a result, a not-unexpected increase in the non–CGT vote. This did not overturn the union's virtual monopoly of steward positions, but it represented the first perceptible challenge to its hegemony.[64]

The union leadership, though, did little to shore up its crumbling base in the plants. Fearing provocations or production disruptions, it made little effort to regroup its forces, defend the besieged Matignon system, or reassert itself on the shop floor. Even in August, after Daladier threatened to suspend the forty-hour law, union leaders merely issued a platonic counter-threat which they had no intention of carrying out. Once again, political considerations demanded restraint. Communist policy remained geared to military preparedness against Germany—and this meant augmenting armament output, keeping the factories peaceful, and making more efficient use of manpower and materials. Union leaders, however, were not indifferent to declining worker morale. To mitigate the onerous implication of their productionist policies, as well as ward off employer demands for additional revisions of the Matignon system, they touted the cause of rationalization, mechanization, and technological innovation, as well as lobbied for new measures to retrain the unemployed and expand the number of skilled workers.[65] Employers, however, preferred their traditional method of speeding up assembly lines and sweating their workforce.[66]

Whenever the ranks spontaneously resisted faster-moving lines or diminished piece rates, communists preached calm and discipline. They, in fact, spent much of their energy after April policing the ranks and maintaining production levels. Those advocating a riposte to beat back the reassertion of *patronal* authority or the intensification of the labor process were routinely labeled Trotskyists, fascists, or provocateurs—which was usually enough to get them fired or ostracized. As rank-and-file militants experienced union complicity in the new work regime, they began to wonder if the union had not become more concerned with solving management's production problems than with serving as "an organ of struggle."[67] Only in the court of public opinion—in newspapers, public statements, and the conference rooms of various state ministries— did communist union leaders rally in defense of the June conquests. But, as oppositionists and shop floor militants repeatedly pointed out, it was in the plants alone, through direct action, that this defense needed to be waged.

The large number of communists in the union ranks, along with the party's control of most steward positions and *sections,* enabled the leadership to carry out its increasingly unpopular policies, but these policies did not go unchallenged. After April, oppositionists displayed a renewed vigor in contesting the leadership. In factories where communists were a minority, such as Citroen, they began to assume a role in the *sections* and even in party strongholds like Renault, they started winning steward positions. Disillusionment with the existing leadership did not, however, translate into significantly more members for the Cercle Syndicaliste, the *Syndicats* group, or the Amicales. Broadly speaking, those turning away from unionism after the failed strikes of March and April did so not as unionists disgusted with a particular leadership, but as those disillusioned with unionism per se. This was a bitter disappointment to the opposition, but it logically followed from the type of unionism established in June 1936: for once the mystique wore away—the mystique that unity would resolve the social problems of industrialism, that the People's Front was some sort of Second Coming, that the communist political project was a proper basis for unionism—the inevitable result was lassitude and lethargy.

If oppositionists failed to recruit the disaffected, communist support for national defense nonetheless continued to divide the union, augmenting the audience of the anti-communists and keeping union leaders on the defensive. To disarm their critics and defend their flank, communists now resorted to increasingly underhanded measures. Besides physical intimidation, which they were not above using, their most common method was to direct a barrage of vituperation against anyone questioning their leadership.[68] In this spirit, the PCF drew up a secret document on "provocateurs, spies, crooks, and Trotskyites," a blacklist in effect, designed to keep non-conformists and oppositionists out of the industry. If a newly hired metal worker found himself on this list, he was likely to be hounded from the factory.[69] Communist unionists also tried to isolate their critics through a process of "decentralization." By splitting up and reducing the size of the *sections syndicales*—which was done in the name of democratization—dissidents were cut off from the larger workforce.[70] The new arenas created by these decentralized *sections* were usually too small in which to stage a revolt. In factories where communists did not control the *section* and decentralization could not be carried out, other means were used. For example, at union meetings, where attendance had slipped to 10 to 20 percent of the increasingly apathetic membership, important decisions were commonly left to the very last, when only the party faithful remained in attendance. If this did not insure the party line, the factory-level leadership was appointed by the *section*'s executive committee or the Paris office and important decisions were made behind closed doors, instead of by vote, as statute designated.[71]

In such a situation, a showdown between the leadership and the opposition became inevitable. On 12 June 1938, at a meeting of the Metal Federation's Comité Nationale, it was impossible not to see the formation of two hostile blocs, although communists steeped in unity rhetoric refused to acknowledge it. It nonetheless became glaringly apparent when Marcel Roy led the opposition in attacking the union leadership for its role in the April strikes and its acceptance of the disastrous settlement. Roy criticized the CGT's subordination to governmental imperatives and called for a withdrawal from the People's Front. In urging labor to defend its interests irrespective of political considerations, Roy struck at the very foundations of communist labor policy. But the position that irked communists the most and threatened to split the union apart was the international question. Based on their integral pacifism, Roy and other oppositionists claimed France had no stake in the latent quarrel between Russia and Germany. In their view, the Versailles Treaty was at the root of the international disorder and needed to be revised. They thus opposed the aggressive foreign-policy measures that communists advocated to defend the Versailles order and instead called for an arbitrated solution to the growing international crisis.

For communists, the opposition's position was tantamount to a rejection of anti-fascism. They refused to believe that war, rather than fascism, was the principal danger menacing the labor movement. Turning the tables on the opposition, they denounced factional strife and cloaked themselves in the rhetoric of working-class unity. They then passed resolutions defending their leadership of the April strikes and their acceptance of the strike settlement—admitting in effect that they had something to be defensive about. They also passed resolutions calling for the revocation of non-intervention, a boycott of Japanese goods, firmness to the fascist powers, and maintenance of France's alliance with Czechoslovakia, now threatened by German irredentists. Oppositionists lacked the votes to defeat these resolutions, but in formally resisting them, they refused to identify trade-union interests with the imperatives of Soviet foreign policy.[72]

Munich

By the fall of 1938, the attention of most Frenchmen was directed not at the faction-ridden metal union but at the deepening crisis in Czechoslovakia. In early September, after announcing he would tolerate no further Czech assaults on the Sudeten Germans, Hitler demanded that the Czech Sudetentland be annexed to Germany. Unlike previous revisionist assaults on the Versailles state system, this one constituted a direct threat to the Western alliance—for Czechoslovakia was formally allied with France. As Hitler readied his army, Britain and France responded by mobilizing theirs. For a moment, Europe seemed to teeter on the verge of another holocaust. Only the hastily arranged Munich conference and the accords signed on 30 September managed to defuse the crisis.

Compounding the extreme social divisions tearing at the fabric of French society, new and equally divisive antagonisms now arose in contention over

Munich. For those viewing the disorders in the European state system from the perspective of anti-fascism or from the liberal Versailles settlement, the accords were a shameful betrayal; war to them seemed inevitable.[73] Most Frenchmen, however, were unwilling to consider the possibility of another massive blood-letting. The Great War, which had killed or mutilated a fifth of France's adult male population, was still too vivid in popular memory. In every area of French life, on the right and the left, at the top and the bottom of the social order, a majority of the population supported the Munich compromise.[74] Given this polarization between the supporters and opponents of the accords—between the *munichois* and *anti-munichois*—the Czech crisis served less to prepare France for the prospect of another war or the acceptance of German revisionism than to further divide her.[75] These divisions began tearing at the metal union even before the signing of the accords. Pacifists among the Amicales, the Cercle Syndicaliste, and especially in the *Syndicats* group, all of whom saw Munich as the last hope for peace, lined up against those agitating for "firmness" in the face of German expansionism (principally among communists, whose party would be the only one in parliament to reject the accords).

Prior to 30 September, as the world awaited the outcome of the Munich Conference, the PCF and its union supporters had demanded that France reject Hitler's ultimatum in support of France's Czech alliance. The party organized large demonstrations in Paris and the suburbs and the union leadership announced that aircraft and armament workers would put in extra hours for the defense effort. Then, on 30 September, after all they had worked for at the level of foreign policy was repudiated at Munich, communists launched a strident campaign against the accords, characterizing them as a scandalous betrayal of the anti-fascist front and a threat to lasting peace. The concessions made to Hitler, they predicted, would lead to a reactionary assault on the June reforms and the interests of the entire working class.[76] As the former CGTU leader Gaston Monmousseau put it: "The 'peace' of Munich has been transformed into a domestic war against the France of May and June 1936 . . . against the People's Front and the social laws, against trade-union and democratic freedoms."[77] Communists next reversed their position vis-à-vis the government's armament program. On 1 October, the Metal Federation announced it would allow no further abridgment of the forty-hour law—which it had previously tolerated in the name of national defense.[78] Any further mitigation of the social laws, it argued, would simply encourage Daladier and the anti-labor policies inherent in the "reactionary principles" accepted at Munich.[79]

While communist unionists urged firmness to Hitler in the days leading up to the Munich Accords, anti-communists took the opposite tract in arguing that an "artificial" nation like Czechoslovakia, a majority of whose population wanted it to break up, was not worth the risk of war.[80] These militants refused to identify the labor movement with either the defense of Czechoslovakia or the maintenance of the Versailles order, and instead called for a Franco-German rapprochement to preserve the peace. They also denounced unionists favoring an aggressive anti-German foreign policy as "Stalinist mercenaries"—ready "to use the labor movement to further Soviet foreign policy interests."[81] At virtually every union meeting in this period, oppositionists proposed resolutions critical of PCF efforts to resuscitate the *union sacrée*. They also took their anti-war politics into the streets. Supported by the Centre d'Action Contre la Guerre (close to the *Syndicats* group), they demonstrated against war preparations, posted the walls of Paris with placards calling for "a general mobilization for peace," and distributed a half million leaflets urging a peaceful resolution of the international crisis.[82] At the same time, they made common cause with politicians sharing their viewpoint, such as those belonging to the large pacifist wings of the Radical and Socialist parties. In seeking out these politicians and urging them to broker some sort of international conciliation, they began mixing politics and unionism—in ways they had always condemned when communists had done so.[83] That these unionists had become so engaged indicates the degree to which the internal dynamic of the metal union had become irreparably bound to the logic of the political system.

Against this background of union dissension, Daladier again applied himself to rectifying the French economy and preparing the country for war. Unlike the general public and some members of his own government, the premier believed the Munich Accords had not preserved the peace, but only temporarily averted a general conflagration. As an artilleryman in the previous war, Daladier well knew what armed conflict would entail and had no desire to sacrifice another generation of Frenchmen. But as the former defense minister and proponent of the anti-fascist line, he thought war avoidable only through an overwhelming show of force.[84] The armament sector, however, was in complete disarray. In June 1938, the production index for metal stood at 69, compared to 78 and 88 in 1936 and 1937 (100 = 1928). Every month of 1938 had witnessed an additional drop in the production index. By August, when hardly a war plane was produced, the index fell to a dismal 66.[85] These depressing figures, in Daladier's eyes, reflected the damaging effects of the on-going social contest in the metal industry and the negative legacy that had come with the reforms of the People's Front. As a step toward preparing the industrial mobilization needed to put France on a war footing, Daladier asked the Chamber of Deputies for additional plenary powers and a formal abridgment of the forty-hour law. Only a strong executive and the mitigation of the social laws, he claimed, would enable France to compete with the larger, more disciplined workforce of Nazi Germany. Once these powers were granted, he set about mobilizing the country for the possibility of war. His armament plans, however, took little account of the Paris *métallos*, who comprised the bulk of the nation's defense workers.

30 November

To stimulate economic recovery, calm the social situation, and ready France for war, Daladier's government needed to become more authoritarian—for the parliamentary system, after experiencing fifteen ministerial crises between 1932 and 1938, had clearly failed.[86] Daladier's intervention in the April strike, as well as his willingness to modify the social laws and rule by decree, constituted successive stages in the inauguration of this more authoritarian style of government. Such a course, to be sure, was unacceptable to his former coalition partners, but the People's Front at this point had become an empty shell of an alliance. Moreover, the Radical party had fallen into the hands of its anti-communist wing which was then preparing to disassociate the party from the left alliance, thereby clearing the way for Daladier's metamorphosis into the *taureau de Vaucluse,* who would rearm and rally the country. The final break with the Marxist parties came at the annual Radical congress in late October, when Daladier delivered a stridently anti-communist speech assailing the PCF's opposition to his Munich policy.[87]

After the People's Front was formally sundered, Daladier's government shifted noticeably rightward. On 1 November 1938, Paul Reynaud, a center-rightist from the Alliance Démocratique, was appointed finance minister. The appointment of Reynaud, who had opposed the People's Front from its inception, finalized Daladier's break with the two "worker parties." Reynaud would henceforth serve as the linchpin in Daladier's effort to revive the economy, put France on a war footing, and discard the social legacy of June. The anti-labor implications of Reynaud's appointment were not long in coming. On 12 November, the new finance minister addressed the French people in a national radio broadcast detailing his rearmament plan. "Do you believe," he asked the nation, "that in the Europe of today France can maintain her standard of living, spend 25 billion *francs* for armaments, and rest two days per week, all at the same time? . . . The week of two Sundays has got to cease."[88] Reynaud's message was unambiguous: national defense was incompatible with social reform.

Reynaud then issued thirty-two decree laws, which raised taxes, shifted funds from public works to armament production, provided new mechanisms to regulate industrial conflict, and, most significantly, established a six-day work week. The Reynaud decrees also gave employers the right to fire and blacklist defense workers refusing overtime or obstructing production, provided fines and imprisonment for unionists advocating resistance to the decrees, imposed new controls against foreigners and "undesirables," and freed piece rates and labor-saving mechanization from contract provisions. Because these decrees favored the *patronat* and put the burden of defense on the shoulders of the popular classes, they were viewed as a consummation of the employers' two-year project to avenge the June occupations, even though in actuality the decrees had been motivated by the war danger and the industrial imperatives of rearmament. Nonetheless, through longer hours, higher taxes, and more repressive working conditions, labor was now expected to carry the lion's share of the defense burden.[89] Workers, one historian later remarked, "could be forgiven for feeling that they, and not the Nazi regime, were the intended victims of the government's offensive."[90]

The Reynaud decrees could not have been announced at a worse time. From 14 to 17 November, the CGT's biennial congress was in session at Nantes. The decrees stunned the assembled leaders of the French labor movement and produced a reaction that might not have occurred if they had been announced just a week later.[91] Unlike the Unity Congress of 1936, the Congress of Nantes witnessed an acrimonious and divisive confrontation between the opposed factions. On several occasions, as debates over national and international issues, especially over Munich, threatened to become violent, Jouhaux resorted to words stronger than any he had previously used to warn his fellow delegates against the possibility of schism. Yet despite the internecine strife dominating the congress, all wings of the CGT stood together in opposition to the Reynaud decrees. A communist-sponsored resolution proposing a general strike to oppose them was passed by unanimous vote. Although the strike's preparation was left to a later meeting of the Commission Administrative, all the assembled CGT leaders agreed—or felt obliged to agree—that the Reynauld decrees had to be resisted. Pacifists in the *Syndicats* group, however much they differed with their rivals, were no less concerned with defending the social legacy of the People's Front and warding off what looked like a frontal assault on the entire labor movement. Revealingly, communists who denounced the decrees and characterized them as the reactionary consequence of Munich were not altogether unhappy with them. Since 30 September, they had waged a vitriolic campaign against Daladier's government, accusing it of serving the interests of British imperialists, German Nazis, and French reactionaries; their primary concern after Munich had in fact been to dispose him from power. Based on a recent parliamentary incident linking the SFIO and certain Radical deputies critical of Daladier, the PCF now hoped to bring down his government and form one based on the chamber's left-leaning majority.[92] The CGT resolution provided the ideal justification for mobilizing the labor movement against Daladier and forcing a crisis that might bring the People's Front back to power.

In the shops reaction to the Reynaud decrees was considerably more straightforward.[93] Despite employer professions to the contrary, workers had not the slightest doubt that the decrees were being used to undermine the June reforms, rather than augment defense production. In Paris and in several provincial cities, spontaneous strikes with occupations broke out every day between 21 and 24 November—involving 100,000 workers at their peak. As these protests gained momentum, numerous rank-and-file voices demanded the implementation of the general-strike proposal made at Nantes. Like the anti-communist *Syndicats* group, workers in various trades and regions who might not otherwise have supported the PCF's confrontation with the government were nonetheless willing to do so for the sake of their social conquests.[94]

Daladier, though, turned a deaf ear to their protests. The shop floor of industry, he decided, had influenced public policy long enough. On 21 November, he ordered his *prefects* to evacuate the occupied factories. In succeeding days, as additional plants went out, police resorted to their truncheons. Then, on 24 November, Renault, Citroen, Caudron, Blériot, and Bloch were occupied. The police again forcibly evacuated these plants—except Renault, where the decisive confrontation was about to occur. For several days, communist agitators outside the gates of Renault had preached against the decrees. On 22 November, a large prohibited meeting of Renault workers was violently dispersed by the police.[95] As tensions escalated in the plant, several thousand engaged in spontaneous workstoppages. Management then poured oil on the smoldering conflict by announcing that hours in the main factory would be raised from thirty-two to forty per week and spread over six days in accordance with the provisions of the Reynaud decrees—a deliberately provocative arrangement that provoked another round of strife.

As Renault workers halted production on the 24th, union officials entered the plant and urged them on. Yet once police and *gardes mobiles* arrived to evict them, union leaders had a sudden change of heart. As much as they opposed Daladier, they did not seek a frontal confrontation with the state. A violent clash, they feared, might benefit their leftist critics who were hankering for a showdown with the government or else alienate those Radical deputies with whom the PCF hoped to form a new government. They therefore advised the strikers to peacefully evacuate the plant. They had, however, underestimated the ranks' commitment to the June reforms. At this crucial juncture, as union leaders tried to exercise restraint, the ranks abandoned them. Extremist elements among the Amicales, the Cercle Syndicaliste, and dissident communists, supported by a large number of workers intent on making a last-ditch stand, now came forward to organize an occupation in a spirit considerably different from June 1936 or April 1938.[96] As they readied themselves in anticipation of the police attack, women, apprentices, and older workers were ordered out of the factory. Factory gates were then welded shut or barricaded (except two through which the police later entered the plant). Various machine parts were collected and stockpiled as projectiles. Trucks and cars were rolled into place to form barricades or block entrances. While more than 6,000 police and *gardes mobiles* were being deployed outside Renault, 10,000 to 15,000 auto workers, led by dissident militants, prepared to hold their "fortress" by force.

Between eight and one o'clock that evening, the police besieged the giant auto plant, resolved to "chuck the strikers out." Workers were no less determined to hold their ground. In barricaded workshops and behind a hail of flying metal parts, they desperately fought off the guardians of order, giving vent to the weight and edge of successive retreats. One Trotskyist *métallo* later said, "We decided to fight to the death." The "Battle of Renault," as a result, turned into one of the most violent conflicts of the period. Police freely used their clubs and resorted to tear gas, a then novel means of crowd control, while auto workers responded in kind, unleashing a barrage of steel bars, iron parts, crankshafts, and whatever else they could hurl. When the siege ended late that night, thanks largely to the gas, forty-six police lay seriously injured, twenty-two workers were in need of hospitalization, hundreds of others had been hurt, and a large part of the plant damaged. Of the 500 arrests, 283 were later charged and sentenced to jail terms. The next day, the Renault management locked out 28,000 of its workers and declared the contract null and void. Boulogne-Billancourt was then occupied by the *gardes mobiles,* the local union office was surrounded by troops, and the city took on the air of an armed camp. The government had shown it meant business; the CGT now had to decide if it was prepared to defend its social conquests.[97]

Between 22 and 25 November, the CGT national office began polling the lower-level leadership on the desirability of a general strike. The spontaneous rank-and-file resistance helped convince union leaders who had hesitantly went along with the general strike resolution at Nantes to come out in favor of its implementation. Yet no wing of the union movement, except among the revolutionaries to the left of the PCF, was prepared to wage a direct assault on the government. The Battle of Renault had demonstrated the need for some sort of riposte, but Daladier's readiness to use force also alerted them to the cost of a possibly uncontrolled protest. Even the PCF, which wanted to "chase the premier from power," was cautious in its call for action. This was evident when the Metal Federation, the first to demand a general strike, advised prudence.[98] Aware that the international and domestic situations were extremely volatile, communists hoped to avoid potentially unpredictable actions. The spontaneous strikes of 21–24 November, which escaped union control, had also alerted them to the danger of possible "incidents" that might alienate public opinion, create an opening for the far left, and undermine their leadership.

Following the Battle of Renault, the Commission Administrative met to consider the general-strike resolution. Frachon wanted the strike scheduled for Monday, 28 November, but Jouhaux, Belin, and other non-communist leaders, who thought the government might still be persuaded to moderate its decree laws, insisted on 30 November.[99] All the CGT leaders, however, conceived of the general strike in purely symbolic terms. It was thus limited to twenty-four hours, occupations were prohibited, and no street demonstrations planned. Union leaders also emphasized that the strike was to be calm, dignified, and peaceful—in effect, innocuous. Neither the communists nor the ex-confederals were willing to face down the government and "force it to submit." The logic of the People's Front, never more contradictory, precluded such a recourse.[100] With exemplary shortsightedness, the leadership acted as if it merely needed to repeat its performance of 12 February 1934 in order to reverse the decrees and bring down the government.[101] But nothing could have been more quixotic. Daladier had shown he meant business and platonic protests were obviously not the stuff to move him.[102] Moreover, by the 25th, the spontaneous strikes had begun to subside. Workers were therefore called into battle at the very moment they had begun to retreat. By not striking immediately as Frachon had urged, the government was given five days to prepare its own counter-measures. The leadership's bankruptcy was never more glaringly evident than in the *folie de grandeur* it planned for 30 November.

In Daladier's eyes, the spontaneous strikes opposing the Reynaud decrees had been part of a larger communist scheme to break the Munich Accords. That the Renault conflict occurred the night British Prime Minister Neville Chamberlain was in Paris to discuss peace did not appear coincidental to him. Believing the Comintern was bent on reversing his government, Daladier now dug in his heels.[103] His newfound allies on the right encouraged him in this. During the Renault occupation, Reynauld told him: "If we let the country slide into the troubles of '36 again, if the Renault factory is not evacuated tonight, my experiment is over."[104] Such sentiments would shape his response to the general strike. But what he and other politicians erred in assuming was that resistance to the decrees had been orchestrated to serve Soviet foreign-policy interests. Worker defense of the June reforms had only incidentally coincided with the PCF's international commitments.

In the days following the Commission Administrative's announcement, Daladier prepared the government's resistance. Using his decree powers, he requisitioned railroad workers, miners, and public-service workers. He ordered his *prefects* to threaten immigrants with deportation if they should observe the forthcoming strike. He called troops and *gardes mobiles* into Paris and other industrial centers. Then, in a radio speech on 27 November, he dismissed the CGT's contention that the general strike had been called to defend the social laws. This, he claimed, was an "absurd pretext," for there were no justifiable corporate reason for the strike, which he described as a form of blackmail against his "peace policy." After calling the announced strike a detriment to "the life of the nation," he vowed to uphold "republican law."[105] This was no bluff. With public service and transport workers under military requisition and the army alerted for possible intervention, Daladier was prepared to confront labor with considerably more resolve than he had shown in his recent encounter with Hitler.

On the eve of the general strike, the government began deploying troops throughout the capital, commandeering key intersections and boulevards, and occupying train stations, bus depots, and subways. This show of force could not but intimidate potential strikers. Then, on the morning of the 30th, Daladier activated his preventative measures. The army was mobilized to insure the normal operation of public transport, eliminating one of the most persuasive features of a general strike. Water, gas, and electricity, also under military requisition, were likewise furnished without interruption. Police, stationed throughout the industrial districts and around most large plants, controlled the streets. Finally, the state-controlled radio reported the strike in disparaging terms, discouraging many would-be strikers. So successful were these measures that only the keen-eyed Parisian was able to detect the strike's effect in the capital.

Technically, though, the strike was not a failure, especially in the suburbs. Although police and troops had been deployed throughout the Red Belt, CGT pickets succeeded in shutting down most large factories. In at least a half-dozen suburban towns, violent confrontations broke out between pickets and the police, but this did little to erode strike solidarity. The industrial federations making up the great battalions of June 1936, by and large, kept faith with the CGT and honored the strike order—although the turnout was not quite as overwhelming as union leaders had hoped. In metal, the federation estimated a 90 percent observance, but 75 percent for the Paris Region and 70 percent for the rest of French metal were probably closer to the mark.[106] Strikers in other industries and trades ranged from 40 to 65 percent. This again put the *métallos* in the vanguard of the strike movement. But it was to no avail. The protest had been waged at the symbolic level and here the unions were thoroughly outmatched by the government, which not only repressed the most important aspects of the strike and blunted its economic effects, but shaped the public's perception of it. With some justice, Daladier was able to call the general strike "a total defeat."

Revenge of the *Patronat*

The CGT's miscarried attempt to dislodge the government and reverse its anti-labor decrees gave the employers a free hand in exacting revenge.[107] As the government stood shoulder to shoulder with the *patronat*, that revenge followed hard at heel.[108] Mass firings, recommended by the CGPF, were the first line of retribution. In plants where a majority of workers had struck, employers locked-out their entire workforce; in plants where only a minority observed the strike, strikers alone were victimized. The extent of these lockouts was unprecedented. The labor minister estimated that 800,000 French workers (9 percent of the entire working class) were temporarily or permanently locked out after 30 November. The CGT claimed 500,000 of these were *métallos*.[109] In the Paris Region, forty large-scale metal factories locked out the entirety and twenty dismissed the majority of their workforce. In nearly all cases, union secretaries and shop stewards were hit hardest by the firings, for employers lost no opportunity in ridding their plants of "troublemakers." The government repression was equally severe.[110] In nationalized armament plants, as well as in public sector jobs, the government fired or penalized all who had participated in the strike. The government also sent its troops into Boulogne-Billancourt and other metal-working towns to insure order and prevent the outbreak of spontaneous demonstrations. Finally, 500 strikers in the Paris Region (1,000 according to the CGT) were arrested and sentenced to short prison terms for their part in the strike.[111]

Because the government declared the strike politically motivated and thus not a genuine corporate conflict, employers were authorized to annul union contracts. When locked-out workers presented themselves for rehire, they were placed under a different contract, often without their former seniority, vacation time, or right to elect stewards; some had their jobs redefined or were reassigned to more demanding tasks. At Renault, 28,000 workers were rehired in three days, 60 percent of them under a contract that lacked significant provisions of the old one. But the worst aspect of the repression remained the victimization. Guy Bourdé, in his study of the general strike, characterizes the employer repression as falling into the following stages. Initially, from 1 to 10 December, the lockouts were general, involving massive sectors of the entire workforce. This was followed by a second stage, from mid-December to mid-January 1939, when victimized strikers were slowly allowed back under new contract.[112] At the end of this stage, only a few thousand metal workers, mainly shop stewards and union secretaries, had yet to be rehired, but these militants would remain unemployed throughout the winter of 1939; only with the enormous increase of defense production in the months preceding the Second World War were they finally reintegrated into the workforce.[113]

The repression had a devastating effect on the metal union. With *section* leaders and stewards driven from the factories and the government mobilizing its police and courts against them, the *métallos* took cognizance of the new power relations and sank into a kind of stupor.[114] It was not long before social relations in the Paris metal industry reverted back to their pre-June condition. At the same time, union leaders were shut out of the higher institutional chambers of the state and the various consultative bodies in which they had previously participated. Lacking power in the plants and denied institutional access, the union's single remaining option after the 30th was to beg employers to respect contractual relations, which they now had no incentive to do. To compound matters, union membership experienced a massive hemorrhage, dropping another 25 to 30 percent.[115] These losses were followed by a sharp rise in worker apathy, the virtual cessation of workshop conflict, and the unchallenged imposition of managerial authority. At this point, our history comes full circle, for the Paris metal union, the largest and most important of all French unions, virtually overnight ceased to be a factor in French national life.

The Demobilization of the Labor Movement

In one of the last works of his life, the eminent historian and essayist Daniel Halévy wrote that on 30 November 1938 all Europe waited to see if there were still a state in France.[116] In Halévy's view, the general strike was a contest of wills to determine who would control the nation's destiny: labor agitators in the factories or elected representatives in the Palais Bourbon. The strike's real stakes, in other words, were not over the decree laws or the Munich Accords, but over who would determine France's future. From Halévy's perspective, Daladier's victory on 30 November and the subsequent restoration of the old factory regime represented the triumph of liberal democracy over the labor movement, and thus the curtailment of union power in the production process and in the institutions of industrial society.

As the political system adjusted to labor's crushing defeat, Daladier and his Radical party realigned themselves with various right parties to form a government of National Union. Given the nature of the recent social confrontation, this realignment was entirely pillared on anti-communism, which had taken hold not only of the government but also of the public. As 432 French newspapers campaigned for the PCF's interdiction, Daladier's new coalition refused to forgive the CGT for the general strike and proceeded to eradicate the legislative record of the People's Front. This boded ill for the labor movement. Even the timid Radical governments of the previous year and a half had governed in consultation with the unions and respected the social legacy of June. But now, as the CGT was shut out of the higher institutional chambers of the state and the political system repositioned itself along anti-communist lines, the labor movement was to suffer the full brunt of its political affiliations.

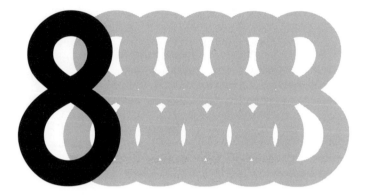

The Battle for the War Factories

THE FAILED STRIKE OF 30 NOVEMBER 1938 TERMINATED the period of labor activism opened by the general strike of 12 February 1934. The republican mobilizations following the first strike had created many new arenas for the unions and given them a powerful means of mobilizing workers; the successful occupations of June 1936 and the social legislation of the People's Front then turned them into a force of national significance. Yet their corporate interests were no sooner institutionalized than they began to collide with the altered exigencies of the left alliance. This collision reached its crescendo on 30 November. After that, the unions faced a hostile political system and a *patronat* intent on revenge. Union membership henceforth dwindled, union meetings and activities nearly ceased, and the CGT was locked out of the inner chambers of the state. The worst, though, was still to come.

National Defense

Even after its crushing defeat in the general strike, the metal union remained torn between its divided commitments to rank-and-file interests and national defense. Because each new month brought a worsening of the international situation and an enhanced need to augment armament production, national defense tended to prevail. For the sake of French preparedness, the union willingly tolerated longer hours, speed-ups, and deteriorated conditions—and not simply because it lacked the power to challenge the *patronat* in the plants.[1] Then, in March 1939, after Hitler occupied the rump of Czechoslovakia and the British abandoned their peace policy, French defense efforts shifted into high gear. At this point, as storm clouds gathered on the horizon, Daladier introduced a series of decrees that made all metal works part of the national-defense system and subject to a sixty-hour week.[2] These decrees had an extremely curative effect on the economy. In the six months following the general strike, metal production climbed 21 percent, and the production index, for the first time since the advent of the depression, regained its 1928 level. Although the cost of living continued to mount, longer hours meant higher wages and bigger take-home packets.[3] It also improved the labor market, creating new employment opportunities. The economic upturn, however, came at a cost. With six-day weeks, ten-hour shifts, lines running at higher speeds, and additional decrees enhancing the employers' disciplinary powers, workers faced not merely a restoration but an intensification of the old factory regime.[4] Subsequent decrees authorized penalties for refusing overtime, preventing technological innovation, and obstructing industrial reorganization. In most plants, the stopwatch engineer reappeared. Foremen and section managers reasserted their former unchallenged supervision of the shop floor. Work rules and employment policies were reformulated to reflect the new relations of power. Only the tightness of the job market, which enhanced the bargaining power of skilled workers, prevented a complete restoration of the old regime. But every increase in the defense effort seemed to come at worker expense. Given their recent defeat and the reversal of power relations in the plants, they had little choice but to accept their worsening lot. Their acquiescence, however, was not solely the result of the forces arrayed against them. With longer hours and a good deal of overtime pay, skilled workers were now earning more than a thousand *francs* a week—a sum greater than what many civil servants and shopkeepers took home.[5] For younger workers, unfamiliar with the boom years of the 1920s, these rates were without precedent. Bigger pay checks, combined with longer hours and employer hegemony, helped, as a result, mute whatever grievance they may have had against the new factory regime.

Union leaders were also a force for acquiescence. They disagreed with management and government over how production ought to be organized and who should bear the brunt of the new burdens, but they wholeheartedly supported the defense effort. In this spirit, they criticized employers for sweating workers rather than spending money to modernize equipment and rationalize production processes. They also charged the government with being "class-biased" in giving *carte blanche* to the industrialists. In favoring a well-armed France, however, they studiously avoided actions that might have disrupted production. Again, foreign-policy considerations took precedent over rank-and-file concerns. In the words of their critics, communist metal leaders "submitted body and soul to Comintern policies"—and those policies dictated military preparedness, even under a *munichois* regime like Daladier's.[6] Thus, instead of regrouping their forces for another confrontation, communists welcomed the introduction of new technologies, complained when output was slowed by outdated machinery or ill-conceived policies, and urged workers to make Stakhanovite efforts for the sake of defense.

As the metal union pursued its productionist policy, the PCF veered progressively rightward. Hoping the French political class might be won back to a policy of anti-fascist frontism, the party repeatedly brought out its nationalist and patriotic credentials, sounding the Jacobin alarm that the country was in danger, that war was imminent, that political unity was more necessary than ever.[7] Yet in view of its recent record, the party had trouble convincing anyone that the People's Front represented the best approach to national defense.[8] Moreover, the class antagonisms spawned by the April and November strikes had thoroughly alienated labor's middle-class allies, making future coalition unfeasible. Public opinion also came to believe that an insurmountable contradiction existed between the social legacy of the People's Front and the imperatives of national defense.[9] This sentiment, in fact, animated Daladier's defense program. As a result, communist enthusiasm for armament production served only to sanction the government's own anti-labor policies.

Daladier, however, realized that defense preparations depended on a modicum of labor content. The Matignon system was thus not entirely abolished. To provide an outlet for worker grievances, shop stewards were retained (even if their powers were curtailed). State directives also continued to influence industrial relations and aspects of the annulled contract helped set the standard for wage rates and conditions. More importantly, the union still existed and had a not inconsiderable following. Membership figures for the period after 30 November are extremely unreliable, but the most authoritative estimates indicate that total CGT membership fell from a high of 4,989,000 in 1937 to 2,855,000 on the eve of the Second World War; (Lefranc believed the number might have been as low as 1,700,000).[10] The Metal Federation suffered a comparable loss, falling from 815,000 in early 1938 to 415,000 in 1939.[11] Estimates for the Paris metal union, harder to come by, suggest its membership dropped to about 125,000. Far-left critics, hostile to the communist leadership and anxious to discredit it, put the figure at 100,000 or 110,000.[12] Yet even if the union possessed but 40 percent of its post-June membership (as the far left contended), its following was significantly larger than in the days when its 3,000–4,000 members constituted a mere splintering of the total workforce. This led some *métallos* to believe that however much the pre-June regime had been restored, the social equation remained open to revision. In reality, though, the metal union, like the labor movement as a whole, had become but a remnant of its former self.

Remnants of the Labor Movement

The masses who flocked to the CGT in June 1936 won their first great victories nearly without effort. Then, after a long series of defeats, of which 30 November represented the culmination, the CGT was no longer able to perform the role it had under the People's Front, when the government actively sympathized with it.[13] As the metal union was forced to retreat and union membership became increasingly perilous, many of the "Blum promotion" bade *adieu* to the labor movement.[14] This reflected not only the degree to which fatigue and disillusionment had spread over the ranks, but also the shallowness of their original commitment. As the *sections* were depleted, few came forward to collect dues, call meetings, distribute *Le Métallo,* or challenge management. Employers, moreover, started monitoring their plants for union activity. Those distributing leaflets, organizing meetings, or opposing management were summarily dismissed. Stewards were rendered powerless and management abided no interference in its affairs. Prudence now dictated that unionists keep a low profile. In such an environment, many *sections* simply withered and died. Even in large plants like Renault, where numerous party members were available to replace purged unionists, the *sections* were only able to carry out a minimal operation.[15] With this *grand silence* descending over the labor movement, the Paris metal leadership sank into a kind of torpor, able to follow but no longer influence governmental and *patronal* direction of the defense effort.[16]

Some resistance, though, was inevitable in a workforce that had experienced two and a half years of occupations and mass actions. At the Lorraine aviation plant, for example, a half-hour workstoppage occurred in early February when a worker was fired for striking another accused of being a fascist. At Hispano-Suiza, in late April, a short strike protested long hours. At Kellner, which made auto bodies, an abusive firing caused a workstoppage for a morning and a lock-out for an afternoon. The most consequential action after 30 November came at Sautter-Harlé, when 700 armament workers briefly occupied their plant to protest long hours, layoffs, and non-recognition of shop stewards.[17] These incidents, however, were relatively isolated and unrepresentative of the rest of the metal industry. The Labor Ministry, inaccurately but revealingly, registered no metal strikes for the whole of 1939.

The Moscow-Berlin Pact

The defeat of 30 November and the gathering storm clouds did little to reduce factional strife. Although all wings of the labor movement maintained a
public image of unity, factionalism had become so rampant that schism seemed
imminent. This was especially evident at the Federal Metal Congress held
shortly after the general strike, when anti-communists, led by Marcel Roy, aggressively attacked the leadership for its disastrous mix of politics and unionism. Only a communist-brokered compromise prevented a split.[18] The unity
that was saved, though, was purely formal. Jouhaux and his centrist faction,
constituting the main bulwark against the centrifugal forces, had lost most of
its authority at this point, while Belin of the *Syndicats* group and Frachon of
the communists concentrated their forces on antagonistic wings of the CGT. In
this heavily polarized environment, where each faction maneuvered for strategic position, polemics and policy disputes progressively shifted from programmatic and organizational matters to explicitly political issues, particularly in
respect to foreign policy.[19]

In these factional clashes, communists continued to campaign for a militarized Franco-Soviet Pact and collective security,[20] while their rivals in the
Syndicats group, like much of the non-Stalinist left, rallied to the side of pacifism and revisionism.[21] By the summer of 1939, these international issues mo-
nopolized both the public and internal life of the union. Yet neither partisan in
these skirmishes quite realized it was fighting a hopeless cause, for the forces of
pacifism and anti-fascism were each about to give way to a new alignment in
the international arena. Basic to this realignment was the failure of the
People's Front strategy to forge an effective collective security alliance between
the Western democracies and the Soviet Union. Since the signing of the
Franco-Soviet Pact in May 1935, the French and British governments had compromised with the fascist powers, reneged on pledges to their allies, and done
nothing to enhance their relations with the Soviets. More damaging, the
Munich conference, following the charade of non-intervention, suggested that
the Western democracies were unwilling to resist German expansionism.[22]
This led the Soviets to fear they might be dragged "into a conflict with Germany
as a 'cat's paw' to pull Britain and France out of the fire."[23] Sooner or later,
Moscow was bound to conclude that if the Western democracies were not to be
trusted, then perhaps allies would have to be sought in other quarters.[24] As
early as March 1939, in a secret speech to the Russian party congress, Stalin
had hinted as much.[25] When his Jewish foreign minister, M. M. Litvinov, "resigned" in May 1939, the way suddenly cleared for just such a realignment.
Meanwhile, Hitler, having set his sights on Danzig and the Polish Corridor, was
seeking an arrangement that would neutralize the threat of Soviet attack in

case a European-wide war broke out over Poland. In the summer of 1939, international imperatives of the most Machiavellian kind unexpectedly drew the two dictators together, upsetting the schemes of both the anti-fascists and pacifists in the French labor movement.

The union's polarized factions now experienced a rude awakening. At midnight on 21 August 1939, Radio Berlin announced that Joachim von Ribbentrop, the Nazi foreign minister, was en route to Moscow to sign a non-aggression pact, the news of which struck France—and particularly the PCF—like a bolt from the blue. Few could believe that "the leader of international anti-fascism" had agreed to such a deal. For years, fascism had been stigmatized as the chief enemy of "the international working class." Then, without warning, Stalin reconciled with Hitler. As the *parti de Staline en France* groped for an explanation of this perplexing turn of events, the rest of the world rushed to condemn the pact. Daladier, for one, labeled it a treasonous assault on French national interests and accused its French supporters of subversion.

As the public succumbed to another wave of anti-communist frenzy and political tensions inside the CGT approached the breaking point, the Commission Administrative convened to discuss the non-aggression pact. Belin now demanded a purge of the "traitors." The pact, he argued, proved without the slightest ambiguity that communists were willing to betray the labor movement for the sake of Soviet interests.[26] Members of Frachon's faction tried to deflect Belin's charges, but they were as taken aback by the pact as other Frenchmen. The only way they were able to make sense of it was by rendering it in terms of the anti-fascist line that had guided the PCF over the past five years—even if the pact made nonsense out of that line. For the next several weeks, before they were informed otherwise, communists would justify the pact as a tactical maneuver designed to prevent a Nazi attack on the Soviet Union— a maneuver, they insisted, that was "a victory for the forces of peace and anti-fascism."[27] This argument, however, carried little weight with the centrists holding the swing votes in the Commission Administrative. Fearing the wrath of the French state, and behind it, the rising tide of anti-communism, Jouhaux and his followers harshly condemned the pact and those who supported it. But they resisted Belin's demand for a purge.

Inside the PCF, the pact wrecked havoc.[28] Nearly a third of the party's deputies and elected officials resigned in protest. The rank-and-file was equally stunned, but less likely to defect. This, of course, disrupted numerous facets of communist activity, but the PCF was spared the full brunt of Stalin's unprincipled alliance. On 25 August, Daladier ordered the seizure of *L'Humanité* and *Ce Soir*, the party's two Paris dailies, and threatened communists with imprisonment if they publicly defended the pact. Because the crackdown effectively silenced the most significant of the party's media, the PCF was spared further embarrassment in the court of public opinion. The repression also gave the PCF an image of martyrdom, victim of "Daladier's anti-labor government," which prompted many communists, in an act of reflexive solidarity, to suppress their doubts and rededicate themselves to the "party of the working class."

The PCF, however, did not escape the world-shaking consequences of the realignment. Scarcely a week after the pact's signing, Hitler's Wehrmacht invaded Poland. With this, the house of cards that for two decades had been the European state system came tumbling down. Dragged along by the British war party, France was compelled to honor her treaty obligations to Poland—although it did so with considerable hesitation and uncertainty, for anti-war sentiment remained strong, even at the highest levels of the state.[29] Then, on 2 September, Daladier ordered the mobilization of the French Army. The next day, without a vote in the chamber, France joined Britain in declaring war on Germany.[30] As the long-dreaded Armageddon descended on Europe, communists proclaimed their solidarity with the threatened *patrie* and rallied in its defense.[31] Several days later, after Maurice Thorez and twenty-two deputies accepted their mobilization orders, the party reaffirmed its support for the war effort, called for national unity, and announced its intention of standing in the front ranks of the nation's defenders. The war, however, was not to be fought with "national unity." Even if Stalin had no other plans in mind, French society and politics were far too polarized to permit national reconciliation.[32] Following the war's declaration, Daladier is reported to have told General Pierre Hering, the military governor of Paris, that: "We have to fight [this war] on two fronts: internationally against the Germans, domestically against the communists."[33] In the premier's view, communists were bound by Soviet, not French interests, and these now collided with those of the nation. Therefore, while communists rallied to national defense, Daladier and that large part of the political establishment holding the PCF responsible for "abetting" the enemy sought to exclude them. Yet in doing so, Daladier's government effectively arrayed itself against much of the French working class.

Schism

On 24 and 31 August and for a third time on 1 September, the CGT national office issued formal condemnations of the Moscow-Berlin Pact. But eight communist-led federations, including metal, defiantly voted counter-resolutions rejecting the substance of these condemnations. Because Daladier viewed the pact as a subversion of French national interest and branded its supporters traitors, these counter-resolutions immediately compromised the CGT.[34] In some provincial cities, the government had already begun occupying communist-controlled labor councils *(union departementale)*.[35] If the CGT was to maintain its legality, it had to distance itself from the PCF and its union supporters.

The *Syndicats* group now declared that there was only one course left for the labor movement: to break with *les communazis* and rid the unions of Soviet influence.[36] Yet as pressure for a purge mounted, Jouhaux continued to temporize, unable to bring himself to expel the communists and split the labor movement a second time. His patience, however, had limits and these were finally breached on 17 September. On that day, in solidarity with Hitler's war on the "plutocratic democracies," the Soviet Union—"the greatest bulwark of peace"—invaded eastern Poland. As the Red Army claimed its share of the spoils, Moscow sent the PCF its first communique since the signing of the pact. The war between France and Germany, it was informed, was not an "anti-fascist people's war but a classic imperialist war," for French politicians, subservient to English financial interests and indifferent to the welfare of the French people, had allegedly joined British imperialists in a struggle against German imperialism.[37] Given this view of the war as a sordid squabble among imperialist rivals, with Germany playing the less villainous role, the PCF was ordered to stop attacking Hitler and adopt a policy of revolutionary defeatism—which meant, in effect, opposition to the French war effort and an irreparable break with the anti-fascist line, for it was now held that *l'ennemi est à l'intérieur du pays.*[38] In another of those extraordinary zigzags characteristic of communist history, the French "border guards of the Soviet Union" unhesitatingly swung back to the revolutionary orientation of the 1920s. Only this time revolution would serve the forces they had previously opposed.[39]

The Soviet invasion of Poland forced the hand of Jouhaux and the centrists in the CGT national office. On the 18th, they issued another statement condemning the Moscow-Berlin Pact, but now added that there could "no longer be any possible collaboration with those who did not condemn" Soviet collaboration with fascist aggression. Unionists who refused to disavow the pact were then denounced as traitors and formally expelled from the CGT.[40] Having straddled the factional divide since 1936, Jouhaux and his tendency at last cast their lot with Belin. As they did, communists, after denouncing their attack as part of an oligarchic assault on labor unity, were expelled from the CGT and the union split along the fault lines created during the period of the People's Front.[41] Like the unity achieved in 1936, the schism involved neither trade-union principles nor industrial imperatives, but followed entirely from ideological controversies remote to the social world of the factory.[42]

Repression

Prior to their exclusion, communist unionists attempted to integrate themselves into the burgeoning war effort. On 2 September, the Paris metal union, along with party-loyal delegations from the Paris construction union and the Paris chemical products union, presented the Labor Ministry with suggestions for improving war production. Several days later, the metal union issued a statement criticizing the *patronat* for obstructing production and asked the government to take measures against it. At the same time the union launched a solidarity campaign for families of mobilized workers, set up professional-training centers for women likely to enter the workforce, and established a placement office to service the manpower needs of the war industry. It also issued a directive to its factory *sections* asking them to do their utmost to support the mobilization.[43] Each of these measures was taken in a spirit of national unity, which, communists argued, was crucial to the success of the war effort and realizable only with their participation.

As the metal union prepared opinion for communist participation in the war effort, members of the *Syndicats* group, who formally supported the government's war effort, but behind the scenes continued to promote its peace policy, staged an attack on the communist rear. With government compliance, they seized the union's Paris office (although not before their rivals absconded with its treasury). Then, after the formal expulsion of the communists on 18 September, the anti-communists attempted to mobilize the ranks behind the purge and consolidate their influence in the plants. Communists in the *sections*, although disorganized and hamstrung by the opinion that had turned against them, fought back with a "campaign of calamity" that depicted the former confederals as "government agents," "valets of Anglo-French capitalism," and "wreckers of the labor movement."[44] This, combined with the ineffectiveness of the anti-communist offensive and the general disarray in the plants provoked by the mobilization, was enough to blunt the anti-communist attack and prevent the former confederals from regrouping the ranks in the shops. On 26 September, the government disbanded the metal union and all other communist-dominated organizations.

Besides forcing the PCF underground, the government's anti-communist repression had the effect of alienating workers from the state, which appeared more concerned with suppressing the PCF and crushing the institutions of the labor movement than with waging war against the Germans. This impression was massively reinforced by the realities of the homefront. While not a shot was fired across the Rhine and civilian life went on much as usual, military discipline was imposed in the factories, civil liberties were suspended, and numerous repressive bodies were organized to ferret out dissenters on the shop floor. Equally disconcerting, the repression was carried out in scatter-shot fashion, striking at all unionists, irrespective of political affiliation; internment camps set up to imprison communists soon included unionists of every stripe. At the same time, collective bargaining and strikes were made illegal, wages were frozen, labor was excluded from any meaningful role in the war effort, and workers were subjected to an immediate deterioration of their standards. Finally, Daladier's government, riddled with defeatists, made little effort to overcome the disunity and divisiveness that had plagued the nation in the years leading up to the war.[45]

"Class Collaboration"

Once the metal union was outlawed and the PCF forced underground, the former confederals attempted to regroup and rebuild the shattered union. As early as 20 October 1939, the CGT's Commission Administrative announced that the regrouping was "almost total."[46] This, however, was an utter exaggeration. The largest industrial federations had all been under communist leadership; once they were destroyed by the government ban, confederals succeeded only in reorganizing their central offices.[47] In addition to the purge, the military mobilization of five and a half million men, which in some cases emptied the factories of their entire workforce, completely disrupted their efforts. Called to the colors or under military requisition in the war plants, they were in complete disarray. They lacked the resources and cadre to rebuild the union, they were caught in the crossfire directed against the communists, and they had to deal with a workforce scattered by the mobilization (which conscripted half the metal workforce) or hastily reconstituted with women, boys, and "militarized workers." On the shop floor their forces were so depleted that in most cases they lacked the personnel to staff the government-mandated steward positions.[48] The reorganization of the Paris metal union was also hindered by clandestine communist agitation, which accused the anti-communists of being employer agents and union-wreckers. Although they were more spontaneous than organized, given the PCF's clandestine status, and although they were initially carried out in an environment critical of the party's anti-war position, this agitation contributed to stymieing the rebuilding effort.[49]

Clandestine communist agitation would not, however, have found an audience in the factories if the government had handled the mobilization with greater sensitivity to labor, for divisive social relations continued to influence defense production and poison industrial relations. Unlike 1914, the state made little effort to implement a *union sacrée* or incorporate the unions in the war effort. This failure to foster national solidarity followed from the same short-sightedness that had gotten the country into a war from which it had nothing to gain. Moreover, Daladier's government opted to regulate production by bureaucratic fiats that ignored labor concerns and left most discretionary powers in the hands of public authorities and employers. It thus allowed prices to inflate, controlled wages, suspended social legislation pertinent to hours and conditions, introduced fines and punishments for poor workmanship and undisciplined behavior, eliminated contracts, arbitration, and overtime pay, outlawed strikes, and used compulsion, not incentives, to induce higher productivity. Even these unilateral measures might have been less divisive if there had been some "equality of sacrifice." But as war workers were requisitioned and subjected to quasi-military discipline in the plants, spied on and supervised with unparalleled rigor, employers were given a relatively free hand.[50] Whenever unionists spontaneously defended labor interests in the plants, where workers had been deprived of the most elementary rights, they were likely to be sent to the front or imprisoned. The suspicions and antagonisms of the People's Front thus continued to divide the nation as it prepared to confront the enemy on the border.

The war, however, did not entirely obliterate the labor movement. As anti-communists took up their awesome task, they succeeded in reconstituting the CGT national office and the Paris office of the metal union. They even established a certain presence in the plants. While most *sections*, already decimated by the general strike, failed to survive the mobilization or became part of the communist underground, the anti-communists did manage to organize three dozen *comités de liaison* in the largest auto and aviation works.[51] A Comité Régionale de Liaison des Métallurgistes de la Région Parisienne was then set up to link these *comités de liaison* to the union's Paris office.[52] In December 1939, the anti-communists attempted to reconstitute the *sections* on the basis of the *comités.* This process continued until the spring of 1940, when the German invasion terminated all union activities. In general, though, they failed to reestablish links with the ranks. Among the thousands of shops and factories making up the Paris metal industry, the anti-communists ended up with less than forty *sections.*[53] Their record was equally dismal in other areas. In early 1940, for example, they tried reviving the *unions locales,* but managed to breathe life into a mere half dozen.[54] The newly formed *sections* and *unions locales,* in other words, touched but a tiny minority of the wartime workforce. There are no reliable figures, but the reconstituted union probably counted less than a thousand members in late 1939—the majority of whom were invariably veterans of the old Confederal Metal Union (although communists attempting to "bore from within" also found a place in their ranks). Most *métallos,* though, were scattered by the war and the schism.[55]

The failure to rebuild the union's factory-level organization and the general disarray of the labor movement did not mean that rank-and-file *métallos* were totally crushed by the wartime regime. Enough skilled workers and unionists remained in the plants to preserve the memory of the former Matignon system. Early in the war, brief slowdown strikes were reported at aircraft plants in Issy-les-Moulineaux, Aubervillier, and Argenteuil. At Lorraine and at Renault, workers on several occasions stopped production and sang the "Internationale" to protest wage cuts. At Gnome-et-Rhône, similar protests took place for non-respect of the conditions of hire. At Petites Voitures in Aubervillier, there was an hour workstoppage over excessive overtime. At Compteurs de Montrouge, a twenty minute strike occurred in reaction to abusive fines. In another factory in the west suburb, a *métallo* sympathetic to Daladier was sent to the hospital by his workmates. These spontaneous protests pale in comparison with the great occupations of the People's Front era, but in conditions of wartime, especially in the opening months when patriotic feeling was at its peak, they revealed that some fight remained in the metal ranks.[56]

Notwithstanding the government's neglect of social issues, worker discontent was a matter of utmost concern to the authorities, who feared communists would exploit it to sabotage the war effort. Communists, however, were extremely disorganized by the repression and the mobilization, and their clandestine apparatus, which did not become operational until late October, was able to carry out only a limited range of activities. While some individual communists succeeded in preserving their influence on the shop floor, their actions rarely threatened the integrity of the war effort, although they might have occasionally hampered it and certainly contributed to the prevailing disaffection.[57] Most communists lost contact with the party after it went underground. Those succeeding in linking up with the illegal apparatus were able to do little more than distribute mimeographed leaflets propounding anti-war and defeatist themes, wage whisper campaigns that reviled the CGT leadership, denounce collaboration with the employers, and, more cautiously, advocate sabotage of armament production. These same communists also formed an unspecified number of secret *comités de defense syndicale* and attempted to rebuild party influence in the plants by championing workshop demands and disparaging CGT and government conduct of the war effort.[58]

Clandestine communist actions, combined with draconian conditions, made themselves felt in low productivity and low morale. But draconian conditions were undoubtedly the decisive factor affecting output, even if the CGT, the government, and the employers remained obsessed with communist machinations; in fact, their obsession with illegal communist activities seemed greater that their concern for low productivity. To combat communist influence, as well as mitigate the social problems of production, Raoul Dautry, the armament minister, and, to a lesser degree, Charles Pomaret, the labor minister, endeavored, despite the absence of a *union sacrée*, to convey the image of a socially responsible war effort. In this vein, they recruited unionists to sit on the Permanent Economic Committee, the Committee for the Study of Social Questions, and Labor Courts.[59] More importantly, they worked out a labor-management accord known as the Majestic Agreement, which was signed on

7 October 1939 by Léon Chevalme of the reconstituted Metal Federation and a UIMM delegate.[60] Couched in a number of high-sounding generalities, the signatories to this agreement promised to engage in a forum of mutual consultations to aid and abet the war effort.[61]

The Metal Federation was quick to hail the Majestic Agreement as "a new Matignon Accord."[62] But the two were hardly comparable. Similar to the *politique de présence* in the 1922–1935 period, which had imbued the CGT with public influence in lieu of rank-and-file influence on the shop floor, the language of collaboration contained in the Majestic Agreement gave confederal leaders an authority denied them by the character of the war effort, even if it granted few actual rights. Employers, however, had little interest in collaboration, despite public professions to the contrary, and signed the accord only under government pressure. Memories of the People's Front still rankled them and most remained distrustful of, if not hostile to the metal union.[63] Since the failed strike of 30 November, they had enjoyed a free hand in their plants, which allowed them to render shop steward positions innocuous, ignore government directives, slash wages, and subject workers to an iron discipline. Collaboration with the CGT could only compromise such conditions. The Majestic Agreement, as a result, promised more than what the employers were prepared to deliver.

Nonetheless, at higher levels, outside the plants, some tentative forms of labor-management cooperation developed. Beginning in November 1939, weekly meetings between the UIMM and the Metal Federation were held at the Labor Ministry. In these meetings devoted to the problems of war production, union leaders appealed to management and government representatives to recognize that the sixty-hour work week, in some cases the seventy-two-hour week, was counterproductive. They argued for a more benign model of war production. If work conditions were improved and government decrees respected, if stewards were allowed to do their job, and if the general interests of the nation took priority in the plants, they claimed workers would automatically intensify their efforts, productivity would rise, and managers would have a less difficult time.[64] The CGT metal leaders also beseeched government and employer representatives to cease treating workers like pariahs and give labor a more meaningful role in the common struggle. If these reforms were implemented, they promised communist propaganda would lose its audience in the factories.[65] Their endeavors to collaborate, however, would neither mitigate the authoritarian character of the war effort nor alleviate the deep social antagonisms within the relations of productions.

The Final Struggle

By the spring of 1940, French aircraft and tank production, despite its low productivity, began to exceed that of Germany.[66] But the war itself—the

"Phony War"—went on without any shots being fired. In September 1939, the ninety-five divisions of the French Army marked time on their border while all but forty German divisions attacked Poland. After squandering the one opportunity to strike a blow against the enemy's rear, the French general staff sat on its heels and waited for the Germans to respond—hoping a bloodless solution would be found before the fighting began.[67] The Armée, moreover, lacked the will to fight what was widely recognized as a suicidal war.[68] On the front, behind the secure ramparts of the Maginot Line, French soldiers kept busy playing football or getting drunk, trying not to think of flying bullets and torn flesh.[69] The civilian population displayed a similar lassitude. After the harshest winter in a half century, most people appeared more interested in the arrival of spring than the prospect of an imminent bloodletting. Sidewalk cafes were unusually busy, parks were full of strollers, the streets of Paris, minus a sandbagged structure here and there, bustled with the usual commerce and traffic. The hit song that year was "Paris Will Always Be Paris." Across France, people seemed to live only in the distant shadow of war, nearly indifferent to the impending catastrophe.[70] The Paris metal industry, by contrast, bellowed and roared, night and day, as if the fate of the nation depended on its output.

As the first weeks of the "Sitzkrieg" stretched into months, the CGT leadership endeavored to address the social problems specific to production. Although excluded from all official decision-making bodies, it drew on the language of "collaboration" in the Majestic Agreement to identify itself with the war effort and develop a means of influencing its course.[71] "Collaboration" was ostensibly based on the recognition that the principal question facing the labor movement was no longer that of class collaboration or class struggle, but rather collaboration or liquidation—for allegedly only contractual agreements between labor and management, "loyally signed, loyally executed," could hold off the onslaught of German fascism.[72] While clandestine communist agitation made hay out of the term, which had an extremely negative connotation in the labor movement, and many older confederals found the term sticking in their throats, Roy and Chevalme, at the helm of the reconstituted Metal Federation, took the lead in convincing the ranks that collaboration was no longer synonymous with union subordination to state and *patronat*, but rather requisite to an equable functioning of the war effort. True to their roots in the *Syndicats* group, Roy and Chevalme also tried to infuse the term with a sense of economic reform, such as related to the corporatist schema of the earlier CGT Plan.[73] Nevertheless, even these metal leaders were forced to acknowledge that collaboration was an ideal for which employers had little regard. Their most persuasive argument always turned on the fact that there was no effective alternative to it.[74] In the factories, moreover, workers showed not the slightest interest in collaboration. The term seemed academic in a situation where they had been deprived of all rights. Only in weekly meetings at the Labor Ministry, where

CGT leaders and industrialists met to discuss production problems, did the language of collaboration acquire a resonance. Here unionists were able to exploit the notion of collaboration to press for a reduction of the work week, the implementation of health and safety legislation, cost-of-living adjustments, and the development of an arbitration system. But even in this realm metal leaders rarely had anything to show for their efforts. On numerous occasions, the war minister and labor minister promised to examine union recommendations or look into worker grievances, but except for certain minor concessions on hygiene and female labor, nothing tangible was ever forthcoming.[75] It was simply easier for the government and the employers to plod along with business as usual, rather than risk imposing a new regime in the war factories—even if this had saved the French in 1914. Collaboration, as a result, remained without much substance.

Yet without real collaboration, labor lacked a voice in production and this could not but deter the war effort. Government officials and plant managers, though, did not seem to care. When faced with production problems or low productivity, they preferred to blame communists rather than confront the inadequacies of their own policies. Production problems may have occasionally resulted from their clandestine activities but the real problem facing the war industry, as reformist union leaders repeatedly but vainly explained, involved abusive, arbitrary, and condescending attitudes toward labor on the shop floor. As even conservative unionists acknowledged, the victimization, arrests, and threats of being sent to the front created a psychology of terror in the plants that was anything but conducive to a loyal war effort.[76]

In its clandestine leaflets and publications, the communist underground exploited the inevitable discontent fostered by this "terror," and, to a degree difficult to access, succeeded in restoring some of their former influence. In a few notable cases, communists succeeded in disrupting and even sabotaging production. At the Farman aircraft works, for example, six workers were caught damaging airplane engines, three of whom were eventually executed. It was never discovered if they were under party orders or merely responding to party propaganda.[77] At Renault, cases of broken machine tools, faulty wiring, defective parts, and tanks with damaged transmissions occurred often enough for management to suspect sabotage. At Gnome-et-Rhône, several aviation workers were arrested for tampering with motors. The slowdown was another, certainly more common form of resistance; "an hour lost to production," according to one clandestine tract, "was an hour gained for the Revolution."[78] Slowdown, however, was also a response to long hours, overwork, and grueling production norms. Absenteeism was another. In many plants it averaged between 10 percent and 20 percent—several times the prewar rate. In general, though, overt forms of disruption were few and far between. Communist agitation, to the degree it was effective, seemed to take its greatest toll at the level of morale.[79]

In some large plants, the party still controlled the *sections syndicales*, which operated secretly as *comités de defense syndicale*. Elsewhere, communists infiltrated into positions of authority within the reconstituted metal union by "boring from within."[80] During the dreary months of the Phony War, they even took on the allure of martyrdom, assuming the self-image of intractable defenders of the working class, unwilling to cooperate with "warmongers . . . armament manufacturers . . . [and] enemies of the people."[81] Persisting government and employer attacks on labor rights only contributed to this allure. Many workers, to be sure, remembered that communist policies had repeatedly sidetracked labor during the period of the People's Front and played a dubious role in the war's opening stage, but such memories were increasingly mitigated by the recognition that communists alone condemned Daladier's anti-labor policies and unreservedly championed their interests.

Although it is difficult to gauge the degree to which war workers sympathized with communists after September 1939, a significant number evidently remained true to "the party of the working class." The superficial character of PCF activities also meant that communist defeatism was never serious enough to antagonize the popular classes, whose patriotism and neo-Jacobinism, despite the character of the war effort, tended to supersede whatever class or social resentment grieved them in the factory. The party, moreover, attempted no mutinies in the army. Few actual cases of sabotage were reported (although the few that did occur made an enormous impression on the political and *patronal* milieu). Slowdowns and production delays were barely distinguishable from normal production problems. Illegal leafleting, clandestine publications, and demoralizing whisper campaigns, the core activities of the communist underground, were enough to sustain their image as martyrs of the "bourgeois government," dampen morale, and perhaps restore part of their tarnished reputation, but they did little to estrange their sympathizers in the plants, whose disaffection rarely translated into outright sabotage. That such activities troubled the government, the employers, and the CGT was due mainly to the fear that these discontented workers might respond to communist agitation and rebel against the class-biased war effort.

Strange Defeat

On a bright spring morning in May 1940, after eight months of Sitzkrieg, the Wehrmacht unleashed a storm of fire and steel against the Western alliance. Belgium and Holland collapsed in days. Only the races of Dunkirk spared the British Expeditionary Force. The French Army—demoralized by the same divisions that had racked French society, incompetently led, unable to counter the formidable German use of tanks and planes, and uncertain why it was fighting—caved in all along the front.[82] Within weeks the marching boots of triumphant Nazism could be heard thundering down the Champs-Elysées. Soon all France lay prostrate before the invader.

The ignominious debacle that left France a German vassalage was, as numerous commentators beginning with Marc Bloch have noted, not explicable by military reasons alone, for the collapse of the French nation in May and June 1940 occurred not merely on the battlefield.[83] The failure of spirit that had weakened French resistance and rent the fabric of national resolve, as chronicled in the above pages, owed much to those divisive events, the *guerre franco-française,* that began in February 1934 and continued up until the Battle of France.[84] This half decade of violent contention—with its sitdown strikes and vengeful lock-outs, mass demonstrations and street murders—undermined whatever community of sentiment and self-sacrifice had previously defined the nation.[85] Now, as the divided and defeated French settled accounts with their past, the great mass-production plants of the Paris Region, having ceased to be the occupied fortresses of an insurgent labor movement, turned to producing tanks and planes for those who had come to occupy the country.

Excursus

THE LABOR MOVEMENT WAS FUNDAMENTALLY A CONSERVA-
tive movement, opposed to the proliferation of capitalist market relations and
the triumph of purely economic values. At the heart of every trade union, even
revolutionary ones formed by communists, there existed an unconscious effort
to prevent the dissolution of meaningful social relations that had come with
marketization. In fighting for better wages, more humane conditions, job security, and all the little things associated with their organizations, unionists
fought off efforts to commodify their lives. Characteristically, their unions
rested on the solidarity of the group, not the individual precious to liberal
thought. Moreover, their efforts in the mills and factories were engaged not
simply to enhance the value of their labor, but to overcome the market's atomizing forces and return men to the communities arising from their common
work experience. Communism, like fascism and various forms of populism and
nationalism, were likewise born of this impulse to reconnect life and labor, individual and community, value and destiny. But unlike these political ideologies, with their economic or racial utopias, unions were without dogmas,
motivated almost entirely by those small-scale endeavors that aimed to make

work and the world surrounding work more amenable to the things that mattered.

Not coincidentally, the labor movement arose in reaction to English liberalism and the Bourgeois Revolution of 1789, both of which accompanied the new individualistic market economy heralded by Adam Smith. As these two movements, with their exchange values and their Rights of Man, destroyed the old social moorings and cast workers adrift in a world drained of ethical purpose, unions responded by offering working people the means of recapturing something of the customary values and symbolic significances that had been lost with rapid growth, economic insecurity, and the triumph of the market's monetary calculus. In England, where the liberal market initially took root, there emerged the first expressions of the labor movement, as workers struggled to preserve the "moral economy" of the pre-capitalist era. Where its implications were most severe, in late nineteenth-century Germany, labor staged its most impressive resistance. Even in the United States, whose civilization was founded on a rejection of the older culture (some say a rejection of all culture) and on a privileging of liberal economic values, a militant labor movement struggled against the market's relentless extension, posing, in the process, an alternative model of production.

Because France industrialized less abruptly than elsewhere, the history of its labor movement assumed a character much unlike that of the other industrial powers. Up to the advent of the twentieth century, much of France and more than half its workforce remained tied to an agrarian economy in which property ownership possessed a significance not to be found in urban capital markets. Although often ravaged by the new economic forms, the highly skilled working class in French towns and cities touched by liberal capitalism was able to buffer itself from the full brunt of marketization. The most jarring and consequential expression of liberalism's "peaceful conquest" came only with the development of mass production during the Great War and the 1920s. Within the technical and social systems of the new large-scale, metal-fabricating plants, Paris workers, for the first time, experienced an industrializing process that cut them off entirely from the customs and sensibilities of the past, subjecting them to forces controlled by the money powers.

The actual birth of the modern French labor movement occurred only in the wake of the general strike of 1934. Workers rallying in defense of the republic did so not to defend the liberal principles undergirding the Third Republic—they, in fact, had been responsible for the conditions fueling their movement—but instead to support a social notion of the republic that only incidentally accorded with the dominant conception. Given their weak corporate and strong political consciousness, it was not surprising that republicanism spurred their movement. When communists raised the Jacobin banner in the red suburbs, when they mobilized the *petits* against the *gros*, when their militants fought for decent relations on the shop floor and demanded a say in managerial direction, they evoked the social notion of the republic and workers responded accordingly. Through this social model of republicanism, labor found a way to express its aspirations and sentiments. Contemporary observers were nearly unanimous in noting the élan and enthusiasm that suddenly moved these previously inert *métallos* and the sense of belonging and emotional attachment that henceforth imbued them with the ambition to reshape their working lives. At one level, these feelings testified to their longing for an honorable place in the national community; at a higher level, that of historicity, they manifested a will to beat back the heartless egoism and authoritarian economic forms that had become a part of French life.

While republicanism stimulated the development of the labor movement, it nonetheless did so with a good deal of complication. The Jacobin heritage and the traditions of 1789 were rich and multiform. Communists and liberals made what they would of them. So too did workers. To the degree that labor's vision differed from the prevailing notions, it put workers on a collision course with the People's Front and its politicians. But because the campaigns and mobilizations of the People's Front were also responsible for the cohesion and confidence that had enabled them to assert themselves in the factory, their movement was predicated on an insupportable contradiction.

The first significant hint of this incompatible mix of political and social objectives came with the June occupations. After playing a critical role in instigating the strikes, communists guided them according to political considerations that marginalized the strikers' own demands. Tensions between the summit and the base of the labor movement further escalated under Blum, as ongoing strife in the plants undermined the newly institutionalized system of labor-management relations and as international events subordinated shop-floor interests to foreign-policy concerns. In time, as these divergences grew in number and intensity, the labor movement collided not only with the "parties of labor," but with the state, the *patronat,* and the middle class. Because these divisive sectional interests took increased precedence over national unity, the French nation would confront its greatest challenge with a highly fractured polity and a polarized social system. The failure to implement a *union sacrée* and the implicit standoff between the working class and the war government represented the most tragic culmination of these divisions.

In other ways as well, the labor movement of the 1930s must be judged a failure. Propelled into positions of influence after June, the CGT declined once the political alignment shifted against it. More seriously, it did little during its brief hegemony to educate its membership, instill in it a higher conception of the labor movement, or deepen its roots in the social system. In consequence, its subsequent collision with the state and management's successful offensive on the shop floor led not only to the erosion of the June conquests, but to a depletion of its ranks. Institutionally, its legislative legacy was somewhat more enduring, but even here the reforms it won were more a sign of senility than of renewal, insofar as they mitigated liberalism's more destructive tendencies while maintaining its underlying principles. As to the deracination and deculturation that infected working-class life, it is difficult to judge the degree to which the labor movement in the Paris metal industry was able to overcome this most characteristic feature of the liberal order. Undoubtedly, at its zenith, it nurtured forms of community and identity that helped compensate for the anomic effects of large-scale production and the anarchy of its labor markets. But here too labor failed to secure its conquests.

In the highest scheme of things, however, labor's failures—and they were numerous—are less important than the possibilities they suggest for our own age, for today problems not unlike those faced by Paris metal workers in the 1920s and 1930s are again being posed, as postmodern liberalism, with its program of global economic integration, multiculturalism, and human rights, threatens even more titanic forms of deracination and deculturation. Although there can be little doubt that the movement to combat these epochal threats will not come from the factories and that the tattered slogans of democracy will count for less than communatarian claims to bio-cultural identity, one might reasonably hope that the story of the *métallos* will at least have its reverberations in the coming struggles against the liberal Moloch.

Notes

Preface

1. Simeon Larson and Bruce Nissen, eds. *Theories of the Labor Movement* (Detroit, 1987).

2. This concept of the labor movement is central to the many works constituting Touraine's vast scholarly opus. It is best elaborated in *Production de la Société* (Paris, 1973), *The Voice and the Eye: An Analysis of Social Movements* (Cambridge, 1981), and, in collaboration with Michel Wieviorka and François Dubet, *Le Mouvement Ouvrier* (Paris, 1984).

Chapter One

1. Gilbert Hatry, *Renault, Usine de Guerre 1914–1918* (Paris, 1978), 29; Anthony Rhodes, *Louis Renault: A Biography* (London, 1969), 77–81.

2. H. Sellier, A. Bruggeman, and M. Poëte, *Paris Pendant la Guerre* (Paris, 1926), 2.

3. W. F. Ogburn and William Jaffé, *The Economic Development of Postwar France* (New York, 1929), 318. In 1915, there were 25,000 factories and shops involved in war production. By 1918, after considerable expansion of the workforce, the number had fallen below 15,000. See Hatry, *Renault, Usine de Guerre*, 33.

4. Sellier, et al., *Paris Pendant la Guerre*, 10.

5. The annual tonnage of imported machine-tools jumped from 23,735 tons in 1913 to 58,216 in 1918. See Arthur Fontaine, *French Industry during the War* (New Haven, 1926), 448. Also Godfrey Carden, *Machine Tool Trade in Germany, France, Switzerland, Italy, and United Kingdom* (Washington, 1909).

6. Sylvie Van de Casteele-Schweitzer, "Management and Labour in France 1914–1939," in *The Automobile Industry and Its Workers*, ed. S. Tolliday and J. Zeitlin (Cambridge, 1986), 57; John F. Godfrey, *Capitalism at War: Industrial Policy and Bureaucracy in France, 1914–1918* (Leamington Spa, 1986), 106.

7. Martin Fine, "Guerre et Reformisme en France, 1914–1918," *Recherches* 32/33 (September 1978), 313.

8. Hyacinthe Dubreuil, *J'ai Fini Ma Journée* (Paris, 1971), 87.

9. Prior to the war, French aviation produced fifty planes per month. By 1918, that figure had climbed to 629. See Edmond Petit, *La Vie Quotidienne dans l'Aviation en France au Début du XXe Siècle (1900–1935)* (Paris, 1977), 158.

10. William H. McNeill, *The Pursuit of Power: Technology, Armed Force, and Society Since A.D. 1000* (Chicago, 1982), 322.

11. The number of French aircraft workers dropped from a high of 190,000 in 1918, to 19,200 in 1920, and then to 3,700 in 1921. See Petit, *La Vie Quotidienne dans l'Aviation en France*, 159; Emmanuel Chadeau, *La Rêve et la Puissance: L'Avion et son Siècle* (Paris, 1996), 104–105.

12. *Bulletin du Ministère du Travail* 28 (1921): 19.

13. *Le Front Populaire, C'est la Guerre*, Fortune Reprint, June 1937, 2. See also Pierre Saly,

"Poincaré Keynésien?" in *Le Capitalisme Français XIXe–XX Siècle: Blocages et Dynamismes d'un Croissance*, ed. Patrick Fridenson and A. Straus (Paris, 1987); Thomas W. Grabau, *Industrial Reconstruction in France After World War One* (New York, 1991).

14. French metal producers had a major advantage over foreign competitors in that France was the last European country to stabilize her currency. This allowed them to sell their products abroad for gold and cover industrial expenditures inside the country with highly devalued paper. On the currency disturbances, see Ogburn and Jaffé, *The Economic Development of Post-War France*, 48–58. On the relation between exports and devaluation, see Arno Burmeister, *Die Entwicklung der französischen Maschinen-Industrie* (Rostock, 1929), 33–34. On industrial modernization, see Aimée Moutet, "Introduction de la Production à la Chaîne du Début du Siècle à la Grande Crise en 1930," *Histoire Economique et Sociale* (1983).

15. Its annual growth rate was doubled that of the prewar period. See T. J. Markovitch, *L'Industrie Française de 1789 à 1964* (Paris, 1966), 3: table 1. On the rationalization movement, see Charles S. Maier, "Between Taylorism and Technology: European Ideologies and the Vision of Industrial Productivity in the 1920s," *Journal of Contemporary History* 5 (1970).

16. By 1927, 40 percent of French metallurgical products were sold abroad. See P. Gancarz, "La Métallurgie Française face à la Crise des Années Trente," *Le Mouvement Social* 154 (January–March 1991), 201; also, Ogburn and Jaffé, *The Economic Development of Post-War France*, 315.

17. Ministère du Travail, *Statistique Générale de la France* 54 (1938): 73*.

18. *Le Peuple*, 13 June 1936.

19. *Les Industries Mécaniques: Révue Mensuelle*, June 1938. See also Fédération des Industries Mécaniques et Transformatrice des Métaux, *La Mécanique dans l'Economie Française* (Paris [1962?]).

20. Henry Coville, *Le Syndicat des Industries Méchanique: Cents Ans d'Action Syndicale (1840–1940)* (Paris, 1944).

21. Yves Laquin, "Social Structures and Shared Beliefs: Four Worker Communities in the Second Industrialization," *International Labor and Working Class History* 22 (Fall 1982): 7; Michelle Perrot, "From the Mechanic to the Metallo," in *Strikes, Wars and Revolution in an International Perspective*, ed. L. H. Haimson and C. Tilly (Cambridge, 1989).

22. In British terminology, mechanical engineering refers to the production of machinery, electrical apparatus, metallic structures, armaments, and sometimes transportation equipment, such as ships and rail cars, as well as planes and autos. The UIMM, by contrast, tended to designate auto and aviation as separate industrial activities and here I follow their designation.

23. Statistique Générale de la France, *Résultats Statistiques du Recensement de la Population* (Paris, 1931) 12:3, 7.

24. *L'Union des Métaux*, August 1935; *L'Humanité*, 30 June 1934; Charles Rist and G. Piron, "De la France d'Avant-Guerre à la France d'Aujourd'hui," *Revue d'Economie Politique* (January–February 1939), iv, v, xxii. In the interwar period, there were an estimated 14,000 metal-working establishments in the Paris Region, the vast majority of which were small shops with less than twenty workers. See Statistique Générale de la France, *Résultats Statistiques du Recensement de la Population*, 12:3, 7, 11.

25. According to H. Pasdermadjian, Smith's division of labor was "horizontal," aimed at fragmenting labor into elementary operations that enhanced productivity. Rationalization, by contrast, was "vertical," designed for the maximum utilization of available personnel, skills, and machines, and based on the already-existing system of parceled labor, extensive mechanization, and "transferable" knowledge. See *La Deuxième Révolution Industrielle* (Paris, 1959), 67.

26. Harry Braverman, *Labor and Monopoly Capitalism: The Degradation of Work in the Twentieth Century* (New York, 1974). More generally, Paul Thompson, *The Nature of Work: An Introduction to Debates on the Labour Process* (London, 1983).

27. Stephen Meyer, *The Five Dollar Day: Labor Management and Social Control in the Ford Motor Company, 1908–1921* (Albany, 1981); Lindy Biggs, *The Rational Factory: Architecture, Technology, and Work in America's Age of Mass Production* (Baltimore, 1996).

28. David A. Hounshell, *From the American System to Mass Production, 1800–1932* (Baltimore, 1984), 249–61.

29. This term was popularized in the 1970s by France's "regulation economists"—principally Robert Boyer, Michel Aglietta, Alain Lipietz, and Benjamin Coriat—and inspired by Antonio Gramsci's early characterization of these innovations in "Americanism and Fordism," *Selections from the Prison Notebooks* (New York, 1971), 277–320. It should not, however, be confused with the Gramscian notion of "Fordism." The Fordist-Taylorist mode of production relates to the technological-managerial character of production, while Fordism connotes social policies that came to preeminence in New Deal America and did not take root in France until after the Second World War.

30. Citroen, as an exception, introduced American mass-production techniques as early as 1919 and the moving assembly line in 1923. See John Reynolds, *André Citroen: The Henry Ford of France* (New York, 1996), 54. The three stages noted above serve only as an ideal characterization of the industry's rationalization.

31. Gramsci, "Americanism and Fordism," 302–303; also Touraine, *L'Evolution du Travail Ouvrier aux Usines Renault*, 109.

32. Prior to 1914, the French factory, as J. Wolff describes it, was "only a group of workshops, characterized by their independence from the supervisory personnel and the initiative of their workers, with no organ linking the shop foreman and the boss." Quoted in Claude Fohlen, "The Industrial Revolution in France 1700–1914," in *The Fontana Economic History of Europe*, ed. C. Cipolla (London, 1973), 4:38. This artisanal system of production dominated even the new auto plants established at the turn of the century; see Patrick Fridenson, *Histoire des Usines Renault: Naissance de la Grande Entreprise 1898–1939* (Paris, 1972), 38.

33. James M. Laux, *The European Automobile Industry* (New York, 1992), 52.

34. *L'Humanité*, 10 April 1925. On the foreman, see Touraine, *L'Evolution du Travail Ouvrier aux Usines Renault*, 151–59.

35. Félix Guillot, *La Rationalisation et Ses Consequences pour l'Ouvrier* (Lyon, 1934).

36. Maurice Bouvier-Ajam, *Histoire du Travail en France depuis la Révolution* (Paris, 1969), 297.

37. *Les Industries Mécaniques: Révue Mensuelle*, June 1930.

38. Touraine, *L'Evolution du Travail Ouvrier aux Usines Renault*, 34. See also Jean-Louis Platet, *L'Industrie Automobile Française Depuis la Guerre* (Paris, 1934), 49; Fridenson, *Histoire des Usines Renault*, 288. Among luxury and custom car builders, such as Hispano-Suiza, skilled workers remained a significant part of the workforce (50 percent to 60 percent).

39. *L'Union des Métaux*, May–June 1923.

40. Biggs, *The Rational Factory*, 131.

41. Georges Navel, *Travaux* (Paris, 1945), 64–65.

42. Simone Weil, *La Condition Ouvrière* (Paris, 1951), 227.

43. Annie Fourcaut, *Femmes à l'Usine en France dans l'Entre-Deux-Guerres* (Paris, 1982), 100–101, 124–26.

44. Even Adam Smith believed the minute division of labor beckoned social degradation. In his words: "The minds of men [subject to highly divided labor] are contracted and rendered incapable of elevation, education is despised or at least neglected, and heroic spirit

is almost utterly extinguished." See his *Lectures on Jurisprudence* (Indianapolis, 1982), 540.

45. See for example, Navel, *Travaux*, 72–73.

46. Weil, *La Condition Ouvrière*, 222.

47. "On the assembly line, every man aspires to the perfection of the machine and at the same time silently every man yells 'I am not a machine'." Robert Linhart, *The Assembly Line* (Amherst, 1981), 31. See also Alain Touraine and O. Ragazzi, *Ouvriers d'Origine Agricole* (Paris, 1961).

48. This characterization of the OS and the OP owes a good deal to Alain Touraine, Michel Wievioka, and François Dubet, *Le Mouvement Ouvrier* (Paris, 1984), 74–76.

49. Louis Bergeron, *Les Capitalistes en France* (Paris, 1978).

50. André Philip, *La Gauche: Mythes et Réalities* (Paris, 1964), 59.

51. Louis Bergeron, "Vers un Renouvellement des Enterprises et des Hommes," in *Histoire des Français XIXe–XXe Siècles*, ed. Yves Lequin (Paris, 1983), 1:291.

52. Weil, *La Condition Ouvrière*, 149.

53. Adeline Daumard, "La Bourgeoisie et les Classes Dirigentes: Permanence, Evolution ou Mutation?" in *Histoire Economique et Sociale de la France*, by Jean Bouvier, et al. (Paris, 1979), 4:pt. 1, p.54.

54. "The French engineer is more a product of the age of enlightenment than of the industrial era. He has kept the prestige attached to it and, in a manner of speaking, its character." Marc Maurice and François Sellier, "Societal Analysis of Industrial Relations: A Comparison Between France and West Germany," *British Journal of Industrial Relations* 17 (November 1979), 324. See also Claude Fohlen, "Entrepreneurship and Management in the Nineteenth Century," in *The Cambridge Economic History of Europe*, ed. P. Mathias and M. M. Postan (Cambridge, 1978), 7:pt. 1, pp.373–80.

55. *Le Syndicalisme Chrétien*, January 1934; *Le Peuple*, 14 January 1929; *L'Age de Fer*, 10 April 1920; Patrick Fridenson, "L'Idéologie des Grands Constructeurs dans l'Entre-Deux-Guerres," *Le Mouvement Social* 81 (October–December 1972): 6. Cf. Jean Lhome, "La Grande Bourgeoisie et Ses Pouvoirs," *Cahiers Internationaux de Sociologie* (July–December 1960); E. Carter, R. Forster, J. Moody, eds., *Entreprise and Entrepreneurs in Nineteenth- and Twentieth-Century France* (Baltimore, 1976).

56. Gérard Dehove, *Le Contrôle Ouvrier en France* (Paris, 1937), 106; Jules Zirnheld, *Cinquante Années de Syndicalisme Chrétien* (Paris, 1937), 135.

57. Paul Vignaux, *Traditionalisme et Syndicalisme* (New York, 1943), 62–63.

58. *L'Union des Métaux*, January 1931. In the words of one trade-union militant, "We have the dubious distinction of being arrayed against the most powerful, reactionary, and intransigent of all employer organizations." Fédération des Ouvriers des Métaux (CGT), *VIe Congrès Fédéral* (Versailles, 1924), 117.

59. *L'Age de Fer*, 25 November and 25 December 1923.

60. Zirnheld, *Cinquante Années de Syndicalisme Chrétien*, 135. Cf. Henry Donald Peiter, *Men of Good Will: French Businessmen and the First World War* (Ph.D. diss., University of Michigan, 1973), 274–79.

61. Robert Pinot, *Les Oeuvres Sociales des Industries Métallurgiques* (Paris, 1924); Jean Duporcq, *Les Oeuvres Sociales dans la Métallurgie Française* (Paris, 1936).

62. Michele Aumont, *Femmes en Usine. Les Ouvrières de la Métallurgie Parisienne* (Paris, 1953), 14.

63. August Gillot, *Un Forgeron dans la Cité des Rois* (Paris, n.d.), 46.

64. In 1914, there were 86,608 accidents in the French metal industry, 118 of which resulted in death. In 1926, there were 351,673 accidents and 368 deaths. Employers claimed these accidents were due to worker negligence and inexperience; union leaders blamed the

authoritarian way in which the new technologies were imposed. See *Le Métallurgiste*, December 1930–January 1931; *L'Age de Fer*, 25 December 1923.

65. Ministère du Travail, *Statistique Générale de la France* (Paris, 1931), 46:271.

66. Danielle Tartakowsky and Claude Willard, *Des Lendemains Qui Chantait? La France des Années Folles et du Front Populaire* (Paris, 1986), 18. See also Gary Cross, *Immigrant Workers in Industrial France: The Making of a New Laboring Class* (Philadelphia, 1983).

67. At Renault, for instance, 60 percent of the 25,000 workers comprising the labor force in 1927 were foreign. Of these, 5,000 were Russian and Ukrainian, 3,000 Italian, 2,000 Polish, 2,000 colonial (mainly North African and Indochinese), 800 Hungarian, and 500 Armenian. See *Bulletin Régional: Cahier du Militant de la Région Parisienne du PCF*, 18 March 1927.

68. Madeleine Guilbert, *Les Fonctions des Femmes dans l'Industrie* (Paris, 1966). Within the industry, women metal workers were seen and treated as an "inferior order," paid low wages, and assigned the most difficult and disagreeable work; see *L'Ouvrière: Organe Communiste des Travailleuses Manuelles et Intellectuelles*, 16 and 31 May 1930; M. Dubesset, F. Thébaud, and C. Vincent, "The Female Munitions Workers of the Seine," in *The French Home Front 1914–1918*, ed. Patrick Fridenson (Providence, 1992).

69. Madeleine Guilbert, "Les Problèmes du Travail Industriel des Femmes et l'Evolution des Techniques," *Le Mouvement Social* 61 (October–December 1967).

70. *La Vie Syndicale*, December 1923; *L'Avant-Garde Ouvrière et Paysane: Organe Officiel de la Fédération des Jeunesse Communistes*, 24 December 1927.

71. Fédération Unitaire des Métaux, *Rapports sur la Questions à l'Ordre du Jour du Comité Fédéral* (Paris, 1927), 7.

72. Weil, *La Condition Ouvrière*, 147.

73. *Le Peuple*, 4 August 1922; *La Vie Syndicale*, August 1927.

74. *L'Humanité*, 22 April 1929. See also François Sellier, "The French Workers' Movement and Political Unionism," in *The International Labor Movement in Transition*, ed. A. Sturmthal and J. Scoville (Urbana, 1973), 97.

75. *L'Humanité*, 2 April 1929.

76. Van de Casteele-Schweitzer, "Management and Labour in France 1914–1939," 65.

77. The significance of turnover in this period is emphasized by Gérard Noirel, *Les Ouvriers dans la Société Française: XIXe–XXe Siècle* (Paris, 1986), 126.

78. Lequin, "Social Structures and Shared Beliefs," 8.

79. The French industrial workforce grew at an imperceptible rate before the war. Between 1876 and 1906, the workforce increased from 3,150,000 to 3,385,000, while the German workforce more than doubled in the same period. See François Sellier, *La Confrontation Sociale en France 1936–1984* (Paris, 1984), 17–19. In general, France lacked the great urban concentrations of industrial workers of Germany and England. This had a marked effect on the character of the French labor movement and on the nature of popular culture and sensibilities, always more populist than proletarian.

80. Lequin, "Social Structures and Shared Beliefs," 12.

81. Gérard Jacquemet, "Belleville Ouvrier à la Belle Epoque," *Le Mouvement Social* 118 (January–March 1982); *Belleville au XIXe Siècle: Du Faubourg à la Ville* (Paris, 1984). See also William J. Goode, "A Theory of Role Strain," *American Sociological Review*, 25, no. 4 (August 1960).

82. Centre de Documentation d'Histoire des Techniques, *Evolution de la Geographie Industrielle de Paris et Sa Poche Banlieue au XIXe Siècle*, 351–58, 593–95; Claudine Fontanon, "L'Industrialisation de la Banlieue Parisienne," in *Un Siècle de Banlieue Parisienne (1859–1964)*, ed. Annie Fourcaut (Paris, 1988), 66–69.

83. Antoine Audit, *Les Fédérations Confédérées et Unitaires des Métaux. Lieu d'Emission d'Analyses Socio-Economique 1922–1935* (Mémoire, Paris I, 1986), 86; Michel Collinet, *L'Ouvrier Français: Essai sur la Condition Ouvrière (1900–1950)* (Paris, 1951), 109–16. Tyler Stovall, "'Friends, Neighbors, and Communists: Community Formation in Suburban Paris During the Early Twentieth Century," *Journal of Social History* 22 (Winter 1988): 239.

84. The near suburb of Paris (Seine) grew 35 percent between 1921 and 1931. The far suburb (Seine-et-Oisie) by 48 percent. See Annie Fourcaut *Bobigny, Banlieue Rouge* (Paris, 1986), 19.

85. The worker population of Paris was mainly located in the eleventh, thirteenth, fourteenth, fifteenth, nineteenth, and twentieth *arrondissements*. There small shops, still largely governed by the artisanal system of production, prevailed.

86. La Courneuve, Saint-Ouen, Gennevilliers, Asnières, Suresnes, Bois-Colombes, Puteaux, Neuilly, Courbevoie, Colombes, Bézon, Argenteuil, Nanterre, Levallois-Perret, Issy-les-Moulineaux, and Montrouge were the more consequential of the smaller metal-working towns.

87. Claude Fohlen, *La France de l'Entre-Deux-Guerres 1917–1939* (Paris, 1972), 87. It was actually Dublin's working class that had the best claim to this "distinction."

88. Maurice Thorez, *Son of the People* (New York, 1938), 179. See also Etienne Videcoq, *Les Aspects Permanents de la Crise du Logement dans la Région Parisienne* (Paris, 1932).

89. In the representative formulation of Louis-Ferdinand Céline, the suburbs are "benumbed with factories, overflowing with muck, tattered and torn . . . a soulless land, an accursed workcamp, where a smile is vain, effort lost, suffering drab." Quoted in Fréderic Vitoux, *Céline: A Biography* (New York, 1994), 366.

90. Jacquemet, *Belleville au XIXe Siècle*, 387.

91. Max Horkheimer and Theodor W. Adorno, *Dialectic of Enlightenment* (New York, 1972), 120–67.

92. Edouard Blanc, *La Ceinture Rouge: Enquête sur la Situation Politique, Morale et Sociale de la Banlieue de Paris* (Paris, 1927), 50.

93. Georges Dumoulin, *La CGT et le Parti Socialiste* (Paris, 1935), 20–21; Robert Garric, *Belleville: Scènes de la Vie Populaire* (Paris, 1928), 100–101.

94. By 1931 there were 500,000 radios in France (out of a population of 39 million) and by 1939, 5.5 million. See Tartakowsky and Willard, *Des Lendemains Qui Chantait?* 217.

95. Garric, *Belleville*, 106; Georges Altman, *Ça, C'est du Cinéma* (Paris, 1931).

96. *The Road to Wigan Pier* (1937; reprint London, 1962), 69–70

97. "Men who lose traditions," G. K. Chesterton writes, "abandon themselves to conventions." See *The Common Man* (New York, 1950), 44.

98. Fédération de Ouvriers des Métaux (CGT), *XIe Congrès Fédéral* (Versailles, 1933), 154.

99. *Le Peuple*, 3 January 1928; Garric, *Belleville*, 100–109.

100. Jacques Valdour, *Atleiers et Taudis de la Banlieue de Paris* (Paris, 1923), 94–95, 97, 168; Garric, *Belleville*, 198. The left and labor press of the period chanted a similar refrain. See, for example, *Le Populaire*, 8 January 1933.

101. Collinet, *Essai sur la Condition Ouvrière*, 122–28; Fédération des Ouvriers des Métaux (CGT), *VIIe Congrès Fédéral* (Versailles, 1925), 5–6; Jacques Valdour, *L'Ouvrier Français* (Paris, 1927), 10; Georges Lefranc, *Histoire du Travail et des Travailleurs* (Paris, 1975), 336; Garric, *Belleville*, 206.

102. *The Revolt of the Masses* (New York, 1932). See also Hannah Arendt, *The Origins of Totalitarianism* (New York, 1958), 305–16.

103. Louis Dumont, *From Mandeville to Marx* (Chicago, 1977).

104. Tyler Stovall, "French Communism and Suburban Development: The Rise of the Red Belt," *Journal of Contemporary History* 24 (July 1989).

105. *L'Humanité*, 13 May 1924. See also Annie Kriegel, "The French Communist Party and the Problems of Power," in *Contemporary France*, ed. John Cairns (New York, 1978); Fourcaut, *Bobigny*, 45–78. The development of this ideological identification mirrors, in many ways, the revival of Islam, Hinduism, and Confucianism that is presently occurring in those parts of the world touched by intensive "modernization." See Samuel P. Huntington, *The Clash of Civilization and the Remaking of World Order* (New York, 1996), 95–101.

106. "Socialism for Marx is capitalism minus private property." See Robert A. Nisbet, *The Sociological Tradition* (New York, 1966), 58. The liberal premises of Marx's project led Spengler, in *Preussenthum und Sozialismus* (Munich, 1920), to characterize him as an English Jew rather than a German—a characterization more philosophical than racial. See also Jean Baudrillard, *The Mirror of Production* (St. Louis, 1975).

107. Fourcaut, *Bobigny*, 35–40; Louis-Marie Ferré, *Les Classes Sociales dans la France Contemporaine* (Paris, 1936), 210–11; Jean-Paul Brunet, *Saint-Denis, La Ville Rouge 1890–1939* (Paris, 1980), 337–62; Jacques Girault, ed., *Sur l'Implantation du Parti Communiste Français dans l'Entre-Deux-Guerres* (Paris, 1977), 61–117; Bernard Bastien, "Sociabilities Populaires dans l'Espace de la Banlieue Parisienne," in *Un Siècle de Banlieue Parisienne*, 214–16.

108. Aristide Zolberg, in his foreword to Annie Kriegel, *The French Communists: Profile of a People* (Chicago, 1972), ix.

109. The party frequently noted the discordance between its electoral influence and its meager recruitment. See, for example, *Cahiers du Bolchevisme*, March 1930.

110. A. Losovsky, *Les Tâches du Mouvement Syndical Révolutionaire* (Paris [1931?]), 17; *Le Populaire*, 8 January 1933.

111. Dubreuil, *J'ai Fini Ma Journée*, 193–95.

112. Léon Mauvais, "Dans l'Enterprise des Années Vingt: Interview de," *Cahiers d'Histoire de l'Institut Maurice Thorez* 8 (January 1974), 48–49.

Chapter Two

1. Val Lorwin, *The French Labor Movement* (Cambridge, 1954), 37.

2. Charles A. Micaud, *Communism and the French Left* (New York, 1963), 7.

3. Jean Maitron, *Paul Delesalle: Un Anarchiste de la Belle Epoche* (Paris, 1985), 26–27.

4. François Sellier, "The French Workers' Movement and Political Unionism," 98.

5. Henri Dubief, *Le Syndicalisme Révolutionnaire: Textes Choises* (Paris, 1969), 71.

6. *La Révolution Prolétarienne*, 1 January 1930.

7. Michelle Perrot, "From the Mechanic to the Metallo," 262. Because these "syndicalists" oriented to the "labor aristocracy," they were not at all comparable to syndicalists in Spain, Italy, and the English-speaking world, who based their program on the "primitive revolt" of the worst-paid, most grievously exploited strata of the working class.

8. Robert Goetz-Girey, *La Pensé Syndicale Française: Militants et Théoriciens* (Paris, 1948); Lorwin, *The French Labor Movement*, 37. On revolutionary syndicalism, see F. F. Ridly, *Revolutionary Syndicalism in France* (Cambridge, 1970); Lewis L. Lorwin, *Syndicalism in France* (New York, 1914); Jeremy Jenkins, *Syndicalism in France* (Oxford, 1990).

9. André Philip, *Trade-Unionisme et Syndicalisme* (Paris, 1936), 255.

10. A British unionist once characterized his French counterparts as always being "the first to raise their hands for some revolutionary measure, but the last to put them in their pocket when contributions were demanded." Quoted in Rhodes, *Louis Renault*, 134.

11. Quoted in Bruce Vandervort, *Victor Griffuelhes and Revolutionary Syndicalism*

1895–1922 (Baton Rouge, 1996), xiii. See also V. Griffuelhes, "Le Syndicalisme Révolutionnaire" (1909), in *Anarcho-Syndicalisme et Syndicalisme Révolutionnaire,* by I. Mercier et al. (Paris, 1978), 93–94.

12. Peter Stearns, *Revolutionary Syndicalism and French Labor: A Cause Without Rebels* (New Brunswick, 1971); Jacques Julliard, *Fernand Pelloutier et les Origines du Syndicalisme d'Action Directe* (Paris, 1971).

13. *L'Eveil des Ouvriers en Instruments de Précision,* March 1914. See also Christian Gras, "La Fédération des Métaux en 1913–1914 et l'Evolution du Syndicalisme Révolutionnaire Français," *Le Mouvement Social* 77 (September–October 1971): 98; Eric Guerber, *Les Fédérations des Métaux: Lieux d'Emission d'Analyses Socio-Econmiques 1892–1914* (Mémoire, Université de Paris, 1985).

14. James M. Laux, "Travail et Travailleurs dans l'Industrie Automobile jusqu'en 1914," *Le Mouvement Social* 81 (October–December 1972).

15. Edward Shorter and Charles Tilly, *Strikes in France 1830–1968* (Cambridge, 1974), 219.

16. Christian Gras, "La Fédération des Métaux en 1913–1914," 104–6.

17. Annie Kriegel and Jean-Jacques Becker, *1914, la Guerre et le Mouvement Ouvrier Français* (Paris, 1964); Jacques Julliard, "La CGT devant la Guerre (1900–1914)," *Le Mouvement Social* 49 (October–December 1964); Susan Milner, "August 1914: Nationalism, Internationalism and the French Working Class," in *War and Society in Twentieth Century France,* ed. M. Scriven and P. Wagstaff (New York, 1991); Jean-Jacques Becker, *1914: Comment les Français Sont Entrée dans la Guerre?* (Paris, 1977).

18. Jean-Louis Robert, *Les Ouvriers, la Patrie et la Révolution: Paris 1914–1919* (Paris, 1995), 85–86, 95–97.

19. André Marchal, *Action Ouvrière et Transformation du Régime Capitaliste* (Paris, 1943), 5.

20. The price index rose from 102 in 1914 to 390 in 1918 (100 = 1913), while wages consistently lagged behind, rising only to 187 in 1918.

21. Roger Picard, *Le Mouvement Syndical durant la Guerre* (Paris, 1927), 110–12; Gilbert Hatry, "Shop Stewards at Renault," in *The French Home Front 1914–18,* ed. Patrick Fridenson (Providence, 1992).

22. Metal workers throughout war-torn Europe constituted the most militant opponents of the war effort and, not unrelatedly, provided the principal working-class base for the Communist parties formed after 1918. See Jane Bond-Howard, "Le Syndicalisme Minoritaire dans les Usines d'Armement de Bourges de 1914 à 1918," *Le Mouvement Social* 148 (July–September 1989): 33. See also Dick Geary, "Radicalism and the Worker: Metalworkers and Revolution 1914–23," in *Society and Politics in Wilhelmine Germany,* ed. Richard Evans (London, 1978), 277–79.

23. William Oualid, "The Effect of the War upon Labour in France," in *Effects of the War upon French Economic Life,* ed. Charles Gide (Oxford, 1923), 178–87.

24. See for example, *L'Humanité,* 5 February 1918; Roberts, *Les Ouvriers, la Patrie et la Révolution,* 194–96. See also, Max Gallo, "Quelques Aspects de la Mentalité et du Comportement Ouvrier dans les Usines de Guerre," *Le Mouvement Social* 56 (July–September 1966).

25. Jean-Jacques Becker, *The Great War and the French People* (Leamington Spa, 1985), 205–11, 260–65.

26. Paul Louis, *Le Déclin de la Société Bourgeoise* (Paris, 1923), 24; Michel Collinet, *L'Ouvrier Français: Essai sur la Condition Ouvrière (1900–1950),* 15–22; Daniel Halévy,

Décadence de la Liberté (Paris, 1931), 87–88; V.I. Lenin, "Letters from Afar" (1917) in *Collective Works* (Moscow, 1964), vol. 23.

27. Henri Barbé, *Souvenirs de Militant et de Dirigeant Communiste* (Typescript MS, Hoover Institution Archives, n.d.), 3–4. Cf. Jean-Paul Brunet, *Jacques Doriot: Du Communisme au Fascisme* (Paris, 1986), 23.

28. Dubreuil, *J'ai Fini Ma Journée*, 12–14, 41, 62; Valdour, *Ateliers et Taudis de la Banlieue de Paris*, 168–69; Fohlen, *La France de l'Entre-Deux-Guerres (1917–1939)*, 40.

29. This had been the rationale justifying the CGT's reformist turn. See John N. Horne, *Labour at War: France and Britain 1914–1918* (Oxford, 1991).

30. Jean-Louis Robert, "Les Programmes Minimum de la CGT de 1918 à 1921," *Cahiers d'Histoire de l'Institut de Recherche Marxiste* 16 (1984); Georges Lefranc, *Le Mouvement Syndical sous la Troisiènne République* (Paris, 1984), 215–39; John N. Horne, "The Comité d'Action (CGT–Parti Socialiste) and the Origins of Wartime Labour Reformism (1914–1916)," in *The French Home Front*.

31. Brunet, *Saint-Denis*, 214–15.

32. On the 1919 strikes, see *Union des Métaux*, June–July 1919; *La Vie Ouvrière*, 11 June, 25 June 1919; *La Voix du Peuple*, July 1919; *L'Humanité*, 2–30 June, 2 and 7 July 1919. See also Bertrand Abherve, "Les Origines de la Grève des Métallurgistes Parisiens, Juin 1919," *Le Mouvement Social* 93 (October–December 1975); Nicholas Papayanis, "Masses Révolutionnaires et Directions Réformistes: Les Tensions au Cours des Grèves des Métallurgies Français en 1919," *Le Mouvement Social* 93 (October–December 1975). For the most authoritative treatment, see Roberts, *Les Ouvriers, la Patrie et la Révolution, 292–374*.

33. Robert Verdier, *Bilan d'une Scission: Congrès de Tours* (Paris, 1981) and Jean-Louis Robert, "Nouveaux Elements sur les Origines du PCF," *Cahiers d'Histoire de l'Institut de Recherches Marxistes* 3 (1980). The PCF was first known as the Section Française de l'Internationale Communiste (SFIC) and did not receive its later appellation until 1935. For simplicity sake, I refer solely to its more commonly known name.

34. George Lichtheim: "If it has been said of the early Christians that they awaited the coming of the Savior and instead got the Church, it may be said of the French proletariat that it expected the Revolution and instead got the Communist Party." *Marxism in Modern France* (New York, 1966), 68.

35. Laurent Batsch and Michele Bouvent, *CGT: Autour de la Scission de 1921* (Paris, 1983); Pierre Monatte, *Trois Scissions Syndicales* (Paris, 1958); Jean-Louis Robert, *La Scission Syndicale de 1921: Essai de Reconnaissance des Formes* (Paris, 1980); Maurice Labi, *La Grande Division des Travailleurs: Première Scission de la CGT (1914–1921)* (Paris, 1964).

36. The best expression of this position, debated in the pages of *La Vie Ouvrière* in 1921–22, can be found in "Letter to Comrade Monatte," in Leon Trotsky, *The First Five Years of the Communist International* (New York, 1945), 2:158–61. Cf. Antoine Prost, *La CGT à l'Epoch du Front Populaire 1934–1939* (Paris, 1964), 129–30.

37. See, for example, *La Révolution Prolétarienne*, 1 January 1930.

38. Kathryn E. Amdur, "Le Tradition Révolutionnaire entre Syndicalisme et Communisme dans la France de l'Entre-Deux-Guerres," *Le Movement Social* 139 (April 1987). On the international relations between syndicalists, anarchists, and communists in this period, see Wayne Thorpe, *"The Workers Themselves": Revolutionary Syndicalism and International Labour, 1913–1923* (Dordrecht, 1989).

39. This, at least, was the case after 1924, when the anarchists split from the CGT. Without their departure, the CGTU would certainly have floundered, for relations between communists and anarchists were marked by extreme violence. In early 1924, for example, an-

archists disrupted a communist meeting with twenty revolver shots, killing two. See Georges Gogniot, *Parti Pris* (Paris, 1976), 72. With the departure of the anarchists, factional tensions between communists and syndicalists were henceforth played out in more restrained measures.

40. *La Vie Ouvrière*, 22 June 1928, 18 January 1929. A Central Committee report from the late 1920s indicates that only 3.5 percent of the total PCF membership was made up of unskilled or semi-skilled workers. We lack comparable figures for the Unitaire Metal Union, but impressionistic sources suggest that the figure was perhaps even lower. See R. Dufraisse, "Le Mouvement Ouvrier Française 'Rouge' Devant la Grande Dépression Economique," in *Mouvements Ouvriers et Dépression Economique de 1919 à 1939* (Assen, 1966), 169. This point needs emphasizing in view of the frequently made contention that the fledgling communist movement attracted mainly young, unskilled workers.

41. Louis Chagnon, *Les Fédérations des Métaux CGT et CGTU de 1922 à 1935: Organisation et Militants* (Mémoire, Université de Paris, 1985), 16. See also Barbé, *Souvenirs de Militant*, 10–15. Cf. R. F. Wheeler, "German Labor and the Comintern: A Problem of Generations?" *Journal of Social History* 37 (Spring 1974).

42. *L'International Syndical Rouge*, September–October 1924 and April 1925. Because membership figures had political significance, all estimates need to be treated with caution; see Prost, *La CGT à l'Epoch du Front Populaire*, 2.

43. *L'Information Sociale*, 23 March 1923; *L'International Syndical Rouge*, April 1925; *La Voix du Peuple de Paris*, 10 February 1933. By 1925, it is estimated that the CGT Metal Federation climbed to 25,000–30,000 members and the CGTU Federation dropped to 40,000. See Third International Conference of Revolutionary Metal Workers, *Report of the Secretariat of the International Propaganda Committee of Revolutionary Metal Workers* (Moscow, 1925), 35.

44. Michel Dreyfus, *Histoire de la C.G.T.* (Brussels, 1995), 121–22.

45. Albert Vassart, *Mémoirs* (Typescript MS, Hoover Institution Archives, n.d.), pt. 1, p.7; *La Vie Ouvrière*, 3 August 1923.

46. Vassart, *Mémoirs*, pt. 2, p.25. Also *L'Union des Métaux*, March–April 1924; *Le Peuple*, 14 March 1929; and *Le Révolution Prolétarienne*, January 1926.

47. See Alain Dewerpe, *Le Monde du Travail en France 1800–1950* (Paris, 1989), 163. The Soviets were especially solicitous about metal production, especially in countries likely to pose a military threat to the Socialist Fatherland. Because metal production was essential to the life and military strength of the modern economy, it was not fortuitous that in the struggle against capitalism, metal workers were called on "to march in the vanguard." See *Report of the Secretariat of the International Propaganda Committee of Revolutionary Metal Workers*. Communist interest in the *métallos* was also conditioned by early Bolshevik successes in the prewar Petersburg metal industry. See Victoria E. Bonnell, *Roots of Rebellion: Workers' Politics and Organization in the St. Petersburg and Moscow 1900–1914* (Berkeley, 1983), 393–98.

48. Vassart, *Memoirs*, pt. 2, p.2. Also *L'Union des Métaux*, January–February 1930; Lefranc, *Le Mouvement Syndical sous la Troisiènne République*, 278.

49. *L'Union des Métaux*, January–February 1930.

50. Jane Degras, ed., *The Communist International: Documents* (London, 1960), 2: 188–200. The "Twenty-One Conditions" of 1921 had also called for a bolshevization of party organization, but it was not carried out.

51. E. H. Carr, *The Interregnum, 1923–24* (Hammonsworth, 1969), 222.

52. Léon Mauvais, "Dans l'Entreprise des Années Vingt: Interview de," *Cahiers d'Histoire de l'Institut Maurice Thorez* 8 (January 1974), 44.

53. Degras, *The Communist International*, 2:79–82. Cf. Barbé, *Souvenirs de Militant*, 69–71.

54. Bolshevization caused PCF membership to drop from 76,000 in January 1925 to 55,000 in June 1926. See Degras, *The Communist International*, 2:291–94.

55. *Cahiers du Bolchevisme*, September 1926; O. Piatnitsky, *The Immediate Tasks of the International Trade Union Movement* (New York [1930?]); Sylvie Schweitzer, "Regards sur la Bolchevisation: Le Cas de la Cellule 410 de l'Usine Citroen (1924–1925)," *Cahiers d'Histoire de l'Institut de Recherches Marxistes* 5 (1981); Gogniot, *Parti Pris*, 1:84–86.

56. *Cahiers du Bolchevisme*, 15 October 1932.

57. *Cahiers du Bolchevisme*, 28 February 1927.

58. Vassart, *Mémoirs*, pt. 2, p.8. Other sources indicate that the figures might have been lower. For example, *La Révolution Prolétarienne* (1 January 1927) claimed there were only 137 in the metal industry, of which but eighty-seven had a functional existence. Moreover, these cells were mostly located in small plants, outside the mass-production sector. The party's dismal record of cell formation in the Paris metal industry was still better than that of any other trade or region.

59. *Bulletin Régional: Cahier du Militant de la Région Parisienne*, April 1926; also "Circulaire Letter on Factory Cells," in Degras, *The Communist International*, 3:141–49.

60. PCF, *Les Cellule Communistes d'Entreprises* (Paris, 1924); *Cahiers du Bolchevisme*, 28 January, 30 April 1926. Cf. T. Ferlé, *Le Communisme en France: Organisation* (Paris, 1937), 54–59.

61. The *section syndicale* was originally called a *section d'usine* or a *section syndicale d'usine*; to avoid confusion, I use only the first term.

62. *L'Humanité*, 29 June 1925.

63. Union Syndicale des Travailleurs de Métallurgie (CGTU), *Statuts* (Courbevoie, n.d.).

64. Piatnitsky, *The Immediate Tasks of the International Trade Union Movement*, 23; *Report of the 4th Congress of the RILU* (Essex, 1928), 68.

65. *La Révolution Prolétaire*, 15 May 1927. Of the 4,000 Paris *métallos* affiliated with the CGTU in the mid 1930s, 2500 were reputedly PCF members. See Michel Collinet, "Masses et Militants: La Bureaucratie et la Crise Actuelle du Syndicalisme Ouvrier Français," *Revue d'Histoire Economique et Sociale* 29 (1951): 69. Also *Bulletin Régional*, 15 February 1927.

66. *La Lutte des Classes*, July 1928.

67. *L'Humanité*, 29 April 1923; *La Vie Syndicale*, November 1923, July 1925.

68. Lucien Monjauvis, *Jean-Pierre Timbaud* (Paris, 1971), 42; Gillot, *Un Forgeron dans la Cité des Rois*, 88–89.

69. Piatnitsky, *The Immediate Tasks of the International Trade Union Movement*, 8.

70. For example, the Talbot auto strike of 1926. See *L'Union des Métaux*, March–April 1926.

71. Brunet, *Saint-Denis*, 270–71.

72. Prost, *La CGT à l'Epoque du Front Populaire*, 63–64.

73. For example, *L'Union des Métaux*, September–October 1927.

74. No matter how craft-oriented, the prewar CGT unions adhered to an industrial conception of unionism. In the heady days of 1919, the CGT resolved to abolish all vestiges of craft unionism and impose a purely industrial form of union organization. In 1920, thirteen craft unions in the Paris Region were fused into a single metal union. After the schism, the CGTU continued this practice, but not the CGT. See Fédération des Ouvriers des Métaux (CGT), *VIe Congrès Fédéral* (Versailles, 1924), 259–61. Also Chagnon, *Les Fédérations CGT et CGTU*, 58–59.

75. Syndicat des Ouvriers en Instruments de Chirurgie (CGT), [No Title] (Paris, 1924).

76. Fédération des Ouvriers des Métaux, *VIe Congrès Fédéral* , 43, 259, 260.

77. Michelle Perrot, "On the Formation of the French Working Class," in *Working-Class*

Formation: Nineteenth-Century Patterns in Western Europe and the United States, ed. I. Katznelson and A. R. Zolberg (Princeton, 1986), 91.

78. Maxime Leroy, *Les Techniques Nouvelles du Syndicalisme* (Paris, 1921).

79. *L'Union des Métaux*, July–August 1926.

80. See, for example, Dubreuil, *J'ai Fini Ma Journée*, 49–62, 203–11.

81. The Paris metal worker Hyacinthe Dubreuil played a major role in promoting rationalization. See his *Standards: Le Travail Américain Vu par un Ouvrier Français* (Paris, 1929). Although historians frequently assume that his view typified the confederal response to the new technologies, Dubreuil represented a minority. Paris confederals occasionally paid lip service to rationalization, but their lack of enthusiasm for, if not their hostility to the new production technologies is evident in the many discussions of this subject that took place in the pages of *L'Union des Métaux* throughout the late 1920s and early 1930s.

82. Confederals and *unitaires* were not the only ones trying to organize Paris metal workers. Anarchists who split from the CGTU in 1924 and formed the Confédération Générale du Travail Syndicaliste Révolutionnaire (CGTSR) in 1926 were also active. They, however, were few in number (their stronghold was Lyon) and had little overall impact on the metal industry. See Jean Maitron, *Le Mouvement Anarchiste en France* (Paris, 1983), 2:65–71. Catholic *métallos* in the Confédération Française des Travailleurs Chrétiens (CFTC) were a somewhat more serious alternative, but until the era of the People's Front, they numbered less than 600 and limited their activities to the parish. See Pierre Trimouille, *Les Syndicats Chrétiens dans la Métallurgie de 1935 à 1939* (Mémoire, Université de Paris, 1949).

Chapter Three

1. On the peculiarities of the French depression, see Alfred Sauvy, *Histoire Economique de la France entre les Deux Guerres* (Paris, 1967), vol. 2.

2. Julien Jackson, *The Politics of Depression in France 1932–1936* (Cambridge, 1985), 23.

3. Bureau International du Travail (BIT), *Annuaire des Statistiques du Travail: 1935–1936* (Geneva, 1936), table 1.

4. *Bulletin de la Statistique Générale de la France* 25 (1936): 484. More generally, see Gancarz, "La Métallurgie Française face à la Crise des Années Trente."

5. UIMM, *Reclassement de la Main-d'Oeuvre* (Paris, 1937), 5.

6. BIT, *Annuaire des Statistiques du Travail: 1935–1936*, table 1.

7. International Labour Office, *Yearbook of Labour Statistics, 1935–1936* (Geneva, 1936), 36.

8. BIT, *Annuaire des Statistiques du Travail: 1935–36*, table 10.

9. Fédération des Ouvriers en Métaux, *Congrès d'Unité* (Versailles, 1937), 62. Management and labor drew radically different conclusions from the government's economic statistics. Subjective perceptions, however, were nearly as important as objective realities.

10. Henri Vieilledent, *Souvenirs d'un Travailleur Manuel Syndicaliste* (Paris, 1978), 117–24.

11. Evident on every page of virtually every labor paper in this period.

12. *Le Prolétaire*, 19 November 1933.

13. All wings of the labor movement complained of the humiliating conditions facing workers in the depressed factory system. See, for example, *Le Syndicalisme Chrétien*, February 1934; *Le Prolétaire*, 10 October 1932.

14. Van der Casteele-Schweitzer, "Management and Labour in France," 66.

15. *Le Prolétaire*, 2 May 1931.

16. Durand, *La Lutte des Travailleurs de chez Renault*, 41–42, 45; CGTU, *Congrès National Ordinaire* (Paris, 1931), 152–59.

17. *L'Ouvrière*, 10 July 1930.

18. CGTU, *La CGTU Contre les Ammendes* (Paris, c.1932).

19. Gary Cross estimates that foreign workers went from 13 to 7 percent of the metal workforce between 1931 and 1936, dismissed from industry at nearly two and a half times the rate of French workers. See *Immigrant Workers in Industrial France*, 188, 204–5.

20. *La Voix du Peuple*, March 1931, March 1932, March 1935.

21. Noirel, *Les Ouvriers dans la Société Française*, 175; *L'Union des Métaux*, March 1932.

22. See, for example, Comité Républicain, *La Crise Economique* (Rouen, 1933). The overproduction thesis is today held by few economic historians. See Jacques Néré, *La Crise de 1929* (Paris, 1968), 61–72. Some employers, however, had lost all confidence in liberal principles and began toying with corporatist and planist ideas. See Richard Kuisel, *Capitalism and the State in Modern France* (Cambridge, 1981), 98–107.

23. *Le Peuple*, 16 February, 13 April, 21 December 1931.

24. CGT, *Congrès Confédéral de Paris: XXVIIe Congrès* (Versailles, 1931); also Bernard Georges, Denise Tintant, and Marie-Anne Renaud, *Léon Jouhaux dans le Mouvement Syndical Français* (Paris, 1979), 91.

25. CGT, *Congrès Confédéral de Paris: XXVIIIe Congrès* (Versailles, 1933), 78.

26. See, for example, *Le Peuple*, 5 October 1932.

27. Fédération des Ouvriers des Métaux (CGT), *XIe Congrès Fédéral* (Versailles, 1933), 233–34; Chagnon, *Les Fédérations des Métaux CGT et CGTU de 1922 à 1935*, ch. 5.

28. Fédération des Ouvriers en Métaux (CGT), *Xe Congrès Fédéral* (Versailles, 1931), 83.

29. *Le Travailleur Parisien*, April–June 1934.

30. "Theses of the Sixth Comintern Congress on the International Situation and the Tasks of the Communist International," in *Soviet Russia Masters the Comintern: International Communism in the Era of Stalin's Ascendancy*, ed. Helmut Gruber (New York, 1974), 215–21.

31. Thorez, *Son of the People*, 53.

32. Barbé, *Souvenirs de Militant*, 243.

33. Philippe Robrieux, *Histoire Intèriere du Parti Communiste 1920–1945* (Paris, 1980), 404.

34. *Le Cri de Peuple*, 2 April 1930; *L'Humanité*, 24 February 1930.

35. Vassart, *Mémoirs*, pt. 3, p.20.

36. CGTU, *5e Congrès National* (Paris, 1929), 544–48.

37. RILU, *Report of the Fourth Congress of the RILU* (Essex, 1928), 15–16.

38. RILU, *Report of the Fourth Congress*, 29.

39. *Le Cri de Peuple*, 18 June 1930; *Le Peuple*, 6 July 1929.

40. For example, their disastrous leadership of the Laboratoires Standard du Material Telephonique strike. See *L'Union des Métaux*, January–February 1930.

41. Thorez, *Son of the People*, 67.

42. Vassart, *Mémoirs*, pt. 2, pp.12–14.

43. Quoted in Pierre Naville, *L'Entre-Deux-Guerres: La Lutte des Classes en France 1926–1939* (Paris, 1975), 194.

44. *Le Métallurgiste*, September–October 1930.

45. *International Press Correspondence*, 10 June 1931.

46. *Le Prolétaire de Clichy: Organe Local du Parti Ouvrier-Paysan*, 5 June 1931. Socialists affiliated with this journal pointed out that the new line was "uniquely oriented toward causing workers to fight among themselves."

47. *Le Prolétaire de Clichy*, 1 January 1930.

48. Edward Mortimer, *The Rise of the French Communist Party 1920–1947* (London, 1984), 143–44.

49. *Le Peuple*, 26, 28 February, 1 April 1929; *L'Humanité*, 23 June 1929; CGTU, *Congrès National Ordinaire* (Paris, 1929). For a critique, see Leon Trotsky, "The 'Third Period' of the Comintern's Errors," in *Writings: 1930* (New York, 1975), 27–68.

50. Vassard, *Mémoirs*, pt. 3, p.35.

51. E. H. Carr, *Twilight of the Comintern, 1930–1935* (New York, 1982), 18–19.

52. Gérard Walter, *Histoire du Parti Communiste Français* (Paris, 1948), 214–15.

53. RILU, *Every Factory a Fortress! The Tasks of the Revolutionary Trade Union Organizations in the Work at the Factory* (London [1931?]), 2. See also RILU, *The Way Forward: Position of the RILU Sections and Their Role in the Leadership of the Economic Struggle and Unemployment Movement: These Adopted by the Eight Session of the CC of the RILU* (London [1931?]); *Resolutions of the Fifth Congress of the RILU* (London, 1931).

54. A. Losovsky, *Les Tâches du Mouvement Syndical Révolutionnaire: Discours et Resolutions Adoptées par le Bureau Executif de l'ISR après Discussions avec la Delegation de la CGTU (Juin 1931)* (Paris [1931?]).

55. *Cahiers du Bolchevisme*, 1 November 1931.

56. In Leninist parlance, as described by Thomas Taylor Hammond, *economism* "placed less emphasis on the political struggle and more on the economic struggle, less on the party and more on the trade union, less on ideological questions and more on practical everyday problems, less on the importance of leadership by the party and more on the spontaneous movement of the workers." See *Lenin on Trade Unions and Revolution 1893–1917* (New York, 1957), 16.

57. PCF, *Le Parti Communiste Français devant l'Internationale* (Paris, 1931). Cf., Carr, *Twilight of the Comintern*, 34.

58. Barbé believed his demise was brought about by his refusal to cooperate with Soviet espionage; see *Souvenirs de Militant*, 263–64, 288–89.

59. Philippe Robrieux, *Maurice Thorez: Vie Secrète et Vie Publique* (Paris, 1975), 153–54. A generation of American social historians, animated by what Nietzsche would have called the "plebeianism" of the academic bourgeoisie, has gone to great lengths to document the distances—the autonomy—that separated the various Communist parties from the Russian-dominated Comintern, rejecting the older anti-communist view that the different national sections of world communism were the willing instrument of Moscow. Their efforts, however, have been even less credible than those of the anti-communists of the 1950s. Stéphane Courtois, the founder of the review *Communisme* and one of the leading authorities on French communist history, has, after surveying the recently opened Russian archives, "discovered with stupor," the total control which the Soviet apparatus exercised over the most minute aspects of the PCF's domestic policies. "Their [i.e. the French communist] margin of maneuver and autonomy vis-a-vis Moscow," he concludes, "was virtually nil." See "Les Archives du Communisme: Entretien avec Stéphane Courtois," *Krisis* 20–21 (November 1997): 83. This, of course, does not reflect on the sincerity of the communist ranks nor does it diminish the significance of their opposition to bourgeois society.

60. Degras, *The Communist International: Documents*, 3:203–208.

61. *Le Prolétaire de Clichy*, 26 September 1930.

62. See, for example, *Cahiers du Bolchevisme*, 1 November 1931.

63. *Cahiers du Bolchevisme*, May 1932. See also PCF, *Les Communistes et les Syndicats: Le Travail des Fractions Syndicales* (Paris, 1932), 5–6, 24. As E.H. Carr argues, this reorientation

was anything but clear and consistent. Many top Soviet officials, like Pianitsky, continued to emphasize the "revolutionary way out of the crisis." See, for example, *International Press Correspondence*, 10 June 1931. Until the Comintern formally abandoned the Third Period line at its 1935 World Congress, Soviet policy continued to lunge back and forth between contrary orientations. The gradual adoption of an "economist" strategy in the unions is evident in both the programmatic and practical developments of this period, but its official reformulation had to wait until the World Congress. Carr's depiction of the Comintern's hesitancy and ambiguity before 1935, as it tried to square its own interest with the situation in the West, best explains why historians have been so divided in their characterization of communist activity in the early 1930s. See his *Twilight of the Comintern*.

64. *Cahiers du Bolchevisme*, May 1930.

65. Jacques Girault, *Benoît Frachon, Communiste et Syndicaliste* (Paris, 1989), 127.

66. Jacques Chambraz, *Le Front Populaire pour le Pain, la Liberté et la Paix* (Paris, 1961), 20; Jacques Duclos, *Mémoires: 1896–1934* (Paris, 1968), 387.

67. Thorez, *Son of the People*, 68.

68. CGTU, *6e Congrès National* (Paris, 1931), 560, 588. Earlier, the congress of the Unitaire Metal Federation passed a similar resolution: see *L'Humanité*, 24, 27 February 1931.

69. *L'Humanité*, 3, 9, 10 October 1932.

70. Bertrand Badie, *Stratégie de la Grève* (Paris, 1976), 55–59.

71. Daniel Guérin, "Une Tentative de Réunification Syndicale, 1930–1931," *Revue d'Histoire Economique* 1 (1966).

72. Daniel Guérin, *Front Populaire, Révolution Manquée: Témoignage Militant* (Paris, 1970), 48.

73. Synoptic biographies of all these figures can be found in Jean Maitron, ed., *Dictionnaire Biographique du Mouvement Ouvrier Français. Quatrième Partie: 1914–1939* (Paris, 1981–86).

74. *Le Cri du Peuple*, 4 March 1931.

75. *The Red International of Labour Unions*, 15 July 1932; CGTU, *6e Congrès National*, 156; *La Voix du Peuple de Paris*, 3 March 1933.

76. *Cahiers du Bolchevisme*, 1 June 1933.

77. *L'Humanité*, 2 December 1932.

78. *La Voix du Peuple de Paris*, 28 July 1933.

79. CGTU, *VIIe Congrès National Ordinaire* (Paris, 1933), 395.

80. Both the CGTU and the RILU had inscribed the sitdown tactic in the original formulation of their programs. In the 1920s, there are several references to sitdowns, such as among assembly line workers at Citroen during a 1926 strike, but these workstoppages seem to have been entirely incidental. The Talbot strike, launched without union inspiration, represented the first authentic sitdown in the Paris metal industry. See *L'Humanité*, 16 January and 8 February 1931. See also H. Desbrousses, *Le Mouvement des Masses Ouvrières en France Entre les Deux Guerres d'après "La Vie Ouvrière"* (Saint Germain de Calberte, 1975), 2:57–58.

81. 100 = 1913. See Ministère du Travail, *Statistique Générale de la France: Annuaire Statistique* 54 (1938), 73*.

82. *L'Humanité*, 7–12, 19 March 1931; *Cahiers du Bolchevisme*, 1 October 1931.

83. *L'Humanité*, 12 July 1931.

84. *L'Humanité*, 21 August 1931.

85. *Cahiers du Bolchevisme*, 15 July 1932.

86. On the Renault strike, see *L'Humanité*, November 1931–January 1932; A. Picard,

"The Struggle of the Workers in the Renault Factories," *The Red International of Labor Unions*, 15 March 1932; Jean-Paul Depretto and Sylvie Schweitzer, *Le Communisme à l'Usine: Vie Ouvrière et Mouvement Ouvrier chez Renault 1920–1939* (Paris, 1984), 153–77. *Le Communisme à l'Usine* is one of the very few books devoted to the labor movement in the Paris metal industry. My own work is much indebted to it.

87. On the Citroen strike, see *L'Humanité*, 28 March to 30 May 1933; *Le Peuple*, 31 March to 5 May 1933; *Cahiers du Bolchevisme*, 15 April, 1 June, 1 August 1933; *La Voix du Peuple de Paris*, 12, 19 May, 30 June 1933; *L'Union des Métaux*, May 1933; *L'Aube Nouvelle*, 15 April 1933; *La Vie Ouvrière*, 12 May 1933 and 20 July 1934; *International Press Correspondence*, 16 June 1933 and 5 March 1934; *La Révolution Prolétarienne*, 25 April, 25 May 1933; CGTU, *VIIe Congrès National Ordinaire*, 170–79, 190–97, 273; Sylvie Schweitzer, *Des Engrenage à la Chaîne; Les Usines Citroen 1915–1935* (Lyon, 1982), 160–65.

88. *La Vie Ouvrière*, 20 July 1934.

89. CGTU, *VIIe Congrès National Ordinaire*, 395; *La Voix du Peuple de Paris*, 10 February, 3 March 1933.

Chapter Four

1. Danielle Tartakowsky and Claude Willard, *Des Lendemains Qui Chantent? La France des Années Folles et du Front Populaire* (Paris, 1986), 110–12.

2. See Georges Michon, *Les Puissances d'Argent et l'Emeute du 6 Février* (Paris [1934?]). The labor movement had an equally critical view of the situation. In the words of one trade unionist: "The status quo today is synonymous with reaction and the decay of democracy. . . . [It] is gangrene . . . unable to function because of the crooks who dominate it." R. Lenoir in *L'Union des Métaux*, May 1933. Yet unlike the right, labor faulted the regime not because it was democratic, but because it lacked genuine democracy.

3. René Rémond, *The Right Wing in France: From 1815 to De Gaulle*, trans. James Laux (Philadelphia, 1969), 254–307. Cf. William D. Irvine, "French Conservatives and the 'New Right' During the 1930s," *French Historical Studies 8* (Fall 1974); Robert Soucy, *French Fascism: The Second Wave, 1933–1939* (New Haven, 1995), 1–25. Unlike Irvine, Soucy, and many liberal American interpreters of fascism, Rémond sees fascism not simply as a reactionary movement definable in terms of its rejection of the eighteenth-century Enlightenment project championed by Marxists and progressives—a rejection fascists shared with conservatives— but also as a revolutionary movement opposed to traditional elites, anti-capitalist, and oriented to a New Order based on a "heroic nationalism" and an anti-cosmopolitan socialism. In this sense, historians like Irvine and Soucy, guided by simplistic right-left dichotomies, bear an uncanny resemblance to Stalinist interpreters, who fixate on fascism's anti-liberalism to the neglect of its revolutionary project and its deep roots in the popular classes. Zeev Sternhell, a critic of Soucy who has gained the greatest notoriety in the current debate over French fascism, simply inverts the narrow categories in which the debate has been conducted and errs in the opposite direction by seeing only the "left" facets of fascism. See his *Neither Right nor Left: Fascist Ideology in France* (Berkeley, 1986). In my view, fascism, to use the prevailing categories, was a highly complex and diverse historical phenomenon that was both right and left, insofar as it tried to harness the left's opposition to the money powers and the right's concern with restoring the integrity of the national community. To see only one facet of fascism is to misunderstand it. See Maurice Bardéche, *Qu'est-ce Que le Fascism?* (Paris, 1970); Roger Griffin, *The Nature of Fascism*, 117–18; Jean-Christian Petitfils, *La Droite en France* (Paris, 1973), 87–93; Armin Mohler, "Le 'Style' Fasciste," *Nouvelle Ecole 42* (1985); Ernst Nolte, Theorien über den Faschismus (Cologne, 1967).

4. The leagues, by definition, were unlike political parties in that they did not participate in parliamentary or electoral activities.

5. Jacques Droz, *Histoire de l'Antifascisme en Europe 1923–1939* (Paris, 1985), 178. See also Ernst Nolte, *Der Europäische Bürgerkrieg 1917–1945* (Berlin, 1988).

6. Thorez, for example, called it a prepared "coup." See Maurice Thorez, *France Today and the People's Front* (London, 1936). See also, Marcel Le Clère, *Le 6 Février* (Paris, 1967). Few historians, however, accept this characterization. See Serge Berstein, *Le 6 Février 1934* (Paris, 1975); Max Beloff, "The Sixth of February," in James Joll, ed., *The Decline of the Third Republic* (London, 1959). The parliamentary commission that investigated the event also refuted the idea of a planned insurrection; see Laurent Bonnevay, *Les Journées Sanglants de Février 1934* (Paris, 1934).

7. Marc Rucart, *Rapport Général: Les Causes et les Origines des Evenements du 6 Février* (Paris, 1934).

8. Elisabeth du Réau, *Edouard Daladier 1884–1970* (Paris, 1993), 127–35.

9. Stanley Hoffmann, "Paradoxes of the French Political Community" in *In Search of France* (Cambridge, 1964). According to Trotsky: "The capitulation of the most powerful parliamentary party before the guns and knives of the fascists is an external expression of the complete upset in the political equilibrium of the country." See *On France* (New York, 1979), 74.

10. See, for example, *La Verité*, 16 February 1934.

11. Pierre Frank, *La Semaine du 6 au 12 Février* (Paris, 1934); Georges Michou, *Les Puissances d'Argent et l'Emeute du 6 Février* (Paris [1934?]).

12. Yves Simon, *The Road to Vichy 1918–1938*, rev. ed. (Lanham, Md., 1988), 93.

13. André Delmas, leader of the CGT Teachers Federation, described Paris on 7 February as having undergone an utter transformation. "The curious and the indifferent have disappeared. One part of Paris ferociously confronts the other. Republican and revolutionary Paris [on one side] . . . fascist Paris [on the other] . . . Two hostile factions prepared to square off in a test of strength." See *A Gauche de la Barricade. Chronique Syndicale de l'Avant-Guerre* (Paris, 1950), 15.

14. *Le Peuple*, 1 April 1933. The CGT Metal Federation adopted a similar resolution; see *L'Union des Métaux*, May 1933.

15. *La Voix du Peuple*, January 1934.

16. *Le Peuple*, 8 February 1934.

17. Frank, *La Semaine du 6 au 12 Février*, 13.

18. In the same issue of *L'Humanité*, André Marty declared that "one cannot fight against fascism without also fighting against social democracy."

19. Speech collected in Nicole Racine and Louis Bodin, *Le Parti Communiste Pendant l'Entre-Deux-Guerres* (Paris, 1982), 214.

20. *L'Humanité*, 8 February 1934.

21. Jules Fourrier, *Graine Rouge* (Paris, 1983), 34.

22. Barbé, *Souvenirs de Militant*, 234. See also J. P. Brunet, *Jacques Doriot* (Paris, 1986), 150–51.

23. Its reverberations were felt as far away as Moscow. See Branko M. Lazic, *Information Fournées par Albert Vassart sur la Politique du PCF entre 1934 et 1938* (Typescript MS, Hoover Institution Archives, n.d.), 13–14.

24. Philippe Robrieux, "1934, On Tourne à Moscou," *Cahiers Léon Trotsky* 27 (September 1986): 20–22.

25. *Le Populaire*, 10 February 1934; M. de Framond, *La Journée Communiste du 9 Février et les Incidents Communistes du 12 en Banlieue* (Paris, 1934).

26. Robert C. Tucker, *Stalin in Power: The Revolution from Above, 1928–1941* (New York, 1990), 228–37, 338. See also Carr, *Twilight of the Comintern*, 116; Cilly Vassart, *Le Front Populaire en France* (Typescript MS, Hoover Institution Archives, 1962), 22–29. It is significant to note that up to this period, the Soviet Union had been a "revisionist" power, ardently opposed to the Versailles settlement. Russian foreign policy, however, was inevitably affected by German relations to the Soviet Union; see Robert Coulondre, *De Staline à Hitler: Souvenirs de Deux Ambassades 1936–1939* (Paris, 1950), 16.

27. Vassart, *Le Front Populaire en France*, 25–27.

28. Vassart, *Mémoirs*; Georges, Tintant, and Renaud, *Léon Jouhaux dans le Mouvement Syndical Français*, 126; Jean Bruhat and Marc Piolot, *Esquisse d'une Histoire de la CGT* (Paris, 1966).

29. Robrieux, *Histoire Intérieure du Parti Communiste*, 453; Vassart, *Le Front Populaire en France*, 18; Barbé, *Souvenirs de Militant*, 336; Victor Barthélemy, *Du Communisme au Fascisme: L'Histoire d'un Engagement Politique* (Paris, 1978), 58.

30. *Le Prolétaire*, 10 February 1934; Barbé, *Souvenirs de Militant*, 334–36; Daniel R. Brower, *The New Jacobins: The French Communist Party and the Popular Front* (Ithaca, 1968), 41.

31. Henry Ehrmann, *French Labor from Popular Front to Liberation* (New York, 1947), 28.

32. Bruhat and Piolot, *Esquisse d'une Histoire de la CGT*, 118.

33. *Le Populaire*, 18 February 1934.

34. Maurice Agulhon, *The Republican Experiment 1848–1852* (Cambridge, 1983), 188–91.

35. Peter L. Berger, *Invitation to Sociology: A Humanistic Perspective* (New York, 1963), 98–102.

36. *Le Populaire*, 13 February 1934.

37. Petrus Faure, *Les Manifestations du 12 Février* (Paris, 1934); Framond, *La Journée du 9 Février et les Incidents Communistes du 12 en Banlieue.*

38. Raoul Dubois, *Au Soleil de 36* (Paris, 1986), 79.

39. This was symbolized by Dimitrov's appointment to the ECCI presidium in April 1934.

40. On the genesis of this policy change, see Vassart, *La Front Populaire en France*, 31–41; Lazic, *Information Fournées par Albert Vassart*, 13–14; Robrieux, "1934, On Tourne à Moscou."

41. Degras, *The Communist International: Document*, 3:296–99; Claude Willard, "Les Réaction du PC et de la SFIO à l'Arrivée de Hitler au Pouvoir," in *Mélanges d'Histoire Sociale Offerts à Jean Maitron* (Paris, 1976), 269.

42. PCF, *Le Triomphe du Front Populaire* (Paris, 1935), 8. As they took up the banner of anti-fascism and rallied in defense of the French Republic, communists conveniently "forgot" Lenin's contention that democracy was a "simple camouflage for the dictatorship exercised by the bourgeoisie." See his *State and Revolution* (1918) and *The Proletarian Revolution and the Renegade Kautsky* (1918).

43. Trotsky, who closely followed French events in this period, was the first to point out that the new anti-fascist line was simply "a means by which the Stalinists could justify their collaboration with the [bourgeois] Radicals"—a collaboration necessary if the Soviet Union were to win France to a system of collective security; see Jean-Paul Joubert, "Trotsky et le Front Populaire," *Cahiers Léon Trotsky* 9 (January 1982): 40.

44. *Le Front populaire* is usually rendered in English as "the Popular Front." I prefer the less common rendition "People's Front." The word *populaire* is, of course, the adjective from

peuple, but "popular" suggests "popularity" rather than "of the people." This is because *le pe-uple* is not equivalent to "the people" but to our now lost sense of "the folk." The English "people" is equivalent to the French *gens* (or the German *Leute*), which means a "group of individuals," not an organic body of human beings related by blood and soil, history and destiny. The inadequacies of English in rendering *le peuple* (or *das Volk*)—a product of Protestant individualism, a mercantile model of society, and an imperial maritime tradition that, as Carl Schmitt argues in *Land und Meer* (Cologne, 1981), obliterated the feeling for *Blut und Boden* that figures prominently in the concerns of the continental powers—are apparent in both renditions but "people" is more suggestive than "popular" in conveying the nationalist, communitarian, and populist connotations of *le Front populaire.*

45. On 10 October 1934 Thorez stated: "We are proposing the idea of a vast popular movement *(rassemblement)* for bread, peace, and liberty. In order to defeat fascism, let us constitute, at any price, a massive People's Front." Quoted in Jacques Fauvet, *Histoire du Parti Communiste Français 1920–1976* (Paris, 1977), 142. Unlike the "united front," which played a significant role in the early history of the Comintern (and should be distinguished from the later "united front from below"), the People's Front was multi-class—allying the working class with "progressive" sections of the bourgeoisie. In adopting this line, the PCF effectively relegated the party's revolutionary strategy to a back burner in order, it was rationalized, to safeguard the opportunity of making a revolution at some later date. At this stage in the history of the world communist movement, the old Bolshevik forms developed by Lenin, with their rigid class barriers and revolutionary ruptures, were superseded by the less consistent, but more pliable "menshevik" ones favored by Stalin. French communist historians have repeatedly claimed that the People's Front was purely a French initiative and that the PCF eventually swung the Comintern around to its position. The documents, however, suggest that the initiative lay where it always lay—in Moscow. See Branko Lazitch, "La Stratégie du Komintern," in *Les Années Trente,* by Michel Winock, et al. (Paris, 1990), 47–48. See also Jiri Hochman, *The Soviet Union and the Failure of Collective Security, 1934–1938* (Ithaca, 1984), 84; Robrieux, *Maurice Thorez,* 193; Jean-Jacques Becker, *Le Parti Communiste Veut-il Prendre le Pouvoir? La Stratégie du PCF de 1930 à Nos Jours* (Paris, 1981), 48–50; "Les Archives du Communisme: Entretien avec Stéphane Courtois," 86–87.

46. Peter J. Larmour, *The French Radical Party in the 1930s* (Stanford, 1964), 162–72; Serge Berstein, *Histoire du Parti Radical* (Paris, 1982), 2:354–89.

47. *Verité,* July 1934; *L'Union des Métaux,* October 1935.

48. PCF, *Le Triomphe du Front Populaire.*

49. Benoît Frachon and Gaston Monmousseau, *Pour une CGT Unique! Pour l'Action de Masse: Discours Pronouncé à la Conference Nationale du PC* (Paris, 1934). By emphasizing working-class unity, *unitaires* tried to bridge the ideological differences that separated them from confederals. As Frachon told the National Party Conference: "We must present our policies in such a way that the socialist worker, the Radical worker, the popular democrat, or the Christian will have not the slightest reproach to make against us for neglecting his interest for the sake of our party."

50. CGT, *La CGT et l'Unité Syndicale* (Versailles, n.d.).

51. *Cahiers du Bolchevisme,* 15 September 1934.

52. *L'Humanité,* 1 October 1934.

53. *Le Peuple,* 16, 30 June, 7, 18 July, 6 October 1934.

54. *Le Peuple,* 8 October 1934; *L'Union des Métaux,* June, August, October, November 1934.

55. Georges Lefranc, *Juin 36* (Paris, 1966), 22.

56. Danielle Tartakowsky, "Stratégies de la Rue: 1934–1936," in *La France en Mouvement 1934–1938*, ed. Jean Bouvier (Paris, 1986), 32.

57. Frank Tannenbaum, *A Philosophy of Labor* (New York, 1951), 78.

58. Vieilledent, *Souvenirs d'un Travailleur Manuel Syndicaliste*, 218.

59. The plan can be found in CGT, *Congrès Confédéral de Paris—1935* (Versailles, 1935), 56–73. See also CGT, *Contre la Crise, Pour l'Economie Dirigée* (Versailles, 1934); Henri de Man, *Planned Socialism: The Plan du Travail of the Belgium Labour Party*, trans. and intro. G. D. H. Cole (London, 1935); Georges Lefranc, "Le Courant Planiste dans le Mouvement Ouvrier Français de 1933 à 1936," *Le Mouvement Social* 54 (January–March 1966).

60. *Le Peuple*, 17 December 1934.

61. *Le Populaire*, 11 November 1934; *Le Peuple*, 16 July 1935. In the words of Trotsky: "The best of plans is only a scrap of paper if it doesn't have the worker masses behind it." See "Du Plan de la CGT à la Conquête du Pouvoir," in *Le Mouvement Communiste en France (1919–1939)*, ed. Pierre Broué (Paris, 1967), 485.

62. By May 1934, there were 143 compared with 109 in late 1933. See *La Voix du Peuple de Paris*, 15 May 1934. Party membership also took a big leap forward. See *L'Humanité*, 1 March 1934.

63. *Cahiers du Bolchevisme*, 1 May 1934; *L'Union des Métaux*, January 1935; Durand, *La Lutte des Travailleurs de Chez Renault*, 58.

64. *Le Prolétaire de Clichy*, 16 March 1934; *L'Humanité*, 23 June 1934.

65. *Syndicalisme: Organe Mensuel de la CFTC*, March 1936.

66. *L'Humanité*, 30 June 1934; *Cahiers du Bolchevisme*, 1 May 1934.

67. *Le Métallo*, June 1935.

68. The highly skilled aviation workers, as a result, faced an increasingly tight labor market, which considerably enhanced their bargaining power. At the same time, the introduction of metal planes in the late 1920s and the progressive Taylorization of the labor process brought about by metal construction threatened or offended their artisanal sensibilities. This combination of factors, which both favored and jeopardized their interests, made aviation an ideal site for *unitaire* efforts. See *L'Humanité*, 4, 15, and 16 December 1934. See also Chadeau, *La Rêve et la Puissance*, 224–29.

69. On the 1931 strike, see ch. 3.

70. Confederals criticized communists for allowing so many unorganized workers to sit on the strike committee. They considered this an abnegation of trade-union responsibility. Confederals would have preferred that *unitaires* direct the strike and assume responsibility for it, rather than leave the formal leadership in the hands of the unorganized. But *unitaires* knew better. Their use of "democratically elected" committees enhanced the strike's legitimacy and gave them more effective control over the ill-disciplined strikers. See *Le Peuple*, 13 April 1935.

71. On the Chenard strike, see *L'Humanité*, 13–25 March 1935; *Le Peuple*, 17–21 March, 12–13 April 1935; *Le Travailleur de la Banlieue Ouest*, April 1935; *Le Prolétaire*, 16 March 1935; *Le Populaire*, 12–3 April 1935.

72. Simone Weil had an interesting premonition about the pact's implications: "Every military alliance is odious, but an alliance with Germany would probably be a lesser evil; for in that case a war between Russia and Germany (with Japan participating too, no doubt) would remain comparatively localized; on the other hand, if France and Russia marched together against Germany and Japan it would be another conflagration which would spread to the whole of Europe and beyond—an incredible catastrophe. As you can imagine, these con-

siderations do not make me a fascist. But I refuse to play the game of the Russian general staff on the pretext of opposing fascism." Simone Weil, *Seventy Letters* (London, 1965), 7. Some confederal leader, such as Raymond Bouyer, the general secretary of the CGT's *Mécaniciens* union, saw the pact in a similar light. See, for example, *L'Union des Métaux*, May 1935.

73. *L'Humanité*, 17 May 1935. See also Fernando Claudin, *The Communist Movement: From Comintern to Cominform* (New York, 1975), 180; and Tucker, *Stalin in Power*, 343, 345. Trotsky called the PCF's embrace of French defense "a rabidly social-patriotic policy" which, he believed, would spread the "conviction in all layers of society that another world war was in the making." See *The Crisis of the French Section (1935–1936)* (New York, 1977), 22. In a similar vein, some confederals saw *unitaire* unity proposals as a means by which the "Russians sought to link the masses to the French bourgeoisie." See *Le Peuple*, 16 October 1934.

74. Doriot claimed the pact "marked the end of an era and the end of the Communist International as a revolutionary organization of the international proletariat." Quoted in Brunet, *Jacques Doriot*, 183.

75. "If the proletariat according to Marx 'has no fatherland,' they have now as internationalists something to defend: that is, the cultural patrimony of France, the spiritual wealth, the works of its artisans, its workers, its artists, and its thinkers." Brian Jenkins, *Nationalism in France: Class and Nation Since 1789* (Savage, Md., 1990), 144. The nation, in other words, was grafted onto and partially displaced the class, in a manner not dissimilar to the way fascists used nationalism to mitigate social antagonisms. For a characteristic display of this tendency, see *L'Humanité*, 13 April 1935.

76. For doctrinaire Marxists, the People's Front represented a grievous betrayal of the PCF's revolutionary mission and would cause them to leave or be expelled from the party. See René Garmy, *Pourquoi J'ai Été Exclu du Parti Communiste* (Paris, n.d.). Some of these former communists would find their way into the ranks of the various ultra-left sects that proliferated in depression France, while others turned to fascism as a means of carrying on the revolutionary cause. See Barthélemy, *Du Communisme au Fascisme*. But whether as Marxists or embryonic fascists, these ex-communists resented the way in which the People's Front blunted the PCF's opposition to liberal society.

77. *L'Humanité*, 14 May 1935. See also T. Ferlé, *Le Communisme en France: Organisation* (Paris, 1937), 153–60.

78. Michel Collinet, "Masses et Militants: La Bureaucratie et la Crise Actuelle du Syndicalisme Ouvrier Français," *Revue d'Histoire Economique et Sociale* 28 (1950), 70.

79. *Le Métallo*, June, July 1935; *La Voix du Peuple de Paris*, June 1935.

80. *L'Etincelle de Boulogne-Billancourt*, June 1935.

81. Herrick Chapman, "The Political Life of the Rank and File: French Aircraft Workers during the Popular Front, 1934–38," *International Labor and Working Class History* 30 (Fall 1986).

82. *Le Métallo*, June 1935; *L'Humanité*, 15 June 1935.

83. *La Barricade: Organe de Défense des Travailleurs des 13e et 15e*, June 1935; *L'Humanité*, 2 June 1935.

84. *Le Métallo*, June 1935.

85. *L'Humanité*, various issues for early August 1935.

86. *Le Peuple*, 15 July 1935.

87. David A. L. Levy, "The French Popular Front, 1936–37," in *The Popular Front in Europe*, eds. H. Graham and P. Preston (London, 1987), 62–64.

88. As Jacques Doriot sarcastically described it, in the People's Front coalition the most

sectarian communists became little lambs, hardly distinguishable from the faint-hearted Radicals. See *La France Ne Sera un Pays d'Esclaves* (Paris, 1936), 15.

89. *Révolution*, 17 January 1936.

90. An English translation of this program can be found in Julian Jackson, *The Popular Front in France: Defending Democracy, 1934–1938* (Cambridge, 1988), 299–302.

91. Lenin was wont to describe the Bolsheviks as Jacobins of the proletarian revolution. The affinities, real and imaginary, between the Revolution of 1789 and that of 1917 played a major role in the PCF's adaptation to the French republican tradition. Among the numerous discussions of these, one of the better recent examples is François Furet, *Le Passé d'une Illusion: Essai sur l'Idée Communiste au XXe Siècle* (Paris, 1995), 81–99.

92. On Jacobinism, see François Furet, "Jacobinism" in *A Critical Dictionary of the French Revolution*, ed. F. Furet and M. Ozouf (Cambridge, 1989). See also Augustin Cachin, *L'Esprit du Jacobinisme* (Paris, 1979).

93. Pierre Birnbaum, *Le Peuple et les Gros: Histoire d'un Mythe* (Paris, 1984).

94. This was made clear at the Comintern's Seventh World Congress in July 1935. See Georges Dimitrov, *Oeuvres Choisies* (Paris, 1972), 108–19. See also Brower, *The New Jacobins*, 198.

95. Malcolm Anderson, "The Myth of the 'Two Hundred Families'," *Political Studies* 11 (June 1965). The figure "200" was based on the number of shareholders controlling the powerful *Banque de France*, the so-called kingpin of French financial capitalism. In actuality, the *Banque de France* was neither the most important financial institution (rather it was the Rothschild's Paribas group, close to the left alliance and favoring a pro-Russian foreign policy) nor was it controlled by 200 (but only forty) families. One of the best short treatments of the French financial elite is in Carroll Quigley, *Tragedy and Hope: A History of the World in Our Time* (New York, 1966), 515–29.

96. Léon Jouhaux, *La CGT et la Front Populaire* (Paris, n.d).

97. *L'Union des Métaux*, September 1935.

98. See, for example, *Le Peuple*, 7, 26, 30 August 1935, 12 January, 24 February 1936.

99. According to Jouhaux: "Between the position of the political parties, created for politics and to make politics, and the situation of the CGT, created to defend worker interests, translate their aspirations [into actions], materialize them, and lead the working class to emancipation, there is a difference in principle and a difference in activity." CGT, *Congrès Confédéral de Paris: XXIXe Congrès, 24–27 Septembre 1935* (Versailles, 1935), 246.

100. Jean-Pierre Rioux, *Révolutionnaires du Front Populaire: Choix de Documents 1935–1939* (Paris, 1973), 174.

101. The political integration of the French working class into the republican political community was the other side of labor's non-integration into French society. The political consciousness of French workers and their social consciousness, as a consequence, have rarely corresponded. Jacques Julliard sees this as the basis for the "schizophrenic" character of the French labor movement—its oscillation between reformist and revolutionary tendencies, its strong political integration in the national community and its weak class consciousness in the factory. Julliard writes: "The proletarians have a country; any effort to persuade them otherwise is resented as an attempt to rob them of their identity. This is why, even when condemned to opposition, the French working class does not feel excluded from French political life; this is why a number of its heroic leaders, like Jaures or Thorez, have always considered the 'people's front' as the natural political formula for the French left." See "Diversité des Réformistes," *Le Mouvement Social* 87 (April–June 1974). Not coincidentally, the introduction

of the People's Front line ushered in the period of "Thorezianism" in the PCF's history. "Thorezianism," according to I. Aviv, "designates a Communist doctrine and a behavior appropriate to the framework of non-Communist society—in such a framework, revolution becomes an affirmative myth for the working class, but no longer a concrete goal. Thorezian Communism, like the People's Front, gave French workers a positive image of themselves as they reconciled themselves to French capitalism." See "Le PCF dans le Système Français des Années 1930 à la Fin de IVe République," *Le Mouvement Social* 104 (July–September 1978), 85. A key element in Thorezianism unemphasized in Aviv's insightful discussion is nationalism, which merged the worker's class identity with his cultural identity as a Frenchman.

102. Thierry Maulnier, *Au-Delà du Nationalisme* (1938; reprint Paris, 1993), 133–45. In the labor movement, this was a view shared only by anti-Marxist Catholics in the CFTC and expressed in various numbers of *L'Ouvrier Métallurgiste* in 1936 and 1937.

103. For Marc Bloch, it was this messianic component of the left alliance that "was the real Popular Front, not the one exploited by the politicians . . . [and here] something lived again of the spirit that had moved men's hearts on the Champ-de-Mars under the hot sun of 14 July 1790." *Strange Defeat* (New York, 1968), 167. See also *L'Ouvrier Métallurgiste*, September 1937.

104. This was sheer demagoguery and followed from the imprecise way in which the Comintern defined "fascism"—as any type of "open offensive" against the working class by the most retrograde agents of the bourgeoisie. See Robrieux, *Maurice Thorez*, 170, 173. Often, their use of the term lacked even this precision. André Marty, for example, characterized "fascists" as being simply "the paid agents of big capital." See his preface to Ralph Fox, *France Faces the Future* (London, 1936). This would have made the entire liberal bourgeoisie fascist and emptied the term of any significance. An ironic twist to this propensity to label "fascist" everything that stood in the way of the labor movement was its self-defeating implication. René Rémond, among others, has argued that the so-called "fascism" of the anti-republican leagues (not to mention that of the *patrons*) was actually a vestige of traditional French authoritarianism and as such helped "immunize" the French against the more serious German or Italian forms of fascism. See *Notre Siècle 1918–1991* (Paris, 1991), 176–78.

According to Trotsky, "Antifascism, like fascism, are for Stalinists not concrete conceptions but two great empty sacks into which they stuff anything that comes into their hands." See *On France*, 43. This made "fascism" a term of abuse, without any descriptive basis. It thus became synonymous with everything oppressive, violent, rapacious, or at odds with the self-appointed champions of the anti-fascist crusade. This is why I write "fascism" with quotation marks. See also George Orwell, "Politics and the English Language" (1946), in *A Collection of Essays* (New York, 1953), 162.

105. *La Commune: Organe Centrale du Parti Communiste Internationaliste*, 3 January 1936; *L'Humanité*, 21 November to 25 December 1935; *Le Prolétaire de Clichy*, 13, 20, 27 December 1935, and 3 January 1936; *Le Métallo*, January 1936.

106. Suggestive of the union's growth in this period are the following figures. In February 1935, in the metal plants of the suburban town of Courbevoie, five *sections syndicales* contained a hundred members; in August, eight *sections* and 500 members; by February 1936, on the eve of the legislative elections, seventeen *sections* and a thousand members. See *La Vie Ouvrière*, 28 February 1936.

107. *La Révolution Prolétarienne*, 25 April 1936.

108. *Révolution*, December 1935, January 1936; *Syndicalisme*, February 1936; *Le Combat Syndicaliste*, March 1936.

109. *L'Union des Métaux*, April 1936.

110. *Cahiers du Bolchévisme*, 1 November 1934.

111. Vassart, *Le Front Populaire en France*, 44; Degras, *The Communist International*, 3:384.

112. *L'Humanité*, 8 June 1935.

113. The reader will remember that *unitaire* and confederal unions were most sharply differentiated in the metal trades.

114. *L'Union des Métaux*, October 1935; *Le Métallo*, December 1935, January 1936.

115. After July 1935, every issue of the Confederal Metal Federation's monthly *L'Union des Métaux* contained elaborate discussions on the impossibility of reconciling these differences. See also *L'Humanité*, 18, 19 December 1935, 2 January 1936.

116. See, for example, *Le Populaire*, 11 January 1936; *L'Humanité*, 18, 19, 29 December 1935.

117. *L'Humanité*, 24 February 1936; *Le Peuple*, 23 February 1936.

118. *Le Peuple*, 29 January 1936.

119. *Syndicalisme*, March 1936; *Le Combat Syndicaliste*, 6 March, 4 April 1936.

120. *Le Peuple*, 8 March 1936. On the congress, see CGT, *Congrès Confédéral d'Unité* (Versailles, 1936).

Chapter Five

1. According to Jean Legrendre, a conservative republican deputy: "The People's Front divides France into two irremediably opposed clans: those of the Republic and those of the dictatorship of the proletariat. Between the two, one has to take sides. One has to choose. All intermediary positions, all equivocations are reproachable." Quoted in Maurice C. Charvades, *Eté 1936: La Victoire du Front Populaire* (Paris, 1966), 62. See also Samuel M. Osgood, "The Popular Front: Views from the Right," *International Review of Social History* 9 (1964); and J. Touchard and L. Bodin, "L'Etat de l'Opinion au Début de l'Année 1936" in *Léon Blum, Chef de Gouvernement 1936–1937*, ed. P. Renouvin and R. Rémond (Paris, 1967), 49.

2. Of the seventy-five deputies representing the Paris Region, forty-one went to the PCF, sign that the party had become the Region's dominant political force. See *Cahiers du Bolchevisme*, 15 May 1936.

3. *L'Humanité*, 2 May 1936; *Le Travailleur Parisien: Bulletin de l'Union des Syndicats Confédérés de la Région Parisienne*, October–December 1936.

4. Croizat's presence in Le Havre is revealing. It indicates, contrary to subsequent accounts, that the occupation was not purely a local action whose significance had escaped the attention of the federal leadership.

5. Jules Moch, *Rencontres avec Léon Blum* (Paris, 1970), 151.

6. *Le Métallo* (Le Havre), February 1937; *Le Peuple*, 15 May 1936; Louis Eudier, "Bréguet-Le Havre: Première Occupation en 1936," *Cahiers d'Histoire de l'Institut Maurice Thorez* 1 (NS) (November–December 1972); Louis Eudier, *Notre Combat de Classes et de Patriotes (1934–1945)* (Le Havre, 1982), 63–64; Herrick Chapman, *State Capitalism and Working-Class Radicalism in the French Aircraft Industry* (Berkeley, 1991), 75–80.

7. Daniel R. Brower, *The New Jacobins: The French Communist Party and the Popular Front* (Ithaca, 1968), 145.

8. *L'Humanité*, 23 May 1936; *Le Peuple*, 15 May 1936.

9. This thesis was initially propounded by the ex-confederals. It was then academically reformulated by Saloman Schwarz in "Les Occupations d'Usines en France de Mai et Juin 1936," *International Review for Social History* 2 (1937) and Henri Prouteau in *Les Occupations d'Usines en Italie et en France, 1920–1936* (Paris, 1938). The most notable recent version can be

found in Georges Lefranc, *Juin 36: "L'Explosion Sociale" du Front Populaire* (Paris, 1966) and Antoine Prost, "Les Grèves de Juin 1936" in *Léon Blum, Chef de Gouvernement* .

10. *La Voix Populaire*, 6 March 1936; *La Commune*, 22 May 1936.

11. *Révolution Prolétarienne*, 10 July 1936; Benoît Frachon, "Juin 1936 . . . Histoire et Enseignements," *Les Cahiers de l'Institut CGT d'Histoire Sociale* 17 (March 1986), 29, 31; Bertrand Badie, "Les Grèves du Front Populaire aux Usines Renault," *Le Mouvement Social* 81 (October 1972), 83. The strikes and occupations of May 1968 involved more workers, but their social significance was considerably less. Moreover, the 1968 strikes were less an expression of the labor movement than an anticipation of the "new social movements" of postindustrial or technocratic society. See Alain Touraine, *Le Communisme Utopique: Le Mouvement de Mai 68* (Paris, 1972).

12. *La Commune*, 22 May 1936; *Révolution*, 22 May 1936; *L'Humanité*, 15 to 17 May 1936; *La Voix Populaire*, 22 and 29 May 1936.

13. *Le Prolétaire*, 16 May 1936, *L'Aube Nouvelle*, 16 May 1936; *L'Ouvrier Métallurgiste*, September 1937; *Le Peuple*, 5, 8, 14, 22 May 1936; Fourrier, *Graines Rouge*, 44.

14. Durand, *La Lutte des Travailleurs de Chez Renault*, 63; *Le Peuple*, 6, 8 May 1936; *Le Travailleur Parisien*, October–December 1936; Tristan Rémy, *La Grande Lutte* (Paris, 1937), 103.

15. "Exposé au Conseil National SFIO (10 Mai)," in Léon Blum, *L'Exercice du Pouvoir* (Paris, 1937), 45.

16. Quoted in Ingo Kolboom, *Frankreich Unternehmer in der Periode der Volksfront 1936–1937* (Rheinfelden, 1983).

17. Jean Bron, *Histoire du Mouvement Ouvrier Français* (Paris, 1970), 2:222.

18. *L'Humanité*, 15 May 1936; Serge Wolikow, "Le PCF et le Front Populaire," in *Le PCF: Etapes et Problèmes 1920–1972*, ed. R. Bourdeon (Paris, 1981), 175; Cogniot, *Parti Pris*, 1:254–55.

19. Maurice Jacquier, *Simple Militant* (Paris, 1974), 94–95; *L'Union des Métaux*, May 1936; *L'Humanité*, 12 May 1936. Worker impatience was also fostered by the SFIO's left wing, which pressed for bold and sweeping reforms.

20. Vieilledent, *Souvenirs d'un Travailleur Manuel Syndicaliste*, 128; Guérin, *Front Populaire, Révolution Manquée*, 121; Maurice Moissonnier, "1936: Les Grèves d'Occupation des Usines," *Les Cahiers de l'Institut CGT d'Histoire Social* 19 (September 1986): 13; "Discussion de M. Yves Chataigneau," in *Léon Blum, Chef de Gouvernement*, 102.

21. Robert Mossé, *L'Experience Blum: Un An de Front Populaire* (Paris, 1937), 33.

22. Rémy, *La Grande Lutte*, 108.

23. *L'Aube Nouvelle*, 23 May 1936. Cf. Touchard and Bodin, "L'Etat de l'"opinion au Début de l'Année 1936," 59.

24. *Le Peuple*, 25 May 1936.

25. Few contemporary commentators seemed to have noticed the irony of commemorating an event carried out not only against the Marxist notion of socialism, but against the republicanism of the Third Republic.

26. Brian Rigby, *Popular Culture in Modern France: A Study of Cultural Discourse* (London, 1991), 68–95.

27. Quoted in Jacques Delperrié de Bayac, *Histoire du Front Populaire* (Paris, 1972), 101.

28. Quoted in Danielle Tartakowsky, "Des Grèves de Juin à la Pause, 'Le Ministère des Masses' au Coeur des Contradictions," *Cahiers d'Histoire de l'Institut de Recherches Marxistes* 24 (1986): 38. When the People's Front strategy was formalized at the Comintern's Seventh World Congress in July 1935, George Dimitrov specified that communists should approach it with their attention fixed mainly "on the development of mass actions." See Georges

Dimitrov, *Oeuvres Choisies* (Paris, 1972), 64. The problem with this strategy in France was that Radicals and socialists prevented the local People's Front Committees from becoming mass organizations. If the populace therefore could not be recruited directly to these committees, it had to be organized at the level of the workshop and the trade union. Communist efforts to build a mass movement would thus be premised on the development of the labor movement.

29. Quoted in Tartakowsky, "Des Grèves de Juin à la Pause," 39–40. This general line had already been sketched out by the PCF's annual congress at Villeurbanne in January 1936. In late May, however, it took on a specificity that the earlier congress could not have anticipated.

30. Pierre Monatte, *La Lutte Syndicale* (Paris, 1976), 226.

31. *L'Aube Nouvelle*, 23 and 30 May 1936; *L'Humanité*, 27 May 1936; *Le Populaire*, 27 May 1936; *Léon Blum Before His Judges at the Supreme Court of Riom March 11th and March 12th 1942* (London, 1943), 133; Schwarz, "Les Occupation d'Usine," 63; Jacques Danos and Marcel Gibelin, *Juin 36* (Paris, 1986), 43.

32. *L'Humanité*, *Le Populaire*, 27 May 1936; *Le Prolétaire de Clichy*, *La Commune*, 29 May 1936.

33. *L'Humanité*, 27 May 1936; Schwarz, "Les Occupations d'Usine," 64.

34. *L'Humanité*, *Le Populaire*, *Le Peuple*, 27 May 1936.

35. *Le Peuple*, 28 May 1936.

36. *L'Humanité*, *Le Peuple*, *Le Populaire*, 28 May 1936.

37. *Le Peuple*, 28 May 1936.

38. Delperrié de Bayac, *Histoire du Front Populaire*, 104–105.

39. *L'Humanité*, 29 May 1936.

40. The conservative argument that the strikes were part of a communist bid to seize power received its fullest treatment in Jacques Bardoux, "Le Complot du 12 Juin," *Revue de Paris*, 15 August 1936. But this was a view shared mainly by "liberal" and traditionalist rightists. Those affiliated with Jacques Doriot's Parti Populaire Français or the weekly *Candide* (e.g., 25 June 1936), not to mention elements from the Croix-de-Feu, the Union Nationale des Combattants, and even the Action Française, looked at the strikes from the perspective of revolutionary nationalism, seeing them as a revolt against the atomized conditions of liberal society and the money powers—and to this degree sympathized with them.

41. *Le Peuple*, 28 May 1936.

42. *Le Populaire*, 28 May 1936.

43. Alexander Werth, *Which Way France?* (New York, 1937), 294–95; "Les Conflits de Juin dans le Région Parisienne," 656–57.

44. Badie, "Les Grèves du Front Populaire aux Usines Renault," 83.

45. Depretto and Schweitzer, *Le Communisme à l'usine*, 182–83.

46. *L'Humanité*, 29 May 1936; Werth, *Which Way France?* 296–97; Durand, *La Lutte des Travailleurs de chez Renault*, 64–66.

47. *L'Aube Nouvelle*, 6 June 1936.

48. Vassard, *Le Front Populaire en France*, 54.

49. See, for example, *Le Peuple*, 28, 29, 31 May, 9 June 1936.

50. The Soviet Foreign Ministry was reportedly alarmed by the strikes which "alerted all bourgeois Europe to the fact that the Communist specter was alive and well." See Jonathan Haslam, "The Soviet Union, the Comintern and the Demise of the Popular Front 1936–39," in *The Popular Front in Europe*, ed. H. Graham and P. Preston (London, 1987).

51. *Le Populaire*, 6 June 1936; Becker, *Le Parti Communiste Veut-il Prendre le Pouvoir?*, 93–99; Claudin, *The Communist Movement*, 206.

52. *Le Populaire*, 29 May 1936. The Paris branch of the UIMM was called the Groupe des Industries Métallurgiques et Mécaniques de la Région de Paris or GIMM; here I refer to it simply by its national appellation.

53. *L'Humanité*, 30 May 1936; Danos and Gibelin, *Juin 36*, 47–48; Schwarz, "Les Occupations d'Usine en France de Mai et Juin 1936," 69; Rioux, *Révolutionnaires du Front Populaire*, 46.

54. *L'Humanité*, 30 May 1936.

55. Rioux, *Révolutionnaires du Front Populaire*, 146; *Que Faire?* July 1936.

56. *La Commune*, 5 June 1936.

57. Werth, *Which Way France?* 298.

58. Frachon, "Juin 1936 . . . Histoire et Enseignements," 32.

59. *Le Peuple*, 3 June 1936.

60. Prouteau, *Les Occupations d'Usines en Italie et en France*, 103; "Les Conflits de Juin dans la Région Parisienne," *Etudes: Revue Catholique* 5 (December 1936): 660–65.

61. *Le Prolétaire*, 13 June 1936; *Le Prolétaire de Clichy*, 12 June 1936.

62. Quoted in Charvardes, *Eté 1936*, 132.

63. The strike movement, combined with the excitement of the election and the impending change of government, had apparently shattered the normal "psychological levers of command." According to Jean Coutrot, an engineering consultant in the Paris metal industry: "The workers no longer thought to obey, the employers to give orders. Supervisors and workers . . . had the impression of living in an unreal atmosphere, not a nightmare, but a dream, like in a play by Pirandello." *Les Leçons de Juin 1936: L'Humanisme Economique* (Paris, 1936), 15.

64. *Que Faire?* July 1936.

65. Robert Francotte, "A l'Usine Renault: Souvenirs de," *Cahiers d'Histoire de l'Institut Maurice Thorez* (January 1973): 140–41; *Lutte Ouvrière*, 10 June 1936.

66. According to Simone Weil, "The workers struck, but they let the militants take care of the details. Passivity nurtured day after day for many years is not given up in a few days, even in days as beautiful as these. And, of course, when you escape slavery for a short while, you haven't the courage to study the conditions under which you had to submit day after day, under which you will again submit." *La Condition Ouvrière*, 233. See also *Le Combat Syndicaliste*, 12 June 1936.

67. Charles F. Sabel, *Work and Politics: The Division of Labor in Industry* (Cambridge, 1982), 110; Danos and Gibelin, *Juin 36*, 148.

68. One conservative observer later said of the occupations that "as in Russia, one replaces liberty with happiness—orchestras, dances, boxing matches—anything to keep the slave from thinking." See *Le Figaro*, 28 March 1938. What this conservative failed to add was that such practices had been pioneered and perfected in the capitalist West.

69. *Le Peuple*, 5 June 1936; Depretto and Schweitzer, *Communisme à l'Usine*, 188–89.

70. Durand, *La Lutte des Travailleurs de chez Renault*, 66.

71. "La Vie et la Grève des Ouvrières Métallos" originally appeared under the pseudonym of S. Galois in *Révolution Prolétarienne*, 10 June 1936 and was later collected in Weil, *La Condition Ouvrière*, 219–38.

72. Weil, *La Condition Ouvrière*, 231–32.

73. Vieilledent, *Souvenirs d'un Travailleur Manuel Syndicaliste*, 129–36.

74. Van de Casteele-Schweitzer, "Management and Labour in France," 70. Cf. Joseph Wilbois, *La Nouvelle Organisation du Travail* (Paris, 1937).

75. *Le Peuple*, 4 June 1936.

76. *The Red International of Labor Unions*, July 1936; *Que Faire?* July 1936.

77. See, for example, Jacquier, *Simple Militant*, 96–97.

78. *Le Travailleur Parisien*, October–December 1936; *Le Peuple*, 8 June 1936. See also Paolo Spriano, *The Occupation of the Factories: Italy 1920* (London, 1975).

79. *Le Peuple*, 5 June 1936.

80. Ibid.

81. Blum, "Exposé au Conseil National," 46; *Léon Blum Before His Judges at the Supreme Court of Riom*, 58. Neither labor leaders nor those to the left of the SFIO thought Blum the right man for the job. Trotsky was not alone in believing that: "Although he is educated and, in his way, an intelligent man, he seems to have set himself the aim in life of uttering nothing but parlor trivialities and pretentious nonsense. . . . His minuscule talents, suitable for parliamentary lobbying, seems wretched and paltry in the awesome whirlpool of our days." See *Trotsky's Diary of Exile: 1935* (New York, 1963), 4. For labor's negative view of Blum, see Delmas, *A Gauche de la Barricade*, 84–86.

82. "Allocution Radiodiffusée sur les Projets Sociaux du Gouvernement (5 Juin 1936)" in Blum, *L'Exercice du Pouvoir*; LeFranc, *Juin 36*, 129.

83. *Léon Blum Before His Judges at the Supreme Court of Riom*, 30–32.

84. The Masonic Order, the Third Republic's secret liberal elite, held up to twenty-five of the thirty-five cabinet positions in Blum's government. See Jacques Kergoat, *La France du Front Populaire* (Paris, 1986), 111. See also, A. Foucher and A. Ricker, *Histoire de la Franc-Maçonnerie en France* (Paris, 1968); Trotsky, *The First Five Years of the Communist International*, 2:124–84.

85. Georges Lefranc, *Les Organizations Patronale en France du Passé au Présent* (Paris, 1976), 104. The employers were also represented by the UIMM, the Paris Chamber of Commerce, and the *Comité des Forges*.

86. "Réponse aux Interpellations sur les Grèves et Occupations à Usines (6 Juin)," in Blum, *L'Exercice du Pouvoir*.

87. The text of the Matignon Accords first appeared in *Le Populaire* on 8 June 1936 and then in the *Bulletin du Ministère du Travail* (Paris, 1936), 222. It has been reprinted many times, such as in Jean Bruhat and Marc Piolot, *Esquisse d'une Histoire de la CGT* (Paris, 1966), 144–45. An English translation is annexed to Ehrmann, *French Labor from Popular Front to Liberation*, 284–85.

88. Lefranc, *Juin 36*, 158; Lefranc, *Les Organisations Patronales*, 105–106; Adrian Rossiter, "Popular Front Economic Policy and the Matignon Negotiations," *The Historical Journal* 30, no. 3 (September 1987).

89. *Le Peuple*, 9 June 1936.

90. *L'Humanité*, 9 June 1936.

91. *Journée Industrielle*, 9 June 1936, quoted in Lefranc, *Juin 36*, 161.

92. *Le Prolétaire*, 13 June 1936; Prouteau, *Les Occupations d'Usines en Italie et en France*, 128. On the different motivation of the two business groups, see Jean Dessirier, "Secteurs 'Arbités et Non-Arbités' dans le Déséquilibre de l'Economie Française," *Revue d'Economie Politique* (1935).

93. Vinen, *The Politics of French Business*, 37. See also R. P. Ducheim, "'L'Accord Matignon,' Ce Que J'ai Vu et Entendu," *Revue de Paris*, February 1937, 587.

94. Quoted in Joel Colton, *Léon Blum, Humanist in Politics* (New York, 1966), 152.

95. *Le Libertaire*, 19 June 1936; *Que Faire?* June 1936.

96. Depretto and Schweitzer, *Le Communisme à l'Usine*, 196.

97. Pierre Brouè and Nicole Dorey, "Critiques de Gauche et Opposition Révolutionnaire au Front Populaire," *Le Mouvement Social* 54 (January–March 1966): 100.

98. Vassart, *Le Front Populaire en France*, 58.

99. *Le Peuple*, 10 June 1936.

100. *Elan Social*, 14 May 1938.

101. *Que Faire?* July 1936.

102. André Ferrat, quoted in Rioux, *Révolutionnaires du Front Populaire*, 202. Cf. Werth, *Which Way France?*, 310.

103. *L'Humanité*, 10 June 1936; Danos and Giberlin, *Juin 36*, 160.

104. *L'Humanité*, *Le Peuple*, 11 June 1936.

105. Trotsky, *On France*. This was also the opinion of revolutionary workers refusing to toe the Stalinist line. See, for example, Jacquier, *Simple Militant*, 96; Guérin, *Front Populaire, Révolution Manquée*, 122–34.

106. *L'Humanité*, *Le Peuple*, 12 June 1936.

107. *Daily Worker* (New York), 10 June 1936.

108. *Le Travailleur Parisien*, October–December 1936; Badie, "Les Grèves du Front Populaire aux Usines Renault."

109. Delperié de Bayac, *Histoire de Front Populaire*, 235.

110. Quoted in Colton, *Leon Blum*, 158.

111. Danos and Gibelin, *Juin 36*, 113.

112. This should not imply that the PCF had now eschewed its revolutionary principles. Rather, in the situation it found itself, it did not consider revolution a viable option. See Becker, *Le Parti Communiste Veut-il Prendre le Pouvoir?*, 91–95.

113. *L'Humanité*, 12, 13 June 1936; *Que Faire?*, July 1936.

114. As one left socialist lamented: "The Revolution, which was there within arm's reach, has just been betrayed." Jacquier, *Simple Militant*, 98. The PCF's left wing shared this sentiment; see *Que Faire?* July 1936.

115. In a letter to Auguste Detoeuf, written shortly after she visited the occupied Renault plant, Simone Weil wrote: "Maurice Thorez had made a speech which is a clear invitation to end the strike. This makes me wonder if the lower levels of the Communist Party have escaped from the Party's control and fallen under some unidentified influence. Because it is clear enough that everything is still being done in the name of the Communist Party (hammer and sickles, banners, the "Internationale," etc., everywhere), and yet one hears rumors that Costes [the Communist president of the Paris Metal Union] got a bad reception [when he tried to end the strike]." *Seventy Letters* (London, 1965), 59.

116. Helmut Gruber judiciously points out that the halting of a vast popular movement cannot be laid at the feet of a single leader or his organization. See *Léon Blum, French Socialists and the Popular Front: A Case of Internal Contradiction* (Ithaca, 1986), 16. To argue, however, that the "creative force" of the working class is the decisive force shaping events not only mirrors the egoism of the workerist, it ignores the utterly indispensable role played by organizations and institutions in channelling popular social movements. In the absence of organizations leading the way beyond the status quo, such movements almost always flounder and retreat under their own rudderless propulsion, or else fragment into anarchistic forces. Once the PCF threw itself into the peaceful and orderly resolution of the strike movement, its days were inevitably numbered.

117. *Le Populaire*, 13 June 1936.

118. *L'Aube Nouvelle*, 20 June 1936.

119. See, for example, *Le Peuple*, 28, 29, 31 May 1936.

120. *Le Combat Syndicaliste*, 5 June 1936; *La Voix du Peuple*, July 1936; Delmas, *A Gauche de la Barricade*, 99.

121. Prost, "Les Grèves de Juin 36," 145.

122. *La Voix du Peuple*, October 1936.

123. *L'Etincelle de Boulogne-Billancourt*, 9 January 1937. PCF membership increased as well, from 120 Renault workers in May to 6,000 by late 1936.

124. Quoted in Brower, *The New Jacobins*, 146. The Pivertists on the SFIO's left wing claimed that nearly half the Paris *métallos* were members or supporters of the PCF. My impression is that it was well below a fifth. In any case, communist influence in the metal union was not merely a matter of having captured the executive offices, but also involved a significant rank-and-file constituency.

125. *Syndicats*, 15 July 1937.

126. *L'Ouvrier Métallurgiste*, September 1937.

127. *Le Populaire*, 28 June 1936; *Le Peuple*, 28 June 1936.

128. Alfred Costes, now a PCF deputy, was elected president of the union, a position more ceremonial than functional; Robert Doury, another ex-*unitaire*, was elected general secretary. Gauthier, Collin, and Poirot, all communists, were elected to fill the remaining executive offices.

129. *Le Peuple*, 28, 30 June 1936.

130. These ex-confederals later complained that they encountered "suspicion, duplicity, and hypocrisy" from the ex-*unitaires* whenever they attempted to participate in the actual governance of the union. See *Le Populaire*, 20 September 1939.

131. Depretto and Schweitzer, *Le Communisme à l'Usine*, 214.

132. *Le Peuple*, 27 May, 26 June 1936; *L'Union des Métaux*, December 1936. The 1935 and May 1936 figures include both wings of the then divided labor movement.

133. *L'Unité Renault*, September 1937.

134. Edouard Dolléans and Gérard Dehove, *Histoire du Travail en France: Mouvement Ouvrier et Legislation Sociale* (Paris, 1955), 2:88.

135. *Syndicats*, 1 June 1938, 22 March 1939.

136. *Le Réveil Syndicaliste*, 24 April 1939.

137. *Syndicats*, 21 January 11937; Delmas, *A Gauche de la Barricade*, 105–106.

138. Michel Collinet, *Esprit du Syndicalisme: L'Ouvrier Français* (Paris, 1951), 73.

139. *La République*, 24 March 1938.

Chapter Six

1. C. J. Gignoux, *Patrons, Soyez Patrons* (Paris, 1937). As early as 1933, metal producers expressed alarm at the state controls which Roosevelt and Hitler had implemented to gain control of their national economies. See, for example, *La Métallurgie Transformatrice*, April 1933.

2. Quoted in Joel Colton, *Compulsory Labor Arbitration in France, 1936–1939* (New York, 1951), 28. Cf. Weil, *La Condition Ouvrière*, 255–65.

3. Henry W. Ehrmann, *Organized Business in France* (Princeton, 1957), 23–32; Ingo Kolboom, *Frankreich Unternehmer in der Periode der Volksfront*, ch. 3; Vinen, *The Politics of French Business*, 38–44.

4. Lefranc, *Les Organisations Patronales en France*, 109.

5. *Le Travailleur Parisien*, October–December 1936.

6. *La Voix du Peuple*, March 1937; *L'Atelier pour le Plan*, 15 March 1937.

7. *Les Travailleurs de la Banlieue Ouest*, 29 August 1936; *L'Union des Métaux*, August 1936.

8. These incidents were reported as early as July. See, for example, *Le Peuple*, 2 July 1936; *Le Prolétaire*, 4 July 1936; *L'Union des Métaux*, June–July 1936.

9. *L'Humanité*, 16 October 1936. Many of these complaints were simply the result of the inexperience which the union and the employers had in handling grievances.

10. C. J. Gignoux, *L'Economie Français Entre les Deux Guerres 1919–1939* (Paris [1942?]), 309.

11. Navel, *Travaux*, 242, 247.

12. *Le Peuple*, 26 September 1936. See also "Discussion de Robert Blum" in *Léon Blum, Chef de Gouvernement*, 103.

13. Pierre Laroque, *Les Rapports entre Patrons et Ouvriers* (Paris, 1938); *L'Ouvrier Métallurgiste*, November 1936; *Prolétaire de Clichy*, 30 October 1936.

14. Patrick Fridenson, "Automobile Workers in France and Their Work, 1914–83," in *Work in France*, ed. S. L. Kaplan and C. J. Koepp (Ithaca, 1986), 528.

15. Weil, *La Condition Ouvrière*, 267–74.

16. *Le Prolétaire*, 11 July to 29 August 1936.

17. *Le Travailleur de la Banlieue Ouest*, 12 August 1936.

18. *Le Populaire*, 3 August 1936.

19. Fédération des Ouvriers en Métaux (CGT), *Congrès d'Unité: Tenu à Paris 25–27 Novembre 1936* (Versailles, 1937), 68.

20. *L'Eveil des Techniciens et Employées*, September 1938. Trotskyists, anarchists, and others to the left of the PCF spent the next two years denouncing *unitaires* and confederals for restraining worker actions. See, for example, *La Commune*, 13 November 1936; *Le Libertaire*, 6 November 1936.

21. *L'Union des Métaux*, June–July 1936.

22. *Syndicats*, 23 October 1936.

23. *Le Peuple*, 16 July 1936.

24. *Le Populaire*, 26 August 1936.

25. Jean Casson, *La Mémoire Courte* (Paris, 1953), 9.

26. Throughout a part of 1937 and for a month in 1938, even France began clandestine arms shipment in violation of its non-intervention policy, but by then the game was almost up.

27. L. Bodin and J. Touchard, *Front Populaire 1936* (Paris, 1961), 170.

28. *Le Peuple*, 24 August 1936.

29. *Le Peuple*, 29 July, 20 August 1936.

30. *Cahiers du Bolchevisme*, 25 August 1936.

31. Sylvie Schweitzer, "Les Ouvriers des Usines Renault de Billancourt et la Guerre Civile Espagnole," *Le Mouvement Social* 103 (April–June 1978): 112.

32. Rumor had it that Thorez was ahead of Stalin in supporting intervention, although the Soviet Politburo was already moving in this direction. See Jonathan Haslam, *The Soviet Union and the Struggle for Collective Security, 1933–39* (New York, 1984), 115. Stalin's eventual intervention, it bears emphasizing, had less to do with his desire to preserve Spanish democracy, as the European left claimed, than with his intention of keeping the Western powers embroiled in war that would drain their resources and keep them distracted. Among the numerous memoirs and histories that remove the veil from the sordid machinations that lay behind the Spanish Civil War, George Orwell's *Homage to Catalonia* (London, 1938) remains a key text. See also Armaud Imatz, *La Guerre d'Espagne Revisitée* (Paris, 1989).

33. André Delmas, *Mémoires d'un Instituteur Syndicaliste* (Paris, 1979), 293–94.

34. *Le Populaire*, 6 September 1936. In the People's Front period, Stalinists revamped the purpose of the general strike—which had traditionally been an exceptional and heroic exercise of labor power, suitable for revolutionary assaults or extraordinary events, like the defense of the Republic. Under their leadership, it became a mundane exercise in symbolic theatrics, designed to influence parliamentary combinations and ministerial policies. Cf. Robert Brécy, *La Grève Générale en France* (Paris, 1969).

35. *L'Humanité*, 8 September 1936.

36. *Le Populaire*, 8 September 1936. In a long report on the strike in the communist weekly *Le Travailleur de la Banlieue Ouest* for 12 September 1936, which emphasized the contractual issues at stake, no mention at all was made of Spain. Not until 19 September, in a report on the one-hour workstoppage at the Aubert-et-Duval metal works, was Spain discussed in relation to the strike. This suggests the duplicitous manner in which communists used corporate demands to promote their political agenda.

37. *La Révolution Prolétarienne*, 25 September 1936.

38. *Le Populaire*, 10 September 1936. Although a majority of the CGT's post-June membership was pro-communist, the CGT national office, elected in March 1936, contained an ex-confederal majority: of the forty-three seats on the Commission Administrative, thirty-three were held by former confederals. Moreover, even if the vote had been taken after June, the fact that proportional representation was not used in such leadership elections meant non-communists, in control of numerous smaller unions, each of which had a vote, would have still been able to hold onto the CGT national office.

39. *Le Populaire*, 8–10 September 1936.

40. *Le Populaire*, 19 September 1936.

41. *Le Prolétaire de Clichy*, 6 November 1936.

42. *Le Populaire*, 2 February 1937.

43. *Le Prolétaire de Clichy*, 5 February 1937.

44. Donald N. Baker, "The Socialists and the Workers of Paris," *International Review of Social History* 24 (1979): 15; *Le Populaire*, 17 October 1937; Jean Pierre Rioux, "Les Socialistes dans l'Entreprises au Temps du Front Populaire: Quelques Remarques sur les Amicales Socialistes (1936–1939)," *Le Mouvement Social* 106 (January–March 1979); *Le Prolétaire de Clichy*, February, March, July 1937.

45. Marie-France Rogliano, "L'Anticommunisme dans la CGT: 'Syndicats'," *Le Mouvement Social* 87 (April–June 1974); René Belin, *Du Secretariat de la CGT au Gouvernment de Vichy: Mémoires 1933–1942* (Paris, 1978), 13–14, 67–73.

46. Beginning in January 1937, these anti-communist metal leaders organized Amis du Syndicats in the factories to mobilize rank-and-file *métallos* behind their tendency. Although they recruited but a few thousand members out of a workforce of over a quarter million, they nonetheless gained a voice on the shop floor.

47. *L'Union des Métaux*, September 1936.

48. Nathanael Greene, *Crisis and Decline: The French Socialist Party in the Popular Front Era* (Ithaca, 1969), 98.

49. Without the threat of revolutionary strikes, the *patronat* saw little reason to make additional concessions. See Ehrmann, *Organized Business in France*, 37.

50. On the Sautter-Harlé strike, see *Le Peuple*, 19, 25 September, 5, 12, 17, 21 October 1936; *La Révolution Prolétarienne*, 10 October, 10 November 1936; *La Populaire*, 18 October 1936; Lefranc, *Juin 36*, 262–66.

51. On the socialist interpretation of the depression, see Julian Jackson, *The Politics of Depression in France 1932–1936* (Cambridge, 1985), 37–41.

52. Only in a few nationalized aviation plants and in the *Office du Blé* (which regulated the grain trade) did Blum's government tentatively introduce forms appropriate to managerial capitalism. On the latter, see James Burnham, *The Managerial Revolution* (New York, 1941). On Roosevelt's labor policy, see Thomas K. McCraw, "The New Deal and the Mixed Economy" in *Fifty Years Later: The New Deal Evaluated*, ed. Harvard Sitkoff (Philadelphia, 1985).

53. *The Economist*, 5 February 1938.

54. Greene, *Crisis and Decline*, 74. Cf. Michel Margairaz, "Les Socialistes face à l'Economie et à la Société en Juin 1936," *Le Mouvement Social* 93 (October–December 1975).

55. *Le Populaire*, 23 August 1936.

56. *Les Industries Mécaniques*, September 1936. See also "Lettre de l'UIMM au Ministre du Travail sur l'Application des 40 Heures," and Pierre Waline, "Le Patronat Français et l'Application des 40 Heures," in *Léon Blum, Chef de Gouvernement*, 207–32. Economic historians have subsequently affirmed the validity of employer fears. See Sauvy, *Histoire Economique de la France entre les Deux Guerres*, 2:533–35.

57. Rossiter, "Popular Front Economic Policy and the Matignon Negotiations," 678–79, 681.

58. Bernard Georges, "La CGT et le Gouvernment Léon Blum," *Le Mouvement Social* 54 (January–March 1966), 52.

59. Fédération des Ouvriers des Métaux, *L'Application des 40 Heures dans la Métallurgie* (n.p. [1936?]).

60. J.-C. Asselain, "Une Erreur de Politique Economique: La Loi des Quarante Heures de 1936," *Révue Economique* 25, no. 4 (1974).

61. *Le Populaire*, 17 February 1937. Symptomatic of labor's refusal to acknowledge the detrimental effects of the forty-hour law is the totally misleading treatment of this subject offered in the CGT's official history. See Bruhat and Piolot, *Esquisse d'une Histoire de la CGT*, 149.

62. Thorez's speech is reprinted in Tartakowsky, "Des Grèves de Juin à la Pause," 42–48.

63. In a letter addressed by the Central Committee to Daladier, published in *L'Humanité* on 18 October 1936, the PCF declared: "Like you, we think that public order is indispensable. . . . Public order is only possible [though,] if the laws are respected and this is why we are in complete accord with you in demanding that everyone respect the law." In other words, the party—"the party of the working class"—was ready to turn the law against workers if it would calm the factories and appease the Radicals.

64. Larmour, *The French Radical Party in the 1930s*, 214–18; Berstein, *Histoire du Parti Radical*, 2:487–88.

65. *La Révolution Prolétarienne*, 25 December 1936. Lemire would describe future congresses as having "an atmosphere of pogrom;" see *La Révolution Prolétarienne*, 10 July 1937.

66. *Syndicats*, 4 December 1936.

67. *La Voix du Peuple*, November 1936; *Le Peuple*, 27 November 1936.

68. Fédération des Ouvriers en Métaux (CGT), *Congrès d'Unité*; Benoît Frachon, *La Rôle Sociale des Syndicats* (Paris, 1937).

69. Vernon L. Lidtke, *The Alternative Culture: The Socialist Labor Movement in Imperial Germany* (New York, 1985).

70. Gary Cross, *Time and Money: The Meaning of a Consumer Society* (London, 1993), 249.

71. Catholic metal unionists in the CFTC opposed to the CGT's "class struggle" ideology, as well as the employers' predatory liberalism, usually placed the blame for these conflicts on both parties. See, for example, *L'Ouvrier Métallurgiste*, October 1937.

72. On the Panhard strike, see *L'Humanité*, 3–19 November 1936; *Le Peuple*, 3–19 November 1936; *Le Populaire*, 3–19 November 1936; *Syndicats*, 13 and 20 November 1936.

73. Colton, *Compulsory Labor Arbitration in France*, 21.

74. Francis Hordern, *Pouvoir Patronale, Contrôle Ouvrier et Delegation du Personnel 1880–1938* (Aix-en-Provence, 1979).

75. Léon Jouhaux, *L'Arbitrage Obligatoire* (Paris [1937?]).

76. Blum, *L'Exercice du Pouvoir,* 107–15.

77. *L'Humanité,* 21, 29 December 1936, 6, 9 January 1937.

78. See, for example, *Le Travailleur de la Banlieue Ouest,* 13 February 1937.

79. Colton, *Compulsory Labor Arbitration in France,* 76.

80. *L'Humanité,* 11 February 1937.

81. *Drapeau Rouge: Journal Communiste Révolutionnaire,* 19 March 1937.

82. *La Commune: Organe Central du Parti Communiste Internationaliste,* 19 February 1937.

83. Georges Lefranc, *Histoire du Front Populaire,* 2d ed. (Paris, 1974), 228–31.

84. Quoted in Greene, *Crisis and Decline,* 99–100. See also Danos and Gibelin, *Juin 36,* 223–25; J. M. Jeanneney, "La Politique Economique de Léon Blum," in *Léon Blum, Chef de Gouvernement,* 220–21.

85. *La Commune,* 26 February 1937.

86. *Syndicats,* 8 April 1937.

87. *La Commune,* 19 January 1937.

88. See, for example, *La Commune,* 26 February 1937; *Le Travailleur de la Banlieue Ouest,* 20 February 1937; *L'Etincelle de Boulogne-Billancourt,* 6 February 1937.

89. *Drapeau Rouge,* 19 March 1937; *Syndicats,* 27 May 1937.

90. *Le Populaire,* 4 March 1937.

91. *L'Humanité, Le Peuple, Le Populaire,* 4 March 1937; *Le Travailleur de la Banlieue Ouest,* 6 March 1937; *La Vie Ouvrière,* 11 and 18 March 1937.

92. *Que Faire?* April 1937.

93. A conservative journalist, who happened to be on the scene, claims to have seen armed workers prepared to shoot it out with the police. See Pierre Lagareff, *Deadline: The Behind-the-Scenes-Story of the Last Decade in France* (New York, 1942).

94. *Le Prolétaire de Clichy,* 26 March 1937; *La Révolution Prolétarienne,* 10 April, 25 May 1937; André Cherasse, *La Hurle: La Nuit Sanglante de Clichy* (Paris, 1983). Anarchists associated with the *Libertaire* would now compare Blum to "Bloody Noske," the patriotic Social Democrat who crushed the German Revolution of 1918–19.

95. *Le Prolétaire,* 20 March 1937; *La Voix Populaire,* 25 March 1937; *L'Eveil des Techniciens et Employées,* March–April 1937; *La Commune,* 16 April 1937.

96. *Que Faire?* April 1937.

97. Irwin M. Wall, "French Socialism and the Popular Front," *Journal of Contemporary History* 5 (1970), 15.

98. *Quatrième Internationale,* March 1937, reprinted in Naville, *L'Entre-Deux-Guerres.* This was a view shared by various far-left groups. See, for example, *Que Faire?* April 1937.

99. *L'Humanité, Le Populaire,* 18 March 1937.

100. *La Lutte Ouvrière,* 19 March 1937; *Le Populaire,* 24 March 1937; *Drapeau Rouge,* 2 April 1937.

101. *Le Travailleur de la Banlieue Ouest,* 10 April 1937; *L'Unité Renault,* 1 April 1937; *Syndicats,* 22 April 1937.

102. *Drapeau Rouge,* 23 April 1937. This sentiment touched more than one party member. See Fourrier, *Graine Rouge,* 57.

103. *L'Humanité,* 19 March 1937.

104. *Le Libertaire,* 1 April 1937.

105. *Le Travailleur de la Banlieue Ouest,* 27 March 1937; *Le Peuple,* 20, 21 March, 16, 23 April 1937.

106. *L'Ouvrier Métallurgiste,* April 1937.

107. *Syndicats,* 6 May 1937.

108. See, for example, *L'Humanité,* 7, 13, 21, 26 April 1937; *Le Peuple,* 13, 20, 21 April 1937.

109. *Syndicats,* 8 April 1937.

110. *L'Humanité,* 19 April 1937.

111. Blum's resignation was also an act of personal and political despair; see Irwin M. Wall, "The Resignation of the First Popular Front Government, June 1937," *French Historical Studies* 6 (Fall 1970).

112. *Le Libertaire,* 24 June 1937.

113. Greene, *Crisis and Decline,* 102–103.

114. *Le Peuple,* 10 July 1937.

115. *Le Peuple,* 20 August 1937; *Syndicats,* 9 September 1937.

116. *Le Peuple,* 20 August 1937; *La Révolution Prolétarienne,* 10 August 1937; *Le Travailleur de la Banlieue Ouest,* 9 September 1937; *La Vie Syndicale,* August 1937.

117. Fédération des Ouvriers en Métaux, *XIVe Congrès Fédéral* (Versailles, 1939), 22.

118. See, for example, *Le Populaire,* 7, 11, 23 September 1937.

119. Syndicat des Techniciens . . . de la Métallurgie, *L'Evolution des Revendications depuis Juin 1936* (Paris, 1938), 1.

120. *La Commune,* 22 October 1937.

121. *Le Peuple,* 8 to 17 October 1937; *Le Populaire,* 17 October 1937.

122. *La Commune,* 29 October 1937; *Syndicats,* 18 November 1937; *La Révolution Prolétaienne,* 10 November, 25 November 1937.

123. *Union des Métaux,* November 1937; *L'Humanité,* 11 November 1937.

124. *L'Ouvrier Métallurgiste,* November 1937.

125. Syndicat des Techniciens, *L'Evolution des Revendications depuis Juin 1936,* 7. Cf. *Le Populaire,* 17 November 1937.

126. See, for example, *La Commune,* 3 December 1937.

127. Jourdain, *Comprendre pour Accomplir,* 31.

128. *Le Métallo,* November 1937.

129. *L'Union des Métaux,* December 1937. See also *Que Faire?* February 1938.

130. *Le Réveil Syndicaliste,* 15 January 1938; *La Lutte Ouvrière,* 26 December 1937; cf. *La Voix Populaire,* 30 December 1937.

131. Alexander Werth writes that these strikes "showed that the CGT included certain unruly and irresponsible elements capable of taking grave decisions without asking the advice of the trade union leaders. M. Jouhaux was as displeased with the strike[s] as anybody else, and so were the Communists—or, at any rate, their leaders." See *Twilight of France,* 131. See also Lefranc, *Histoire du Front Populaire,* 264.

132. *Le Réveil Syndicaliste,* 31 January 1938; *Le Populaire,* 25 November, 8 December 1937, 7 January 1938.

Chapter Seven

1. For Adolf Sturmthal, this largely explained *The Tragedy of European Labor, 1918–1939* (New York, 1943).

2. René Girault, "Les Relations Internationales et l'Exercice du Pouvoir pendant le Front

Populaire, Juin 1936–Juin 1937," *Cahiers Léon Blum* 1 (May 1977). On 6 February 1936, in his first address as premier, Blum laid out his foreign-policy orientation in the following terms: The People's Front "identifies peace with respect for international law and international contracts and with fidelity to engagements and to the given word. It ardently desires that the organization of collective security should permit the end of the unbridled armaments race in which Europe is involved and lead to an international agreement for the publication, progressive reduction, and effective control of national armaments." See *Le Populaire*, 7 June 1936. More generally, see Blum, *L'Exercice du Pouvoir*, 125–72. Cf. Martin S. Alexander, *The Republic in Danger: General Maurice Gamelin and the Politics of French Defense* (Cambridge, 1992), 80–109; R. Gombin, *Les Socialistes et la Guerre* (Paris, 1970). Like the National Union governments that preceded him, Blum nonetheless continued, despite these fine words, to support augmented armament production, which rose steadily after mid-1934.

3. *L'Humanité*, 13 March 1938.

4. *Le Matin*, 13 March 1938. As P.-E. Flandin, spokesman for the right, said: "There is only a single peril: the Communist peril." Quoted in Delperrié de Bayac, *Histoire du Front Populaire*, 440. This statement reflects a cruel irony. Committed to fighting fascism, the People's Front not only failed to enhance the country's defenses, it provoked a shift within the political system that helped disarm France before the aggressive powers. Before 1936, the traditionally nationalist right had supported a policy of rearmament and firmness toward Germany. But the advent of the People's Front, and behind it, the rise of the Communist party, dislodged the right from its traditional position. Rightists henceforth assumed that communist enthusiasm for national defense was a ploy to get France to fight Stalin's battles. A resolute strategy against Hitler became, in other words, identified with the left, its program of social reforms, and the bitter legacy of class antagonisms that followed from the People's Front experiment. This led many on the right to believe that only communists and Jews would profit from another European war. The right, as a consequence, swung away from belligerent opposition to Hitler and toward appeasement. "Rather Hitler than Blum" was, unsurprisingly, a sentiment that not infrequently found its way into right-wing ranks in the years leading up to the Second World War. The People's Front, as Issac Deutscher succinctly put it, "had set out to reconcile the bourgeois West with Russia . . . [but] only increased the estrangement." Quoted in Kevin McDermott and Jeremy Agnew, *The Comintern: A History of International Communism from Lenin to Stalin* (Basingstoke, 1996), 138.

5. *L'Humanité*, 7 March; *Le Peuple*, 3, 11 March 1938.

6. Jacques Duclos, *Mémoires: 1935–1939* (Paris, 1969), 292–94. After the Franco-Soviet Pact of 1935, the Soviets tried to lure France into a preventative war against Nazi Germany. See Coulondre, *De Staline à Hitler*, 13. See also Paul Reynaud, *In the Thick of the Fight* (New York, 1955), 182.

7. *Le Métallo*, March 1938; *Le Peuple*, 13 March 1938.

8. *La Voix Populaire*, 24 March 1938.

9. *L'Humanité*, 14 March 1938.

10. *Le Populaire*, 16 March 1938.

11. *L'Humanité*, 11 March 1938.

12. *Syndicats*, 23 March 1938. For many non-communist union leaders, the PCF's position on national defense and its implicit identification of working class interests with French imperialism was totally insupportable. War, they argued—even against fascism—would be worse than anything fascism might bring about. See, for example, *Syndicats*, 20, 27 April 1938.

13. *Drapeau Rouge,* 19 March 1937. Even though communists repeatedly played on French fears of war—*Le fascisme, c'est la guerre*—their anti-fascism and the bellicose foreign-policy measures they proposed helped push the country toward war. No Frenchmen, whatever his politics, welcomed such a prospect, but French communists consoled themselves with the thought that another war would almost certainly bring about a revolution. See Claude Jamet, *Notre Front Populaire: Journal d'un Militant (1934–1939)* (Paris, 1977), 112.

14. *Le Peuple,* 24 March 1938; *Le Populaire,* 24 March 1938; Union Syndicale des Ouvriers et Ouvrières Métallurgistes . . . de la Région Parisienne, *Conférence Fait aux Elus du Rassemblement Populaire sur l'Etat de la Production dans les Industries de Défense National* (Paris, March 1938).

15. Parti Communiste Internationaliste, *La Grève de la Métallurgie Parisienne* (Paris, 1938), 17.

16. *Le Populaire,* 25 March 1938; *Le Peuple,* 25 March 1938.

17. *Le Matin,* 25, 26 March 1938; *L'Action Française,* 25, 26 March 1938.

18. Of all the strikes and labor conflicts of the period, the metal strikes of March and April 1938 were one of the most ignored by the major left and union papers. What is known about them mainly comes from the papers and publications of the union opposition, the far left, and the far right.

19. *Le Peuple,* 26 March 1938.

20. *L'Ouvrier Libre,* May 1938; *La Lutte Ouvrière,* 21 April 1938.

21. *Le Matin,* 25 March 1938.

22. *L'Eveil des Techniciens et Employées,* May 1938; *La Commune,* 5 April 1938; *Le Réveil Syndicaliste,* 23 May 1938; *La Lutte Ouvrière,* 21 April 1938.

23. *La Lutte Ouvrière,* 31 March 1938. The Trotskyist slogan of "Not one hour for national defense under a capitalist regime"—i.e., no abridgement of the forty-hour law for the sake of capitalist defense preparations—was like a red shirt before the bullish communists.

24. Brunet, *Jacques Doriot,* 245–67.

25. *L'Emancipation Nationale,* 22 April 1938; *L'Humanité,* 7 April 1938.

26. *Le Populaire,* 13 April 1938.

27. *L'Action Française,* 3, 12 April 1938. These committees reportedly succeeded at Salmson, Flertex, Rateau, Peugot, Bréguet, Laffly, Telephones de Bezon, et al.

28. *L'Eveil des Techniciens,* May 1938.

29. *Le Réveil Syndicaliste,* 11 April 1938.

30. *Le Métallo,* April–May 1938.

31. *Le Matin,* 29 March 1938.

32. *La Commune,* 7 April 1938; *Monde Ouvrier,* 9 April 1938.

33. *Le Matin,* 8 April 1938. Not only did the *patrons* refuse to negotiate, they rejected recommendations by other *patronal* bodies to resolve the conflict. The PCF even claimed Gignoux of the CGPF was using the strikes to bring down the government. *L'Humanité,* 10 April 1938.

34. *L'Humanité,* 27 March 1938. This accusation, however, was contradicted by other party publications. See, for example, *La Vie du Partie: Bulletin Mensuelle Reservé aux Sections et Cellules du PCF,* April 1938.

35. *Le Populaire,* 28 March 1938; *Juin 36,* April 1938.

36. *Juin 36,* 22 April, May 1938; *La Révolution Prolétarienne,* 10 May 1938; *La Lutte Ouvrière,* 31 March 1937. Doury, the general secretary, later admitted as much. See *L'Humanité,* 11 May 1938. Interestingly, the main challenge to the communists on the shop floor came from the Cercle Syndicaliste, which the PCF deliberately ignored.

37. The communist tendency to turn strikes on and off to suit their particular needs is inadvertently documented in the autobiographical reflections of a top metal leader; see Henri Jourdain, *Comprendre pour Accomplir*, 29–30.

38. *Le Matin*, 30 March 1938.

39. *Le Peuple*, 1 April 1938.

40. *Le Réveil Syndicaliste*, 11 and 25 April 1938.

41. *Le Peuple*, 7 April 1938; *L'Action Française*, 10 April 1938.

42. *L'Humanité*, 1–7 April 1938; *Candide*, 17 March 1938.

43. Werth, *Twilight of France*, 162.

44. *Le Populaire*, 11 April 1938.

45. *L'Humanité*, 11 April 1938.

46. "With the *Anschluss*, a turning point was reached that drastically altered the conditions of French politics. Domestic affairs lost their significance, foreign affairs changed their focus. . . . The Radicals did not break the Popular Front; the *Anschluss* made it irrelevant." See Peter J. Larmour, *The French Radical Party in the 1930s*, 237–38. At the same time, however, the social factor was crucial in shaping the Radicals' orientation to the republican union. Two and a half years of labor unrest had thoroughly estranged them from the PCF and the unions. This, as much as the altered international situation, accounts for their disaffection. See Alexandre Zévaés, *Histoire de Six Ans (1938–1944)* (Paris, 1944), 17; "Communication de Roger Génébrier" in *Edouard Daladier, Chef de Gouvernment*, ed. by R. Rémond and J. Bourdin (Paris, 1977), 75–76.

47. *Le Peuple*, 15 April 1938.

48. *La Commune*, 14 April 1938.

49. *La Révolution Prolétarienne*, 10 May 1938.

50. *L'Humanité*, 18 April 1938.

51. *Le Réveil Syndicaliste*, 23 May, 6 June 1938; *Le Prolétaire de Clichy*, 29 April, 6 May 1938; *La Révolution Prolétarienne*, 25 July 1938.

52. *Le Réveil Syndicaliste*, 25 April 1938.

53. *L'Humanité*, 27 May 1938; *Le Populaire*, 26 May 1938; *La Vie Ouvrière*, 5, 12, 26 May 1938.

54. *La Commune*, 21 April 1938.

55. *Le Réveil Syndicaliste*, 3 July 1938; *La Révolution Prolétaienne*, 10 May, 25 August 1938; Rioux, *Révolutionnaires du Front Popular*, 244.

56. Virtually every non-communist tendency in the union movement criticized the leadership of the April strikes. See, for example, *L'Eveil des Techniciens et Employés*, May 1938; *L'Ouvrier Métallurgiste*, April 1938; *Le Réveil Syndicaliste*, 25 April 1938; *La Commune*, April 1938; *La Lutte Ouvrière*, 3 May 1938.

57. On membership figures, see Prost, *La CGT à l'Epoque du Front Populaire*, 45. The strike movement of April was poorly covered in the daily papers of the left and the CGT: i.e., *L'Humanité*, *Le Populaire*, and *Le Peuple*. The best journalistic account appeared in *La Lutte Ouvrière*, 31 March, 7, 14, 21 April 1938. Two indispensable pamphlets on the strike are: Syndicat des Techniciens . . . de la Métallurgie, *L'Evolution de Révendications depuis Juin 1936 et les Grèves de la Métallurgie Parisienne de Mars-Avril 1938* (Paris [1938?]); Parti Communiste Internationale, *La Grève de la Métallurgie Parisienne, 24 Mars–16 Avril 1938* (Paris, 1938). For an insightful fascist account, see *L'Emancipation Nationale: Hebdomadaire du PPF*, 1, 9, 15, and 22 April 1938.

58. *Syndicats*, 18 May 1938.

59. *L'Union des Métaux*, May 1938; *Le Prolétaire de Clichy*, 13 May 1938.

60. *Le Prolétaire de Clichy*, 29 April 1938.

61. *La Commune*, 24 May 1938.

62. *L'Humanité*, 26 June 1938.

63. Philippe Machefer, "Les Syndicats Professionnels Français (1936–1939)," *Le Mouvement Social* 19 (April–June 1982).

64. *La Lutte Ouvrière*, 28 April 1938; *Le Réveil Syndicaliste*, 6 June 1938; *La Commune*, 24 May 1938.

65. See, for example, *L'Humanité*, 27 June 1938; *La Vie Ouvrière*, 21 July 1938; *Le Peuple*, 2 July 1938; Gillot, *Un Forgeron dans la Cité des Rois*, 169.

66. Jean-Louis Crémieux-Brilhac, *Les Français de l'An 40: Ouvriers et Soldats* (Paris, 1990), 24–25. A government study of the unemployed in 1938 showed a third of them were over 60, half over 50, and the rest female and unskilled—which meant, contrary to union suggestion, that they were not the type of workers who could be easily retrained. The metal union, which had proposed the study, refused to accept its findings, holding to its belief that the unemployed constituted a suitable reserve army of labor. This reflected the pervasive anxiety of unemployment which still affected most workers in the late 1930s. As for modernization, the employers usually lacked the investment capital to purchase new machinery and reorganize production.

67. *La Révolution Prolétarienne*, 10 May 1938; *Le Réveil Syndicaliste*, 6 June 1938.

68. *Juin 36*, 5 August 1938.

69. *Le Réveil Syndicaliste*, 18 July 1938.

70. *Le Réveil Syndicaliste*, 1 August 1938; *La Commune*, 1 July 1938; *L'Humanité*, 6 July 1938.

71. *Syndicats*, 16 March, 1 June 1938.

72. On the Comité Nationale meeting, see *La Révolution Prolétarienne*, 26 June, 10 July 1938; *Le Peuple*, 13 June 1938; *Syndicats*, 15 and 22 June 1938; *L'Union des Métaux*, June 1938.

73. George Orwell, *The Lion and the Unicorn* (1941; reprint Harmondsworth, 1982), 78.

74. Henri Michele, *La Drôle de Guerre* (Paris, 1971), 52–58.

75. Guérin, *Front Populaire, Révolution Manquée*, 215–19.

76. *L'Union des Métaux*, October 1938.

77. *La Vie Ouvrière*, 6 October 1938; *L'Humanité*, 5 October 1938.

78. *Le Réveil Syndicaliste*, 10 October 1938. The union, however, continued to waffle on this issue. Because it opposed Daladier's Munich policy yet favored a well-armed France, its subsequent policy tended to oscillate back and forth, sometimes emphasizing higher war production, sometimes stressing the need to oppose Daladier's appeasement. It thus took a hard stance in defense of the forty-hour week, but repeatedly acquiesced to longer hours—a contradictory position that followed from its divided allegiances. See *La Lutte Ouvrière*, 28 October 1938.

79. *L'Union des Métaux*, October 1938; *L'Humanité*, 2 October 1938.

80. *Syndicats*, 21 September 1938; *Feuille Bimensuelle d'Information Syndicaliste: Editée par le Centre d'Action Contre la Guerre*, 14 July 1938. Contrary to a good deal of current thinking, this was not a position held solely by rightists and pacifists, but also by many liberals who put the survival of Europe above the triumph of any particular ideology. See, for example, Maurice Cowling, *The Impact of Hitler: British Politics and British Policy 1933–1940* (Chicago, 1977), 349.

81. *La Révolution Prolétarienne*, 10 October 1938.

82. *Syndicats*, 5 October 1938. Earlier, far-left unionists formed a *Comité d'Action Syndicale* whose slogan was "the struggle against war is inseparable from the struggle against the *patronat*." See *La Lutte Ouvrière*, 31 March 1938.

83. *Que Faire?* November 1938.

84. This later became the reigning orthodoxy of the Cold War establishment, even after A. J. P. Taylor's *The Origins of the Second World War* (London, 1961) thoroughly discredited it.

85. Fédération des Ouvriers en Métaux, *XIIe Congrès Fédéral* (Paris, 1938), 72; *Syndicats*, 14 September 1938.

86. R. Rémond and J. Bourdin, eds., *La France et les Français en 1938–1939* (Paris, 1978), 139.

87. Berstein, *Histoire du Parti Radical*, 2:535–64.

88. Reynaud, *In the Thick of the Fight*, 200.

89. *Syndicats*, 29 November 1938; *L'Union des Métaux*, October 1938.

90. Mortimer, *The Rise of the French Communist Party*, 276.

91. On 16 November, Jouhaux told the CGT Congress: "Trade union labor is ready to take a large share in a program of sacrifices but it does not accept sacrifices that are contrary to the general interest. A sound economy cannot be built on the basis of 'Get rich, you capitalists, and may the working class sink lower than ever'. . . . The decrees in their present form are unacceptable." Quoted in Werth, *Twilight of France*, 291. See also *Le Peuple*, 17 November 1938; Lefranc, *Mouvement Syndicale sous la Troisième République*, 282.

92. S. Courtois and D. Peschanski, "La Dominante de l'Internationale et les Tournants du PCF" in *Le Parti Communiste Français des Années Sombres 1938–1941*, ed. J. P. Azéma, et al. (Paris, 1986), 253.

93. *La Vie Ouvrière*, 24 November 1938.

94. *La Commune*, 25 November 1938.

95. *L'Humanité*, 23 November 1938.

96. *Syndicats*, 2 December 1938.

97. On the Renault occupation, see *La Commune*, December 1938; *Le Peuple*, 25 November 1938; *La Vie Ouvrière*, 29 November 1938; *Le Réveil Syndicaliste*, 5 December 1938; Robert Francotte, "L'Usine Renault: Souvenirs," *Cahiers d'Histoire de l'Institut Maurice Thorez* (January 1973), 146–47; Depretto and Schweitzer, *Le Communisme à l'Usine*, 264–71; Guy Bourdé, *La Défaite du Front Populaire* (Paris, 1977), 143–49.

98. *Le Peuple*, 26 November 1938.

99. Delmas, *A Gauche de la Barricade*, 181; "Intervention de René Belin," in *Edouard Daladier, Chef de Gouvernment*, 199.

100. *Juin 36*, 16 June 1939.

101. *Révolution*, December 1938.

102. *La Lutte Ouvrière*, 25 November 1938.

103. Edouard Daladier, *In Defense of France* (Freeport, 1939), 62–66.

104. Quoted in Bourdé, *La Défaite du Front Populaire*, 146.

105. Daladier, *In Defense of France* , 66.

106. *L'Union des Métaux*, December 1938.

107. *L'Union des Métaux*, January 1939; Patrick Fridenson, "Le Patronat Français," in *La France et les Français en 1938–1939*, 139.

108. *Le Prolétaire de Clichy*, 9 December 1938.

109. *Le Peuple, Le Populaire*, 2 December 1938.

110. *Le Peuple*, 2 December 1938, 8 February 1939.

111. *L'Aube Nouvelle*, 10 December 1938; *L'Humanité*, 31 December 1938.

112. At the end of December 1938, 20,000 Paris *métallos* had still not been rehired. See *L'Union des Métaux*, February 1939.

113. The three above paragraphs follow Bourdé, *La Défaite du Front Populaire*, 223–31.

114. *Le Prolétaire de Clichy*, 9 December 1938.

115. *Le Réveil Syndicaliste*, 17 July 1939.

116. Daniel Halévy, *1938: Une Année d'Histoire* (Paris, 1938), 57.

Chapter Eight

1. See, for example, *Le Populaire*, 4 March 1939.

2. Union Syndicale des Ouvriers et Ouvrières Métallurgiques... de la Région Parisienne, *Ce Que Sont les Décrets-Lois Daladier* (Paris, 1939).

3. The decrees of 12 November 1938 opened the way for the forty-eight-hour work week. The decrees of 20 March and 21 April 1939 extended the work week to sixty hours. Overtime pay, calculated after the forty-fifth hour, was only 5 percent above the regular wage, but longer hours made for fatter pay checks.

4. *Le Peuple*, 16 April 1939; *International Press Correspondence*, 22 April 1939.

5. *L'Aube Nouvelle*, 7 January 1939.

6. *La Révolution Prolétarienne*, 25 May 1939; *Le Réveil Syndicaliste*, 27 March 1939.

7. *La Lutte Ouvrière*, 10 July 1939; Stéphane Courtois, *Le PCF dans la Guerre: De Gaulle, la Résistance, Staline* (Paris, 1980), 30–31.

8. This obuseness obviously followed from the PCF's dependence on Moscow. Without a signal to act otherwise, it was duty bound to uphold the Comintern line. The Soviet bureaucracy, on the other hand, was already in the process of reconsidering its objectives in the West.

9. Pierre Laborie, "Images et Crise d'Identitie du PCF," in *Le Parti Communiste Français des Années Sombres*, 118.

10. Bourdé, *La Défaite du Front Populaire*, 250; Prost, *La CGT à l'Epoch du Front Populaire*, 47–48; Lefranc, *Le Mouvement Syndical sous la Troisième République*, 415.

11. Prost, *La CGT à l'Epoch du Front Populaire*, 196.

12. *Le Réveil Syndicaliste*, 31 July 1939.

13. *L'Union des Métaux*, April 1939.

14. *Le Peuple*, 6 December 1938.

15. In August 1939, there were 3,500 PCF'ers at Renault, compared to 6,500 before November 30. See Depretto and Schweitzer, *Le Communisme à l'Usine*, 279.

16. *Le Réveil Syndicaliste*, 27 March, 10 April 1939.

17. *La Vie Ouvrière*, 18 May 1939.

18. *Le Peuple*, 11 December 1938; *Syndicats*, 21 December 1938; CGT/Fédération des Ouvriers des Métaux, *XIVe Congrès Fédéral* (Versailles, 1939).

19. *L'Union des Métaux*, April 1939; *Le Réveil Syndicalist*, 31 July 1939.

20. The Franco-Soviet Pact of 1935 lacked a military clause providing mutual military assistance in case of attack.

21. Fédération des Techniciens, *Pourquoi la Guerre Menace* (Paris [1939?]).

22. Geoffrey Roberts, *The Unholy Alliance: Stalin's Pact with Hitler* (Bloomington, 1989), 92–93.

23. Associated Press, Moscow, 11 March 1939, quoted in R. F. Keeling, *Gruesome Harvest* (Chicago, 1947). See also Walter Isaacson and Evan Thomas, *The Wise Men: Six Friends and the World They Made* (New York, 1986), 175.

24. Coulondre, *De Staline à Hitler*, 164–71.

25. Vassart, *Le Front Populaire en France*, 66; Haslam, *The Soviet Union and the Struggle for Collective Security*, 204–5. After the Munich Conference, the ever perspicacious Trotsky prophesied that: "The collapse of Czechoslovakia is the collapse of Stalin's international policy of the last five years. . . . We may now expect with certainty Soviet diplomacy to attempt a *rapprochement* with Hitler at the cost of new retreats and capitulations." See *Writings of Leon Trotsky, 1938–1939* (New York, 1974), 29. Even earlier, *le bête noir* of the anti-fascists, Charles Maurras, had made an identical prediction. See Pierre Monnier, *A l'Ombre des Grandes Têtes Molles* (Paris, 1987), 272. Although Stalin began reappraising the viability of the People's Front policy in March, he nonetheless kept his options open. Not until late July or early August was a decision made to break with the Western allies.

26. *Syndicats*, 15 September 1939.

27. *L'Humanité*, 26 August 1939; *La Vie Ouvrière*, 31 August, 7, 16 September 1939; *Le Progrès*, 2, 9 September 1939.

28. For the pact's impact on the PCF, see Wolfgang Leonhard, *Betrayal: The Hitler-Stalin Pact of 1939* (New York, 1989), 107–20; Durant, *La Lutte des Travailleurs de chez Renault*, 89–90; Jourdain, *Comprendre pour Accomplir*, 36; Fourrier, *Graine Rouge*, 87.

29. Jean-Pierre Azéma and François Bedarida, *La France des Années Noires* (Paris, 1993), 31; Cowling, *The Impact of Hitler*, 310–12, 343.

30. Taylor, *Origins of the Second World War*, 257–68; Coulondre, *De Staline à Hitler*, 309.

31. *La Vie Ouvrière*, 27, 31 August, 7, 16 September 1939; *Le Populaire*, 9 September 1939; *International Press Correspondence*, 30 September 1939.

32. Fohlen, *La France de l'Entre-Deux-Guerres*, 185.

33. Quoted in Zévaés, *Histoire de Six Ans*, 19. Throughout the war, as he repeatedly confided to the American ambassador, Daladier feared a possible communist rebellion. See Orville H. Bullitt, ed., *For the President, Personal and Secret: Correspondence between Franklin D. Roosevelt and William C. Bullitt* (Boston, 1972), 432.

34. *Syndicats*, 15 September 1939.

35. *Le Peuple*, 1 September 1939.

36. *Syndicats*, 15 September 1939.

37. *International Press Correspondence*, 28 October 1939.

38. *L'Humanité*, December 1939.

39. *Cahiers du Bolchevisme*, January 1940.

40. *Le Peuple*, 5 October 1939.

41. For the PCF declaration of 30 September 1939, see Courtois, *Le PCF dans la Guerre*, 496–98.

42. Monatte, *Trois Scissions Syndicales*, 8.

43. *La Vie Ouvrière*, 7 September 1939.

44. A. Rossi [Angelo Tasca], *Les Communistes Français pendant la Drôle de Guerre* (Paris, 1951), 99.

45. Michel, *La Drôle de Guerre*, 192.

46. *Le Peuple*, 26 October 1939; cf. *Syndicats*, 12 October 1939.

47. *International Press Correspondence*, 9 December 1939.

48. The CGT was able to name no more than 200 stewards in over 14,000 metal plants and shops. See Lefranc, *Les Organisations Patronales en France*, 120.

49. *L'Union des Métaux*, January 1940; *Le Peuple*, 27 February 1940.

50. Crémieux-Brilhac, *Les Français de l'An 40*, 115–131.

51. *Syndicats*, 5, 12, 25 October 1939.

52. *Syndicats*, 25 October 1939; *Le Populaire*, 27 November 1939; *L'Union des Métaux*, January 1939.

53. *Le Populaire*, 9 November 1939.

54. In La Courneuve, Clichy, Courbevoie, Argenteuil, Gennevillier, and Boulogne-Billancourt.

55. The Metal Federation dropped from its 1937 high of 800,000 members to 30,000 in May 1940. Given the greater concentration of communists in the Paris Region, the membership of the reconstituted Paris metal union was proportionally lower. These figures, however, are all speculative. Cf. Bruhat and Piolot, *Esquisse d'une Histoire de la CGT*, 168.

56. *L'Humanité*, 26 October 1939; *International Press Correspondence*, 16 December 1939; *L'Etincelle: Organe des Comités de la 4e Internationale*, 15 November 1939; *La Vie Ouvrière*, February 1940.

57. *L'Union des Métaux*, January 1940.

58. Courtois, *Le PCF dans la Guerre*, 103-13.

59. Ehrmann, *French Labor from Popular Front to Liberation*, 188.

60. Rémi Baudouï, *Raoul Dautry 1880–1951: Le Technocrate de la République* (Paris, 1992), 194–96. It was Chevalme, not the Federation, that accepted the agreement,which meant, it had no *legitimité syndicale*, although Dautry treated it as such and afforded it contractual significance.

61. *Syndicats*, 28 December 1939; *Le Peuple*, 19 October 1939.

62. *L'Union des Métaux*, January 1940.

63. Georges Lefranc, "Inquietudes Ouvrières," *Nouveau Cahiers* 57 (April 1940): 3.

64. *Le Peuple*, 19 October 1939, 22 February 1940; *Le Populaire*, 16 January 1940; *Syndicats*, 15 February 1940.

65. *Syndicats*, 21 December 1939, 17 May 1940.

66. German armament production did not become "total" until 1942.

67. Michel, *La Drôle de Guerre*, 193, 195.

68. Donald Cameron Watt, *Too Serious A Business: European Armed Forces and the Approach to the Second World War* (Berkeley, 1975).

69. The army's escapist mentality is probably best captured in the novel by Julien Gracq, *Un Balcon en Forêt* (Paris, 1958).

70. Michel, *La Drôle de Guerre*, 193–98.

71. Cf. Ehrmann, *French Labor from Popular Front to Liberation*, 200.

72. Lefranc, "Inquietudes Ouvrières," 2.

73. Ehrmann, *French Labor from Popular Front to Liberation*, 205; *Le Peuple*, 18 January 1940; *Syndicats*, 30 November 1939, 15 February 1940.

74. *Syndicats*, 9 May 1940.

75. *Le Peuple*, 4, 11 April 1940.

76. *Syndicats*, 18 April 1940.

77. *La Révolution Prolétarienne*, May 1949.

78. Quoted in Georges Lefranc, *Les Experiences Syndicales en France de 1939 à 1950* (Paris, 1950), 32. See also Rossi, *Les Communistes Français pendant la Drôle de Guerre*, 206–10.

79. Werth, *Twilight of France*, 346.

80. *L'Union des Métaux*, January 1940; Louis Eudier, *Notre Combat de Classes et de Patriotes* (Le Havre, 1982), 53–59.

81. *International Press Correspondence*, 28 October 1939; "Peuple de France," PCF declaration of February 1940, in Courtois, *Le PCF dans la Guerre*, 498–511.

82. Michel, *La Drôle de Guerre*, 203; John Laffin, *Jackboot: The Story of the German Soldier* (New York, 1995), 176.

83. Bloch, *Strange Defeat*; Jacques Benoist-Méchin, *Soixante Jours qui Ebranlérent l'Occident* (Paris, 1956); *International Press Correspondence*, 2 November 1940. See also

Larmour, *The French Radical Party in the 1930s,* 254; Henri Amouroux, *Le Peuple du Désastre: 1939–1940* (Paris, 1976), 15–51. Cf. Robert Frank, "Le Front Populaire A-t-il Perdu la Guerre?" in *Les Années Trente: De la Crise à la Guerre,* ed. Michel Winock, et al. (Paris, 1990).

84. In 1939, as in 1870, the French entered the war with as much hatred for one another as for the enemy on the border. See Julien Gracq, *Lettrines* (Paris, 1967), 14. In this vein, Marc Ferro bitterly observes, "France is gifted not so much for battle as for civil war." Quoted in Richard Bernstein, *Fragile Glory: A Portrait of France and the French* (New York, 1990), 235–36.

85. That is, in the liberal sense. See Ernest Renan, "What Is a Nation?" (1882) in *The Poetry of the Celtic Race and Other Studies,* trans. W. G. Hutchison (Port Washington, 1970), 81.

Bibliography

I. Newspapers and Periodicals

L'Age de Fer: Industriel Bi-Mensuel (UIMM).

L'Atelier pour le Plan (CGT).

L'Aube Nouvelle: Organe Communiste d'Information des Cantons de Montrouge et Vanves.

L'Aube Social: Hebdomadaire Communiste des Travailleurs de la Banlieue Nord-Ouest.

L'Aube Social: Organe de la Fédération Communiste de la Région Parisienne.

L'Automotrice: Ile Seguin Secteur No. 4 (CGT).

L'Avant-Garde: Organe de Défense des Jeunes Travailleurs (PCF).

La Barricade: Organe de Défense des Travailleurs des 13e et 5e (PCF).

Bulletin Communiste: Organe du Communisme International (Trotskyist).

Bulletin de la Fédération Nationale des Syndicats Ouvriers de la Bijouterie-Orfèvrerie-Horlogerie (CGTU).

Bulletin d'Information Socialiste: Education, Discipline, Propagande (SFIO).

Bulletin Régional: Cahiers du Militant de la Région Parisienne du Parti Communiste.

Cahiers du Bolchevisme: Organe Théorique du PCF.

La Chaîne Rouge: Organe de Défense des Jeunes Ouvriers des Usines Citroen (PCF).

Le Combat Syndical: Secteur du Hameau (CGT).

Le Combat Syndicaliste: Organe Official de la CGTSR.

La Commune: Organe Centrale du Parti Communiste Internationaliste (Trotskyist).

Le Cri du Peuple: Hebdomadaire Syndicaliste Révolutionnaire (dissident CGTU).

Drapeau Rouge: Journal Communiste Révolutionnaire (dissident PCF).

Drapeau Rouge: Journal du Socialisme Révolutionnaire (SFIO).

L'Elan Social: Organe du Comité de Prevoyance et d'Action Sociale.

L'Emancipation: Journal d'Unité Ouvrière et Socialiste (SFIO).

L'Emancipation Nationale: Hebdomadaire du PPF.

L'Embouti: Journal des Sections Syndicales de l'Usine Citroen St-Ouen (CGT).

L'Etincelle: Journal du Syndicat Unique des Métaux de St. Chamond (CGTU).

L'Etincelle de Boulogne-Billancourt (PCF).

L'Evolution: Organe du Sections Syndicales, Rue de l'Ile (CGT).

L'Eveil de Seine-et-Oise: Organe du Front Populaire (PCF).

L'Eveil des Ouvriers en Instruments de Précision (CGT).

L'Eveil des Techniciens et Employés (CGT).

L'Eveil du XVIIIe (PCF).

Feuille Bimensuelle d'Information Syndicale: Edité par le Centre Syndical d'Action Contre La Guerre.

Le Guide du Métallurgiste (CGT).

L'Homme Réel: Révue du Syndicalisme et de l'Humanisme.

L'Humanité (PCF).

Les Industries Mécaniques: Révue Mensuelle (UIMM).

L'Information Sociale: Action Syndicale, Organization du Travail, Evolution Economique.

International Press Correspondance (CI).

L'International Syndical Rouge (RILU).

Juin 36: Organe de la Fédération Socialiste de la Seine (SFIO).

Le Libertaire (Anarchist).

La Lutte Ouvrière: Organe du Parti Ouvrier Internationaliste (Trotskyist).

Le Métallo (CGTU/CGT, Paris).

Le Métallo (CGT, Le Havre).

La Métallurgie Transformatrice (UIMM).

Le Métallurgiste (CGTU).

Monde Ouvrier: L'Hebdomadaire de la Famille et du Travail (Catholic).

L'Ouvrier Libre: Organe du PSF pour les Ouvriers de la Région Parisienne.

L'Ouvrier Métallurgiste (CFTC).

L'Ouvrière (CGTU).

Le Peuple (CGT).

Le Prolétaire: Hebromadaire Communiste des Cantons d'Argenteuil (PCF).

Le Populaire (SFIO).

Le Prolétaire de Clichy: Organe locale du Parti Ouvrier-Paysan.

Le Prolétaire Drancéen (PCF).

Que Faire? Révue Communiste Mensuelle (dissident PCF).

The Red International of Labor Unions.

Le Réveil Syndicaliste (Cercle Syndicaliste "Lutte de Classe").

Révolution (Trotskyist).

La Révolution Prolétarienne: Révue Mensuelle Syndicale Communiste (Revolutionary Syndicalist).

Soviet des Usines Citroen (Trotskyist).

Syndicalisme: Organe Mensuel de la CFTC.

Le Syndicalisme Chrétien: Organe Mensuelle de la CFTC.

Syndicat des Mécaniciens, Chaudronniers, et Fondeurs de France (CGT).

Syndicats: Hebdomadaire du Monde du Travail (CGT).

Le Travailleur de la Banlieue Ouest (PCF).

Le Travailleur de Seine et Oise (SFIO).

Le Travailleur Parisien (CGT).

L'Union des Métaux (CGT).

L'Unité Renault (CGT).

La Vague: Organe du Rassemblement Révolutionnaire (SFIO).

La Verité (Trotskyist).

La Vie du Parti (PCF).

La Vie Ouvrière (PCF).

La Vie Socialiste (SFIO).

La Vie Syndicale (CGTU).

La Voix du Peuple (CGT).

La Voix du Peuple de Paris (CGTU).

La Voix Populaire (PCF, Colombes).

II. Union Documents

Bothereau, Robert. *L'Organization de la CGT et du Mouvement Syndical.* Paris: CCEO, 1937.

Bouyer, Raymond. *Le Capitalisme Contemporain: Fiction et Realité.* Paris: CCEO, [1937?].

Confédération Générale du Travail. *La Confédération Générale du Travail et le Mouvement Syndical.* Paris, 1925.

———. *Congrès Confédéral de Paris. XXVIe Congrès, du 17 au 20 Septembre 1929.* Versailles: La Gutemberg, 1929.

———. *Congrès Confédéral de Paris: XXVIIe Congrès National Corporatif, 15–18 Septembre 1931.* Versailles, La Gutenberg, 1931.

———. *Congrès Confédéral de Paris: XXVIIIe Congrès, 26–29 Septembre 1933.* Versailles: La Gutenberg, 1933.

———. *La CGT et l'Unité Syndical.* Versailles: La Gutenberg, [1934?].

———. *Contre la Crise, Pour l'Economie Dirigée.* Versailles: La Gutenberg, 1934.

———. *Congrès Confédéral de Paris. XXIXe Congrès, 24–27 Septembre 1935.* Versailles: La Gutenberg, 1935.

———. *Congrès Confédéral d'Unité. À Toulouse, du 2 au 5 Mars 1936.* Versailles: La Gutenberg, 1936.

———. *Congrès Confédéral de Nantes: XXXIe Congrès, 14–17 Novembre 1938.* Versailles: La Gutenberg, 1938.

Confédération Générale du Travail/Fédération des Ouvriers des Métaux. *Les Méthodes Scientifiques Appliquées au Travail.* Paris: Maison des Syndicats, 1920.

———. *Une Demande de Contrôle Ouvrier en France.* Geneva: BIT, 1921.

———. *Ve Congrès National: Tenu à Lille les 20–23 Juillet 1921.* Paris: Maison des Syndicats, [1921?].

———. *VIe Congrès Fédéral: Tenu à Paris les 11–13 Octobre 1923.* Versailles: La Gutenberg, 1924.

———. *VIIe Congrès Fédéral: Tenu à Paris les 23–25 Août 1925.* Versailles: La Gutenberg, 1925.

———. *VIIIe Congrès Fédéral: Tenu à Paris les 24–25 Juillet 1927.* Versailles: La Gutenberg, 1927.

———. *IXe Congrès Fédéral: Tenu à Paris les 15–16 Septembre 1929.* Versailles: La Gutenberg, 1930

———. *Xe Congrès Fédéral: Tenu à Paris les 13–14 Septembre 1931.* Versailles: La Gutenberg, 1931.

———. *XIe Congrès Fédéral: Tenu à Paris les 24–25 Septembre 1933.* Versailles: La Gutenberg, 1933.

———. *XIIe Congrès Fédéral: Rapport Moral et Administratif, Exercise 1933–1935.* Versailles: La Gutenberg, 1935.

———. *L'Application des 40 Heures dans la Métallurgie.* [1936?].

———. *Congrès d'Unité: Tenu à Paris les 25–27 Novembre 1936.* Versailles: La Gutenberg, 1937.

———. *XIVe Congrès Fédéral: Tenu à Paris du 8 au 11 Décembre 1938.* Versailles: La Gutenberg, 1939.

Confédération Générale du Travail/ Fédération des Techniciens, Dessinateurs, et Assimilés de l'Industrie et des Arts Appliqués. *Les Nationalisations: Aviation, Armament.* Paris, 1937.

———. *Pourquoi la Guerre Menace.* Paris, [1939?].

Confédération Générale du Travail/Fédération des Travailleurs de la Métallurgie. *L'Aviation Française en Danger: Les Travailleurs de la Métallurgie Accusent* Paris, [1947?].

Confédération Générale du Travail/ Syndicat des Ouvriers en Instruments de Chirurgie,

Orthopedie, et Parties Similaires du Département de la Seine. [No Title.] Paris: Imp. Cooperative Ouvrière, 1924.

Confédération Générale du Travail/ Syndicat des Techniciens, Employés et Assimilés de la Métallurgie de la Région Parisienne. *L'Evolution des Revendications Depuis Juin 1936 et les Grèves de la Métallurgie Parisienne de Mars–Avril 1938.* Paris, [1938?].

Confédération Générale du Travail/Union Syndicale des Ouvriers et Ouvrières Métallurgistes et Similaires de la Région Parisienne. *Conférence Fait aux Elus du Rassemblement Populaire sur l'Etat de la Production dans les Industries de Défense Nationale.* Paris, 1938.

———. *Ce Que Sont les Décrets-Lois Daladier.* Paris, 1939.

Confédération Générale du Travail Unitaire. *1er Congrès Tenu à Saint-Etienne du 25 Juin au 1er Juillet 1922.* Paris: Maison des Syndicats, [1922?].

———. *4e Congrès National: Ordinaire (Bordeaux, 19–24 Septembre 1927).* Paris: Maison des Syndicats, [1927?].

———. *5e Congrès National: Ordinaire (Paris, 12–15 Septembre 1929).* Paris: Maison des Syndicats, [1929?].

———. *6e Congrès National Ordinaire (Paris, 8–14 Novembre 1931).* Paris: Maison des Syndicats, 1931.

———. *La CGTU Contre les Ammendes.* Paris: Rédaction de la Révue "L'I. S. R." [1932?].

———. *Les Documents du VIIe Congrès de la CGTU (23–29 Septembre 1933).* Paris: Maison des Syndicats, 1933.

———. *VIIe Congrès National Ordinaire (Paris, 23–29 Septembre 1933).* Paris: Maison des Syndicats, 1933.

———. *VIIIe Congrès National Ordinaire (Issy-les-Moulineaux, 24–27 Septembre 1935).* Paris: Maison des Syndicats, [1935?].

———. *Une Date: 27 Septembre 1935.* Paris: Ed. de la CGTU, [1935?].

Confédération Générale du Travail Unitaire/Fédération Unitaire des Métaux. *IIIe Congrès National (1–3 Septembre 1925).* Paris: Maison des Syndicats, 1925.

———. *Rapports sur les Questions à l'Ordre du Jour du Comité National Fédéral des 26–27 Janvier 1929.* Paris: Maison des Syndicats, 1929.

Confédération Générale du Travail Unitaire/Union Syndicale des Travailleurs de la Métallurgie de la Région Parisienne. *Statuts.* Courbevoie: Société Ouvrière d'Imprimerie, n.d.

———. Confédération Générale du Travail Unitaire/XXe Union Régionale. *Ce Que les Ouvriers Doivent Savoir, Pourquoi Il Faut Se Syndiquer.* Paris: Maison des Syndicats, n.d.

Frachon, Benoît. *Le Rôle Sociale des Syndicats.* Paris: CCEO, 1937.

———. *De Toulouse à Nantes: Deux Ans d'Activité Confédéral au Service de la Classe Ouvrière.* Paris: L'Union Syndicale de la Métallurgie Parisienne, 1938.

Frachon, Benoît, and Gaston Monmousseau. *Pour une CGT Unique! Pour l'Action de Masse!* Paris: Les Publications Révolutionnaires, 1934.

Gaillard. *L'Attaque Patronale et Gouvernementale Contre la Classe Ouvrière.* Paris: Maison des Syndicats, 1927.

Jouhaux, Léon. *Le Syndicalisme et la CGT.* Paris: Eds. de la Sirène, 1920

———. *Le Syndicalisme: Ce Qu'il Est, Ce Qu'il Doit Etre.* Paris: Flammarion, 1937.

———. *L'Arbitrage Obligatoire.* Paris: CCEO, [1937?].

———. *La CGT et Front Populaire.* Paris: Petite Bibliothèque du Militant Syndicaliste, n.d.

Monmousseau, Gaston. *Le Contrôle Syndicale et les Comités d'Usines.* Paris: Union Departmentale de la Seine, 1922.

———. *Du Réformisme à la Lutte des Classes.* Paris: Maison des Syndicats, 1927.

Philip, André. *Le Renouvellement des Conventions Collectives du Travail: Leçons des Experiences.* Paris: CCEO, 1937.

Racamond, Julien. *Le Plan de Salut Economique et de Défense Nationale.* Paris: Ed. de la CGTU, [1935?].

———. *Le Syndicalisme et les Revendications Immediates.* Paris: C.C.E.O., n.d.

III. Governmental, Political, and *Patronal* Documents

Bulletin de la Statistique Générale de la France. Vols. 7–28. Paris: Librairie Félix Alcan, 1918–39.

Blum, Léon. *L'Exercice du Pouvoir: Discours Proncés de Mai 1936 à Janvier 1937.* Paris: Gallimard, 1937.

Bulletin du Ministère du Travail. Vols. 27–46. Paris, 1920–39.

Bureau International du Travail. *Annuaire des Statistiques du Travail: 1935–1936.* Geneva: Kundig, 1936.

Cachin, Marcel. *Oui! Nous Organiserons le Front Unique de la Classe Ouvrière.* Paris: Les Publications Révolutionnaires, 1934.

Chavaroche, J. *L'Economie et Lutte Politique en France.* Paris: Bureau d'Editions, [1929?].

Daladier, Edouard. *Ce Que Veut la France.* Montrouge: Fasquelle Editeurs, 1939.

———. *In Defense of France.* New York: Doubleday, 1939.

Degras, Jane. *The Communist International: Documents.* 3 vols. London: Oxford University Press, 1956–65.

Dimitrov, Georges. *Oeuvres Choisies.* Paris: Eds. Sociales, 1972.

Dubief, Henri. *Le Syndicalisme Révolutionnaire: Textes Choisis.* Paris: Armand Colin, 1969.

Duclos, Jacques. *En Avant pour le Front Union d'Action Antifasciste.* Paris: Les Publications Révolutionnaires, 1934.

Framond, M. de. *La Journée Communiste du 9 Février et les Incidents Communistes du 12 en Banlieue.* Paris: Imprimerie de la Chambre, 1934.

French Subject Collection. Boxes 22–30. Hoover Institution Archives.

Gardiol, Amat, and M. de Framond. *Les Victimes du 6 au 12 Février 1934.* Paris: Imprimerie de la Chambre, 1934.

Garmy, René. *Pourquoi J'ai Eté Exclu du Parti Communiste.* Paris: Impressions Modernes, [1937?].

Georges Lefranc Papers. Hoover Institution Archives.

Gignoux, C. J. *Patrons, Soyez des Patrons!* Paris: Flammarion, 1937.

Gitton, Marcel. *Après les Evénements de Février: Le Parti Communiste dans la Lutte Antifasciste et l'Unité de la Classe Ouvrière.* Paris: Les Publications Révolutionnaires, 1934.

Institut Scientifique de Recherches Economiques et Sociales. *Chronologie Economique Internationale.* 5 vols. Paris: Recueil Sirey, 1934–38.

International Labour Office. *Yearbook of Labour Statistics, 1935–1936.* Geneva, 1936.

———. *Yearbook of Labour Statistics, 1939.* Geneva, 1939.

Leon Blum Before His Judges At the Supreme Court of Riom, March 11th and March 12th, 1943. Foreword by Clement Attlee. Introduction by Felix Gouin. London: The Labour Book Service, 1943.

Losovsky, A. *Les Syndicats et la Révolution.* Paris: Librarie du Travail, [1922?].

———. *The World Trade Union Movement.* Chicago: TUEL, 1924.

———. *What Is the Red International Of Labour Unions.* Moscow: RILU, 1927.

———. *Faisons le Point! Rapport Presenté au Ve Congrès de l'ISR.* Paris: Maison des Syndicats, [1930?].

———. *Où Allons-Nous? Les Leçons et les Perspectives des Luttes Economiques.* Paris: Maison des Syndicats, 1930.

———. *La Grève Est un Combat! Essay d'Application de la Science Militaire à la Stratégie des Grèves.* Courbevoie: La Cootypographie, 1931.

———. *Les Tâches du Mouvement Syndical Révolutionnaire.* Paris: Maison des Syndicats, [1931?].

———. *Luttons Pour la Majorité de la Classe Ouvrière.* Paris: Petite Bibliothèque de l'ISR, [1934?].

Manouilski, D. Z. *Les Partis Communistes et la Crise du Capitalisme.* Paris: Bureau d'Editions, 1931.

Ministère du Travail. *Statistique Générale de la France: Annuaire Statistique.* Vols. 36–54. Paris: Imprimerie Nationale, 1921–39.

Moch, Jules. *Socialisme et Rationalisation.* Bruselles: L'Eglantine, 1927.

Naville, Pierre. *L'Entre-Deux-Guerres: La Lutte des Classes en France 1926–1939.* Paris: EDI, 1975.

Parti Communiste Française. *Les Cellules Communistes d'Entreprises.* Paris: Les Cahiers du Militant, 1924.

———. *Le Parti Communiste Français devant l'Internationale.* Paris: Bureau d'Editions, 1931.

———. *Les Communistes et les Syndicats: Le Travail des Fractions Syndicales.* Paris: Bureau d'Editions, 1932.

———. *Le Triomphe du Front Populaire.* Paris: Les Publications Révolutionnaires, 1935.

Parti Communiste Internationale (Fourth International). *La Grève de la Métallurgie Parisienne, 24 Mars–16 Avril 1938.* Paris, 1938.

Piatnitsky, O. *The Immediate Tasks of the International Trade Union Movement.* New York: Workers' Library Publishers, [1930?].

———. *Les Partis Communistes en Lutte Pour la Conquête des Masses.* Paris: Bureau d'Editions, 1934.

"Quelques Documents Relatifs à la Tactique Classe Contre Classe." *Le Mouvement Social* 70 (January–March 1970).

Red International of Labor Unions/International Syndicale Rouge. *Resolutions and Decisions Adopted by the First International Congress of Revolutionary and Industrial Unions.* Moscow, 1921.

———. *Resolutions and Decisions: Second World Congress of the RILU.* Chicago: TUEL, [1922?].

———. *Resolutions and Decisions: Third World Congress of the RILU.* Chicago: TUEL, 1924.

———. *Rapport pour le IIIe Congrès de l'ISR.* Paris: Librairie du Travail, [1924?].

———. *Report of the Secretariat of the International Propaganda Committee of the Revolutionary Metal Workers.* Moscow, 1925.

———. *L'International Syndicale Rouge au Travail, 1924–1928.* Paris: Maison des Syndicats, 1928.

———. *Report of the Fourth Congress of the RILU.* Essex: Cowdray Press, 1928.

———. "France: Capitalist Rationalisation and Wages." *Bulletin of the RILU,* October 1929.

———. *Problem of Strike Strategy.* New York: Workers' Library Publishers, [1929?].

———. *Resolutions of the 5th Congress of the RILU.* London: The Minority Movement, 1931.

———. *The Way Forward: Position of the RILU Sections and Their Role in the Leadership of the Economic Struggles and Unemployed Movement.* London: RILU Publications, [1931?].

———. *Every Factory a Fortress! The Tasks of the Revolutionary Trade Union Organizations in the Work at the Factory.* London: RILU Publications, [1931?].

Renseignements Statistiques Concernant les Métaux. Paris: Minerais et Métaux, 1938.

Rioux, Jean-Pierre. *Révolutionnaires du Front Populaire: Choix de Documents 1935–1938.* Paris: 10/18, 1973.

Rucart, Marc. *Rapport Général: Les Causes et les Origines des Evénements du 6 Février 1934.* Paris: Imprimerie de la Chambre, 1934.

Semard, Pierre. *Front Unique à l'Usine!* Paris, [1928?].

Statistique Générale de la France. *Résultats Statistiques du Recensement de la Population.* Paris: Imprimerie Nationale, 1908–38.

Theses, Resolutions and Manifestos of the First Four Congresses of the Third International. Translated by A. Holt and B. Holland. Introduced by B. Hessel. London, 1980.

Thorez, Maurice. *Le Front Populaire en Marche.* Paris: Les Publications Révolutionnaires, 1934.

———. *La Lutte pour l'Usine Révolutionnaire à la Crise.* Paris: Les Publications Révolutionnaires, 1934.

———. *Par l'Unité d'Action Nous Vaincons le Fascisme!* Paris: Les Publications Révolutionnaires, 1934.

———. *Unir, Unir, Unir, Pour Realiser la Programe du Rassemblement Populaire.* Paris, 1936.

———. *France Today and the People's Front.* London: Victor Gollancz, 1936.

———. *L'Heure de l'Action: Discours Pronouncé au Comité Central du PCF le 21 Novembre 1938.* Paris: Editions Sociales Internationales, 1938.

Union des Industries Métallurgiques et Minière. *Reclassement de la Main-D'Oeuvre.* Paris, 1937.

U.S. War Labor Policies Board. *Report on Labor and Socialism in France.* Washington: Government Printing Office, 1919.

IV. Biographies, Memoirs, and Diaries

Barbé, Henri. *Souvenirs de Militant et de Dirigeant Communiste.* Typescript MS, Hoover Institution Archives, n.d.

Barthélemy, Victor. *Du Communisme au Fascisme: L'Histoire d'un Engagement Politique.* Paris: Albin Michel, 1978.

Baudouï, Rémi. *Rauol Dautry 1880–1951: Le Technocrate de la République.* Paris: Balland, 1992.

Belin, René. *Du Secretariat de la CGT au Gouvernment de Vichy: Mémoires 1933–1942.* Paris: Albatros, 1978.

Berstein, Serge. *Eduoard Heriot ou la République en Personne.* Paris: PFNSP, 1985.

Bousquet, Hadrien. *J'ai Eté Ouvrier.* Avignon: Maison Aubanel, 1941.

Brunet, Jean-Paul. *Jacques Doriot: Du Communisme au Fascisme.* Paris: Balland, 1986.

Carls, Stephen D. *Louis Loucheur and the Shaping of Modern France 1916–1931.* Baton Rouge: Louisiana State University Press, 1993.

Gogniot, Georges. *Parti Pris: Cinquante-Cinq Ans au Service de l'Humanisme Réel—Vol. I: D'Une Guerre Mondiale à l'Autre.* Paris: Eds. Sociales, 1976.

Colton, Joel. *Léon Blum: Humanist in Politics.* 1966. Reprint, Durham: Duke University Press, 1987.

Coulondre, Robert. *De Staline à Hitler: Souvenirs de Deux Ambassades 1936–1939.* Paris: Hachette, 1950.

Dabit, Eugène. *Journal Intime (1928–1936).* Paris: Gallimard, 1939.

Delmas, André. *A Gauche de la Barricade: Chronique Syndicale de l'Avant-Guerre.* Paris: Eds. de l'Hexagone, 1950.

———. *Mémoires d'un Instituteur Syndicaliste.* Paris: Ed. Albatros, 1979.

Dolléans, Edouard. *Alphonse Merrheim.* Paris: CISO, 1939.

Dubois, Raoul. *Au Soleil de 36.* Paris: Eds. Messidor, 1986.

Dubreuil, Hyacinthe. *J'ai Fini Ma Journée.* Paris: Librairie du Compagnonnage, 1971.

Duclos, Jacques. *Mémoires: 1896–1934.* Paris: Fayard, 1968.

———. *Mémoires: 1935–1939.* Paris: Fayard, 1969.

Eudier, Louis. *Notre Combat de Classe et de Patriotes (1934–1945)*. Le Havre: Duboc, 1982.

Frachon, Benoît. *Pour la CGT: Mémoires de Lutte, 1902–1939*. Paris: Eds. Sociales, 1981.

Francotte, Robert. "A l'Usine Renault: Souvenirs." *Cahiers d'Histoire de l'Institut Maurice Thorez* (January 1973).

Fourrier, Jules. *Graine Rouge*. Paris: La Brèche, 1983.

Georges, Bernard, Denise Tintant, and Marie-Anne Renaud. *Léon Jouhaux dans le Mouvement Syndical Français*. Paris: PUF, 1979.

Gillot, Auguste. *Un Forgeron dans la Cité des Roi*. Paris: Eds. des Halles, n.d.

Girault, Jacques. *Benoît Frachon, Communiste et Syndicaliste*. Paris: Presses de la Fondation Nationale des Sciences Politiques, 1989.

Guérin, Daniel. *Front Populaire, Révolution Manquée: Temoignage Militant*. Nouvelle Edition. Paris: Maspero, 1970.

Hatry, Gilbert. *Louis Renault, Patron Absolu*. Paris: Eds. JCM, 1990.

Jacquier, Maurice. *Simple Militant*. Paris: Denoël, 1974.

Jamet, Claude. *Carnets de Déroute*. Paris: Ed. Sorlot, 1942.

————. *Notre Front Populaire: Journal d'un Militant (1934–1939)*. Paris: La Table Ronde, 1977.

Jourdain, Henri. *Comprendre pour Accomplir: Dialogue avec Claude Willard*. Paris: Eds. Socialies, 1982.

Lacouture, Jean. *Léon Blum*. Paris: Seuil, 1977.

Maitron, Jean, ed. *Dictionnaire Biographique du Mouvement Ouvrier Français. Quatrième Partie: 1914–1939*. Vols. 16–28. Paris: Les Eds. Ouvrières, 1981–86.

Mauvais, Léon. "Dans l'Entreprise: Les Années Vingt. Interview de:" *Cahiers d'Histoire de l'Institut Maurice Thorez* (January 1974).

Millet, Raymond. *Jouhaux et la CGT*. Paris: Denoël, 1937.

Monjauvis, Lucien. *Jean-Pierre Timbaud*. Paris: Eds. Sociales, 1971.

Papayanis, Nicholas. *Alphonse Merrheim: The Emergence of Reformism in Revolutionary Syndicalism 1871–1925*. Dordrecht: Martinus Nijhoff Publishers, 1985.

Peneff, Jean, ed. *Autobiographies de Militants CGTU–CGT*. Nantes, 1979.

Réau, Elisabeth du. *Edouard Daladier 1884–1970*. Paris: Fayard, 1993.

Reynauld, Paul. *In the Thick of the Fight 1930–1945*. New York: Simon and Schuster, 1945.

Reynolds, John. *André Citroën: The Henry Ford of France*. New York: St. Martin's Press, 1996.

Rhodes, Anthony. *Louis Renault: A Biography*. London: Cassel, 1969.

Robrieux, Philippe. *Maurice Thorez: Vie Secrète et Vie Publique*. Paris: Fayard, 1975.

Teulade, Jules. *Nous les Croulants*. Typescript MS, Hoover Institution Archives, n.d.

Thorez, Maurice. *Son of the People*. New York: International Publishers, 1938.

Trotsky, Leon. *Diary in Exile: 1935*. New York: Atheneum, 1963.

Vandervort, Bruce. *Victor Griffuelhes and French Syndicalism 1895–1922*. Baton Rouge: Louisiana State University Press, 1996.

Vassart, Albert. *Mémoirs*. Typescript MS, Hoover Institution Archive, n.d.

Vieilledent, Henri. *Souvenirs d'un Travailleur Manuel Syndicaliste*. Paris: La Pensée Universelle, 1978.

Zirnheld, Jules. *Cinquante Années de Syndicalisme Chrétien*. Paris: Eds. Spes, 1937.

V. Select Secondary Sources

Abherve, Bertrand. "Les Origines de la Grève des Métallurgistes Parisiens, Juin 1919." *Le Mouvement Social* 93 (October–December 1975).

Adibekov, G. M. *Die Rote Gewerkschaftsinternationale: Grundriss der Geschichte der RGI*. West Berlin: Das Europäische Buch, 1973.

Alexander, Martin, and Helen Graham, eds. *The French and Spanish Popular Fronts: Comparative Perspectives.* Cambridge: Cambridge University Press, 1989.

Amdur, Kathryn E. "Le Tradition Révolutionnaire entre Syndicalisme et Communisme dans la France de l'Entre-Deux-Guerres." *Le Mouvement Social* 139 (April–June 1987).

Amouroux, Henri. *Le Peuple du Désastre: 1939–1940.* Paris: Ed. Robert Laffont, 1976.

Anderson, Malcolm. "The Myth of the 'Two Hundred Families'." *Political Studies* 11 (June 1965).

Arum, Peter M. "Du Syndicalisme Révolutionnaire au Réformisme: Georges Dumoulin (1903–1923)." *Le Mouvement Social* 87 (April–June 1974).

Audit, Antoine. *Les Fédérations Confédérés et Unitaires des Métaux.* Mémoire de Maitrise, Paris I, 1986.

Aumont, Michele. *Femmes en Usine. Les Ouvrières de la Métallurgie Parisienne.* Paris: Eds. Spes, 1953.

Aviv, Isaac. "Le PCF dans le Système Français des Années 1930 à la Fin de la IVe République." *Le Mouvement Social* 104 (July–September 1978).

Azéma, Jean-Pierre, and François Bédarida, eds. *La France des Années Noires: De la Défaite à Vichy.* Paris: Seuil, 1993.

Azéma, Jean-Pierre, Antoine Prost, and Jean-Pierre Rioux, eds. *Le Parti Communiste Français des Années Sombres 1938–1941.* Paris: Seuil, 1986.

Badie, Bertrand. "Les Grèves du Front Populaire aux Usines Renault." *Le Mouvement Social* 81 (October–December 1972).

———. *Stratégie de la Grève: Pour une Approache Fonctionaliste du Parti Communiste Français.* Paris: FNSP, 1976.

Baker, Donald N. "The Socialists and the Workers of Paris: The Amicales Socialistes, 1936–1940." *International Review of Social History* 24 (1979).

Battestini, Felix. *L'Industrie Française du Gros Materiel Méchanique et Electrique.* Paris: Librairie Technique et Economique, 1937.

Becker, Jean-Jacques. *Le Parti Communiste Veut-il Prendre le Pouvoir? La Stratégie du PCF, de 1930 à Nos Jours.* Paris: Seuil, 1981.

Berlanstein, Lenard R. *The Working People of Paris: 1871–1914.* Baltimore: Johns Hopkins University Press, 1984.

Bernard, Marc. *Les Journées Ouvrières des 9 et 12 Février.* Paris: Grasset, 1934.

Bernard, Philippe, and Henri Dubief. *The Decline of the Third Republic, 1914–1938.* Cambridge: Cambridge University Press, 1985.

Berstein, Serge. *Le 6 Février 1934.* Paris: Gallimard Julliard, 1975.

———. *Histoire du Parti Radical: Crise du Radicalisme 1926–1939.* Paris: Presses de la Fondation Nationale des Sciences Politiques, 1982.

———. *La France des Années 30.* Paris: Armand Colin, 1993.

Bettelheim, Charles. *Bilan de l'Economie Français 1919–1946.* Paris: PUF, 1947.

Birnbaum, Pierre. *Le Peuple et les Gros: Histoire d'un Mythe.* Paris: Grasset, 1984.

Blanc, Edouard. *La Ceinture Rouge. Enquête sur la Situation Politique, Morale, et Sociale de la Banlieue de Paris.* Paris: Spes, 1927.

Bodin, Louis, and Jean Touchard. *Front Populaire 1936.* Paris: Armand Collin, 1985.

Bond-Howard, Jane. "Le Syndicalisme Minoritaire dans les Usines d'Armement de Bourges de 1914 à 1918." *Le Mouvement Social* 148 (July–September' 1989).

Bourdé, Guy. *La Défaite du Front Populaire.* Paris: Maspero, 1977.

Bouvier, Jean, ed. *La France en Mouvement 1934–1938.* Paris: Champ Vallon, 1986.

Bouvier-Ajam, Maurice. *Histoire du Travail en France depuis la Révolution.* Paris, 1969.

Broué, Pierre, and Nicole Dorey. "Critiques de Gauche et Opposition Révolutionnaire au Front Populaire." *Le Mouvement Social* 54 (January–March 1966).

Brower, Daniel R. *The New Jacobins: The French Communist Party and the Popular Front.* Ithaca: Cornell University Press, 1968.

Bruhat, Jean, and Marc Piolot. *Esquisse d'une Histoire de la CGT (1895–1965).* Paris: CGT, 1966.

Brunet, Jean-Paul. *Saint-Denis, la Ville Rouge 1890–1939: Socialisme et Communisme en Banlieue Ouvrière.* Paris: Hachette, 1980.

Burmeister, Arno. *Die Entwicklung der französischen Maschinen-Industrie.* Rostock: Karl Hinstorffs, 1929.

Burnham, James. *The People's Front: The New Betrayal.* New York: Pioneer Publishers, 1937.

Carr, E. H. *Twilight of the Comintern, 1930–1935.* New York: Pantheon, 1982.

Centre de Documentation d'Histoire des Techniques. *Evolution de la Geographie Industrielle de Paris et Sa Proche Banlieue au XIXe Siècle.* Paris, 1976.

Chagnon, Louis. *Les Fédérations des Métaux CGT et CGTU de 1922 à 1935: Organization et Militants.* Mémoire de Maitrise, Paris I, 1985.

Chambaz, Jacques. *Le Front Populaire pour le Pain, la Liberté et la Paix.* Paris: Eds. Sociales, 1961.

Chambelland, C., and J. Maitron, eds. *Syndicalisme Révolutionnaire et Communisme: Les Archives de Pierrre Monatte, 1914–1924.* Paris: Maspero, 1968.

Chapman, Herrick. *State Capitalism and Working-Class Radicalism in the French Aircraft Industry.* Berkeley: University of California Press, 1991.

Chateau, Henri. *Le Syndicalisme des Techniciens en France.* Paris: PUF, 1938.

Chavardes, Maurice C. *Eté 1936: La Victoire du Front Populaire.* Paris: Calmann-Lévy, 1966.

Clark, Marjorie Ruth. *A History of the French Labor Movement (1910–1928).* Berkeley: University of California Press, 1930.

Claudin, Fernando. *The Communist Movement: From Comintern to Cominform.* New York: Monthly Review Press, 1975.

Collinet, Michel. "Masses et Militants: Quelques Aspects de l'Evolution des Minorités Agissante au Syndicalisme de Masse." *Revue d'Histoire Economique et Sociale* 28 (1950).

———. "Masses et Militants: La Bureaucratie et la Crise Actuelle du Syndicalisme Ouvrier Français." *Revue d'Histoire Economique et Sociale* 29 (1951).

———. *L'Ouvrier Français: Esprit du Syndicalisme.* Paris: Eds. Ouvrières, 1951.

———. *L'Ouvrier Français: Essai sur la Condition Ouvrière (1900–1950).* Paris: Eds. Ouvrières, 1951.

Colton, Joel. *Compulsory Labor Arbitration in France, 1936–1939.* New York: King's Crown Press, 1951.

Comment le Parti Communiste Dirige la CGT. Paris: BEIPI, 1953.

"Les Conflicts de Juin dans la Région Parisienne." *Etudes* 5 (December 1936).

Courtois, Stéphane. *Le PCF dans le Guerre: De Gaulle, la Resistance, Staline.* Paris: Ed. Ramsay, 1980.

———. "Les Archives du Communisme: Entretien avec." *Krisis* 20–21 (November 1997).

Coutrot, Jean. *Les Leçons de Juin 1936. L'Humanisme Economique.* Paris, 1936.

Crémieux-Brilhac, Jean Louis. *Les Français de l'An 40: Ouvriers et Soldats.* Paris: Gallimard, 1990.

Cross, Gary S. *Immigrant Workers in Industrial France: The Making of a New Laboring Class.* Philadelphia: Temple University Press, 1983.

Danos, Jacques, and Marcel Gibelin. *Juin 36.* Revised Ed. Paris: La Découverte, 1986.

Degas, Jane. "United Front Tactics in the Comintern 1921–1928." In *International Communism.* Ed. David Footman. London: Chatto and Windus, 1960.

Delperrié de Bayac, Jacques. *Histoire du Front Populaire*. Paris: Fayard, 1972.

Dewerpe, Alain. *Le Monde du Travail en France 1800–1950*. Paris: Armand Colin, 1989.

Depretto, Jean-Paul, and Sylvie Schweitzer. *Le Communisme à l'Usine: Vie Ouvrière et Mouvement Ouvrier chez Renault 1920–1939*. Paris: EDIRES, 1984.

Dolléan, Edouard, and Gérard Dehove. *Histoire du Travail en France: Mouvement Ouvrier et Legislation Social*. Vol. 2. Paris: Domat Montchrestien, 1955.

Downs, Laura Lee. *Manufacturing Inequality: Gender Division in the French and British Metalworking Industries, 1914–1939*. Ithaca: Cornell University Press, 1995.

Dreyfus, Michel. *Histoire de la C.G.T.* Brussels: Eds. Complex, 1995.

Droz, Jacques. *Histoire de l'Antifascisme en Europe 1923–1939*. Paris: Eds. La Découverte, 1985.

Ducheim, René. "L'Accord Matignon, Ce Que J'ai Vu et Entendu." *Revue de Paris* 44 (February 1937).

Durant, Robert. *La Lutte des Travailleurs de chez Renault: Racontée par Eux-même 1912–1944*. Paris: Eds. Sociales, 1971.

Ehrmann, Henry W. *French Labor from Popular Front to Liberation*. New York: Oxford University Press, 1947.

———. *Organized Business in France*. Princeton: Princeton University Press, 1957.

Eudier, Louis. "Bréguet-Le Havre: Première Grève Occupation en 1936." *Cahiers d'Histoire de l'Institut Maurice Thorez* 1 (NS) (November–December 1972).

Eyaud, François. "The Principles of Union Action in the Engineering Industries in Great Britain and France: Towards a Neo-Institution Analysis of Industrial Relations." *British Journal of Industrial Relations* 21 (November 1983).

Faure, Petrus. *Les Manifestations du 12 Février 1934—La Grève Générale*. Paris: Imprimerie de la Chambre, 1934.

Fauvet, Jacques. *Histoire du Parti Communiste Français de 1920 à 1976*. Revised Edition. Paris: Fayard, 1977.

Fédération des Industries Méchaniques et Transformatrices des Métaux. *La Méchanique dans l'Economie Française*. Paris, n.d.

Ferrat, A. *Histoire du Parti Communiste Français*. Paris: Bureau d'Editions, 1931.

Fine, Martin. "Guerre et Réformisme en France, 1914–1918." *Recherches* 32/33 (September 1978).

———. "Hyacinthe Dubreuil: Le Témoignage d'un Ouvrier sur le Syndicalisme, les Relations Industrielles et Evolution Technologique de 1921 à 1940." *Le Mouvement Social* 106 (January–March 1979).

Fohlen, Claude. *La France de l'Entre-Deux-Guerres (1917–1939)*. Paris: Casterman, 1972.

Fontaine, Arthur. *French Industry During the War*. New Haven: Yale University Press, 1926.

Fourcaut, Annie. *Femmes à l'Usine en France dans l'Entre-Deux-Guerres*. Paris: Maspero, 1982.

———. *Bobigny, Banlieue Rouge*. Paris: Eds. Ouvrières, 1986.

———, ed. *Un Siècle du Banlieue Parisienne*. Paris: L'Harmattan, 1988.

Frachon, Benoît. "Juin 1936 . . . Histoire et Enseignements." *Les Cahiers de l'Institut CGT d'Histoire Sociale* 17 (March 1986).

Frank, P. *La Semaine du 6 au 12 Février*. Paris: Ligue Communiste, 1934.

———. *Fallait-il Prendre les Usines? La Grève Générale de Juin 1936*. Paris: Centre Ed. Documentation Révolutionnaire, 1936.

Fridenson, Patrick. *Histoire des Usines Renault 1898–1939*. Paris: Seuil, 1972.

———. "L'Ideologie des Grands Constructeurs dans l'Entre-Deux-Guerres." *Le Mouvement Social* 81 (October–December 1972).

———. "Pour une Histoire de l'Automobile en France." *Le Mouvement Social* 81 (October–December 1972).

————. "France—Etats-Unis: Genese de l'Usine Nouvelle." *Recherches* 32/33 (September 1978).

————. "Automobile Workers in France, 1914–83." In *Work in France: Representations, Meaning, Organization, and Practice.* Eds. S. L. Kaplan and C. J. Koepp. Ithaca: Cornell University Press, 1986.

————, ed. *The French Home Front 1914–1918.* Providence: Berg, 1992.

Furet, François. *La Passé d'une Illusion: Essai sur l'Idée Communiste au XXe Siècle.* Paris: Ed. Robert Lafffont, 1995.

Gallo, Max. "Quelques Aspects de la Mentalité et du Comportement Ouvriers dans les Usines de Guerre." *Le Mouvement Social* 56 (July–September 1966).

Gancarz, Patrick. "La Métallurgie Française face à la Crise des Années Trente (1928–1938)." *Le Mouvement Social* 154 (January–March 1991).

Garmy, René. *Histoire du Mouvement Syndical en France.* 2 vols. Paris: Bureau d'Editions, 1933/1934.

Garric, Robert. *Belleville: Scènes de la Vie Populaire.* Paris: Grasset, 1928.

Gelly, Jean-François. "A la Recherche de l'Unité Organique: La Démarche du Parti Communiste Français (1934–1938)." *Le Mouvement Social* 121 (October–December 1982).

Georges, Bernard. "La CGT et le Gouvernement Léon Blum." *Le Mouvement Social* 54 (January–March 1966).

Gide, Charles, ed. *Effects of the War upon French Economic Life.* Oxford: The Clarendon Press, 1923.

Gignoux, C. J. "CGT 1936 ou le Qauatrième Pouvoir." *Revue de Paris* 43 (October 1936).

————. *L'Economie Française entre les Deux Guerres, 1919–1939.* Paris: Eds. Economiques et Sociales, [1942?].

Gille, Bertrand. *Histoire de la Métallurgie.* Paris: PUF, 1966.

Girault, Jacques, ed. *Sur l'Implantation du Parti Communiste Français dans l'Entre-Deux-Guerre.* Paris: Editions Sociales, 1977.

Girault, René. "Les Relations Internationales et l'Exercise du Pouvoir Pendant le Front Populaire, Juin 1936–Juin 1937." *Cahiers Léon Blum* 1 (May 1977).

Godfrey, John F. *Capitalism at War: Industrial Policy and Bureaucracy in France 1914–1918.* Leamington Spa: Berg Publishers, 1987.

Goetz-Girey, Robert. *Le Mouvement des Grèves en France 1919–1962.* Paris: Eds. Sirey, 1965.

Grabau, Thomas W. *Industrial Reconstruction in France After World War I.* New York: Garland Publishing, 1991.

Graham, Helen, and Paul Preston, eds. *The Popular Front in Europe.* London: Macmillan, 1991.

Gras, Christian. "Merrheim et le Capitalisme." *Le Mouvement Social* 63 (April–June 1968).

————. "La Fédération des Métaux en 1913–1914 et l'Evolution du Syndicalisme Révolutionnaire Français." *Le Mouvement Social* 77 (September–October 1971).

Greene, Nathanael. *Crisis and Decline: The French Socialist Party in the Popular Front Era.* Ithaca: Cornell University Press, 1969.

Guebber, Eric. *Les Fédérations des Métaux Lieux d'Emission d'Analyses Socio-Economiques (1892–1914).* Mémoire de Maitrise, Paris I, 1985.

Guilbert, Madeleine. *Les Fonctions des Femmes dans l'Industries.* Paris: Mouton, 1966.

Guillot, Felix. *La Rationalisation et Ses Consequences Pour l'Ouvrier.* Lyon: Bosc Frères, 1934.

Halévy, Daniel. *1938. Une Année d'Histoire.* Paris: Grasset, 1938.

Hatry, Gilbert. *Renault, Usine de Guerre 1914–1918.* Paris: Eds. Lafourcade, 1978.

Hoffmann, Stanley, ed. *In Search of France.* Cambridge: Harvard University Press, 1964.

Hoisington, W. A. "Class Against Class: The French Communist Party and the Comintern—

A Study of Election Tactics in 1928." *International Review of Social History* 15 (1970).

Horne, John N. *Labour at War: France and Britain, 1914–1918.* Oxford: Clarendon Press, 1991.

Huard, Raymond, et al. *La France Contemporaine: Identité et Mutations de 1789 à Nos Jours.* Paris: Eds. Sociales, 1982.

Humphreys, George G. *Taylorism in France 1904–1920: The Impact of Scientific Management on Factory Relations and Society.* New York: Garland Publishing, 1986.

Huret, Marcel. *Les Industries Méchanique en France.* Paris: PUF, 1951.

Jackson, Julien. *The Politics of Depression in France 1932–1936.* Cambridge: Cambridge University Press, 1985.

———. *The Popular Front in France: Defending Democracy, 1934–38.* Cambridge: Cambridge University Press, 1988.

Jacquément, Gérard. *Belleville au XIXe Siècle: Du Faubourg à la Ville.* Paris: Ed. de EHESS, 1984.

Joubert, Jean-Paul. "Trotsky et le Front Populaire." *Cahiers Léon Trotsky* 9 (January 1982).

Julliard, Jacques. "La CGT Devant la Guerre (1900–1914)." *Le Mouvement Social* 49 (October–December 1964).

———. "Théorie Syndicaliste Révolutionnaire et Pratique Gréviste." *Le Mouvement Social* 65 (October–December 1968).

———. "Diversité des Réformistes." *Le Mouvement Social* 87 (April–June 1974).

———. "Integration Politique et Non-Integration Sociale de la Classe Ouvrière Française." In *Mouvements Sociaux d'Aujoudhui.* Ed. Alain Touraine. Paris: Eds. Ouvrières, 1982.

———. *Autonomie Ouvrière: Etudes sur le Syndicalisme d'Action Directe.* Paris: Gallimard, 1988.

Katznelson, Ira, and Aristide Zolberg, eds. *Working-Class Formation: Nineteenth-Century Patterns in Western Europe and the United States.* Princeton: Princeton University Press, 1986.

Kemp, Tom. *Stalinism in France: The First Twenty Years of the French Communist Party.* London: New Park Publications, 1984.

Kergoat, Jacques. *La France du Front Populaire.* Paris: La Découverte, 1986.

Kolboom, Ingo. *Frankreich Unternehmer in der Periode der Volksfront 1936–1937.* Rheinfelden: Schäuble Verlag, 1983.

Köller, Heinz. *Frankreich zwischen Fascismus und Demokratie (1932–1934).* Berlin (DDR): Akademie Verlag, 1978.

Kriegel, Annie. *The French Communists: Profile of a People.* Chicago: University of Chicago Press, 1972.

———. "The French Communist Party and the Problem of Power (1920–1939)." In *Contemporary France.* Ed. John Cairns. New York: New Viewpoints, 1978.

Kuisel, Richard F. *Capitalism and the State in Modern France: Renovation and Economic Management in the Twentieth Century.* Cambridge: Cambridge University Press, 1981.

Labi, Maurice. *La Grande Division des Travailleurs: Première Scission de la CGT (1914–1921).* Paris: Eds. Ouvrières, 1964.

Lambert, Max. *Structure et Problèmes des Grandes Industries Françaises.* Vol. I. Paris: PUF, 1945.

Larmour, Peter J. *The French Radical Party in the 1930s.* Stanford: Stanford University Press, 1964.

Laux, James M. "Travail et Travailleurs dans l'Industrie Automobile Jusqu'en 1914." *Le Mouvement Social* 81 (October–December 1972).

———. *In First Gear: The French Automobile Industry to 1914.* Montreal: McGill-Queens University Press, 1976.

Lazic, Brankd M. *Information Fournies par Albert Vassart sur la Politique du PCF entre 1924 et 1938.* Typescript MS, Hoover Institution Archives, n.d.

Lecoeur, Auguste. *Le Parti Communiste Français et la Résistance, Août 1939–Juin 1941*. Paris: Plon, 1968.

Lefranc, Georges. "Inquiétudes Ouvrières." *Nouveau Cahiers* 57 (April 1940).

———. *Les Experiences Syndicales en France de 1939 à 1950*. Paris: Aubier, 1950.

———. "Le Courant Planniste dans le Mouvement Ouvrier Français de 1933 à 1936." *Le Mouvement Social* 54 (January–March 1966).

———. *Juin 36: "L'Explosion Sociale" du Front Populaire*. Paris: Julliard, 1966.

———. *Le Mouvement Syndical sous la Troisième République*. Paris: Payot, 1967.

———. *Histoire du Front Populaire (1934–1938)*. Second Ed. Paris: Payot, 1974.

———. *Histoire du Travail et des Travailleurs*. Paris: Flammarion, 1975.

———. *Les Organisations Patronales en France du Passé au Présent*. Paris: Payot, 1976.

Leroy, Maxime. *Les Techniques Nouvelles du Syndicalisme*. Paris: Marcel Rivière, 1921.

Lequin, Yves. "Social Structures and Shared Beliefs: Four Worker Communities in the Second Industrialization." *International Labor and Working Class History* 22 (Fall 1982).

Lorwin, Lewis L. *Syndicalism in France*. New York: Columbia University Press, 1914.

Lorwin, Val. *The French Labor Movement*. Cambridge: Harvard University Press, 1954.

Louis, Paul. *Histoire de la Classe Ouvrière en France de la Révolution à Nos Jours*. Paris: Rivière, 1927.

Machefer, Philippe. "Les Syndicats Professionnels Français (1936–1939)." *Le Mouvement Social* 119 (April–June 1982).

Magraw, Roger. *A History of the French Working Class: Workers and the Bourgeois Republic 1871–1939*. Oxford: Blackwell, 1992.

Maier, Charles. "Between Taylorism and Technocracy: European Ideologies and the Vision of Industrial Productivity in the 1920s." *Journal of Contemporary History* 5 (1970).

Marcus, John T. *French Socialism in the Crisis Years, 1933–1936*. New York: Praeger, 1958.

Markovitch, T. J. *L'Industrie Française de 1789 à 1964*. 3 vols. Paris: Cahiers de L'ISEA, 1965/1966.

Martelli, Roger. "Une Introduction à l'Année 1934: Le PCF, l'Internationale et la France." *Cahiers d'Histoire de l'Institut de Recherches Marxistes* 18 (1984).

Martin-Saint-Léon, Etienne. *Les Deux CGT: Syndicalisme et Communisme*. Paris: Plon, 1923.

Maurice, Marc, and François Sellier. "Societal Analysis of Industrial Relations: A Comparison between France and West Germany." *British Journal of Industrial Relations* 17 (November 1979).

Merkle, Judith A. *Management and Ideology: The Legacy of the International Scientific Management Movement*. Berkeley: University of California Press, 1980.

Micaud, Charles A. *Communism and the French Left*. New York: Praeger, 1963.

Michel, Henri. *La Drôle de Guerre*. Paris: Hachette, 1971.

Milner, Susan. *The Dilemmas of Internationalism: French Syndicalism and the International Labour Movement*. New York: Berg, 1990.

Mitzman, Arthur. "The French Working Class and the Blum Government (1936–1937)." In *Contemporary France*. Ed. John Cairns. New York: New Viewpoints, 1978.

Moch, Jules. *Naissance et Croissance du Front Populaire*. Paris, 1966.

Moissonnier, Maurice. "1936: Les Grèves d'Occupation des Usines." *Les Cahiers de l'Institut CGT d'Histoire Sociale* 19 (September 1986).

Monatte, Pierre. *Trois Scissions Syndicales*. Paris: Eds. Ouvrières, 1958.

———. *La Lutte Syndicale*. Paris: Maspero, 1976.

Mortimer, Edward. *The Rise of the French Communist Party 1920–1947*. London: Faber and Faber, 1984.

Moutet, Aimée. "Les Origines du Système de Taylor en France. Le Point de Vue Patronal (1907–1914)." *Le Mouvement Social* 93 (October–December 1975).

———. "Patrons de Progrès ou Patrons de Combat? La Politique de Rationalisation de l'Industrie Française au Lendemain de la Première Guerre Mondiale." *Recherches* 32/33 (September 1978).

———. "Introduction de la Production à la Chaîne en France du Début du XXe Siècle à la Grande Crise en 1930." *Histoire Economique et Sociale* (1983).

Mouvements Ouvriers et Dépression Economique de 1929 à 1939. Assen: Van Gorcum & Comp., 1966.

Murard, Lion, and Patrick Zylberman, eds. *Le Soldat du Travail: Guerre, Fascisme et Taylorism.* Recherches 32/33 (September 1978).

Noiriel, Gérard. *Les Ouvriers dans la Société Française: XIXe–XXe Siècle.* Paris: Seuil, 1986.

Ogburn, W. F., and William Jaffé. *The Economic Development of Post-War France: A Survey of Production.* New York: Columbia University Press, 1929.

Papayanis, Nicholas. "Masses Révolutionnaires et Directions Réformistes: Les Tensions au Cours des Grèves des Métallurgies Français en 1919." *Le Mouvement Social* 93 (October–December 1975).

Passage, Henri de. "L'Occupation des Usines. La Grève sur le Tas." *Etudes* (5 September 1936).

Philip, André. *Trade Unionisme et Syndicalisme.* Paris: Aubier, 1936.

Picard, Roger. *Le Mouvement Syndicale Durant la Guerre.* Paris: PUF, 1927.

Piettre, André. *L'Evolution des Ententes Industrielles en France depuis la Crise.* Paris: Recueil Sirey, 1936.

Platet, Jean-Louis. *L'Industrie Automobile Française depuis la Guerre.* Paris: PUF, 1934.

Prost, Antoine. *La CGT à l'Epoch du Front Populaire 1934–1939.* Paris: Armand Colin, 1964.

Prouteau, Henri. *Les Occupations d'Usines en Italie et en France.* Paris: Librairie Technique et Economique, 1938.

Racine, Nicole, and Louis Bodin. *Le Parti Communiste Français pendant l'Entre-Deux-Guerres.* Paris: FNSP, 1982.

Rémond, René, and Janine Bourdin, eds. *Edouard Daladier, Chef de Gouvernement Avril 1938–Septembre 1939.* Paris: FNSP, 1977.

———. *La France et les Français en 1938–1939.* Paris: FNSP, 1978.

Rémy, Tristan. *La Grande Lutte.* Paris: Eds. Sociales Internationales, 1937.

Renouvin, P., and R. Rémond, eds. *Léon Blum, Chef de Gouvernement 1936–1937.* Paris: FNSP, 1965.

Ricard, Roger. *Le Mouvement Syndical durant la Guerre.* Paris: PUF, 1927.

Ridley, F. F. *Revolutionary Syndicalism in France: The Direct Action of Its Time.* Cambridge: Cambridge University Press, 1970.

Rioux, J.-P., A. Prost, and J.-P. Azéma, eds. *Les Communistes Français de Munich à Chateaubriant (1938–1941).* Paris: PFNSP, 1987.

Robert, Jean-Louis. "Les Programmes Minimum de la CGT de 1918 et 1921." *Cahiers d'Histoire de l'Institut de Recherches Marxistes* 16 (1984).

———. *Les Ouvriers, la Patrie et la Révolution: Paris 1914–1919.* Paris: Les Annales Littéraires, 1995.

Roberts, Geoffrey. *The Unholy Alliance: Stalin's Pact with Hitler.* Bloomington: Indiana University Press, 1989.

Robrieux, Philippe. *Histoire Intérieure du Parti Communiste 1920–1945.* Paris: Fayard, 1980.

———. "1934, On Tourne à Moscou." *Cahiers Léon Trotsky* 27/31 (September 1986/ September 1987).

Rogliano, Marie-France. "L'Anticommunisme dans la CGT: 'Syndicats'." *Le Mouvement Social* 87 (April–June 1974).

Ross, George. *Workers and Communists in France: From Popular Front to Eurocommunism.* Berkeley: University of California Press, 1982.

Rossi, A. [Angelo Tasca]. *Les Communistes Français pendant la Drôle de Guerre.* Paris: Les Iles d'Or, 1951.

Rossiter, Adrian. "Popular Front Economic Policy and the Matignon Negotiations." *The Historical Journal* 30 (September 1987).

Saint-Germain, Pierre. "La Chaîne et la Parapluie: Face à la Rationalisation (1919–1935)." *Les Révoltes Logiques* 2 (Summer 1976).

Saposs, David J. *The Labor Movement in Post-War France.* New York: Columbia University Press, 1931.

Sauvy, Alfred. *Histoire Economique de la France entre les Deux Guerres.* 4 vols. Paris: Fayard, 1965–1975.

Schwarz, Salomon. "Les Occupations d'Usine en France de Mai et Juin 1936." *International Review for Social History* 2 (1937).

Schweitzer, Sylvie. "Les Ouvriers des Usines Renault de Billancourt et la Guerre Civile Espagnole." *Le Mouvement Social* 103 (April–June 1978).

———. "Regards sur la Bolshevisation: Le Cas de la Cellule 410 de l'Usine Citroën (1924–1925)." *Cahiers d'Histoire de l'Institut de Recherches Marxistes* 5 (1981).

———. *Des Engrenage à la Chaîne: Les Usines Citroën 1915–1935.* Lyon: Presses Universitaires de Lyon, 1982.

Seidman, Michael. "The Birth of the Weekend and the Revolt against Work: The Workers of the Paris Region during the Popular Front (1936–1938)." *French Historical Studies* 12 (Fall 1981).

———. *Workers Against Work: Labor in Paris and Barcelona During the Popular Fronts.* Berkeley: University of California Press, 1991.

Sellier, François. "The French Workers' Movement and Political Unionism." In *The International Labor Movement in Transition.* Eds. A. Sturmthal and J. G. Scoville. Urbana: University of Illinois Press, 1973.

———. *La Confrontation Sociale en France 1936–1984.* Paris: PUF, 1984.

Shorter, Edward, and Charles Tilly. *Strikes in France 1830–1968.* Cambridge: Cambridge University Press, 1974.

Spriano, Paolo. *Stalin and European Communism.* London: Verso, 1985.

Stovall, Tyler. "French Communism and Suburban Development: The Rise of the Red Belt." *Journal of Contemporary History* 24 (July 1989).

———. *The Rise of the Paris Red Belt.* Berkeley: University of California Press, 1990.

Tartakowsky, Danielle. "Des Grèves de Juin à la Pause, 'Le Ministère des Masses' au Coeur des Contradictions." *Cahiers d'Histoire de l'Institut de Recherches Marxistes* 24 (1986).

Tartakowsky, Danielle, and Claude Willard. *Des Lendemain Qui Chantent? La France des Années Folles et du Front Populaire.* Paris: Eds. Sociales, 1986.

Tiersky, Ronald. *French Communism, 1920–1972.* New York: Columbia University Press, 1974.

Touraine, Alain. *L'Evolution du Travail Ouvrier aux Usines Renault.* Paris: CNRS, 1955.

———. *La Conscience Ouvrière.* Paris: Seuil, 1966.

Touraine, Alain, Michel Wieviorka, and François Dubet. *Le Mouvement Ouvrier.* Paris: Fayard, 1984.

Toutain, J. C. *La Population de la France de 1700 à 1959.* Paris: ISEA, 1963.

Trimouille, Pierre. *Les Syndicats Chrétiens dans la Métallurgie de 1935 à 1939.* Mémoire de DES, Paris, 1949.

Trotsky, Leon. *Le Mouvement Communiste en France (19219–1939).* Ed. Pierre Broué. Paris: Les Eds. de Minuit, 1967.

———. *Writings of Leon Trotsky: 1929–1940.* New York: Pathfinder, 1969–75.

———. *The Crisis of the French Section (1935–1936).* New York: Pathfinder, 1977.

———. *On France.* New York: Monad Press, 1979.

Tucker, Robert C. *Stalin in Power: The Revolution from Above, 1928–1941.* New York: Norton, 1990.

Valdour, Jacques. *Ateliers et Taudis de la Banlieue de Paris.* Paris: Ed. Spes, 1923.

Van de Casteele-Schweitzer, Sylvie. "Management and Labor in France 1914–1939." In *The Automobile Industry and Its Workers.* Eds. S. Tolliday and J. Zeitlin. Cambridge: Polity Press, 1986.

Varin, Jacques. *Les Hommes du Métal.* Paris: Fédération des Travailleurs de la Métallurgie/Eds. Messidor, 1986.

Vassart, Célie, and Albert. "The Moscow Origin of the French Popular Front." In *The Comintern: Historical Highlights.* Eds. M. Drachkovitch and B. Lazitch. Stanford: Hoover Institution, 1966.

Vassart, Cilly. *Le Front Populaire en France.* Typescript MS, Hoover Institution Archives, 1962.

Verdier, Robert. *Bilan d'une Scission: Congrès de Tours.* Paris: Gallimard, 1981.

Vichniac, Judith Eisenberg. *The Management of Labor: The British and French Iron and Steel Trade Industries, 1860–1918.* Greenwich, Conn.: JAI Press, 1990.

Vignaux, Paul. *Traditionalisme et Syndicalisme: Essai d'Histoire Sociale.* New York: Ed. de la Maison Française, 1943.

Vinen, Richard. *The Politics of French Business 1936–1945.* Cambridge: Cambridge University Press, 1991.

Wall, Irwin M. "French Socialism and the Popular Front." *Journal of Contemporary History* 5 (1970).

Walter, Gérard. *Histoire du Parti Communiste Français.* Paris: Somogy, 1948.

Weber, Eugen. *The Hollow Years: France in the 1930s.* New York: W. W. Norton, 1994.

Weil, Simone. *La Condition Ouvrière.* Paris: Gallimard, 1951.

———. *The Need for Roots.* London: Ark, 1987.

Werth, Alexander. *Which Way France?* New York: Harper and Brothers, 1937.

———. *France and Munich: Before and After the Surrender.* New York: Harper and Brothers, 1939.

Winock, Michel, et al. *Les Années Trente: De la Crise à la Guerre.* Paris: Seuil, 1990.

Wohl, Robert. *French Communism in the Making, 1914–1924.* Stanford: Stanford University Press, 1966.

Zévaés, Alexandre. *Histoire de Six Ans (1938–1944).* Paris: Nouvelle Revue Critique, 1944.

Index

Amicales Socialistes d'Enterprise, 131, 140, 147, 152, 155–56, 161, 163, 167

Anarchists, 28, 35–37, 92, 111, 140, 143, 149, 203n, 206n, 225n, 228n

Anschluss, 150–51, 153, 232n

Azaña, 127

Bases multiples, 137

Battle of France, 189–90

Belin, René, 131, 146, 169, 178–79, 181

Bloch, Marc, 190

Blum, Léon, 94, 96, 98, 102, 109–16, 126–30, 132, 134–35, 138–39, 142, 145–46, 150–52, 154–57, 222n, 228n, 229n, 230n

Cachin, Marcel, 96

Cahiers du Bolchevisme, 152

Ce Soir, 179

Centre d'Action Contre la Guerre, 164

Cercle Syndicaliste "Lutte de Classes," 141, 147, 152, 161, 163, 167, 231n

Chamber of Deputies, 62, 65, 67, 69, 94, 110, 114, 134, 138, 143, 154, 157, 164, 166

Chamberlain, Neville, 169

Chartre d'Amiens, 29, 33, 36

Chautemps, Camille, 145–46, 148–51

Chevalme, Léon, 132, 137, 185, 187, 237n

Chiappe, Jean, 67

"Clichy, bloody night of," 142–43, 145, 228n

Comité de liaison, 184

Comité National Inter-Fédéral des Métaux, 91

Comité des 22, 58

Comités de defense syndicale, 185, 189

Communist International, 39–40, 52, 54–56, 70, 73

Compulsory arbitration law, 138–39

Confédération Française des Travailleurs Chrétiens, 147, 206n, 227n

Confédération Générale du Production Française, 110–13, 122–23, 133, 144, 148, 155, 171, 231n

Confédération Générale du Travail:
Centres Syndicaux de Propagande, 52
Congress of Nantes, 166
Craft unions, 45, 205n
Factions, 131–32, 161–62
Minimum Program of 1918, 34, 51
Plan, 76–77, 87, 146, 187, 214n
Politique de présence, 46, 51, 186
Reconstitution, 183–84
Reunification, 73–75, 90–92
Schism of 1921, 36
Schism of 1939, 180–81
Unity Congress of Toulouse, 92

Confédération Générale du Travail Unitaire:
Economism, 56–61, 63, 77–78, 208n
Factory committees, 42–43
Origins, 36
People's Front, 40, 147
Relations with PCF, 39, 52, 54, 58
Relations of unitaire unions, 39
Sections syndicales, formation of, 41–42, 56, 59–60, 78, 83
Strike committees, 61–62, 214n
Syndicat unique, 74–75
Union model, 36–38

Coste, Alfred, 58, 99, 101, 103, 108–9, 223n, 224n

Cri du Peuple, Le, 58

Crise du syndicalisme, 30–31

Croizat, Ambroise, 58, 94, 218n

Cuissot, Maurice, 132

Culture industry, 22–24

Daladier, Edouard, 67–68, 114, 156–57, 160, 163–72, 175–76, 179–80, 183, 185, 236n

Dautry, Raoul, 185, 237n

De Man, Henrick, 76

Demonstrations:
Bastille Day, 84, 91
Clichy, 142–43
Mur des Fédérés, 97–98, 117, 219n

Popular Front, 75–76, 114
Processions of June 1936, 116
Spain, 151, 156
6 February 1934, 67–69, 75, 102
9 February 1934, 69–70
12 February 1934, 71–72, 84
Doriot, Jacques, 69, 71–72, 154–55, 215n, 216n
Dormoy, Marx, 143
Doumergue, Gaston, 68, 73
Doury, Robert, 58, 98, 101, 112, 129, 224n, 231n
Ducheim, René, 122
Duclos, Jacques, 100

Employers, metal:
Character, 14–15, 198n
Managerial style, 14–16
Paternalism, 15–16
And Majestic Accords, 186
And Matignon Accords, 111–12, 121–23
And workers, 15
Eudier, Louis, 94

Faubourgs of Paris, 19, 45
Figaro, Le, 97
Flandin, Pierre-Etienne, 230n
Ford, Henry, 3, 8–9
Forty-hour week, 57, 102, 110, 114, 135–36, 144, 148, 152, 160, 163–64, 227n, 233n, 235n
Frachon, Benoît, 57, 74, 90, 101, 111–12, 115, 126, 131, 141, 169, 178–79, 213n
Franco, General Francisco, 127, 151
Franco-Soviet Pact, 80, 82, 91, 178, 215n, 235n
Front Français, 128
Frossard, Ludovic-Oscar, 103–4

Galopin, Gustave, 141
General Strike of:
12 October 1925, 43
12 February 1934, 68–72, 75, 169, 173
7 September 1936, 129
18 March 1937, 143
10 November 1937, 148
31 November 1938, 170–71, 174, 186
Gignoux, C. J., 122–23, 144, 231n
Giraud Sentence, 158
Gitton, Marcel, 102
Goodrich dispute, 149
Gramsci, Antonio, 9
Griffuelhes, Victor, 30

Halévy, Daniel, 172
Hénaff, Eugène, 98
Hering, General Pierre, 180
Hitler, Adolf, 48, 66, 68, 70, 72, 150–51, 162–63, 175, 178–79, 181, 230n, 236n
Humanité, L', 69, 71, 96, 111, 115, 129, 143, 155, 179

Immigrants, 17, 20–21, 50, 170, 207n

Jacobinism, 86
Jacomet Sentence, 157
Jouhaux, Léon, 32, 92, 111–12, 127–28, 132, 141, 146, 166, 169, 178–79, 181, 216n, 229n, 234n

Labor movement, concept of, ix–x
Lambert-Ribot, Alfred, 110
Laval, Pierre, 80
Leagues, right-wing, 66–68, 141, 211n
Lebrun, Alfred, 109
Lemire, Albert, 132, 137, 227n
Litvinov, M. M., 178
Losovsky, Alexander, 55
Lutte Ouvrière, La, 113

Majestic Agreement, 185–87
Marty, André, 118
Masons, 110, 145, 222n
Matignon Accords, 111–13, 115, 121–23, 133, 146, 186
Matin, Le, 154
Metal industry:
Artisanal system, definition of, 9
Depression, 47–50
Concept, 5–6
Conditions, 13, 16, 48–49
Fordist-Taylorist mode of production, 8–14, 197n
Foremen, 9–10, 15, 125
Labor market, 16–18
Rationalization, 4–5, 8–9, 46, 196n, 206n
Sectors, 5–6
Technical system, definition of, 9–10
Turnover, 18, 50
Workforce, size of, 2, 5–7, 48
Metal plants:
Air Liquide, 154
Amiot, 89, 99
Babcock-et-Walcox, 61, 125
Bennes-Pillot, 144

Blériot, 167
Bloch, 78–79, 83, 89–90, 95–96, 129, 157, 167
Bourget, 144
Brandt, 101, 103, 129
Bréguet, 94–95
CAMS, 83, 125
Carnard, 141
Caudron, 89, 101, 158, 167
Chaise, 156
Chausson, 83, 101, 141, 143, 156
Chenard-et-Walker, 60, 78–80, 89, 125
Citroen, 2, 12, 14–15, 18, 49, 62–63, 77–78, 101, 103, 142, 153–55, 161, 167, 209n
Compteurs de Mountrouge, 185
Continentale des Compteurs, 144
Dehouse, 127
Delaunay-Belleville, 2
Electro-Méchanique, 144
Farman, 89, 99–101, 188
Ferodo, 153
Fiat (SIMCA), 89, 101, 141
Flertex, 154, 231n
Forges de Commentry, 144
Franco-Belge, 125
Geoffrey-Delore, 144
Gevelot, 101
Gnome-et-Rhône, 83, 89–90, 101, 103, 128, 154, 157–58, 184, 188
Harriot, 101
Hispano-Suiza, 83, 89, 128, 130–31, 177, 197n
Hotchkiss, 99, 112, 125, 129, 131
Jouet, 144
Kelner, 177
Laffy, 144, 231n
Latécoère, 95
Latil, 130
Levallet, 99, 125
Lioré-Olivier, 49, 77, 83, 89, 157
Livy, 130
Lockheed, 153–54
Lorraine-Dietrich, 89, 177, 184
Messier, 156
Mors, 4
Néoton, 144
Nieuport, 98–101, 103, 125, 154, 158
Panhard, 83, 137–38, 156
Petites Voitures, 185
Peugeot, 12, 90, 231n
Potez, 157
Rameau, 129

Renault, 2, 12, 14, 31, 49, 61–62, 99–101, 103–4, 108, 114, 116, 118–19, 128, 131, 156, 161, 167–69, 171, 177, 184, 188, 199n, 235n
Rosengard, 77, 101, 156
SACEM, 126, 144
Salmson, 89, 101, 231n
Sautter-Harlé, 99, 133–34, 177
SECM, 125
Seignol, 130
SKF, 154
Société d'Outillage, 141, 144
Solex, 130
Talbot, 60, 101, 209n
Metal Union (after 1936):
    Arbitrations, 138–39, 147–48, 157–58
    Colonization, 119–20, 146
    Contracts, 116, 145, 149, 159
    Decentralization of sections, 161
    Federal Congress of 1936, 136–37
    Federal Congress of 1938, 178
    Fusion Congress, 118, 136
    Membership figures, 38, 119, 158, 172, 176, 184, 204n, 237n
    National Defense, 148, 160–61, 174–76, 230n, 233n, 234n
    Shop stewards and section secretaries, 124–26, 159, 171–72, 236n
    Strike committees, 98, 101, 105–6, 119, 154, 214n
Métallo, Le, 78, 177
Molotov, V. M., 55
Monatte, Pierre, 98
Monjauvais, L., 62
Monmousseau, Gaston, 57, 163
Moscow-Berlin Pact, 178–81
Munich Accords, 162–63, 166, 169, 172

Neutralization, definition of, 127
Non-Intervention, 127–28, 132, 151, 162, 178, 225n

Ortega y Gasset, José, 26
Oualid, William, 139
Ouvrier manoeuvrer, definition of, 11
Ouvrier professionnel, definition of, 10–11
Ouvrier spécialisé, definition of, 11–12

Parti Communiste Français:
    Antimilitarism, 54, 80
    Barbé-Célor group, 53, 56
    Bolshevization, 40–42, 58, 69

Cells, formation of, 40–41, 205n
Clandestine activities, 183, 185, 188
Elections of 1935, 82, 117
Elections of 1936, 94, 218n
National Party Conference of 1934, 73–74
Origins, 36, 203n
Party/union relations, 36–37, 39, 52–57, 151
People's Front, 80, 82, 86–87, 115, 176, 220n
Revolutionary defeatism, 181
Sewer socialism, 25
Terre ouvrière, 25
Third Period, 52–54, 69, 72, 209n
United Action Pact with SFIO, 73
Parti Populaire Français, 154–55
Parti Social Français, 141–43, 147, 154–55
People's Front:
Announcement, 73
Collapse of Blum government (1937), 145
Collapse of Blum government (1938), 156
Collapse of Chautemps government, 149
Comité de Rassemblement, 84, 87
Confederal reservations, 87
Internal contradictions, 84, 89, 124, 132, 134, 230n
Pause, 140–41
Program, 85, 146
Worker reaction, 88–89, 96–97, 107, 142, 144, 217n
Peuple, Le, 87, 103–4, 111
Pivert, Marcel, 140
Pivertists, 140, 142
Poincaré, Raymond, 4
Pomaret, Charles, 185
Populaire, Le, 100, 111, 130

Radicals and the Radical party, 65–67, 73–74, 80, 85, 94, 112, 115, 127, 129, 134, 136, 145–46, 148, 155, 157, 164–67, 172, 232n
Ramadier, Paul, 158
Red International of Labor Unions, 36, 39, 55
Rémy, Tristan, 97
Republicanism, worker, 71, 88–89
Révolution Prolétarienne, La, 130
Revolutionary syndicalism and revolutionary syndicalists, 27, 29–30, 37, 41–42, 44, 58, 87, 130, 132–33, 149, 201n
Reynaud, Paul, 165–66, 169
Ribbentrop, Joachim von, 179

Richemond, Pierre, 103–4
Roosevelt, Franklin, 134

Roy, Marcel, 100, 132, 137, 152, 161–62, 178, 187
Russian Revolution, 33, 35–36

Sarraut, Albert, 100, 103, 109
Second Industrial Revolution, 20–21, 28
Section Française de l'Internationale Ouvrière, 70, 72–73, 76, 85, 130–31, 166, 219n
Elections of 1936, 94
Foreign policy, 150–51, 230n
Purchasing-power strategy, 66, 134, 140
Relations with the CGT, 131
Schism of 1920, 36
Salengro, Roger, 114
Stalin, Joseph, 53, 55, 70, 72, 80, 178–80, 225n, 230n, 236n
Stavisky, Serge, 66–67, 69
Suburbs of Paris, 20–21, 25, 45, 59, 82, 90, 116, 170, 200n; Map, 81
Syndicats group, 131–32, 140, 144, 146–47, 152, 161, 163–64, 166, 178, 181–82, 187, 226n

Tardieu, André, 53, 66
Taylor, Frederick W., 8–9
Temps, Le, 113, 140
Thomas, Albert, 32
Thorez, Maurice, 56, 58, 69, 73, 78, 84, 86, 98, 102, 115–16, 129, 136, 180, 223n, 225n
Timbaud, Jean-Pierre, 58, 101
Touraine, Alain, ix–x, 195n
Trotsky, Leon, 113, 211n, 212n, 214n, 215n, 217n, 222n, 235n
Trotskyists, 85, 104, 111, 113, 140, 142–43, 149, 154–55, 160, 168, 225n, 231n

Union des Industries Métallurgiques et Minière, 5–6, 103–4, 112, 116, 123, 135, 139, 145, 155, 185–86, 196n, 221n
Union des Métaux, 87
Union locale, 41, 45, 52, 106, 118, 184
Usine, 104

Vassard, Albert, 39–41, 70
Vigny, Marcel, 101

Weil, Simone, 13, 107–8, 215n, 221n, 223n